PRINCIPLE AND PRAGMATISM IN ROMAN LAW

This edited collection presents an interesting and original series of essays on the roles of principle and pragmatism in Roman private law.

The book traverses key areas of Roman law to examine the explanatory power of – and delineate interactions between – abstract, doctrinal principle, and pragmatic, real-world problem-solving. Essays canvassing sources of law, property, succession, contracts and delicts sketch the varied roles of theoretical narratives – whether internal to Roman doctrine or derived from external influence – and of practical, policy-based solutions in the jurists' thought.

Principled reasoning in Roman juristic argument ranges from safeguarding commerce, to the priority of acts or intentions in property transactions, to notions of *pietas*, to Platonic conceptions of the market. Pragmatism is discernible in myriad ways, from divergence between form and substance, to extension of legal rules for economic, social or political utility, to emphasis on what parties did rather than what they said.

The distinctive contribution of the book is its survey of different manifestations of principle and pragmatism across Roman private law. The essays – by eminent as well as emerging academics – will stimulate debate about the roles principle and pragmatism play in juristic argument, and will be of interest to both scholars and students of Roman law.

Principle and Pragmatism in Roman Law

Edited by
Benjamin Spagnolo
and
Joe Sampson

•HART•
OXFORD • LONDON • NEW YORK • NEW DELHI • SYDNEY

HART PUBLISHING

Bloomsbury Publishing Plc

Kemp House, Chawley Park, Cumnor Hill, Oxford, OX2 9PH, UK

1385 Broadway, New York, NY 10018, USA

HART PUBLISHING, the Hart/Stag logo, BLOOMSBURY and the Diana logo are trademarks of Bloomsbury Publishing Plc

First published in Great Britain 2020

A catalogue record for this book is available from the British Library.

Library of Congress Cataloging-in-Publication data

Names: Spagnolo, B. J. (Benjamin James) editor. | Sampson, Joe, editor.

Title: Principle and pragmatism in Roman law / edited by Benjamin Spagnolo and Joe Sampson.

Description: Oxford, UK ; New York, NY : Hart Publishing, an imprint of Bloomsbury Publishing, 2020. | Includes bibliographical references and index.

Identifiers: LCCN 2020026411 (print) | LCCN 2020026412 (ebook) | ISBN 9781509938957 (hardback) | ISBN 9781509938971 (ePDF) | ISBN 9781509938964 (Epub)

Subjects: LCSH: Roman law—Philosophy. | Principle (Philosophy) | Pragmatism.

Classification: LCC KJA2160 .P75 2020 (print) | LCC KJA2160 (ebook) | DDC 340.5/4—dc23

LC record available at https://lccn.loc.gov/2020026411

LC ebook record available at https://lccn.loc.gov/2020026412

ISBN: HB: 978-1-50993-895-7
ePDF: 978-1-50993-897-1
ePub: 978-1-50993-896-4

Typeset by Compuscript Ltd, Shannon

PREFACE

This volume contains papers from among those presented at a workshop entitled 'Principle and Pragmatism in Roman Juristic Argument', held in Trinity College, Cambridge in August 2019. We were delighted that participants included some of the most distinguished British and continental Romanists, alongside emerging Roman law scholars. Conscious of the existing gender imbalance in our field, we regret that none of the female colleagues invited was ultimately able to join us for the workshop or contribute to this volume. Roman law scholarship has traversed cultures and continents for the better part of two millennia; intellectual diversity is profoundly enriching and is to be pursued and prized in all its forms.

Shaping a new contribution to Roman law scholarship is challenging. The corpus of original source material may be limited but it compresses complex layers of continuity and change in the law of a civilisation whose citizens and circumstances differed as widely from one another as they do from ours. Even if the daunting depth of theoretical and doctrinal scholarship of succeeding centuries were physically and linguistically accessible to the student of Roman law, its range and volume would be formidable. Contextual and comparative enquiries further enrich – but also further compound – these challenges. Nevertheless, insight and inspiration have not been limited by these constraints; in Roman law as in other academic sciences, imperfect understanding has stimulated rather than impeded enquiry, and the mass of past study has fuelled rather than stultified new investigations.

We think that this essentially unbroken and apparently inexhaustible intellectual tradition of Roman law is due to at least two factors, both of them significant motivations for this volume, and for the workshop from which it arises. The first is the enduring relevance of the subject matter: the confluence of principle and pragmatism – as it were – in the substantive content and in the juristic methods of Roman law offers unending potential to human societies ordered by law. The second is the intellectual leadership of senior academic colleagues: teachers who imbue their students with the curiosity, commitment and confidence necessary to confront the challenges involved in contributing to Roman law scholarship. We count ourselves fortunate to have been exposed to both.

Benjamin Spagnolo
Joe Sampson

ACKNOWLEDGEMENTS

The editors and contributors gratefully acknowledge the generous financial contribution of Trinity College's Conference Fund and Marjorie Hollond Fund, in support of the workshop from which this volume arises.

The editors express their warm appreciation to all of the workshop participants – especially those who travelled from Scotland, the Netherlands and Germany to attend. The convivial atmosphere and lively debate that characterised the workshop owes much to the example of established professors and to the enthusiasm of more junior colleagues.

The editors also record their gratitude to Hart Publishing, whose dedicated and professional staff made possible the preparation of this volume in a short time frame and in challenging global circumstances.

TABLE OF CONTENTS

CONTRIBUTORS

Peter Candy is a College Lecturer and Fellow in Law, St Catharine's College, Cambridge

Graeme Cunningham is a Lecturer in Law, University of Abertay

Paul du Plessis FRHistS FSAScot is Professor of Roman Law, University of Edinburgh

Wolfgang Ernst is Regius Professor of Civil Law, University of Oxford, and Fellow of All Souls College, Oxford

David Ibbetson FBA is Regius Professor of Civil Law, University of Cambridge, and President of Clare Hall, Cambridge

Mike Macnair is Associate Professor of Law, University of Oxford, and Ann Smart Fellow and Tutor in Law, St Hugh's College, Oxford

Joe Sampson is Associate Professor of Law, University of Oxford, and Tutorial Fellow in Law, Magdalen College, Oxford

Boudewijn Sirks KNAW is Emeritus Regius Professor of Civil Law, University of Oxford

Benjamin Spagnolo is a Fellow and Lecturer in Law, Trinity College, Cambridge

Constantin Willems is Professor of Civil Law and Roman Law, University of Marburg

ABBREVIATIONS

The following abbreviations are used in the text and footnotes:

AUPA	*Annali del Seminario Giuridico dell'Università di Palermo*
BGU	*Berliner griechische Urkunden*
BIDR	*Bulletino dell'Istituto di diritto romano "Vittorio Scialoja"*
C.	*Codex Iustinianus*
CIL	*Corpus Inscriptionum Latinarum* (1863–)
Coll.	*Collatio Legum Mosaicarum et Romanarum*
CTh.	*Codex Theodosianus*
D.	*Digesta Iustiniani Augusti*
Epit.Ulp.	*Eiptome Ulpiani*
FIRA	Riccobono et al (eds), *Fontes Iuris Romani Antejustiniani*, 2nd, amended edn (Florence, G Barbèra, 1940–1943)
Fr.Vat.	*Fragmenta Vaticana*
G.	Gaius's *Institutiones*
IG	*Inscriptiones Graecae* (1873–)
Index Interpolationum	E Levy, E Rabel, and L Mitteis, *Index interpolationum quae in Justiniani Digestis inesse dicuntur* (Weimar, Böhlau, 1929) and D Broggini, *Index interpolationum quae in Iustiniani Codice inesse dicuntur* (Weimar, Böhlau, 1969)
Index	*Quaderni Camerti di studi romanistici (Indici)*
Inst.	Justinian's *Institutiones*
IVRA	*Rivista internazionale di diritto romano e antico*
Labeo	*Labeo: Rassegna di Diritto Romano*
Leg Hist Rev	*Tijdschrift voor Rechtsgeschiedenis / Revue d'Histoire du Droit / The Legal History Review*
PS	*Pauli Sententiae*

Reg.Ulp.	*Regulae Ulpiani*
RIDA	*Revue internationale des droits de l'antiquité*
SEG	*Supplementum Epigraphicum Graecum* (1923–)
SDHI	*Studia et Documenta Historiae et Iuris*
TAM	*Tituli Asiae Minoris* (1901–)
XII Tables	*Lex Duodecim Tabularum*
ZRG RA	*Zeitschrift der Savigny stiftung für Rechtsgeschichte (Romanistische Abteilung)*

Conventional abbreviations used for other ancient sources are those found in: S Hornlower, A Spawforth and E Eidinow (eds), *Oxford Classical Dictionary*, 4th edn (Oxford, Oxford University Press, 2012).

TRANSLATIONS

Unless otherwise indicated, all translations, including translations from Roman legal sources, are those of the chapter authors. The Latin and Greek text of the *Corpus Iuris Civilis* is taken from the standard edition: P Krueger and others (eds), *Corpus Iuris Civilis* (Berlin, Weidmann, 1872–95).

1

Principle and Pragmatism

BENJAMIN SPAGNOLO AND JOE SAMPSON

I. Introduction

Nineteenth-century scholarship often treats Roman law as 'peculiarly complete and scientific',[1] as 'a system instead of a mere congeries of rules and dicta … [its] conceptions … rational and, so to speak, natural'.[2] Twentieth-century research appreciates that 'the work of the jurists remained overwhelmingly practical',[3] and that the 'Digest is essentially a casebook, though a disorderly one'.[4] While modern Romanists readily accept disagreement between jurists and recognise their individual and often pragmatic approaches, they continue to search for abstract explanatory principle, whether internal to Roman doctrine or to a jurist's own approach, or derived from external influences, such as rhetoric and philosophy, theories of natural law, Stoic causal thinking or Greek perspectives on dowry. The essays collected in this volume traverse Roman private law to examine the explanatory power of – and delineate relationships between – on the one hand, abstract, doctrinal principle and, on the other, pragmatic, real-world problem-solving.

Notwithstanding significant references in the surviving sources to, for example, the concepts of *ratio* and *utilitas*, the Roman jurists rarely frame their arguments explicitly in terms of 'principle' and 'pragmatism'; as Stein says, they

> are noted for their pragmatic approach to cases and for the subtlety of their casuistic reasoning. They did not generally indulge in discussions of legal theory. It should not, however, be assumed that because they did not articulate comprehensive legal theories, they lacked ideas about the nature of law.[5]

Accordingly, the essays in this volume explore the substance and the methods of juristic thought to tease out themes of principle and pragmatism, in different time

[1] JF Stephen, *A History of the Criminal Law of England*, vol I (London, Macmillan, 1883), 50, cited in HF Jolowicz, 'Academic Elements in Roman Law' (1932) 48 *LQR* 171, 171.

[2] J Bryce, 'Inaugural Lecture: The Academical Study of the Civil Law' in J Bryce, *Studies in History and Jurisprudence*, vol II (Oxford, Clarendon Press, 1901) 475, 493.

[3] Jolowicz, 'Academic Elements in Roman Law' (n 1), 172.

[4] WW Buckland, quoted in discussion: HG Hanbury, 'The Place of Roman Law in the Teaching of Law To-day' [1931] *Journal of the Society of Public Teachers of Law* 14, 24.

[5] PG Stein, 'Interpretation and Legal Reasoning in Roman Law' (1995) 70 *Chicago-Kent Law Review* 1539, 1539. See also AM Honoré, 'Legal Reasoning in Rome and Today' (1973) 4 *Cambrian Law Review* 58, 59.

periods and with reference to a range of disciplines within Roman private law, from sources to property, succession, contracts and delicts.

This framework chapter samples relevant jurisprudential and Romanist literature to present a rough working taxonomy of five major, and two minor, senses of 'principle' and 'pragmatism'. It offers a handful of illustrative examples, before surveying the contributions of subsequent chapters in terms of the volume's central concepts.

II. Senses of 'Principle' and 'Pragmatism'

Varying senses of 'principle' and 'pragmatism' are employed in diverse contexts.[6] It is convenient, at the outset, to put some of these aside. The essays in this volume do not, except incidentally, explore 'principles' in the sense of 'the basic views of law and justice animating the Romans responsible for the law ... the true principia, the true "beginnings" of Roman law'.[7] Nor are the contributions concerned to distinguish 'principles' from 'rules',[8] or from 'policies',[9] as is sometimes convenient in legal philosophy. Still less are they concerned with pragmatism in general philosophy, beyond the domain of legal theory.[10] Instead, each author engages with one or more senses of 'principle' and 'pragmatism' in Roman juristic argument, seven of which are characterised in this chapter in stylised pairs: *ratio* and *utilitas* (or logic and experience); objective concepts and factual context; consistency and diversity; reason and tradition; theory and empiricism; form and substance; and rights and remedies.

The paired senses of principle and pragmatism sketched in this chapter overlap; and they do not exhaust the possible significations of these concepts. Moreover, while they are paired in order to bring out contrasting features, principle and pragmatism in each of these senses are by no means incompatible. A given argument and even a given source – notably the praetorian Edict – can often be considered both 'principled' and 'pragmatic', in one or more senses. From competition to

[6] PS Atiyah, 'From Principles to Pragmatism: Changes in the Function of the Judicial Process and the Law' (1980) 65 *Iowa Law Review* 1249, 1250; RA Posner, 'Pragmatic Adjudication' (1996) 18 *Cardozo Law Review* 1, 2; MH Kramer, 'The Philosopher-Judge: Some Friendly Criticisms of Richard Posner's Jurisprudence' (1996) 59 *MLR* 465, 475; S Haack, 'On Legal Pragmatism: Where Does "the Path of the Law" Lead Us?' (2005) 50 *American Journal of Jurisprudence* 71, 71–74.

[7] F Schulz, *Principles of Roman Law* (M Wolff trans, Oxford, Oxford University Press, 1936), 1.

[8] For a flavour of this debate in legal philosophy, see HLA Hart, 'American Jurisprudence through English Eyes: The Nightmare and the Noble Dream' (1970) in HLA Hart, *Essays in Jurisprudence and Philosophy* (Oxford, Clarendon Press, 1983) 123, 134–35; J Raz, 'Legal Principles and the Limits of Law' (1972) 81 *Yale Law Journal* 823, 828, 838–41.

[9] For his proposed distinction between these concepts, see RM Dworkin, *Taking Rights Seriously* (London, Duckworth, 1977), 22–26, 82, 91.

[10] Pragmatism in legal theory is distinct from philosophical pragmatism: TC Grey, 'Freestanding Legal Pragmatism' (1996) 18 *Cardozo Law Review* 21, 21.

symbiosis, relationships between principle and pragmatism often explain the origins, development, contours and conclusions of legal argument. That both principle and pragmatism are necessary and valuable components in legal reasoning arises from the dual ambition of law, as both a rational system (setting standards) and a purposive enterprise (resolving disputes): 'Legal ideas never reach very far beyond practical needs'.[11]

A. *Ratio* and *Utilitas*; Logic and Experience

The first sense of 'principle' and 'pragmatism' contrasts 'reason or rationality or philosophical inquiry … with the pragmatic, the practical';[12] it contrasts 'doctrine [with] policy'.[13] In this sense, 'principle' entails 'conformity to reason, uniformity, and certainty … a reasoned body of principles for the administration of justice'.[14] The 'logic' involved is sometimes syllogistic logic in the strict sense[15] but more commonly signifies that a rule makes sense or is consistent 'with the general policies and principles of the law'.[16] Plainly, in any system, 'reason and rationality are indispensable in the construction and use of law'.[17]

This sense of 'principle' and 'pragmatism' is commonly associated with Holmes's celebrated aphorism: 'The life of the law has not been logic: it has been experience'.[18] By this, Holmes does not denigrate the role of logic or principle but, in historical terms, disparages 'the notion that the only force at work in the development of the law is logic'.[19] With reference to deciding difficult common law cases, he emphasises that 'the simple tool of logic does not suffice, and even if it is disguised and unconscious, the judges are called on to exercise the sovereign

[11] FW Maitland, *Township and Borough* (Cambridge, Cambridge University Press, 1898), 27. See also NR Pound, 'Mechanical Jurisprudence' (1908) 8 *Columbia Law Review* 605, 609; HF Jolowicz, 'Utility and Elegance in Civil Law Studies' (1949) 65 *LQR* 322, 325.

[12] PS Atiyah, *Pragmatism and Theory in English Law* (London, Stevens & Sons, 1987), 6.

[13] BM Hale, 'Principle and Pragmatism in Developing Private Law' (Cambridge Freshfields Lecture 2019), available at: www.supremecourt.uk/docs/speech-190307.pdf, 1.

[14] Pound (n 11), 605.

[15] Atiyah, *Pragmatism and Theory in English Law* (n 12), 44.

[16] DN MacCormick, *Legal Reasoning and Legal Theory* (Oxford, Oxford University Press, 1978), 38–39.

[17] Atiyah, *Pragmatism and Theory in English Law* (n 12), 93.

[18] OW Holmes, *The Common Law* (London, Macmillan, 1882), 1. Holmes has been characterised as '[l]aw's greatest pragmatist': RA Posner, *Overcoming Law* (London, Harvard University Press, 1995), 13. The characterisation may be doubted, in view of Holmes's own attitude to pragmatic philosophical works: TC Grey, 'Holmes and Legal Pragmatism' (1989) 41 *Stanford Law Review* 787, 788.

[19] OW Holmes, 'The Path of the Law' (1897) in OW Holmes, *Collected Legal Papers* (New York, Harcourt, Brace and Co, 1920) 167, 180. For further explanation in context of the 'misused quotation' about logic and experience, see Hart, 'American Jurisprudence through English Eyes' (n 8), 129–30; HLA Hart, 'Diamonds and String: Holmes on the Common Law' (1963) in *Essays in Jurisprudence and Philosophy* (Oxford, Clarendon Press, 1983) 178, 281.

prerogative of choice'.[20] The relevant sense of 'pragmatism' is thus a tempering influence, complementary to principle:

> It is in the formulation, if necessary the adaptation, of legal principle to embrace [the intuitively] just solution that we can see not only the beneficial influence of facts upon the law, but also the useful impact of practical experience upon the work of practising lawyers in the development of legal principles.[21]

Stein suggests[22] that this aphorism about logic and experience may have been influenced by Holmes's reading, two years earlier, similar observations of Jhering's:

> It is to misunderstand the very essence of law, it is to fall into complete error, to wish, in the name of logic, to make jurisprudence into legal mathematics. Life does not bow to principles; it is principles that must model themselves on life. It is not logic, it is life, it is interactions, it is legal sentiment that demand what must be; and logical necessity and impossibility have nothing to do with it. The Romans could have been accused of madness, if they had thought otherwise, and if they had sacrificed the interests of life to the dialectics of the school.[23]

Jhering's plea is closer to the sense in which Holmes's aphorism is usually understood (when taken out of context): a 'reaction against excessive reliance on thought that is deductive, formal, abstract'.[24] As an example, Jhering observes that, while logic would dictate that fruits gathered by a *bona fide* possessor belong not to him but to the owner,[25] in this and other cases, 'it is practical need or legal sentiment that dictates the decision; logic only comes later'.[26]

The predominant view is that the Roman jurists accommodated both principle and pragmatism in this first sense: they worked out logical starting points and a dogmatic framework but took into account social and commer-

[20] OW Holmes, 'Law in Science and Science in Law' (1889) in OW Holmes, *Collected Legal Papers* (New York, Harcourt, Brace and Co, 1920) 210, 239.

[21] RLA Goff, 'The Search for Principle' (1983) 69 *Proceedings of the British Academy* 169, 183.

[22] PG Stein, 'Logic and Experience in Roman and Common Law' in PG Stein, *The Character and Influence of the Roman Civil Law: Historical Essays* (London, Hambledon, 1988) 37, 37. It has equally been noted that Holmes's biographers found no evidence that Holmes recognised the connection between Jhering's thoughts and his own: HLA Hart, 'Jhering's Heaven of Concepts and Modern Analytical Jurisprudence' (1970) in *Essays in Jurisprudence and Philosophy* (Oxford, Clarendon Press, 1983) 265, 267.

[23] CRR Jhering, *Geist des römischen Rechts auf den verschiedenen Stufen seiner Entwicklung*, vol 4 (Leipzig, Breitkopf und Härtel, 1867), 318–19. The translation here is from the French edition Holmes read: CRR Jhering, *L'Esprit du droit romain dans les diverses phases de son développement*, vol 4, 3rd edn (O de Meulenaere trans, Paris, Marescq, 1886), 311–12 ('C'est méconnaître l'essence même du droit, c'est verser dans une erreur complète, que de vouloir, au nom de la logique, faire de la jurisprudence la mathématique du droit. La vie ne doit pas se plier aux principes; ce sont les principes qui doivent se modeler sur la vie. Ce n'est point la logique, c'est la vie, ce sont les relations, le sentiment juridique, qui réclament ce qui doit être; et la nécessité ou l'impossibilité logique n'ont rien à voir ici. L'on aurait pu taxer les Romains de folie, s'ils avaient pensé autrement, et s'ils avaient sacrifié les intérêts de la vie à la dialectique de l'école').

[24] Hart, 'American Jurisprudence through English Eyes' (n 8), 130.

[25] Jhering, *Geist des römischen Rechts* (n 23), 320.

[26] ibid, 320–21; Jhering, *L'Esprit du droit romain* (n 23), 314 ('c'est le besoin pratique ou le sentiment juridique qui a dicté la décision, la logique ne vient qu'après').

cial considerations,[27] deciding 'contrary to the *stricta iuris ratio* or the *subtilis ratio* … in cases in which the application of such rules would have led to a result contrary to the needs of legal practice'.[28] As Birks says:

> Had Gaius been confronted with Holmes's famous aphorism … he might not have been unduly shocked, since the jurists were well aware of the non-logical elements in legal development, which they called, compendiously, *utilitas*.[29]

Ankum translates *utilitas* as '"the necessities" or "the interest of practical juridical life"'.[30] Privileging a pragmatic solution – deviating from *ratio*, general principle[31] – is commonly signalled by references to *utilitas*,[32] from Labeo to Macer.[33] Perhaps the most famous opposition of *ratio* and *utilitas* in this fashion is Julian's: 'That many things have been settled by the civil law contrary to the logic of argument [*contra rationem disputandi*] but on account of common necessity [*pro utilitate communi*] can be shown in innumerable cases'.[34] Stein suggests it was typical for Julian, as head of the Sabinian school, to set *utilitas* 'against Proculian logic'.[35]

Though arising at a time when Greek philosophical thought was influential at Rome, *utilitas* is distinctively Roman,[36] and reflects the law's commitment 'to protecting particular interests judged worthy of being supported, as much at the private level (*utilitas singulorum*) as the public (*utilitas publica*)'.[37] In this sense, it is important to acknowledge that *utilitas* does not denote irrational or unprincipled expediency: it cuts across the logic (principle) of a particular legal rule but does so to protect, for example, legal certainty, good faith conduct, the interests of the vulnerable, the validity of transactions, and the victims of wrongdoing.[38]

[27] U Leptien, '"Utilitatis causa": Zweckmässigkeitsentscheidungen im römischen Recht' (1969) 35 *SDHI* 51, 72.

[28] JA Ankum, 'The Functions of Expressions with *Utilitatis Causa* in the Works of the Classical Roman Lawyers' (2010) 16 *Fundamina* 5, 5–6 (footnotes omitted). See also JA Ankum, '*Utilitatis causa receptum*, On the Pragmatical Methods of the Roman Lawyers' in JA Ankum, R Feenstra and WF Leemans (eds), *Symbolae iuridicae et historicae Martino David dedicatae* (Leiden, Brill, 1968) 1, 2–3, 28–29.

[29] P Birks, 'Fictions Ancient and Modern' in DN MacCormick and PBH Birks (eds), *The Legal Mind: Essays for Tony Honoré* (Oxford, Clarendon Press, 1986) 83, 85.

[30] Ankum, '*Utilitatis causa receptum*' (n 28), 5.

[31] Leptien (n 27), 52; M Navarra, *Ricerche sulla utilitas nel pensiero dei giuristi romani* (Torino, Giappichelli, 2002), 182, 196–97, 205, 206.

[32] For cognate expressions, see Ankum, '*Utilitatis causa receptum*' (n 28), 4–5; Navarra (n 31), 10; Ankum, 'The Functions of Expressions with *Utilitatis Causa*' (n 28), 7, 20–21.

[33] Ankum, 'The Functions of Expressions with *Utilitatis Causa*' (n 28), 5–6. See also Ankum, '*Utilitatis causa receptum*' (n 28), 28; Leptien (n 27), 71–72; Honoré, 'Legal Reasoning in Rome and Today' (n 5), 65; Navarra (n 31), 20–21, 181, 188; AM Honoré, *Ulpian: Pioneer of Human Rights*, 2nd edn (Oxford, Oxford University Press, 2002), 98.

[34] D. 9.2.51.2 (Iul. 86 *Dig.*): *Multa autem iure civili contra rationem disputandi pro utilitate communi recepta esse innumerabilibus rebus probari potest.* See Navarra (n 31), 182–83.

[35] Stein, 'Interpretation and Legal Reasoning in Roman Law' (n 5), 1553.

[36] E Dovere, 'Le discours juridique et moral d'*utilitas* à Rome' (1999) 65 *SDHI* 239, 240.

[37] ibid, 247 ('protéger certains intérêts jugés dignes d'être soutenus, tant sur le plan privé (*utilitas singolorum*) [sic] que public (*utilitas publica*)').

[38] Ankum, '*Utilitatis causa receptum*' (n 28), 29–30.

The precise contours of the role *utilitas* plays in juristic reasoning remain controversial. *Utilitas* might, or might not, suffice when unaccompanied by a plausible dogmatic argument – that is, pragmatism might, or might not, function as more than a tie-breaker between competing principled solutions.[39] *Utilitas* might, or might not, be connected with the concept of *ius singulare* (a privilege or exception[40]).[41] Reference to *utilitas* in conjunction with the phrase *receptum est* might signal only that *utilitas* was the basis for general acceptance by the jurists of a solution, or it might signify that *utilitas* was the argument for that solution.[42] Whatever the resolution of these controversies, *utilitas* plainly denotes preference for a solution that departs from the logic of an applicable general rule.[43]

Utilitas is not the only conceptual tool by which the jurists indicate preference for pragmatism over principle in this first sense. What Honoré characterises as 'open arguments (topoi, principles)',[44] appealing to social values such as *aequitas*, *aequum et bonum*, *animus*, *benignitas*, *bona fides*, *favor libertatis*, *humanum*, *natura* and *necessitas*, are also deployed in juristic reasoning at various times to justify exceptions to general rules.[45] Adopting a different technique, Gaius and Paul often state a general rule and then mark its rejection in a particular case by appending a phrase introduced by 'but' (*sed* or *tamen*).[46] Beyond the scope of juristic argument is a further systemic feature that facilitates pragmatic decision-making: referring to the example of the good faith standard in contracts, Stein points out that, on account of the formulary procedure, juristic logic would be 'tempered by lay experience … the Roman *iudex* provided an input of nontechnical experience of life'.[47]

Among the many *utilitas* cases studied in depth by Ankum, Leptien and Navarra,[48] D. 41.2.1.14 on retention of possession of a runaway slave offers a convenient illustration.[49] While the Proculian Nerva holds that possession could not be obtained through a runaway slave, and the Sabinians Cassius and Julian hold that it could, it is, on account of *utilitas*, settled by the time of Paul – *utilitatis*

[39] See Leptien (n 27), 63, 67, 70, 71. See also WAJ Watson and KA El Fadl, 'Fox Hunting, Pheasant Shooting, and Comparative Law' (2000) 48 *American Journal of Comparative Law* 1, 3, 20–21, suggesting that, in the almost artificial juristic exploration of legal rules and doctrines, practical utility, 'while present, was in the background': ibid, 36.

[40] R Sohm, *The Institutes of Roman Law*, 4th edn (JC Ledlie trans, Oxford, Oxford University Press, 1892), 18.

[41] Navarra (n 31), 202.

[42] Contrast ibid, 179–80, 207 and Ankum, 'The Functions of Expressions with *Utilitatis Causa*' (n 28), 21–22.

[43] Navarra (n 31), 179, 206.

[44] Honoré, 'Legal Reasoning in Rome and Today' (n 5), 60.

[45] M Kaser, 'Sur la Méthode des Jurisconsultes Romains' (1962) 5 *Romanitas* 107, 112; Leptien (n 27), 62; Honoré, 'Legal Reasoning in Rome and Today' (n 5), 61–62; Navarra (n 31), 206.

[46] Navarra (n 31), 185, 190, 201.

[47] Stein, 'Logic and Experience in Roman and Common Law' (n 22), 40.

[48] Ankum, '*Utilitatis causa receptum*' (n 28), 12–13; Leptien (n 27), 58–59; Navarra (n 31), 90–98 (noting further consideration in the literature).

[49] D. 41.2.1.14 (Paul. 54 *ad Ed.*).

causa receptum est – that possession of the runaway slave itself was retained, and so the slave could be usucapted (unless a third party took possession). Following the logic (principle) of the rule that possession requires both physical control (*corpus*) and relevant intention (*animus*), loss of physical control entails loss of possession. In a social context of mass slave-ownership, the economic consequences – of interrupting *usucapio* and, to avoid that, of taking additional steps to keep large numbers of slaves under control – make the pragmatic solution obviously preferable.

B. Concepts and Context

A second sense of 'principle' and 'pragmatism' captures distinct methods of legal analysis: argument by reference to concepts, where legal principles are treated almost as 'objective phenomena';[50] and argument by reference to context, where emphasis is given to achieving 'sensible results in an everyday commercial context',[51] having regard to the purpose of the rule and to the circumstances – πράγματα – of the case. A principled focus on concepts permits law to be structured 'into a system of classification made up of relatively abstract principles and categories';[52] such a system offers coherence and order but, as Pound observes:

> The nadir of mechanical jurisprudence is reached when conceptions are used, not as premises from which to reason, but as ultimate solutions. So used, they cease to be conceptions and become empty words.[53]

In contrast, a pragmatic focus on context – an 'appeal to the facts of the case'[54] – is '[c]haracterized chiefly by its orientation towards the future, its adaptability, its fluidity, and its "down to earth" quality … [it] purports to offer practical solutions to concrete problems'.[55] While a pragmatic, contextual method accommodates 'general principles and systematic thought … [it insists] that the test of abstractions must be their usefulness for action and concrete inquiry'.[56]

Characterisations of the dominant approach in Roman juristic argument have differed starkly. Austin reports the view, popularised by Savigny and Leibniz,[57] that

[50] Atiyah, *Pragmatism and Theory in English Law* (n 12), 99–100.

[51] ibid, 100. See also Kaser (n 45), 113.

[52] Grey, 'Holmes and Legal Pragmatism' (n 18), 822.

[53] Pound (n 11), 620–21.

[54] Honoré, 'Legal Reasoning in Rome and Today' (n 5), 60. See also RA Posner, *The Problematics of Moral and Legal Theory* (London, Belknap Press, 1999), 227.

[55] M Rosenfeld, 'Pragmatism, Pluralism, and Legal Interpretation: Posner's and Rorty's Justice without Metaphysics Meets Hate Speech' (1996) 18 *Cardozo Law Review* 97, 98. See also Atiyah, *Pragmatism and Theory in English Law* (n 12), 76.

[56] Grey, 'Holmes and Legal Pragmatism' (n 18), 824.

[57] F Horak, *Rationes decidendi: Entscheidungsbegründungen bei den älteren römischen Juristen bis Labeo* (Aalen, Scientia, 1969), 65–69; see also PG Stein, 'Franz Horak – Rationes decidendi [review]' (1970) 36 *SDHI* 460, 461–62.

the jurists were 'master[s] of the Roman law in its full extent; each had the whole of its principles constantly present to his mind, and could argue down from them and apply them with the greatest certainty';[58] with the result that 'their successive works have the coherency commonly belonging only to the productions of one master mind'.[59] Jhering explodes this conceptualist view, the view 'that law is fundamentally no more than a creation of juristic discourse, for the understanding of which practical perspectives are not necessary',[60] 'as if Roman law contained the eternal law of all juridical thought!'[61] More recent scholarship concludes that 'the Roman lawyers did not follow the deductive method based on general legal propositions to find the law, but rather solved their legal problems according to the criteria that were decisive for the individual case'.[62] The jurists sometimes justified the solution 'simply by the fact that it is reasonable from a practical point of view and that it takes account of the circumstances of the case'.[63] Even as they developed it into a science distinct from customary practice, the jurists

> used arguments of analogy and contrariety in order to demonstrate the essential similarity or dissimilarity of a new case to an established one, and developed techniques of induction and deduction in order to generate abstract principles from concrete cases and then to reason outwards from these principles to new situations, though invariably tempering these results with a sense of pragmatism.[64]

Only rarely do the classical jurists explicitly abstract principles or formalised rules from the cases they consider; 'rules were tools of reasoning within Roman juristic discourse, rather than end-products'.[65] Rather than adducing a case as illustration of an abstract rule, the jurists' method tends 'to embed the rule in the vicinity of a set of cases and to subject it to the increasingly particular, minor, subtle and technical refinement that these cases enclose'.[66] Those abstract rules that do appear are

[58] J Austin, *Lectures on Jurisprudence*, vol II, 5th edn (R Campbell ed, London, Murray, 1885), 677.

[59] ibid.

[60] Jhering, *L'Esprit du droit romain* (n 23), 309 ('que le droit n'est essentiellement qu'une création de la dialectique juridique, pour l'intelligence de laquelle des vues pratiques ne sont pas nécessaires').

[61] ibid, 311 ('comme si le droit romain contenait la loi éternelle de toute pensée juridique!'). Nonetheless, well into the twentieth century, there persisted the view that Roman law offered 'enduring content of truth with respect to indispensable categories of legal thought, and [the] capacity, based on its absolutely mathematical precision, to initiate beginners into the study of law': L Mitteis, 'Storia del diritto antico e studio del diritto romano' (1929) 12 *AUPA* 477, 493 ('durevole contenuto di verità rispetto alle indispensabili categorie del pensiero giuridico, e [la] capacità, basata sulla sua precisione assolutamente matematica, di avviare i principianti nello studio del diritto').

[62] Leptien (n 27), 52 ('Die römischen Juristen befolgten bei der Rechtsfindung bekanntlich nicht die von allgemeinen Rechtssätzen ausgehende deduktive Methode, sondern lösten ihre Rechtsprobleme jeweils nach den gerade für den Einzelfall maßgeblichen Gesichtspunkten').

[63] Kaser (n 45), 114 ('On justifie la solution simplement par le fait qu'elle est raisonnable du point de vue pratique et qu'elle tient compte des circonstances de la cause').

[64] DJ Ibbetson and ADE Lewis, 'The Roman law tradition' in ADE Lewis and DJ Ibbetson (eds), *The Roman Law Tradition* (Cambridge, Cambridge University Press, 1994) 1, 11.

[65] C Humfress, 'Telling Stories About (Roman) Law' in P Dresch and J Scheele (eds), *Legalism: Rules and Categories* (Oxford, Oxford University Press, 2015) 79, 98.

[66] E Mussawir, 'To isolate the law: the activity of the jurist in Digest 9.2.27.12 and Digest 45.3.18.2' (2019) 10 *Jurisprudence* 54, 54.

often later generalisations of particular decisions, constituting 'a jurisprudence of ends in fact, even if in form it is a jurisprudence of conceptions'.[67] Moreover, what appears as an abstract rule or concept – especially in the abbreviated medium of the Digest – 'might constitute a rule of law in the mouth of one jurist and not in the mouth of another'.[68]

Abundant examples substantiate the view that, in this sense of principle and pragmatism, classical Roman juristic thought is more contextual than conceptual.[69] An illustrative commonplace is *dominium*: problems of acquisition, infringement and loss of ownership are not resolved by arguments derived from this – itself remarkably immutable – concept but by reference to contextual facts. When Proculus discusses taking a wild boar caught in a trap set by another, the answer is given in terms of control ('if it came into my power, it became mine'); he derives this conclusion not from any concept of *dominium* but from contextual questions: was the trap set on public land or private land; if private, the trapper's land or another's; if another's, with that other's permission or without; was the boar capable of escaping?[70]

Nonetheless, the jurists are, of course, not a homogenous group, and methods evolve over time. Stein delineates contrasting movements in the early Empire: one favouring the coherence of rules; the other flexibility 'to concentrate on the decision in the individual case'.[71] By way of illustration, he juxtaposes the Proculian conclusion that a legacy including the phrase 'part of the goods' meant a fraction of the goods themselves, since the testator could easily have given a fraction of the value, had he so intended, with the 'more convenient' Sabinian interpretation of it as referring to a fraction of the value of the estate.[72] The type of work necessarily affects method, too. Juristic works with a pedagogical aim naturally rely on classification and generalisation for explanation; nevertheless, Gaius, for example, does not 'draw binding dogmatic conclusions for the solution of problems, according to the place that a notion or a proposition occupies within his system'.[73]

Different emphases may be discerned in Justinianic law. However, even then, the rethinking of legal materials and the application to them of dialectic method is, for Kaser, only partially realised: the *regulae* and *definitiones* favoured by the Byzantine jurists still do not 'receive a fixed place arising from logical principles, within a closed system'.[74] The leading excerpt that the compilers retained on *regulae*

[67] Pound (n 11), 611.

[68] Honoré, 'Legal Reasoning in Rome and Today' (n 5), 61. See also Humfress (n 65), 96.

[69] For detailed recent analyses of principle and casuistry in two specific cases, D. 9.2.27.12 (Ulp. 18 *ad Ed.*) and D. 45.3.18.2 (Pap. 27 *Quaest.*), see Mussawir (n 66).

[70] D. 41.1.55 (Proc. 2 *Epist.*).

[71] Stein, 'Interpretation and Legal Reasoning in Roman Law' (n 5), 1545.

[72] ibid, 1547. See also Stein, 'Logic and Experience in Roman and Common Law' (n 22), 45–46.

[73] Kaser (n 45), 118 ('Il ne peut être question, pour lui, de tirer des conclusions dogmatiques contraignantes pour la solution des problèmes, en fonction de la place qu'occupe une notion ou une proposition à l'intérieur de son système').

[74] ibid, 119 ('Chez elles, les règles et les définitions de concepts n'ont pas encore reçu de place fixe découlant des principes logiques, à l'intérieur d'un système fermé').

is Paul's affirmation of Sabinus's view (against Labeo's[75]) that *regulae* are derived from the law as it is – and that law is not derived from *regulae*.[76]

Taking a wider perspective still – concerning not conceptual and contextual method in legal reasoning but the compilers' approach to the *Corpus Iuris* itself – Jolowicz considers it the 'supreme example in antiquity … [of a work the method of which] was not that most obviously adapted to the production of a compendium for practical use'.[77] With particular reference to its atavism and archaisms, Jolowicz characterises the *Corpus* as a work in which

> law appears as an object of study whose practical purpose is remote or non-existent; and sometimes this study is 'elegant' in the sense that it consciously strives to rise above the immediate necessities of practice, or at least to adorn what is conceived as a mercenary pursuit with the graces of useless learning.[78]

This conclusion – about law as a concept, more than as a practice in context – is perhaps the ultimate abstract form of this second sense of principle and pragmatism.

C. Consistency and Diversity

Related to both the first and the second senses but distinct from them, a third sense of 'principle' is 'as a requirement for coherence in legal reasoning',[79] emphasising principle as an 'attempt to give some overall structure or rational shape to the law … in the interests of consistency, of the desire to ensure that like is treated alike'.[80] In contrast:

> Pragmatists differ … because they see no inherent virtue in logical consistency if it leads to unacceptable outcomes; what pragmatists seek in legal reasoning is not logical neatness but persuasion in the service of reasonable outcomes.[81]

In this vein, and commenting in a fashion that may echo for Roman law, Holmes identified the

> error of supposing the science of the law to reside in the *elegantia juris*, or logical cohesion of part with part. The truth is, that the law is always approaching, and never reaching, consistency. It is forever adopting new principles from life at one end, and it

[75] See Stein, 'Logic and Experience in Roman and Common Law' (n 22), 49–50; Stein, 'Interpretation and Legal Reasoning in Roman Law' (n 5), 1554.

[76] D. 50.17.1 (Paul. 16 *ad Plaut.*).

[77] Jolowicz, 'Utility and Elegance in Civil Law Studies' (n 11), 323.

[78] ibid, 322.

[79] A Aarnio and DN MacCormick, 'Introduction' in A Aarnio and DN MacCormick (eds), *Legal Reasoning*, vol II (Aldershot, Dartmouth, 1992) xi, xiv.

[80] Atiyah, *Pragmatism and Theory in English Law* (n 12), 27.

[81] DJ Luban, 'What's Pragmatic about Legal Pragmatism?' (1996) 18 *Cardozo Law Review* 43, 45. See also Atiyah, 'From Principles to Pragmatism' (n 6), 1250–51; RM Dworkin, *Law's Empire* (London, Fontana, 1986), 161; Posner, 'Pragmatic Adjudication' (n 6), 5.

always retains old ones from history at the other, which have not yet been absorbed or sloughed off. It will become entirely consistent only when it ceases to grow.[82]

When deciding novel cases, a preference for pragmatism over principle in this sense frequently manifests as rejection of analogy.[83] Consistency is not, however, undermined when an apparently general applicable rule is qualified by reference to some other – perhaps cross-cutting – rule of law.[84]

Though now rejected, it was once maintained that Roman law was a perfect and consistent system of private law.[85] Modern scholarship more sensitive to individual juristic thought credits Labeo and the Proculian school with recognising

> the existence of an unstated structure of basic principles. They sought to apply those principles in circumstances where their rivals saw no connection. They looked for a logical structure to the law, whereas the Sabinians stressed custom and practice. Labeo held that one could use analogy to discover the law applicable to a problem which had not been the subject of a previous ruling. He was familiar with the dispute among grammarians between analogists, who viewed language as a structure of rules, and anomalists, who considered language as based exclusively on popular usage.[86]

Stein adduces examples contrasting the Proculians' preference for analogy and thus consistency (principle) with the Sabinians' tolerance of anomaly and thus diversity (pragmatism). In the case of the legacy of 'part of the goods' mentioned above, the Proculians treated the phrase as straightforwardly indicating a fraction of the goods, while the Sabinians

> considered that the words were capable of a more convenient interpretation than that provided by their precise objective meaning. For these Sabinians the same expression could mean one thing in one testament and another thing in another … In emphasizing the intention of the testator as a criterion of interpretation, Sabinus showed that he was more concerned with arriving at a reasonable decision in the particular case than he was with maintaining consistency of meaning whenever a form of words was given legal effect.[87]

A second example is the schools dispute recorded at G. 3.98, about legacies bequeathed subject to an impossible condition;[88] the Proculians treat the case as analogous to stipulations subject to an impossible condition, and so hold them void, but the legacies are regarded as valid and treated as if they were unconditional by the Sabinians – including Gaius, who nonetheless expresses his unease: 'Though, to be sure, a sound reason for the difference can scarcely be given'.[89]

[82] Holmes, *The Common Law* (n 18), 36.

[83] Atiyah, *Pragmatism and Theory in English* Law (n 12), 50.

[84] ibid, 49.

[85] For a relatively late example, see Mitteis (n 61), 490.

[86] Stein, 'Interpretation and Legal Reasoning in Roman Law' (n 5), 1550–51. See also Stein, 'Logic and Experience in Roman and Common Law' (n 22), 43–44.

[87] Stein, 'Logic and Experience in Roman and Common Law' (n 22), 45–46 (footnote omitted).

[88] Stein, 'Interpretation and Legal Reasoning in Roman Law' (n 5), 1551.

[89] G. 3.98: *Et sane vix idonea diversitatis ratio reddi potest.*

D. Reason and Tradition

A fourth sense of 'principle' and 'pragmatism', canvassing both substance and method, contrasts, on the one hand, juristic argument by reference to reason, where principle connotes the logical, 'the orderly, the systematic, the scientific'[90] and, on the other, argument by reference to tradition, where pragmatism connotes custom and continuity with past decisions.[91] Principle and pragmatism in this sense are not exclusive but complementary: as Holmes observes, 'Everywhere the basis of principle is tradition'.[92] Holmes is concerned to ensure that history is properly understood[93] and not emphasised over 'a study of the ends sought to be attained and the reason for desiring them'.[94] While he thus agrees with Pound that '[r]everence for institutions of the past'[95] will not suffice, Holmes reminds us that:

> The law embodies the story of a nation's development through many centuries, and it cannot be dealt with as if it contained only the axioms and corollaries of a book of mathematics. In order to know what it is, we must know what it has been, and what it tends to become.[96]

Law retains historical artefacts as it develops; and it reflects values and institutions that 'depend to some degree on the very fact of long historical continuity and tradition'.[97] Principle and pragmatism as reason and tradition is especially apposite for Roman law, in view of its longevity and the layered nature of its sources.

Gordon observes that historical artefacts persisting in the Roman legal system – such as *mancipatio* and *stipulatio* – may be understood both in terms of a tendency to layer new institutions over old ones, rather than to replace them, and in terms of retaining institutions that have been approved.[98] Mere survival, however, does not signify a predominant role for tradition: many 'reasons must be considered along with the force of tradition or inertia in assessing what lay behind a particular course of development or a particular cessation of development'.[99]

[90] Atiyah, *Pragmatism and Theory in English Law* (n 12), 7.

[91] Deliberately blurring the line, Holmes suggests a 'peculiar logical pleasure in making manifest the continuity between what we are doing and what has been done before': OW Holmes, 'Learning and Science' (1895) in OW Holmes, *Collected Legal Papers* (New York, Harcourt, Brace and Co, 1920) 138, 139.

[92] Holmes, 'The Path of the Law' (n 19), 191.

[93] Holmes, 'Law in Science and Science in Law' (n 20), 225–26.

[94] Holmes, 'The Path of the Law' (n 19), 195. See Grey, 'Holmes and Legal Pragmatism' (n 18), 805–06.

[95] Pound (n 11), 606.

[96] Holmes, *The Common Law* (n 18), 1. See also Holmes, 'Law in Science and Science in Law' (n 20), 225–26.

[97] Atiyah, *Pragmatism and Theory in English Law* (n 12), 95.

[98] WM Gordon, 'Legal Tradition, with particular reference to Roman Law' in DN MacCormick and PBH Birks (eds), *The Legal Mind: Essays for Tony Honoré* (Oxford, Clarendon Press, 1986) 279, 282. Roman law's preference for 'developing new doctrines and techniques rather than openly modifying or rebuilding the old' is not unique: Atiyah, *Pragmatism and Theory in English Law* (n 12), 123–24.

[99] Gordon (n 98), 285.

Even so revered a cultural artefact – and binding statute – as the XII Tables could be manipulated to sustain novel interpretation, as the pontiffs achieved with voluntary manumission.[100]

The pontiffs were, of course, the earliest Roman legal authorities.[101] While observing that it was accompanied by a rational system no later than the middle of second century BCE, Kaser stresses the foundations of juristic understanding in 'the law already discovered by previous generations, carefully collected and transmitted to posterity, as preserved in the juristic literature'.[102] Exemplifying this dual foundation, in the early Empire, Stein associates the search for *ratio* in the unwritten law with the Proculian school, while the Sabinians 'looked for evidence of its antiquity … [considering] that the validity of the law was somehow connected with its observance from time immemorial'.[103] In a celebrated illustration, Julian's argument in support of the innovative conclusion that both defendants who inflicted successive mortal wounds should count as having slain includes analogy but foregrounds invocation of the authority of the Republican jurists: *Idque est consequens auctoritati veterum*.[104] Scarano Ussani considers that, while the Proculian Celsus perceived as potentially destructive the authority of juristic science:[105]

> From Julian's [Sabinian] perspective, in contrast, an unbroken thread had to tie the present to the past, whose solutions, even if not always acceptable, must be seriously considered: they guaranteed the soundness of learning and its coherent development.[106]

In the subsequent fragment, Julian appeals to policy, considering it absurd to hold neither defendant liable, and difficult to say which, if only one, is the more plainly liable. He then reiterates his appeal to tradition, however illogical, over reason: 'That many things have been settled by the civil law contrary to the logic of argument but on account of common necessity can be shown in innumerable cases'.[107]

The contrasting approaches of reason and tradition were synthesised by the end of the second century CE:

> The jurists no longer had to choose between the methods of one [school] or the other. Instead, they accepted the idea that they had a variety of techniques at their disposal;

[100] HF Jolowicz and JKBM Nicholas, *An Historical Introduction to the Study of Roman Law*, 3rd edn (Cambridge, Cambridge University Press, 1972), 89–90; Stein, 'Interpretation and Legal Reasoning in Roman Law' (n 5), 1541.

[101] Jolowicz and Nicholas (n 100), 88–90.

[102] Kaser (n 45), 114 ('le droit déjà découvert par les générations passées, soigneusement recueillie et transmise à la postérité, telle qu'elle fut conservée dans la littérature juridique').

[103] Stein, 'Logic and Experience in Roman and Common Law' (n 22), 47; see also 45.

[104] D. 9.2.51.1 (Iul. 86 *Dig.*).

[105] D. 45.1.91.3 (Paul. 17 ad Plau.): … *esse enim hanc quaestionem de bono et aequo: in quo genere plerumque sub auctoritate iuris scientiae perniciose, inquit [Celsus], erratur.*

[106] V Scarano Ussani, *L'Utilità e la certezza* (Milan, Giuffrè, 1987), 13 ('Un filo ininterrotto doveva invece legare, nella prospettiva giulianea, il presente al passato, le cui soluzioni, anche se non sempre accettabili, dovevano tenersi nel massimo conto: garantivano la solidità della scienza e del suo svolgersi coerente').

[107] D. 9.2.51.2 (Iul. 86 *Dig.*): … *Multa autem iure civili contra rationem disputandi pro utilitate communi recepta esse innumerabilibus rebus probari potest …*

that in some cases it would be appropriate to rely on established practice or authority, whereas in other cases logical reasoning and analogy were more useful.[108]

Nonetheless, jurists (on both sides of this debate) often prefer the authority of other (earlier) jurists to concrete arguments.[109] To some degree, this is a matter of the 'scientific personalities of the Roman jurists';[110] according to Honoré, 'Proculus likes to argue from the facts, Julian to formulate rules, Pomponius to appeal to open arguments, Ulpian to cite authority, [and] Scaevola disdains giving reasons'.[111] More broadly, however, the phenomenon attests to the centrality of tradition in professional juristic practice. Leptien observes how commonly later classical lawyers cite general (juristic) approval for a solution adopted on account of *utilitas* rather than logic, typically by means of the phrase *utilitas causa receptum est*.[112] While enacted to mitigate dangers of forged and inauthentic sources,[113] the Law of Citations of 426 CE[114] shows persistence of the phenomenon into post-classical law, albeit at a time when argument was reduced to 'rules to operate mechanically'.[115]

E. Theory and Empiricism

A fifth sense of 'principle' and 'pragmatism' considers the relative places of, on the one hand, reasoning *a priori* in light of some system of abstract ideas and, on the other, reasoning directed to the particular end of solving a problem with concrete facts.[116] In this sense, both principle and pragmatism concern law's character as an instrumental social phenomenon:

> Law may be in some respects a highly practical subject, but it is quite impossible that it could exist at all without theory. Law is a *purposeful* enterprise. We live by law in modern societies for *reasons*, because we have intelligible and discoverable human goals. The whole concept of the rule of law requires not just that we have rules, and that government is bound by rules, but also that these rules should be based on purposes and reasons which are open to public debate.[117]

[108] Stein, 'Logic and Experience in Roman and Common Law' (n 22), 50. See also Stein, 'Interpretation and Legal Reasoning in Roman Law' (n 5), 1552.

[109] Kaser (n 45), 112–13; Stein, 'Logic and Experience in Roman and Common Law' (n 22), 47.

[110] Gordon (n 98), 280. As Gordon notes, scholarship has not always distinguished the jurists in this way: see, eg, Schulz, *Principles of Roman Law* (n 7), 107–08.

[111] Honoré, 'Legal Reasoning in Rome and Today' (n 5), 67.

[112] Leptien (n 27), 70. It has been suggested that reference to *utilitatis causa* always denotes the move from *ius controversum* to *ius receptum*, even absent the phrase *receptum est*: Navarra (n 31), 177–78, 206. This is, however, disputed: see, eg, Ankum, 'The Functions of Expressions with *Utilitatis Causa*' (n 28), 6.

[113] AJB Sirks, *The Theodosian Code: A Study* (Friedrichsdorf, Tortuga, 2007), 18–19.

[114] CTh. 1.4.3 (Theodosius and Valentinianus to the Senate of Rome, 7 November 426).

[115] Pound (n 11), 607.

[116] See, eg, W James, *Pragmatism: A New Name for Some Old Ways of Thinking* (London, Longmans, 1907), 51.

[117] Atiyah, *Pragmatism and Theory in English Law* (n 12), 143–44 (original emphasis).

Principle as abstract theory and pragmatism as empirical problem-solving are both purposeful; however, they differ in the degree to which they are purposeful:

> There are those of us who start from a basis of legal principle and those of us who start from a basis of pragmatism – starting from the beginning or starting from the end: what Stephen Sedley called, 'reasoning from a given conclusion'.[118]

The theory–empiricism spectrum in legal reasoning might be measured in three dimensions: the level of generality at which a rule is formulated; the degree to which the rule 'fits' into a superstructure of ideas; and the extent to which that superstructure is internal to the law or is connected to an external system, such as religion, philosophy or ethics. Implicated in the dimension of generality is the stereotypical contrast between top-down and bottom-up reasoning in civilian and common law systems:

> The tradition of the English Common Law has been one of gradual development from decision to decision; historically speaking, it is case-law, not enacted law. On the Continent the development since the reception of Roman law has been quite different, from the interpretation of JUSTINIAN's Corpus Iuris to the codification, nation by nation, of abstract rules.[119]

The continental preference for principle is clear in the famously general article 1240 of the French Civil Code: 'Every act whatever of man that causes damage to another obliges him by whose fault it occurred to repair it'.[120] In contrast, English jurists 'hesitate to accept generalities which are unrelated to concrete facts'.[121]

The epitome of integrating particular rules into a superstructure is the 'rational structure for the law of nature' contrived by Pufendorf and Grotius.[122] On such a view, an individual rule is no more than a manifestation of the principles, derived from rational intuition, that underlie the entire legal system. Pragmatists, however, 'conceive of law as a cluster of activities too complex to be captured and subdued by any theory'.[123] At its most pragmatic, legal reasoning could be viewed as akin to engineering,[124] with each rule a tool perfectly fashioned for the discrete, specific end it is designed to achieve.

A third dimension of the theory–empiricism (principle–pragmatism) spectrum measures purposefulness by the degree to which the relevant superstructure

[118] Hale (n 13), 2, citing S Sedley, 'Declining the brief' in S Sedley, *Ashes and Sparks: Essays On Law and Justice* (Cambridge, Cambridge University Press, 2011) 153, 156.

[119] K Zweigert and H Kötz, *An Introduction to Comparative Law*, 3rd edn (AD Weir trans, Oxford, Oxford University Press, 1998), 69.

[120] *Code civil* (France), art 1240 (formerly art 1382): 'Tout fait quelconque de l'homme, qui cause à autrui un dommage, oblige celui par la faute duquel il est arrivé à le réparer'.

[121] AL Goodhart, *English Contributions to the Philosophy of Law* (New York, Oxford University Press, 1949), 12.

[122] DJ Ibbetson, 'Natural Law in Early Modern Legal Thought' in H Pihlajamäki, MD Dubber and M Godfrey (eds), *The Oxford Handbook of European Legal History* (Oxford, Oxford University Press, 2018) 566, 572.

[123] Grey, 'Freestanding Legal Pragmatism' (n 10), 26.

[124] D Howarth, *Law as Engineering: Thinking About What Lawyers Do* (Cheltenham, Edward Elgar, 2013).

of rules reaches into – or derives from – other disciplines, or is distinctively legal. In a sense, this dimension is no more than an application of the dimensions of generality and rational structure; a system can be regarded as more principled in this sense if its rules derive from, or give effect to, a broader system of norms. The appeal, in centuries past, to natural law and the sometime universal law of the Catholic Church has arguably been replaced, in the modern world, by principled connectedness to norms of human rights and due process.

The form of the Digest as 'essentially a casebook'[125] conveys an overwhelmingly empirical (pragmatic), rather than theoretical (principled), impression of Roman juristic argument. The jurists' method of working and thinking was

> practical, pragmatical: their interest is to find good answers to concrete legal questions, to find solutions that are suitable for practical life. They do not like to make theoretical considerations and often they refuse to suffer decisions in legal disputes to depend only on dogmatic and logical reasonings.[126]

The majority of texts concern points of detail, contain scant relation of the particular to the general, and only infrequently abstract into general principles. Nonetheless, the absence of frequent express formulation of underlying principle does not mean that the jurists as a profession – or even individual jurists – lacked theoretical vision about the place and functions of law. Ulpian, the archetypal doctrinal jurist, expressed their role in notably theoretical terms:

> We [jurists] are deservedly known as priests of [the art of justice], for we cultivate justice and profess knowledge of the good and fair [*boni et aequi*], separating the fair from the unfair, discerning what is lawful from what is unlawful, desiring to make people good not only through fear of punishment but also by appealing to them through rewards, and striving towards a philosophy that, unless I am mistaken, is true, not feigned.[127]

The primary conduit for theoretical influence in Roman juristic argument is thought to have been a scientific method: 'to define, elucidate and enhance existing legal notions'.[128] Beginning in the mid-second century BCE, the Greek schools of philosophy and rhetoric, in particular, provided a 'broader intellectual context in which the Roman jurists operated'.[129] Looking backwards to this period from the early Principate, Stein observes:

[125] Buckland quoted in Hanbury (n 4), 24.

[126] Ankum, '*Utilitatis causa receptum*' (n 28), 2.

[127] D. 1.1.1.1 (Ulp. 1 *Inst.*): *Cuius merito quis nos sacerdotes appellet: iustitiam namque colimus et boni et aequi notitiam profitemur, aequum ab iniquo separantes, licitum ab illicito discernentes, bonos non solum metu poenarum, verum etiam praemiorum quoque exhortatione efficere cupientes, veram nisi fallor philosophiam, non simulatam affectantes.*

[128] J Giltaij, 'Greek Philosophy and Classical Roman Law: A Brief Overview' in PJ du Plessis, C Ando and K Tuori (eds), *The Oxford Handbook of Roman Law and Society* (Oxford, Oxford University Press, 2016) 188, 197.

[129] A Kacprzak, 'Rhetoric and Roman Law' in PJ du Plessis, C Ando and K Tuori (eds), *The Oxford Handbook of Roman Law and Society* (Oxford, Oxford University Press, 2016) 200, 200. See also J Gordley, *The Jurists: A Critical History* (Oxford, Oxford University Press, 2013), 12–18; B Forschner,

> The seeds of Labeo's methodological innovations were planted in the century before he wrote, when the influence of Greek philosophy became dominant in Roman intellectual circles. In the area of law this influence was not directed towards given solutions to specific problems, as it was in other disciplines, but was rather a general, climatic influence. From Greek philosophy the Romans learned that any worthwhile knowledge ought to be organized as a science. Aristotle's work demonstrated the evolutionary development of a body of knowledge into a science. First the common elements which unite individual experiences are identified and then propositions which state those elements in principles are formulated.[130]

It is possible that particular substantive ideas were borrowed from Greek philosophy in the late Republic, too, but in an eclectic rather than a systematic fashion, to explicate particular cases.[131] In the Principate, particular Greek practices may have played a role,[132] and Stoic theories more generally may have been implicated in theories of will and intention,[133] or causation.[134] Naturally, these influences may have been more relevant to some jurists than others.[135] Most commonly, however, even reasoning resting 'on open arguments (topoi, principles)',[136] such as Pomponius's assertion that 'one who suffers loss through his own fault is understood not to have suffered loss at all',[137] is not framed in terms of abstract principle, let alone systematic philosophy, but 'is filtered through the more specific maxim'.[138] While it is conceivable that legal decisions were reached and doctrines formulated with a view to implementing underlying conceptions, a process of juridification – special to the methods, objectives and traditions of the Roman jurists – transforms the extra-legal values into legal maxims, *regulae* that expound the law.[139] As Gordley puts it, the jurists

> were giving their own opinions as jurists as to how legal concepts applied to particular cases. They were neither deducing the results in the cases from the concepts, nor deriving general conclusions about the concepts form the results in the cases.[140]

If Greek philosophy is the enduring – though problematic – candidate for theoretical influence in late Republican and classical law, Christianity is its principal

'Law's Nature: Philosophy as a Legal Argument in Cicero's Writings' in PJ du Plessis (ed), *Cicero's Law: Rethinking Roman Law of the Late Republic* (Edinburgh, Edinburgh University Press, 2016) 50.

130 Stein, 'Logic and Experience in Roman and Common Law' (n 22), 43.

131 Giltaij (n 128), 190–93.

132 See, eg, M Leese, 'Greek Influences on Roman Dowry Law' (2019) 40 *Journal of Legal History* 130.

133 Giltaij (n 128), 195.

134 AJB Sirks, 'The slave who was slain twice: causality and the *lex Aquilia* (Iulian. 86 *dig*. D. 9,2,51)' (2011) 79 *Leg Hist Rev* 313.

135 See, eg, JR Kroger, 'The Philosophical Foundations of Roman Law: Aristotle, the Stoics, and Roman Theories of Natural Law' [2004] *Wisconsin Law Review* 905 (on Gaius and Ulpian); AM Honoré, 'Ulpian, Natural Law and Stoic Influence' (2010) 78 *Leg Hist Rev* 199.

136 Honoré, 'Legal Reasoning in Rome and Today' (n 5), 60.

137 D. 50.17.203 (Pomp. 8 *ad Q. Muc.*): *Quod quis ex culpa sua damnum sentit, not intellegitur damnum sentire.*

138 Honoré, 'Legal Reasoning in Rome and Today' (n 5), 62.

139 See, in particular, PG Stein, *Regulae Iuris: From Juristic Rules to Legal Maxims* (Edinburgh, Edinburgh University Press, 1966).

140 Gordley (n 129), 16.

successor in the post-classical period. Christian principle is detectable in relation to the law of persons – in areas such as *patria potestas*, slavery, marriage and the protection of the vulnerable[141] – though, in some respects, it probably built on Stoic ideas of humanity already present.[142] The prime opportunity to recast the law – in terms of Christian ethics but also Eastern values more generally – was, of course, the compilation of the *Corpus Iuris*. A willing and ambitious architect could have shaped its design and content to a framework of principles and underlying values. However, this did not occur, either in structure or in substance. No extrinsic superstructure of ideas displaces the edictal ordering of topics in the Digest; the nearly 150 references to the XII Tables retained in the *Corpus* show that, a millennium after enactment, the 'fountainhead of all public and private law'[143] remained the subject of 'that blind and partial reverence which the lawyers of every country delight to bestow on their municipal institutions'.[144] Modern scholarship concludes that Byzantine law was characterised by

> internal development of the law rather than external borrowing, evolution rather than reception, '*fusione*' as Riccobono says … eastern influence [had only] a very minor role … The final form that Justinian's law took results from the work of Roman jurists upon their own law.[145]

F. Form and Substance

Related to several others is a sixth, distinct but arguably more minor, sense of 'principle' and 'pragmatism' that takes Holmes's aphorism about logic and experience 'as a kind of anti-formalist banner'.[146] Reflecting law's aspiration 'to be an immanently intelligible normative practice',[147] the formalist

> approaches legal relationships by first discerning their necessary conditions, their internal principles of organization, and their presuppositions. These formal aspects then guide substantive determination.[148]

[141] See, eg, J Highwood, *The Influence of the Christian Religion on Roman and English Law* (Durham, Thomas Caldcleugh, 1903), 26–51; S Riccobono, 'Outlines of the Evolution of Roman Law' (1925) 74 *University of Pennsylvania Law Review* 1, 8.

[142] See, eg, HJS Maine, *Lectures on the Early History of Institutions* (London, Murray, 1875), 62; P Collinet, 'The General Problems Raised by the Codification of Justinian' (1923) 4 *Leg Hist Rev* 1, 15–16; Ibbetson (n 122), 568.

[143] Liv., 3.34.6: *fons omnis publici privatique … iuris.*

[144] E Gibbon, *The History of the Decline and Fall of the Roman Empire*, vol 4 (London, Strahan and Cadell, 1788), 338.

[145] AA Schiller, 'Sources and Influences of the Roman Law, III-VI Centuries A. D.' (1933) 21 *Georgetown Law Journal* 147, 153.

[146] Atiyah, *Pragmatism and Theory in English Law* (n 12), 90.

[147] EJ Weinrib, 'Legal Formalism' in D Patterson (ed), *A Companion to Philosophy of Law and Legal Theory* (Chichester, Blackwell, 2010) 327, 327.

[148] ibid, 328.

The contrasting, pragmatic approach instead assigns priority to substantive – 'moral, economic, political, institutional, or other social'[149] – considerations.

An evolving preference for substance over form is an enduring narrative in Roman legal scholarship. In early Roman law, steeped in public ceremony, '[r]itualism and formalism held the field'.[150] Governing principally the creation of legal relationships and their enforcement by legal proceedings, a failure of form was fatal to legal efficacy. Over time, this dogmatic adherence to form gave way to an analytical focus on the ends the parties sought to achieve. Late Republican doctrines of the *ius gentium* were not formalistic; the *ius honorarium* often tended to expediency.[151] Chapters in this volume explore clear shifts in *stipulatio* and in *mancipatio*, after the creation of the *actio Publiciana* and associated defences.[152] Examples, though, are plentiful: defences of fraud and duress made form inconclusive in stipulations;[153] in rhetorical terms (but with jurists in the background),[154] Crassus's victory in the *causa Curiana*, argued before the centumviral court in 93 BCE, was a victory for the intention of a testator over the literal interpretation advocated by Scaevola.[155]

The contest for primacy between the objective meaning of the written will (principle) and the testator's intentions (pragmatism) remained a live issue in classical law, as is demonstrated by the schools dispute, mentioned above, concerning the phrase 'part of the goods' in a legacy.[156] More generally, for all that the Proculian Celsus proclaimed that *ius est ars boni et aequi*,[157] his school 'consistently advocated a strict, objective interpretation of the words used' in written texts;[158] Stein gives the example of Labeo's refusing to recommend the interdict *unde vi* for a possessor who fled armed men without waiting actually to be evicted by force.[159]

In a more concrete application of 'form' and 'substance', another schools dispute concerned *specificatio*: 'The Sabinians held that the mead would belong to the

[149] PS Atiyah and RS Summers, *Form and Substance in Anglo-American Law: A Comparative Study in Legal Reasoning, Legal Theory, and Legal Institutions* (Oxford, Oxford University Press, 1987), 1.

[150] Jolowicz, 'Academic Elements in Roman Law' (n 1), 176. On distinguishing formality, ritual and symbolism from magic, free of out-dated sociological and anthropological preconceptions, see GD MacCormack, 'Formalism, Symbolism and Magic in Early Roman Law' (1969) 37 *Leg Hist Rev* 439.

[151] Riccobono (n 141), 1–3.

[152] See chs 3 and 6.

[153] WAJ Watson, *The Law of Obligations in the Later Roman Republic* (Oxford, Oxford University Press, 1965), 3, 257–58.

[154] J Hilder, 'Jurors, Jurists and Advocates: Law in the *Rhetorica ad Herennium* and *De Inventione*' in PJ du Plessis (ed), *Cicero's Law: Rethinking Roman Law of the Late Republic* (Edinburgh, Edinburgh University Press, 2016) 166, 173.

[155] See, eg, OE Tellegen-Couperus and JW Tellegen, 'Reading a Dead Man's Mind: Hellenistic Philosophy, Rhetoric and Roman Law' in PJ du Plessis (ed), *Cicero's Law: Rethinking Roman Law of the Late Republic* (Edinburgh, Edinburgh University Press, 2016) 26, 32–35; M Wibier, 'Cicero's Reception in the Juristic Tradition of the Early Empire' in PJ du Plessis (ed), *Cicero's Law: Rethinking Roman Law of the Late Republic* (Edinburgh, Edinburgh University Press, 2016) 100, 112–13.

[156] See text accompanying nn 72 and 87.

[157] D. 1.1.1.pr (Ulp. 1 *Inst.*).

[158] Stein, 'Interpretation and Legal Reasoning in Roman Law' (n 5), 1545.

[159] D. 4.2.9.pr (Ulp. 11 *ad Ed.*).

owner of the wine and honey used [to make it] while the Proculians maintained that it belonged to the maker'.[160] Jolowicz and Thomas associate the Proculian view, perhaps influenced by Aristotelian thinking, with a focus on the identity (form) of the new thing, which could not sensibly be claimed by a *vindicatio* naming the materials from which it was fashioned.[161] The newer Sabinian view, perhaps informed by Stoic thinking, focused on the property rights of the owner of the *materia* and *substantia* (substance) used to create the new thing.[162] Stein's summary of the debate captures the sense of principle and pragmatism as form and substance:

> The Proculians' reasoning was probably grounded in the technicalities of procedure. In an action to claim the statue, the plaintiff would have to describe it as his property. Only A could claim that he owned a statue, since all B had owned was a lump of marble. The Sabinians countered this subtlety by reference to nature, the facts of life and common sense. A thing is a thing is a thing, they said. Without the material of which it is made, there can be no thing. To them, the statue was still just a lump of marble even though its outward form might have been altered by A.[163]

The classical law did not, of course, abandon formality; the rise of praetorian *aequitas* and amelioration of the harshness of the *ius civile* did not obviate the benefits of certainty and outward predictability of rules that emphasise recognition of form:

> During the first three centuries of the Christian era, many formal acts were required by the law of persons, of *iura in re*, of contracts, of succession and finally of procedure, which last was ordinarily the 'formulary' drawing its name from the rigid *formulae* of actions.[164]

By Justinianic law, however, almost all of these formal acts had gone; formality remained for certain matters connected with status and testaments but property and commercial transactions, as well as procedure – now by *libellus* rather than *formula* – were substantively informal.[165] Taking a wider view, however, legal reasoning itself took a final, formal turn: Justinian's *constitutio tanta* forbade reference to sources outside the *Corpus Iuris*, prohibited commentaries on it, and reaffirmed that only imperial legislation could remedy remaining gaps.[166]

G. Rights and Remedies

In a final, also arguably minor but certainly no less applicable, sense, 'principle' consists of a commitment in juristic method to rights and interests, while

160 JAC Thomas, 'Form and Substance in Roman Law' (1966) 19 *Current Legal Problems* 145, 151.
161 Jolowicz, 'Academic Elements in Roman Law' (n 1), 176–77; Thomas (n 160), 158–59.
162 Jolowicz, 'Academic Elements in Roman Law' (n 1), 176–77; Thomas (n 160), 147, 154–56.
163 Stein, 'Logic and Experience in Roman and Common Law' (n 22), 47.
164 Collinet (n 142), 13.
165 ibid.
166 C. 1.17.2.18–19, 21 (Justinian to the Senate and all the people, 16 December 533).

'pragmatism' is the contrasting 'tendency to develop the law by invoking remedies and procedures'.[167] As with several other senses of principle and pragmatism, reasoning in terms of rights is compatible with reasoning in terms of remedies:

> [I]t is of the utmost importance that rights be effectively enforceable by practical remedies; rights without remedies may be meaningless words. But it is equally true that remedies without an adequate theoretical understanding of what they are for, what purposes they serve, what rights and duties they are designed to uphold, are unlikely to serve as a satisfactory basis for the law.[168]

Surveying early legal systems from Iceland to India, Maine concludes that the 'substantive law has at first the look of being gradually secreted in the interstices of procedure; and the early lawyer can only see the law through the envelope of its technical forms'.[169] Roman law was no exception:

> [T]he XII Tables begin with, and appear to deal most fully with, procedure. The Edict and the Digest follow this plan. It is only in the institutional books that procedure takes its place as an instrumental or adjectival law. In Justinian's law the old forms of action are gone … Nevertheless, the Byzantine lawyers still think in terms of actions[.][170]

Sophisticated and creative though they were, the classical jurists are stereotypically 'not so much concerned with laying down rules on rights and duties as with discussing the conditions under which a certain action lies and the redress which might be obtained by it'.[171] Their approach is

> action-oriented rather than right-oriented. Legal discussion … was not in terms of whether a party had a right which the law would protect, but in terms of whether there was a recognized form of action which fitted the facts of the case, what the limits of that action were, and so on.[172]

The jurists' prism of considering the appropriate action nonetheless implies consideration of the scope and limits of the rights and interests an action protects. This is clearest in the demarcation between *actiones civiles*, subject to clearly defined bounds, and *actiones utiles*, which lie outside those bounds, or *actiones fictitiae*, which feign compliance with the prescriptions of the civil law.[173] That a fictitious action must be allowed for damage to property of a non-citizen[174] and a praetorian decretal action for a citizen who was not *erus* (owner)[175] shows that there was, underlying the procedural distinction, principled consideration of rights and

[167] Atiyah, *Pragmatism and Theory in English Law* (n 12), 66.
[168] ibid, 113.
[169] HJS Maine, *Early Law and Custom*, new edn (London, Murray, 1890), 389.
[170] WW Buckland and AD McNair, *Roman Law and Common Law*, 2nd edn (FH Lawson ed, Cambridge, Cambridge University Press, 1952), 399.
[171] F Schulz, *Classical Roman Law* (Oxford, Oxford University Press, 1951), 11.
[172] Stein, 'Logic and Experience in Roman and Common Law' (n 22), 38.
[173] Dovere (n 36), 243.
[174] G. 4.37.
[175] eg, a usufructuary: D. 9.2.12 (Paul. 10 *ad Sab.*).

interests – even if the framing of the discussion at the same time underscores pragmatic development by invoking remedies and procedure.

Moreover, behind the stereotypical jurist, Stein discerns different emphases in the Proculian and Sabinian schools. In relation to the *actio ad exhibendum*, seeking production in court of a disputed thing, the Proculian Labeo appears to hold that production of a damaged thing suffices (the object of the action being production), whereas Sabinus counts this a failure to produce, and allows a remedy (the claimant being worse off with the damaged thing).[176] In Stein's view, the Sabinians are less concerned with the conceptual right or interest (principle) underlying any given action but instead

> preferred to deal with new fact situations by pressing them into the already recognized forms of actions. As a result, Sabinians showed little respect for the limits of contractual or delictual actions and were prepared to extend them as convenience required. For example, Sabinus had no qualms about extending the notion of theft to include the stealing of land as well as moveables. The Proculians, however, refused such a proposition probably because the word for theft – *furtum* – implied originally that the thief carried away the owner's property.[177]

A further example, beyond production and theft, is the Sabinian Julian's preference for holding liable for slaying both defendants who inflicted successive mortal wounds.[178] The policy rationale, that it is better that both be liable when it cannot be said which, if only one, should count as having slain, arguably privileges the pragmatic award of a remedy, and a collective interest in punishment[179] and deterrence, over the principle of the statute, to say nothing of the rights of the defendant.

III. Chapter Survey

Revealing a mild preference for principle over pragmatism, the chapters in this volume are roughly arranged according to the taxonomy of the Institutes, rather than the inherited (edictal) order of topics in the Digest. More pragmatically, no particular sense or senses of the volume's core themes was prescribed, so the chapters exhibit a welcome diversity of approaches.

In chapter two, du Plessis examines the conceptual baggage that German intellectual debates of the late nineteenth and early twentieth centuries import into any discussion of principle and pragmatism. He considers the ways in which Roman juristic method was sidelined by the Pandectists in their ambition to create a rational framework of legal doctrine, dissolving dissent and distilling debate into absolute rules, applicable in any jurisdiction, regardless of time, place or social

[176] Stein, 'Interpretation and Legal Reasoning in Roman Law' (n 5), 1548, with reference to D. 50.16.246.pr (Pomp. 16 *Epist.*) and D. 10.4.9.3 (Ulp. 24 *ad Ed.*).
[177] Stein, 'Logic and Experience in Roman and Common Law' (n 22), 48.
[178] D. 9.2.51 (Iul. 86 *Dig.*).
[179] Scarano Ussani (n 106), 9.

context. The backlash from early legal realists also took the study and teaching of Roman law as a battleground for their insistence on understanding law as a social institution with a particular context. Principle as reason, conceptualism and coherence are themes in du Plessis's account, as are pragmatism as utility, context and diversity. In surveying these debates, and their significance for future Roman law scholarship, du Plessis argues both for a jurist-centric approach and for sensitivity to the open character of the Roman legal reasoning.

Macnair focuses in chapter three on Gaius and, in particular, on the passage in his second-century pedagogical work where the jurist explains 'bonitary ownership' in terms of a purchaser of *res manicipi* who fails to take by formal conveyance. In probing where, how and why Gaius introduces bonitary ownership, Macnair shows how Gaius's treatment is shaped by the lack of any conceptual explanation, by a focus on remedies and, above all, by context. Inadequate attention to Gaius's pragmatic pedagogical choices has, in turn, shaped all subsequent academic treatment of the topic. Macnair argues for a radical refocusing of the traditional textbook accounts of bonitary ownership and the *actio Publiciana*, and for an understanding of Roman conceptions of ownership that is properly sensitive to context, substantive consequences and remedies.

In chapter four, Sampson examines the ways in which successive generations of jurists used the language of *causa* in relation to *usucapio*, noting a shift towards prioritising factual events over the intentions of the parties. This, he suggests, reflects a changing view of the dynamic that existed between the constitutive elements of *usucapio*, as *causa* ceased to be a basis for good faith and became an element in its own right. This conceptual shift is used to explain the disagreement between Julian and Ulpian as to the causal requirement of *traditio*, where Sampson argues that a juristic desire for consistency across the two modes of acquisition is visible at different points in classical law. The chapter engages with themes of tradition, utility and abstraction, as well as consistency and remedial focus; moreover, Sampson's approach stresses the diversity of juristic reasons and the need to approach jurists as individuals, recognising that they formulate doctrines in radically different ways, based on their views about the appropriate outcome and also on their commitment to a structure of ideas.

Cunningham's exploration, in chapter five, of the *querela inofficiosi testamenti* focuses on connections between juristic reasoning and rhetoric, arguing that the characteristically Roman virtue of *pietas*, as a social and cultural construct, was directly implemented by the jurists in the *querela*, including in opposition to the theoretical legal absolutism of *patria potestas*. Cunningham locates the reinvention of methods and extension of remedies – by Republican and Imperial jurists, and by emperors in the post-classical period – against the background of emergent juristic science, and in the context of natural law rhetorical argument. Addressing also the related cultural value of *aequitas*, Cunningham's argument that juristic reasoning was not an internalised science but one open to arguments drawn from practical, social reality deals with tradition, analogy and consistency, as well as the role of theory and context.

In chapter six, Ibbetson addresses a central illustration in Roman law of principle and pragmatism as form and substance, tracing the evolution of the *stipulatio* from the last century BCE to Justinian. His theme is that the juristic literature, which, with the development of legal science, necessarily involves a measure of essentialisation, fails at all times to portray the full picture of *stipulatio*. Ibbetson speculates on the original ritual components of the *stipulatio* in practice and unpacks the contrast between its later written character, in commercial context, and the orality of its conceptualisation, in legal theory. He observes how the essentialised core of *stipulatio* could be accommodated in juristic tradition long after it ceased to resemble the practical reality.

Sirks focuses in chapter seven on the three principal subsidiary pacts in the contract of sale and purchase: the *pactum displicentiae* (sale on approval); the *in diem addictio* (sale subject to a better offer); and the *lex commissoria* (sale subject to forfeiture in default of payment on the due date). He demonstrates that the very validity of the contracts could depend on whether these pacts were interpreted by reference to an abstract, objective notion of a condition, or by reference to the intention of the parties as expressed in the phrasing of the contract. Observing that Stoic causal thinking and the logic of the Greek schools exerted no discernible influence, Sirks reveals disagreement between generations of jurists in construing these *pacta adiecta*. By contrasting these with the interpretation of analogous terms in testamentary dispositions and stipulations, Sirks further shows that the jurists preferred to grapple with conditions in context, rather than to seek consistency across all areas of the law.

The temptation to look for overarching theories that could have shaped Roman law can lead scholars to overlook the extent to which concentrated points of detail were infused with learning. The 'fish law' of Hadrian provides Willems with a platform for examining a particular conflict between principle and pragmatism, in chapter eight. Connecting Hadrian's measure with a fragment from Callistratus, Willems articulates three competing conceptions of socio-economic policy concerned with the division and specialisation of labour, market thickness and the control of prices. One such conception is drawn directly from Plato, from whose *Republic* Willems suggests Callistratus quotes selectively and deceptively, in order to support his own position of principle, over that of the emperor. Greek philosophy, economic efficiency, tradition and empiricism coalesce in a single instance of juristic reasoning, showing how principle and pragmatism can operate hand-in-hand.

In chapter nine, Candy shows how juristic application of the exercitorian edict entailed a careful balancing of principle and pragmatism in the specialised context of maritime trade. The commercial impracticality of the civil law's failure to provide for direct agency led to the praetor's edict, providing an action against the exploiter (*exercitor*) of a ship on contracts entered into by its master within the scope of authority allowed by the *exercitor*. The principle of privity of contract was thus attenuated. In turn, the principle of the *voluntas* of the *exercitor*, in his appointment of a master, on given terms, was challenged on grounds of *aequitas* – fairness – towards third parties, both when they dealt with a sub-appointee instead of the master appointed by the *exercitor*, and when they lent money for the purposes of the ship that were subsequently turned to the master's own use. Candy demonstrates the nuanced and different methods adopted by jurists of the late Republic, high classical period and late classical law, arguing that they were reluctant to venture too far beyond praetorian attenuation of *ius civile* principle but that were prepared to do so, in the practical interests of long-distance trade, within carefully circumscribed factual contexts.

Chapter ten offers a case study of principle and pragmatism as manifested in the amendment of classical texts by Justinian's compilers. Taking its attestation in the Collatio as authentic, Ernst demonstrates that a fragment of Ulpian about burning in the *lex Aquilia* originally concerned something quite different from the focus of the texts retained in the Digest. Ernst's reconstruction illustrates that the easy flow of cases in the Ulpianic original is not merely pragmatic, in the sense of taking πράγματα, circumstances, as a structural guide in expounding a lemmatic commentary, but also principled, in its progressive – and increasingly complex and layered – exposition of elements of location, object, defendant and claimant. His central thesis is that the compilers' changes were not merely cosmetic – pragmatic, incidental changes attending the task of compilation – but entailed a purposive reworking: a legal re-synthesis of facts, rules and results, with the aim of recasting the expository and didactic functions of the text, undertaken by means of principles of method, such as efficiency and avoiding redundancy.

The final chapter of the volume also considers the *lex Aquilia*, focusing not on burning but on bursting, *ruptio*, which the jurists of the late Republic understood to include *corruptio*, spoiling. Spagnolo reconstructs Ulpian's lemmatic commentary on *ruptio* and *corruptio*, with particular attention to the pattern of texts employing the adverb *quasi*, which he argues reveals an 'antiphonal structure' of paired texts, in which affirmation of a principle about *ruptio* or *corruptio* is 'answered' by a text illustrating attenuation of that principle for reasons of practical utility. In so doing, Spagnolo demonstrates the use of *quasi* to mark departure from strict logic, in a manner analogous to the use of *utilitas* or *ius singulare* or *sed/tamen* in other passages. His reconstruction reveals that Ulpian's argument is structured by reference to principle, rather than scenarios linked by mere factual association, and suggests that the jurist's purpose was less likely to be destruction of a view of his predecessor Celsus than exposition of historical layers of juristic interpretation of *ruptio*, *quasi ruptio*, *corruptio* and *quasi corruptio*.

IV. Conclusion

In its different senses, the dynamic, paired perspective of 'principle' and 'pragmatism' organises several connected frames of reference for studying the substance and the methods of Roman legal thought. The chapters that follow illustrate, in different ways and with different emphases, the utility of employing this perspective, the range of its application, and the complex subtleties of Roman juristic argument it reveals.

The cover of this volume depicts part of the procession on the south side of the Ara Pacis Augustae, centred on the figure of Marcus Agrippa:

> Actually, his figure is at the same moment the dividing element and the link between two sectors of the procession: the one reserved to the State officers and the one where the members of the Augustan family are arrayed. Appearing with his head veiled, *capite velato*, Agrippa is portrayed as a priest … but as one of Augustus' relatives he opens the cortege of the members of his family.[180]

The theme of principle and pragmatism is aptly represented by both the Ara Pacis and Agrippa himself. The altar is a monument to the goddess Peace but also to the promise of prosperity under Augustus's formally republican but substantively dynastic constitutional settlement. It at once conforms to the principled demands of *pietas* and civil religion, and to the pragmatic exigencies of propaganda. Agrippa shared Augustus's vision of the restored republic 'but was focused on operational results, on getting things done'.[181] Priest in the traditional order, he is preceded by a *lictor*; son-in-law to the *princeps*, he has clutching his toga Augustus's seven-year-old heir Gaius Caesar.[182] Agrippa stands out as a man of principle, displaying *aequitas* in his treatment of the Jews, and a man of pragmatism, building aqueducts, baths and gardens and supplying them with maintenance crews.[183] The procession advances, as does Roman law, embodying both principle and pragmatism.

[180] Comune di Roma, *Ara Pacis*, new edn (S Fox trans, Milan, Electa, 2009), 55. See also J-M Roddaz, *Marcus Agrippa* (Rome, École française de Rome, 1984), 380.
[181] L Powell, *Marcus Agrippa: Right-Hand Man of Caesar Augustus* (Barnsley, Pen & Sword, 2015), 206.
[182] Comune di Roma (n 180), 55.
[183] Powell (n 181), 207.

2

Modes of Roman Legal Reasoning in Context: A Brief Survey

PAUL J DU PLESSIS

When Fritz Schulz published *A History of Roman Legal Science* in 1946, he began the book by defining its central concept, 'Roman legal science'. He wrote:

> We shall use the term 'legal science' in a wider meaning than the ordinary. Commonly it is confined to systematic thinking about actual law (legal dogmatics), to the exclusion, in particular, of the law-making processes. So at any rate it has been understood in previous accounts of Roman legal science ...[1]

In a volume devoted to 'principle and pragmatism in Roman juristic argument', the decision to start this chapter by reflecting on the concept of 'legal science' needs little justification. As intimated by the quotation from Schulz, the two topics are related. It would be impossible to address modes of Roman juristic reasoning without also examining this larger issue. Phrased differently, one cannot fully explain *what* the Roman jurists were doing without reflecting on *how* they were doing it (or at least how modern scholars *understand* it), since context is vital for the understanding of history.

Traditionally, 'legal science' has been associated with 'systematic thinking', as Schulz shows. Or as Winkel put it: 'Rational reasoning and an uncontested systematical approach are important tools for the development of a science'.[2] Given that Schulz was a Jewish-German émigré who received his training in Germany at the end of the nineteenth century/start of the twentieth century, it goes without saying that Schulz's intellectual conception of 'legal science' was formed against the backdrop of the debates between the Historicist and the Pandectist schools of Roman law, prominent in Germany during the late nineteenth century.[3] This

[1] F Schulz, *History of Roman Legal Science* (Oxford, Oxford University Press, 1946), 1.

[2] LC Winkel, 'The Role of General Principles in Roman Law' (1996) 2 *Fundamina* 103, 105.

[3] See generally J Beatson and R Zimmermann (eds), *Jurists Uprooted: German-speaking Emigré Lawyers in Twentieth-century Britain* (Oxford, Oxford University Press, 2004). The term 'Pandectism' is not without controversy; see generally HP Haferkamp and T Repgen (eds), *Wie pandektistisch war die Pandektistik?* (Tübingen, Mohr Siebeck, 2017).

debate, together with its impact on modern understanding of the modes of Roman juristic argumentation, will form the core of this chapter.

Before progressing to the substance of this piece, however, certain observations concerning terminology are required. The terms 'principle' and 'pragmatism' do not translate well into Latin, even if there is evidence that the underlying ideas were present in the vocabulary of the Roman jurists. Given that these two concepts are associated with 'rational reasoning', to use Winkel's phrase, it stands to reason that they should be viewed in the context of changes to Roman juristic reasoning from the late Republic to the early Empire. In a survey of Roman conceptions of law, Stein identified a change in juristic method between the 'pre-classical' period, mainly the last century of the Roman Republic, and that of the Imperial period, mainly the first century CE. In Stein's view, commenting here on the modes of legal argumentation in the late Republic:

> By the end of the second century B.C. much of private law was covered by juristic opinions, delivered piecemeal, usually in actual cases, but occasionally in hypothetical cases. The next step was to generalize the opinions, and although the material remained Roman, the methods by which it was organized were Greek. The key step in passing from the accumulation of particular cases to universals is induction (*epagōgē*). This process produces certain propositions, of which the most basic are so-called definitions (*horoi*).[4]

A good example of such a 'definition', albeit from a later period, can be seen in the following text by the third-century jurist, Paul, quoting earlier jurists, on the etymology of *furtum*:

> According to Labeo the word 'theft' [*furtum*] comes from the word 'black' [*nigro*], because it is done in secret and typically at night; or from the word 'fraud', as Sabinus says; or from 'taking' [*ferendo*] or 'carrying off' [*auferendo*]; or from the Greek term [φῶρας, *foras*] which is used to describe thieves; indeed, the Greeks speak of carrying things off [ἀπὸ τοῦ φέρειν φῶρας, *apo ton ferein foras*].[5]

The references to Labeo, Sabinus and Greek etymology are all indicative of inductive reasoning. This mode of reasoning came to be supplemented in the first century of the classical period by 'deduction', largely owing to the endeavours of the jurist Labeo. According to Stein, Labeo is responsible for two main innovations in Roman legal thought. The first is the systematic use of analogy as a way to develop law. The second is the deductive mode of legal reasoning:

> Another of Labeo's innovations was the use of the term *regula* in place of *definitio*. *Regula* (and its Greek equivalent *kanon*) had superseded *analogia* in grammatical discourse to

[4] PG Stein, 'The Roman Jurists' Conception of Law' in A Padovani and PG Stein (eds), *A Treatise of Legal Philosophy and General Jurisprudence*, vol 7: The Jurists' Philosophy of Law from Rome to the Seventeenth Century (Dordrecht, Springer, 2007) 1 (reference omitted).

[5] D. 47.2.1.pr (Paul. 39 *ad Ed.*): *Furtum a furuo, id est nigro dictum Labeo ait, quod clam et obscuro fiat et plerumque nocte: vel a fraude, ut Sabinus ait: vel a ferendo et auferendo: vel a Graeco sermone, qui φῶρας appellant fures: immo et Graeci ἀπὸ τοῦ φέρειν φῶρας dixerunt.*

> describe the rules of inflection. There was a subtle difference between *regula* and *definitio*. A *definitio iuris*, as understood by Mucius, was essentially descriptive. A *regula iuris* went further; it was a normative proposition which governed all the situations which fell under its *ratio* or underlying principle. It looked to the future as much as to the past.[6]

It is this deductive mode of legal argumentation that has become inextricably associated with Roman law and with the civilian tradition more generally.

Given the key importance of this mode of legal reasoning, I will therefore define 'principle' as a shorthand reference to 'reasoning from principle', in other words, deductive reasoning. But what of 'pragmatism'? In order to provide a working definition of this concept for the purposes of this chapter, I will use a famous statement by the Roman jurist Julian in the context of the *lex Aquilia* as demonstration:

> However the valuation of what has been destroyed will not be the same for each person; for the person who wounded him first will be liable for the highest value of the slave in the previous year, counting back 365 days from the day of the wound, the one who wounded him afterwards will be liable to the highest value he would have come to in the year before his life ended, in which the value of the inheritance will also be included. Hence for the killing of the same slave one will receive a higher valuation and one a lower. Nor should this be surprising, since each is understood to have killed the slave in a different way and at a different time. And if anyone should think that what has here been laid down by us is absurd, he should reflect that it would be far more absurd to lay down that neither should be liable on the *lex Aquilia*, or one rather than the other; for on the one hand wrongs should not go unpunished, and on the other is it is not easy to lay down which should rather be liable on the *lex*. **And it can be proved by innumerable examples that many things are accepted by the civil law for the common good which are contrary to the logic of argument. I shall for the time being be content with one. Where several people take another's beam with the intention of stealing, which they could not have carried individually, all are treated as liable to an *actio furti*, although by sharp logic it can be said that none of them is liable, since it is true that no one of them took it**.[7]

In the bold portion of this text, which deals with the knotty issue of the quantification of loss, Julian tells us, that there is much in the civil law which does not follow

[6] Stein, 'The Roman Jurists' Conception of Law' (n 4), 7.

[7] D. 9.2.51.2 (Iul. 86 *Dig.*): *Aestimatio autem perempti non eadem in utriusque persona fiet: nam qui prior vulneravit, tantum praestabit, quanto in anno proximo homo plurimi fuerit repetitis ex die vulneris trecentum sexaginta quinque diebus, posterior in id tenebitur, quanti homo plurimi venire poterit in anno proximo, quo vita excessit, in quo pretium quoque hereditatis erit. Eiusdem ergo servi occisi nomine alius maiorem, alius minorem aestimationem praestabit, nec mirum, cum uterque eorum ex diversa causa et diversis temporibus occidisse hominem intellegatur. Quod si quis absurde a nobis haec constitui putaverit, cogitet longe absurdius constitui neutrum lege Aquilia teneri aut alterum potius, cum neque impunita maleficia esse oporteat nec facile constitui possit, uter potius lege teneatur. Multa autem iure civili contra rationem disputandi pro utilitate communi recepta esse innumerabilibus rebus probari potest: unum interim posuisse contentus ero. Cum plures trabem alienam furandi causa sustulerint, quam singuli ferre non possent, furti actione omnes teneri existimantur, quamvis subtili ratione dici possit neminem eorum teneri, quia neminem verum sit eam sustulisse.*

strict deductive logic (*contra rationem*). Nonetheless, the reader is told by Julian, in some instances one must adopt positions which conflict with deductive logic, since a failure to do so would lead to absurd results. Bearing this statement in mind, I will use the following working definition: 'pragmatism' signifies deviations from 'principle-based reasoning'.

Having established these working definitions, the next logical step would seem be to investigate the causes of such deviations in principle-based reasoning, and to assess whether any patterns (either within the works of one jurist or within the works of a group, such as the Proculians or Sabinians) may be detected in this regard. This would then enable us to draw conclusions about the personalities or academic affiliations of specific jurists. As I hope to demonstrate in this chapter, however, the above-mentioned research strategy has, for various reasons, not borne much fruit. Unlike the majority of chapters collated in this volume, therefore, I do not intend to examine specific cases where the Roman jurists chose to employ 'pragmatism' rather than 'principle'. It is my belief that such investigations, while useful, fail to appreciate the larger context in which this debate is located. More specifically, they fail to acknowledge the extent to which the parameters of the topic have been preconfigured by late nineteenth-century debates concerning 'legal science'. To that end, I wish to focus on the intellectual context surrounding these two concepts and to demonstrate how this influences our understanding of the activities of the Roman jurists.

I. The Origins of 'Science'

In the quotation from Schulz at the start of this chapter, mention is made of the traditional conception of 'legal science' which was confined to 'systematic thinking about actual law (legal dogmatics)'. Since 'scientification' as an intellectual process is commonly associated with the late nineteenth century and the pervasive impact of the natural sciences also upon European legal scholarship, we must turn attention to an important debate that took place between prominent German scholars of Roman law towards the end of the nineteenth century.[8] The debate about 'legal science' did not occur in isolation. It was part of a general trend, visible across many academic disciplines in Germany during the late nineteenth century, in which scholars attempted to improve the quality of their discourse by adopting more rigorous methodologies in relation to sources and their interpretation.[9] Nowhere is this more visible than in the discussions about the nature of historical research centred around the German historian, Leopold von Ranke. This debate also affected Roman law, especially in the context of the ongoing efforts to create a

[8] T Giaro, 'Legal Tradition of Eastern Europe. Its Rise and Demise' (2011) 2 *Comparative Law Review* 1, 6.

[9] See generally FC Beiser, *The German Historicist Tradition* (Oxford, Oxford University Press, 2011).

civil code for a newly united German Empire. Because of this contemporary aspect to the debate, two issues were extensively debated, namely how the Romans made law, and whether they developed any theory about legal norms and their hierarchy.

It is not my intention to present a full picture of the two dominant scholarly positions in this chapter.[10] Suffice it to say that one group, the Historical School headed by Savigny, 'displaced the natural law school, and saw a return to the historical approach to the Roman law in order to understand the evolution of legal institutions'.[11] The root of Savigny's criticism of codification may be summarised as follows:

> What he [Savigny] opposed was the disposition to liken law to a system of mathematics that can be deduced from axioms, an analogy that appealed to those who saw in codification the universal remedy for all defects in a legal system. Savigny argued that the character of law is rather like that of language, about which rules can be formulated but whose complexity can never be fully expressed by such rules.[12]

As is well known, Savigny's opposition to codification did not win the day and the German civil code came into force in 1900. Intellectually, however, the disciples of Savigny and of the Historical School made a significant contribution to the concept of 'legal science'. This occurred via an offshoot of the Historical School, known as the Pandectists, who according to Schiller

> employed the systematic structure of the law which had been worked out a century earlier, developed the whole complex of legal rules and institutions to fit the emerging modern life, largely on the framework of the historical development of institutions which had been worked out by the efforts of their teachers; a system of law which resembled that of the natural law school in that it purported to take care of any novel legal situation that might arise.[13]

The approach of the Pandectists was based on the idea of law as a 'system', in other words a fully worked out set of legal rules spanning all of Roman private law that fit together seamlessly and without any gaps, and which could be applied, using the principle of analogy, to any new legal scenario that may arise.[14] It does not take much to appreciate that for such a 'system' to function, one needed, in the words of Winkel, both 'rational reasoning and an uncontested systematical approach'. What this meant, in practical terms, for how Pandectist scholars approached Roman law, is best viewed through the lens of satire. Rudolph von Jhering, a prominent contemporary critic of Pandectism, satirised their methodology as follows. Jhering's criticism of the intellectual approach of the Pandectists

[10] For a survey, see PG Stein, *Roman Law in European History* (Cambridge, Cambridge University Press, 1999), 116–20.

[11] AA Schiller, *Roman Law: Mechanisms of Development* (The Hague, Mouton, 1978), 4.

[12] SR Letwin, *On the History of the Idea of Law* (Cambridge, Cambridge University Press, 2005), 185.

[13] Schiller (n 11), 5.

[14] K Tuori, *Ancient Roman Lawyers and Modern Legal Ideals: Studies on the Impact of Contemporary Concerns in the Interpretation of Ancient Roman Legal History*, 2nd corrected edn (Frankfurt am Main, Vittorio Klostermann, 2007), 21–70.

was threefold.[15] The first point of criticism related to the Pandectist conception of 'legal science' and its boundaries.[16] He wrote:

> Life, as you know it, is synonymous with death for true science. It is bondage to science and compulsory servitude to concepts that, instead of living for themselves as required, are harnessed to the most degrading yoke of dependence upon earthly existence. Here the concepts live for themselves, and if you don't want to cut off your prospects completely, don't ask anyone about the utility of anything you see. Utility! It would be the last straw if the concepts were also useful in our heaven. Here they reign and compensate themselves for the drudgery and servitude they had to suffer on earth.

The point is clear. The Pandectist conception of 'legal science' was exceedingly narrowly drawn. Specifically, 'true science' could only be practised by wholly separating it from real-world concerns. Legal concepts, according to the Pandectists, 'live for themselves' without any reference to their 'utility', which, as we shall presently see, was a particularly important concept in the context of this debate.

This separation between 'true science' and the real world served a very specific purpose in Pandectist legal thought, according to Jhering:

> And, this separation between theory and practice is one of the greatest contemporary achievements. Only because of it has science won the complete freedom of movement that is essential to the interest of investigating truth … However, all this has only been possible since theory has been completely emancipated from practice and has finally become independent. For the condition of this free dialectical, creative activity is the prevention of every contact with practical life, which exerts the same pernicious influence on theoreticians that in the judgment of an expert, war exerts on soldiers. In this respect, the highly praised Roman jurists, who during their lives often allowed themselves to be led by insipid utilitarian principles, serve as a warning. You will not find any of them in our heaven. The abolition of sentencing faculties has eliminated the danger of contact with life for our modern jurisprudence.[17]

While it is difficult not to read this statement against the backdrop of the changing role of Roman law in German law schools post codification, Jhering's point is a broader one. By removing any link between 'true [legal] science' and real-world concerns, scholars became liberated to debate legal concepts in a timeless manner and without dwelling on the fact that Roman law was a functioning legal order, the rules of which must have been applied with regularity to the inhabitants of the Roman Empire. Another consequence of this approach was that, in the spirit of 'legal science', aspects of Roman law could be problematised beyond reason. In a particularly scathing part of Jhering's critique, he attacks the method of the Pandectists, known as 'construction', whereby unexpressed principles of law latent in the Roman legal material could be created:

[15] See generally CRR Jhering, *Ist die Jurisprudenz eine Wissenschaft?: Jherings Wiener Antrittsvorlesung vom 16. Oktober 1868*, 2nd rev edn (O Behrends ed, Göttingen, Wallstein, 2009).

[16] CRR Jhering, 'In the Heaven for Legal Concepts: A Fantasy' (1985) 58 *Temple Law Quarterly* 799, 807.

[17] ibid, 825.

> 'This one is the construction machine. We are lucky to find it in operation right now. We'll soon see what the spirit who works it has in mind'. 'Exalted spirit, permit me to ask you what you are doing at the moment?' 'I am constructing a contract'. 'A contract? That's so simple. What else can be constructed on the machine?' Just because it is so simple, a lot! You must be a neophyte here or you would know that. The art of construction derives its most interesting and rewarding objectives from the simplest things. **Everyone can understand simplicity, but understanding comes later. The expert knows that the simplest legal phenomena involve the greatest difficulties.**[18]

Jhering, an early proponent of legal realism, fervently objected to this approach. As Letwin puts it, according to Jhering, 'their [Pandectists] talk about legal logic and the science of law had no connection with real life'.[19] But do these 'real-world' concerns matter? After all, as Pandectism and its successor, Legal Positivism, have shown, it is perfectly possible to debate rules of law in the abstract without giving any thought to such matters. As I hope to show in the remainder of this chapter, however, it is impossible to examine the modes of reasoning of the Roman jurists solely using a Pandectist (or indeed Legal Positivist) lens.

II. Modes of Legal Reasoning

The narrowness (or not) of one's conception of 'legal science' will affect one's view of the nature of Roman legal reasoning, as well as the modes that were employed. More specifically, it will also colour one's view on the impact of external influences upon these modes of reasoning. Given the pervasive impact of, first, Pandectism and thereafter its successor, Legal Positivism, upon all branches of research into civil law during the first part of the twentieth century, it comes as little surprise that research into Roman juristic reasoning and its modes was almost non-existent during this period.[20] The reasons for this may be traced back directly to the intellectual aims of the Pandectists. If the chief purpose of Roman law was to create modern legal provisions in a civil code, there could be no room for ambiguity. Furthermore, as long as the prevailing legal theory is one that endorses law as the product of the lawgiver (the state), there is little room for debate about the origins or indeed the authors of those rules of law. The consequence of this was that Roman legal reasoning as contained in the texts collected in the Digest became unimportant and was replaced by axiomatic and unambivalent rules of law. In addition, if these rules of law had to form a 'gapless system', juristic controversies had to be smoothed over in order to create one clear position on each issue. This reduction of Roman juristic controversies to axiomatic rules of law with little regard for the authors of these statements or indeed their modes of reasoning came to be known

[18] ibid, 807.
[19] Letwin (n 12), 188.
[20] Winkel (n 2), 107.

in German legal scholarship as the doctrine of '*Fungibile Personen*' (interchangeable persons) – where the author or book from which the relevant Digest passage was taken, was ignored.[21]

III. A Post-War Revival

The scholarly debate concerning the modes of Roman legal reasoning, from Viehweg's work, published in 1953, to Winkel's survey article on the topic in 1996, is well explored and need not be picked over in detail. It is worth pointing out, as Winkel has done in his article, that this revival occurred within the context of renewed interest in the work of Emmanuel Kant. In this section, I will highlight some of the insights which have emerged from this debate. The first notable insight, by Winkel, concerns the way in which the Roman jurists dealt with 'sources of law':

> A theory about the sources of law, however, had hardly been developed in Roman law. This is the reason why topical arguments play a much more important role than we can imagine. For the continental jurist nowadays a hierarchy of juridical norms is quite self-evident. Fixed rules of interpretation were unknown in Roman jurisprudence. The juridical system is a very open one, much more so than in modern times.[22]

The second insight concerns the theoretical bases of the Roman jurists' reasoning. As Honoré had observed already in 1974:

> The Roman jurists probably had no conscious theory about the way in which they reasoned. This does not prevent us from trying to give a systematic account of what they were doing, any more than the fact that in ordinary speech the notion of 'cause' is used unreflectively prevents us from giving a systematic account of the principles on which that unreflective use rests.[23]

Although the Roman jurists may not have had a conscious 'theory' of their own legal reasoning, it is certainly possible to discern different types of argument. Based on the work of Viehweg (1953)[24] and that of Horak (1969),[25] Honoré identified at least five different types of argument used by the Roman jurists. That being said, as his discussion – together with the other contributors to the debate – have shown, there is very little consistency, even within the work of one jurist, to draw any meaningful conclusions, especially concerning 'patterns' or the propensity of

[21] On this entire debate, see the chapters collected in C Baldus and others (eds), *Dogmengeschichte und historische Individualität der römischen Juristen = Storia dei dogmi e individualità storica dei giuristi romani: atti del seminario internazionale (Montepulciano 14–17 giugno 2011)* (Trento, Università degli Studi di Trento, 2012).

[22] Winkel (n 2), 105.

[23] AM Honoré, 'Legal Reasoning in Rome and Today' (1973) 4 *Cambrian Law Review* 58, 59.

[24] T Viehweg, *Topik und Jurisprudenz* (Munich, Beck, 1953).

[25] F Horak, *Rationes Decidendi: Entscheidungsbegründungen bei den älteren römischen Juristen bis Labeo* (Aalen, Scientia, 1969).

certain jurists to use certain types of reasoning. In addition, as Honoré's discussion has demonstrated, it is not the deductive arguments that have been the subject of debate among modern Romanist scholars. Rather, it has been the 'open argument' using *topoi*, another one of the five types, that has been the main source of modern scholarly controversy, primarily because of the different interpretations of modern scholars concerning the extent to which open argument allows the jurists to introduce 'social values' such as good faith and utility into their arguments.

There are two further insights of Honoré's that are worth noting. First, according to Honoré, the Roman jurists had 'a canon of acceptable arguments'.[26] This set them apart from, say, the Greeks, who utilised a wider range of arguments in their legal discourse than is visible in Roman law. In second place, according to Honoré, the Roman jurists over time developed 'conventions concerning the range of acceptable open arguments', as a result of their 'professionalisation' as a group.[27] These two points, in my opinion, should form the backbone of any further investigations into the modes of Roman legal reasoning. More specifically, the relationship between the Roman jurists as a profession and larger societal concerns deserves close scrutiny. After all, as Honoré has observed:

> Given, then, intellectual professionalism it is possible for certain issues to be considered not in isolation from the moral, social, political and religious issues affecting society at large but in such a way that these are allowed to be taken into account only on certain terms and within certain limits.[28]

The link between the reasoning of the Roman jurists and these larger societal concerns is important. As Watson pointed out in 1972:

> [A]t least sometimes, the Roman jurists were more concerned to reach a sensible practical result than to follow the dictates of a rigorous logic … they were not ivory-tower philosophers but sensible men dealing with contemporary problems of living. Though it may be felt that this diminishes the claims of Roman law to be a system of universal unchanging validity, it must make us accept the Roman jurists as individual human beings. And we must give credit to their sophistication.[29]

What remains, therefore, is to determine how to deal with the modes of argumentation of the Roman jurists 'as individual human beings'. One thing is clear, since – with a few exceptions – the real-world impact of the Roman jurists' arguments cannot be ascertained, a different approach is necessary.[30] A popular line of investigation pursued in the past decade has been to investigate the examples of Roman juristic reasoning for signs of patent and latent influences from either philosophy of rhetoric.[31] This has been done because, so the argument goes, the

[26] Honoré (n 23), 65.
[27] ibid, 65–66.
[28] ibid, 65.
[29] WAJ Watson, 'Illogicality and Roman Law' (1972) 7 *Israel Law Review* 14, 24.
[30] For a rare instance where this is possible, see *BGU* II 613 where, in a petition, the opinion of L. Volusius Maecianus is presented.
[31] TG Leesen, *Gaius meets Cicero: Law and Rhetoric in the School Controversies* (Leiden, Brill, 2010).

jurists would have been well-versed in these two branches of knowledge, as a result of their education. Thus far, however, the results of such investigations have been less than promising. The conclusions reached in the most recent surveys of Giltaij (on philosophy)[32] and Kacprzak (on rhetoric)[33] are well worth reading in this regard.

Is there an alternative option? Recent studies in 'law and society' might well provide the way ahead.[34] They cannot, however, end with the now well-rehearsed conclusion that 'law in books' differ from 'law in action'. Rather, the matter will have to be addressed from a different perspective, such as 'legal culture' and the relationship between 'centre and periphery' when dealing with legal knowledge. As Bryen has recently remarked,

> the consequence of the last decade's new work in Roman legal history is that we now have to accept that the legal order as a whole was the product of the participation of many more actors than previous generations of scholars had been prepared to account for, and that these actors' participation in creating a legal culture was not necessarily predicated on their somehow consciously replicating official narratives, which were themselves often shifting and inchoate.[35]

IV. Conclusions

On balance, there is little to be gained from a Pandectist discourse concerning the modes of legal argumentation of the Roman jurists. Both the Pandectists and their intellectual successors, the Legal Positivists, were not interested in juristic controversies. Rather, they were focused on creating unambiguous rules of law, freed from any context and with a sufficient level of abstraction to be utilised across time and space. The downside of this approach, as pointed out by early legal realists such as Jhering, was that the rules themselves became 'otherworldly' and without any thought being given to their 'utility' in the real world. In order to understand the modes of reasoning of the Roman jurists, therefore, a jurist-focused approach is required. This necessarily involves an acceptance that the Roman legal order was different from a modern legal system. It was a more 'open' system, as Winkel has shown, which did not have a hierarchy of sources or, indeed, a theory of legal argumentation. It is this 'openness' that should form the basis of any further discussions concerning modes of argumentation of the Roman jurists. And when it comes to 'openness' context matters.

[32] J Giltaij, 'Greek Philosophy and Classical Roman Law: A Brief Overview' in PJ du Plessis, C Ando and K Tuori (eds), *The Oxford Handbook of Roman Law and Society* (Oxford, Oxford University Press, 2016) 188.

[33] A Kacprzak, 'Rhetoric and Roman Law' in PJ du Plessis, C Ando and K Tuori (eds), *The Oxford Handbook of Roman Law and Society* (Oxford, Oxford University Press, 2016) 200.

[34] J Pölönen, 'Framing "Law and Society" in the Roman World' in PJ du Plessis, C Ando and K Tuori (eds), *The Oxford Handbook of Roman Law and Society* (Oxford, Oxford University Press, 2016) 8.

[35] AZ Bryen, 'Law in Many Pieces' (2014) 109 *Classical Philology* 346, 357.

3

The Case of the Careless Purchaser, or 'Bonitary Ownership' and Ownership

MIKE MACNAIR

The centre of this chapter is a piece of technical ancient Roman property law, which is the subject of a very large literature.[1] Why is this issue worth discussing yet again? The answer is that it seems to me that a pedagogic choice made by the second century CE law teacher Gaius in explaining this bit of technical property law has contributed in a small way to the development in medieval and modern legal thinking of a skewed vision of the legal category 'ownership'. The skew is that medieval and modern accounts focus on ownership as a kind of right (or as a 'bundle of rights', in Tony Honoré's celebrated phrase)[2] and omit its dimension *as a public status* and its dimension as giving rise to *liability*.

The traditional account is one of principle (Roman citizen ownership had to be created by Roman citizen means) modified by pragmatism (the means were inconvenient to the market, and hence displaced). My argument is that the *appearance* to which this traditional account responds was, rather, created by pedagogic choices.

I. The Standard Story

The inevitable starting point is a passage in the Institutes of Gaius, written c 160 CE:

> 40. Next, we must observe that among non-Romans there is only one ownership [*dominium*]; for with them a person either is owner [*dominus*], or is not thought to be

[1] Indeed, the scope of this literature and the range of languages involved is such that I have certainly missed some relevant pieces, and hence may have merely rediscovered a view already argued somewhere. If so, apologies to the author or authors concerned; but the *textbooks* remain dominated by the interpretation criticised here.

[2] AM Honoré, 'Ownership' in AG Guest (ed), *Oxford Essays in Jurisprudence* (Oxford, Oxford University Press, 1961), 107. *cf* also the elaborate discussion of classificatory problems by GL Gretton, 'Ownership and its Objects' (2007) 71 *Rabels Zeitschrift für ausländisches und internationales Privatrecht* 802.

> owner. In the past the Romans had the same law; a person was either owner by Roman-citizen right [or law], or was not thought to be owner at all. But afterwards a division was made of ownership, so that one person can be owner by Roman-citizen right/law, and another can have the thing among his goods. 41. For if I have neither mancipated to you [conveyed to you by *mancipatio*, literally 'taking in hand'], nor ceded to you in court, a thing liable to mancipation, but have merely delivered it, it becomes part of your goods; but it will remain mine by Roman-citizen right/law, until you, possessing it, usucape it [*usucapias*, literally, take it by use]. Once *usucapio* is completed, it becomes yours by full right [*pleno iure*], that is both among your goods and by Roman-citizen right/law, just as if it had been conveyed by *mancipatio* or ceded in court.[3]

To explain briefly and provisionally for those unfamiliar with the issue: *ex iure Quiritium* is a formula used particularly in relation to property rights;[4] the Latin could be translated either as 'by Roman-citizen right' or 'by Roman-citizen law'.[5] *Mancipatio* was a formal oral ceremony required to convey legal title *ex iure Quiritium* to *res mancipi* 'thing[s] liable to conveyance by *mancipatio*', which were: 'Italic' land; certain appurtenances of such land, such as rights of way; and the high-value fixed capital equipment of a farm, ie slaves and draft animals (but not circulating stocks such as flocks or herds of livestock).[6] *In iure cessio*, 'ceding in court', was an alternative to *mancipatio*. It was a conveyance by fictitious litigation. *Usucapio* was prescriptive acquisition. The required period for prescription was at the date Gaius was writing two years for land and one year for movables; there were additional requirements which need not detain us in the instant context, since they were prima facie satisfied in the case Gaius discusses.[7]

[3] G.2.40–41: 40. *Sequitur, ut admoneamus apud peregrinos quidem unum esse dominium; nam aut dominus quisque est aut dominus non intellegitur. Quo iure etiam populus Romanus olim utebatur: aut enim ex iure Quiritium unusquisque dominus erat aut non intellegebatur dominus. Sed postea diuisionem accepit dominium, ut alius possit esse ex iure Quiritium dominus, alius in bonis habere.* 41. *Nam si tibi rem mancipi neque mancipavero neque in iure cessero, sed tantum tradidero, in bonis quidem tuis ea res efficitur, ex iure Quiritium vero mea permanebit, donec tu eam possidendo usucapias: semel enim impleta usucapione proinde pleno iure incipit, id est et in bonis et ex iure Quiritium tua res esse, ac si ea mancipata vel in iure cessa esset.* We will also be concerned with G. 1.17, G. 1.35–36, and G. 1.54; but these are less central to the textbook tradition.

[4] In the words used in the *mancipatio*, G. 1.119, and in the *legis actio sacramentum in rem* (statutory claim by oath to recover a thing), G. 2.24, 4.16, and Cic., *Mur.* 12.26.

[5] *cf* also AHM Jones, 'In eo solo dominivm Populi Romani est vel Caesaris' (1941) 31 *Journal of Roman Studies* 26, 28–29, on the problems of grants of citizenship without Italic status given to the soil.

[6] G. 2.14a–17. It should be noted (a) that 'Italic land' is inferred by modern editors, to occupy part of a legibility gap in the MS, from Pseudo-Ulpian, LSR 19.1 (M Avenarius, *Der pseudo-ulpianische liber singularis regularum: Entstehung, Eigenart und Überlieferung einer hochklassischen Juristenschrift* (Gottingen, Wallstein, 2005), 357; citations hereafter to Ps-Ulp LSR are to this edition), and from the express exclusion of provincial land later in the section; and (b) that some Roman *coloniae*, citizen settlements, outside Italy, had the legal status of Italic land: D. 50.15.1 and 6–8, and TH Watkins, '*Coloniae* and *Ius Italicum* in the Early Empire' (1983) 78 *Classical Journal* 319. Appurtenant rights, 'rustic praedial servitudes', chiefly rights of way; the rights of way for persons, animals, vehicles and water were certainly *mancipi* but whether the other probable rustic servitudes (rights of pasture, etc: Inst. 2.3.3) were, is debated: M Kaser, *Das römische Privatrecht*, 2nd rev edn (Munich, Beck, 1971), 441 fn 13 and accompanying text.

[7] They are conveniently discussed in JAC Thomas, *Textbook of Roman Law* (Amsterdam, North-Holland, 1976), 157–63.

In short, the person who 'has the thing among his goods' (*in bonis habere*) is in this text a purchaser who has taken delivery without a formal conveyance of an item or items of property which legally require a formal conveyance. Legal title to the property remained with the vendor, until the grantee had completed *usucapio*. In the interim, the purchaser had interdicts, remedies to protect his possession which were effectively *in personam* against an immediate dispossessor.[8] From some date before 66 BCE the praetor also provided him with a defence if the vendor were to sue to recover the property, the *exceptio rei venditae et traditae* (defence of thing sold and delivered).[9] At some date either in the first century BCE or the first century CE (the dating issue will reappear later) the praetor also provided the purchaser with an action *in rem* to recover the property, the *actio Publiciana*, good against all the world.[10]

In the 'classical law' of the second to early third centuries CE, the grantee was described, as Gaius does here, as one whose thing it is 'among his goods', *in bonis*.[11] The Emperor Justinian in 530/31 CE formally abolished the distinction between Quiritary *dominium* and holding *in bonis* (by abolishing Quiritary *dominium*).[12]

[8] Summary discussion in the textbooks, eg WW Buckland, *A Text-Book of Roman Law from Augustus to Justinian*, 3rd edn (PG Stein ed, Cambridge, Cambridge University Press, 1963), 192. 'Effectively' because while the interdict *unde vi* for land is clearly *in personam* against the immediate dispossessor, *utrubi* for movables in classical law asks who has had the most possession of the thing in the last year, which was capable of reaching a transferee from an immediate dispossessor if the claimant took quick enough action. In addition, the narrative of the proceedings in Cicero's *Pro Caecina* suggests that at that period *unde vi* was fictionalised to a point analogous to 14th-century English Novel Disseisin, ie that it was sufficient to make a technical entry on the land with a view to being thrown out and then bring *unde vi*: see BW Frier, *The Rise of the Roman Jurists: Studies in Cicero's pro Caecina* (Princeton, Princeton University Press, 1985), 23–25, 78–90 for *unde vi* in the *Pro Caecina*; DW Sutherland, *The Assize of Novel Disseisin* (Oxford, Oxford University Press, 1973), 148–50 for that action.

[9] Thomas (n 7), 136 makes the point that this *exceptio* must antedate the general *exceptio doli*, which is securely dated to 66 BCE and would clearly cover the case of the vendor of property who seeks to reclaim it on a technical ground; HF Jolowicz and JKBM Nicholas, *An Historical Introduction to the Study of Roman Law*, 3rd edn (Cambridge, Cambridge University Press, 1972), 266, makes the analogous point that the *exceptio* is very likely to antedate the *actio Publiciana*.

[10] Jolowicz and Nicholas (n 9), 263–67 is a convenient summary account.

[11] Ankum, van Gessel-de Roo and Pool have conducted an enormously elaborate survey of *in bonis* phraseology: JA Ankum, M Gessel-de Roo and E Pool, 'Die verschiedenen Bedeutungen des Ausdrucks in bonis alicuius esse/in bonis habere im klassischen römischen Recht' (1981) 104 *ZRG RA* 238; JA Ankum, M van Gessel-de Roo and E Pool, 'Die verschiedenen Bedeutungen des Ausdrucks in bonis alicuius esse/in bonis habere im klassischen römischen Recht: Teil 2' (1988) 188 *ZRG RA* 334; JA Ankum, M van Gessel-de Roo and E Pool, 'Die verschiedenen Bedeutungen des Ausdrucks in bonis alicuius esse/in bonis habere im klassischen römischen Recht: Teil 3' (1990) 105 *ZRG RA* 155. Ankum and Pool have summarised this study in English in JA Ankum and E Pool, '*Rem in bonis meis esse* and *rem in bonis meam esse*: Traces of the Development of Roman Double Ownership' in PBH Birks (ed), *New Perspectives in the Roman Law of Property* (Oxford, Oxford University Press, 1989) 5. They argue that *rem in bonis* ***meam esse*** (as distinct from *rem in bonis* ***meis esse***) is an ownership formula equivalent *meum ex iure Quiritium* applied to 'bonitary ownership'. But the expression is rare. Sirks argues for a broader meaning of *in bonis*, at least for the *actio Serviana*, than is used by Ankum, van Gessel-de Roo and Pool: AJB Sirks, 'What did *in bonis* in the *actio Serviana* include?' in H Dondorp, MJ Schermaier and AJB Sirks (eds), *De rebus divinis et humanis: Essays in honour of Jan Hallebeek* (Göttingen, Vandenhoeck & Ruprecht, 2019) 323.

[12] C. 7.25.1 (Justinian to Julianus, 530–31).

In 531 CE, he also abolished the distinction between *res mancipi* and *res nec mancipi* (property not subject to conveyance by *mancipatio*).[13] Some of the other cases in which the distinction between *dominium ex iure Quiritium*, holding *in bonis*, and Gaius's *pleno iure* could arise (to which we will return below) had already disappeared in practice.[14] The topic was therefore largely excluded from Justinian's Digest, except for casual references that the Compilers did not notice and delete or amend. Theophilus in his Greek *Paraphrase* of Justinian's Institutes, in referring to the old law, coined the expression 'δεσπότης bonitarios', 'bonitary owner'.[15] The Latin form *dominium bonitarium*, 'bonitary ownership', was used from the time of the thirteenth century French jurist Jacques de Révigny, at the latest.[16] Although the expressions 'bonitary owner' and 'bonitary ownership' are non-classical and hence arguably misleading, it would be too inconvenient to abstain from using them here, though I mark them with scare quotes.

II. Problems

What I have described so far is pretty much the standard account of 'bonitary ownership' in the modern textbooks of Roman law. The more elaborate textbooks consign to brief side-references and to footnotes the other aspects of the doctrine; the briefer ones may simply leave them out. In the absence of putting these other aspects in an upfront central position in the account, two issues arise.

The first is why Gaius describes this as a *division* of ownership, when the 'bonitary owner' is clearly in modern terms owner in all but name? The second is perhaps a 'common lawyer' question. It is: why should the praetor help out the careless purchaser of land who has not bothered to take a legal conveyance? The *exceptio rei venditae et traditae* is fair enough: the vendor who seeks to reclaim property he has been paid for and has handed over is pretty clearly prima facie fraudulent. But beyond that is less clear.

The usual answer is that *mancipatio* was inconvenient. It required a pair of scales and a piece of copper, the presence of six Roman citizens (five witnesses and a *libripens* to hold the scales);[17] the presence of the thing itself or something that could be said to be a representative part of it (in the case of land a piece of turf or

[13] C. 7.31.1 (Justinian to Johannes, 18 October 531).

[14] *Bonorum emptio/venditio* (below nn 39–41) is said by the compilers to have become obsolete since the disappearance of formulary procedure, being replaced by interlocutory orders in the *cognitio* procedure: Inst. 3.12.pr. This would logically affect also *damnum infectum* and related remedies (below nn 48–51). *Bonorum possessio* contrary to statute (below nn 44–47) was formally maintained by Justinian (Inst. 3.9), but the extensive statutory reforms of inheritance in the later empire *probably* marginalised it as a form of 'bonitary ownership', before Justinian formally abolished Quiritary ownership.

[15] Theophilus, *Paraphrasis Institutionum* 1.5.3 in JHA Lokin, R Meijering and BH Stolte (eds), *Theophili Antecessoris Paraphrasis institutionum* (AF Murison trans, Groningen, Chimaira, 2010), 41.

[16] G D'Amelio, 'Il *Dictionarium Iuris* di Jacques de Revigny' (1972) 40 *Leg Hist Rev* 43, 52–58.

[17] Ps-Ulp LSR 19.4 says that the parties to a *mancipatio* may be citizens, Junian Latins, Latin colonists, or foreigners having an individual grant of *commercium*. In 20.8, on mancipatory wills, the text says

something similar), the presence of transferor and transferee, and for the transferee to speak a specific formula.[18] Hence, economic development and quickening markets led to the substitution of simple delivery.[19]

Remember, however, that this ceremony was in substance a formality for the conveyance of legal title to Italic land and related agricultural fixed capital assets. And the non-land capital assets in question, slaves and draft animals, so far as they were not sold with the land (a *praedium instructum*, a 'fully-equipped farm', included them),[20] were usually sold in organised markets.[21] It cannot in an organised market have been hard to find the requisites of *mancipatio*. Gaius himself comments that this procedure was more convenient and private than the alternative of *in iure cessio*.[22] It is undoubtedly cheaper and more convenient than any procedure which necessitated the employment of a lawyer, and cheaper, quicker and more private than the land title registration systems which are common in modern times. Highly active land markets do not seem to require informality in land transfer.[23] Some fixed-capital movables may also be subject to transfer formalities in modern law; for example, the UK requires a bill of sale to transfer title to ships, and operates registers of mortgages of ships and aircraft, and, while the UK does not operate formalities for the transfer of title to cars, several US states do.[24] *Mancipatio* may have been an *insufficient* formality, providing insufficient publicity and no inherent evidentiary protection;[25] but it can hardly have been a significant *obstacle* to markets in *res mancipi*.

Conversely, assuming that the effect of the praetor's intervention with the *actio Publiciana was* to render *mancipatio* obsolete in practice (and we do not have anything like enough evidence to be confident of this conclusion), is it really

that Junian Latins may be *libripens* or witness. This account would make *mancipatio* still easier than it is in Gaius.

[18] G. 1.119–22.

[19] Thus, eg, JKBM Nicholas, *An Introduction to Roman Law* (Oxford, Oxford University Press, 1962) 125–27; Thomas (n 7), 137 (final para); Jolowicz and Nicholas (n 9), 265.

[20] For this terminology, see DP Kehoe, *Investment, Profit, and Tenancy: The Jurists and the Roman Agrarian Economy* (Ann Arbor, University of Michigan Press, 1997), 97–98. A pertinent example is Fr.Vat. 259 (Pap. 12 *Resp.*), where the land, being provincial, passed, but the slaves and beasts of burden needed to be usucaped.

[21] This can be seen from the fact that remedies for non-disclosure of latent defects were initially provided under the Edict of the Aediles, whose responsibility was for public spaces and markets: R Zimmermann, *The Law of Obligations: Roman Foundations of the Civilian Tradition* (Oxford, Oxford University Press, 1996), 311–18 (slaves) and 318–19 (initially *iumenta*, meaning draft animals, later extended to *pecus* (hoofed stock animals) in general).

[22] G. 2.25.

[23] In fact, it has been argued that the provision in 1190s England of a *highly formal* mode of transfer, the fine recorded in the central common law courts, sharply stimulated land markets; fines were certainly used for quite small quantities of land. See, eg, R Palmer, 'The Economic and Cultural Impact of the Origins of Property: 1180–1220' (1985) 3 *Law and History Review* 375.

[24] For the UK, see: Merchant Shipping Act 1995 (UK), sch 1 paras 1, 7 ff; Mortgaging of Aircraft Order 1972, SI 1972/1268 (UK). For US States, see, eg: Tex. Transportation Code (USA), § 501.071; Cal. Vehicle Code (USA), § 5600; Mass. Gen. Laws (USA), ch 90D § 15.

[25] I owe this point to Professor Helen Scott, in discussion of an earlier version of this chapter at the UCL Thomas Seminar in Roman Law, 22 February 2019.

desirable to abolish all formalities for the transfer of title to land? The government of the Emperor Constantine seems to have come to the opposite conclusion. A law of 313 CE on sales of land required an actual handing over of the land in the presence of the neighbours. Probably aimed at a tax-dodge (to which we will return later), the law justified itself in terms of the fraud risks of informal conveyances. A law of 323 CE on gifts added to this ceremony a requirement of registration in the records of the local municipality.[26] A later law of Zeno of 478 CE dispensed with the requirement of delivery in the presence of the neighbours if the transfer was registered.[27] Registration in municipal records probably continued in operation beyond the fall of the western Roman Empire.[28] Formality in *land transfer* therefore returned, on a more generalised (and better) basis than the old *res mancipi* rules, in spite of its non-appearance in Justinian's Institutes.

In fact, these two questions are posed *because* the textbooks sideline issues other than the careless purchaser and focus mainly on the transfer rules. Once we bring the other aspects of the subject to the forefront, the issues look rather different. There were classes of 'bonitary owner' beyond the case of the careless purchaser of *res mancipi*, and some of them may well have been much more important than this case. And there were real and practically significant differences between 'bonitary ownership' and *dominium ex iure Quiritium* or Gaius's *pleno iure*. The latter justify Gaius's characterisation of 'bonitary ownership' as involving a division of ownership; but they should also force us to ask larger questions about what we do or should mean by 'ownership'.

III. Other Holders *in bonis*

'Bonitary ownership' did not just apply to the careless purchaser of *res mancipi*. It also applied to other cases where the praetor made an order transferring possession to a claimant – *missio in possessionem* – which was inconsistent with the statutory provisions of the XII Tables, the original Roman law-code of 450 BCE. The cases attested in Gaius are *bonorum venditio* or *emptio*, bankruptcy, and

[26] For the law of 313 CE: Fr.Vat. 35, summarised in CTh. 3.1.2. For the law of 323 CE: Fr.Vat. 249, CTh. 8.12.1. Clear discussion in AM Honoré, 'Conveyances of Land and Professional Standards in the Later Empire' in PBH Birks, *New Perspectives in the Roman Law of Property* (Oxford, Oxford University Press, 1989) 137, drawing on WE Voss, *Recht und Rhetorik in den Kaisergesetzen der Spätantike: eine Untersuchung zum nachklassischen Kauf- und Übereignungsrecht* (Frankfurt, Löwenklau, 1982), 131–77.

[27] C. 8.53.31 (Zeno to Sebastianus, 1 March 478).

[28] I Wood, 'Disputes in late fifth- and sixth-century Gaul: some problems' in W Davies and P Fouracre (eds), *The Settlement of Disputes in Early Medieval Europe* (Cambridge, Cambridge University Press, 1986) 7, 12–14. *cf* also N Everett, 'Lay documents and archives in early medieval Spain and Italy, c. 400–700' in WC Brown and others (eds), *Documentary Culture and the Laity in the Early Middle Ages* (Cambridge, Cambridge University Press, 2013) 63, 70–82; WC Brown, 'The *gesta municipalia* and the public validation of documents in Frankish Europe' in WC Brown and others (eds), *Documentary Culture and the Laity in the Early Middle Ages* (Cambridge, Cambridge University Press, 2013) 95.

bonorum possessio, testate and intestate succession under praetorian, as opposed to statutory, rules.[29]

Beyond these, a number of others have been inferred from indirect Digest references:[30] *missio in possessionem* under the second decree in *damnum infectum*;[31] adjudication of property to the claimant under a non-statutory form of action, a *iudicium imperio continens*;[32] perhaps a subset of this, adjudication resting on the decisory oath rather than on a trial;[33] self-help seizure of a slave who has committed a delict, by the authority of a praetorian order where the owner has failed either to pay or surrender the slave to the claimant;[34] tree-prunings (or the whole tree) under a praetorian order permitting the pruning of a defendant's tree overhanging claimant's land;[35] the enforcement of *fideicommissa* (*very* roughly, testamentary trusts) under the *senatus consultum Trebellianum*;[36] and the special provision made by the Emperor Marcus Aurelius for slaves emancipated by will to be protected if the heirs refused the estate.[37]

In each of these cases, the 'bonitary owner' is in possession under a court order. It is the inconsistency with ancient statute, rather than the want of formality, which prevents the court order transferring immediate *dominium ex iure Quiritium* (as *in iure cessio*, and *adiudicatio*, judgment, in a *iudicium legitimum*, a statutory action, did)[38] and hence requires the 'bonitary owner' to usucape the property. It should be obvious that all these cases have a stronger claim on the assistance of the praetor than the careless purchaser. It also seems likely that praetorian successions at least would be a far more common issue in litigation than the careless purchaser.

That said, if it were clear that the *actio Publiciana* for the careless purchaser was developed *before* the appearance of these other cases, the phenomenon of 'bonitary ownership' would have to be explained by the case of the careless purchaser. This makes unavoidable some discussion of those of the other cases which are dateable to an early date, and of the date of the *actio Publiciana* and related remedies.

[29] G. 3.80.

[30] The list following is from CL Appleton, *Histoire de la propriété prétorienne et de l'action publicienne*, vol I (Paris, Ernest Thorin, 1889), 5–6. Those modern textbooks which advert to the issues at all follow this list.

[31] D. 39.2.5.pr (Paul. 1 *ad Ed.*).

[32] D. 6.2.3.1 (Ulp. 16 *ad Ed.*) *ad fin* and D. 6.2.7.pr (Ulp. 16 *ad Ed.*); both these are interpretations beyond the text, supposing that something has been cut by the Compilers, on the basis that Ps-Ulp LSR 19.16 tells us that a civil law *adiudicatio* transfers Quiritary ownership of both *res mancipi* and *res nec mancipi*, so that there would be no need for the *Publiciana*.

[33] D. 6.2.7.7 (Ulp. 16 *ad Ed.*).

[34] D. 6.2.6 (Paul. 19 *ad Ed.*).

[35] Interdictal remedy, and Edict statement that the claimant is entitled *sibi habere* the tree, or prunings, in D. 43.27.1.pr (Ulp. 71 *ad Ed.*). That this is *in bonis habere* seems to be a reasonable inference, though the phrase is not used and the case is not in D. 6.2. on the *Publiciana*.

[36] D. 6.2.12.1 (Paul. 19 *ad Ed.*).

[37] Inst. 3.11.1 (and analogous extensions in D. 40.5.2 (Ulp. 60 *ad Ed.*) ff). There is a plain *analogy* with *bonorum possessio*, so that (as with the trees) that this is *in bonis habere* seems to be a reasonable inference, though again the phrase is not used and the case is not in D. 6.2. on the *Publiciana*.

[38] *In iure cessio*: G. 2.22–24. *Adiudicatio*: summary of the point in Thomas (n 7), 165; Ps-Ulp, LSR 19.16.

(1) *Bonorum emptio* or *venditio*. The XII Tables provision for the debtor unable to pay multiple creditors was that '*partis secanto*', 'cut into pieces'. It is debated whether this was meant literally or metaphorically (the latter either as allowing the creditors to divide the debtor's assets, or to place him in debt-bondage and divide his labour time).[39] Either way, the provision is of very limited use to creditors: if literal, they would get at most the ability to ransom the body parts to relatives for funeral,[40] more likely merely vindicative satisfaction; if metaphorical, it provides no guidance at all about *how to divide* the assets or labour. The praetor provided an alternative remedy. Under this remedy the debtor's goods would be auctioned (*bonorum venditio*) with bidding on the basis of the dividend bidders would offer to pay to creditors. The praetor would put the highest bidder in possession as *bonorum emptor*. Since the procedure was non-statutory, the *bonorum emptor* needed to usucape before he became owner. His remedy, beyond the interdicts, was not primarily the *actio Publiciana*, but an *actio Serviana*, in which the *bonorum emptor* fictitiously claimed the bankrupt was dead and he was his heir, or a variant *actio Rutiliana* in which he claimed in the name of the bankrupt but expressed the *condemnatio* (the remedy demanded) in his own name. Gaius tells us that the praetorian intervention in the field was 'said to be' due to the jurist Publius Rutilius Rufus, who was Praetor in, or at some date shortly before, 118 BCE.[41]

(2) *Bonorum possessio*. This was an order of the praetor to give the claimant possession of a decedent's estate. The probable early context has two elements. The first is that in the claim for an estate, *hereditatis petitio*, which was a *legis actio sacramentum in rem* (statutory action by oath *in rem*), judgment was impossible without the participation of the defendant, and the defendant (the person in possession of the estate) could not be compelled by any statutory means to participate, the claimant being expected to use forcible self-help to get the defendant into court; the apparent absurdity of this rule reflects the general self-help basis of early Roman legal procedure. The praetor would in this situation order possession to the claimant.[42]

The second is that the estate only vested in the heir or heirs automatically if they were *sui heredes* (descendants of the decedent who were emancipated by his death from paternal power) or *necessarii heredes* (slaves emancipated by the will). For other heirs, formal acceptance of the inheritance was necessary and, in the interim before acceptance, the estate and its contents were open to *usucapio* in one year by a person acting in bad faith.[43] Possession and possessory remedies thus became highly important in this context.

[39] Brief discussions of the literature in MH Crawford (ed), *Roman Statutes*, vol 2 (London, Institute of Classical Studies, 1996), 629; H Dondorp, '*Partes secanto*: Aulus Gellius and the Glossators' (2010) 57 *RIDA* 131 (mainly but not exclusively on medieval interpretations).

[40] For McCormack's interpretation, see GD MacCormack, '*Partes secanto*' (1968) 36 *Leg Hist Rev* 509.

[41] G. 4.35: *dicitur*. The dating of Publius Rutilius Rufus's praetorship is in TC Brennan, *The Praetorship in the Roman Republic*, vol II (Oxford, Oxford University Press, 2000), 550.

[42] WAJ Watson, *The Law of Succession in the Later Roman Republic* (Oxford, Oxford University Press, 1971), 198; on self-help, JM Kelly, *Roman Litigation* (Oxford, Oxford University Press, 1966).

[43] Watson, *The Law of Succession in the Later Roman Republic* (n 42), 188.

While the standard case of *bonorum possessio* in the Edict in the form reported by Cicero was to give possession to the heir instituted by will, which was consistent with the statutory context, in certain cases the praetor would act without statutory support. By the classical law, this extended to a major reorganisation of intestate succession, but Watson argues forcibly that this was not in existence until the very end of the Republic or the early Empire.[44] He argues, however, that by 74 BCE at the latest a patron could obtain half his freedman's estate, against the terms of the freedman's will, by *bonorum possessio*.[45] This was an extension of the XII Tables provision which gave the patron the entire estate if the freedman died *intestate*, leaving no children. The fact that this was against the terms of the will and not a statutory provision means that the patron must have had to usucape the property, as was the case with *bonorum possessores* in classical law (who are also clearly identified as holding *in bonis* by Gaius).[46] The *bonorum possessor*'s remedy beyond the interdicts was another fictional action, not given a name or date by Gaius, in which the fiction was that the *bonorum possessor* had title as statutory heir to the estate in question.[47]

(3) *Damnum infectum*. This was a remedy for what would be called in English law a form of private nuisance, where the state of the defendant's property threatened to cause damage to the claimant's neighbouring property. There was an old statutory remedy – *legis actio* – which Gaius tells us was (unusually for *legis actiones*) still available in his time; Watson argues that it was the self-help remedy of *pignoris capio*, which corresponds very roughly to common law extrajudicial distraint.[48] The praetor provided an alternative remedy by way of interdict whose purpose was to force the defendant to give security to pay damages if the loss in fact arose. If the defendant was completely recalcitrant, the praetor could order *missio in possessionem* in favour of the claimant; on a second decree, if the defendant remained recalcitrant, the claimant would be given the right to usucape the property.[49]

The basic praetorian remedy is dated by Watson as existing at the latest by c 73–70 BCE.[50] However, the juristic texts discussing the *missio in possessionem* aspect of the procedure start later, and this procedure is absent from the relevant provisions of the *lex de Gallia Cisalpina* (between 49 and 42 BCE), which were based on the Edict of the Peregrine Praetor; while this may be a peculiarity of the *lex*, or of the Edict of the Peregrine Praetor, as Watson argues, it cannot be completely excluded that the procedure had not yet been applied to *damnum infectum*.[51]

[44] ibid, 176.

[45] WAJ Watson, *The Law of Persons in the Later Roman Republic* (Oxford, Oxford University Press, 1967), 231–34.

[46] G. 3.80.

[47] G. 4.34.

[48] WAJ Watson, *The Law of Property in the Later Roman Republic* (Oxford, Oxford University Press, 1968), 127–31; G. 4.26–29.

[49] Watson, *The Law of Property in the Later Roman Republic* (n 48), 125, 136–37.

[50] ibid, 141.

[51] MH Crawford (ed), *Roman Statutes*, vol 1 (London, Institute of Classical Studies, 1996), 461, text at 464–66, translation at 469–70; Watson, *The Law of Property in the Later Roman Republic* (n 48), 136–38.

(4) The date of the *actio Publiciana*. The conventional date for the *actio Publiciana* is 67 BCE, on the bases that (a) a Quintus Publicius is known to have been Praetor at that date, and (b) the character of the reform fits with late Republican praetorian innovations.[52] As will be seen from what has just been said, by this date possession under *bonorum emptio/venditio* had certainly been in existence for some time, and *bonorum possessio* not supported by statute (in the case of freedmen) may well have been in existence for some years; the interdictal remedy on *damnum infectum* was also certainly in existence, though it is not so clear whether the *missio in possessionem* procedure in that remedy was already in existence.

Watson tentatively suggests that the date of the *actio Publiciana* might be much later, since: (a) there was also a Praetor Publicius Certus in 93 CE (and in any case knowledge of the names of praetors in the first century CE is very limited); and (b) there is no surviving juristic discussion of the action before Neratius, writing c 100 CE.[53] If this were the case, the developed form of *bonorum possessio* superseding the XII Tables intestacy rules would also have been in existence for some time.

(5) What about dating *traditio* of *res mancipi*? The answer is that we have no evidence of the dating of this problem before Gaius, writing c 160 CE and certainly well after the creation of the *actio Publiciana*, and no evidence at all of its frequency.[54] It is clear from Gaius that *mancipatio* was still in use (he advises its use as more convenient than *in iure cessio*),[55] and there are several surviving examples of wills in the *mancipatio* form from Egypt, as well as slave sales by *mancipatio* from the mid-second century CE from Dacia (Transylvania), out on the borders.[56] Maria Nowak argued in 2011 that these are merely examples of documentary forms taken (often inappropriately) from formularies (books of conveyancers' precedents), rather than implying actual performance of the *mancipatio* ceremony.[57] Even such formulaic use is still surprising if the inconvenience of *mancipatio* had produced a *common* practice of *traditio* of *res mancipi* in the late second to early first centuries BCE that had in turn led to the *actio Publiciana* in 67 BCE, though it would be less surprising if the date of the *actio* were in the first century CE. If, of course, the form of words in a document gave rise to a presumption of the performance of the oral

[52] The second point is in PJ du Plessis, *Borkowski's Textbook on Roman Law*, 5th edn (Oxford, Oxford University Press, 2015), 195.

[53] Watson, *The Law of Property in the Later Roman Republic* (n 48), 104–07.

[54] Cic., *Top.* 5.28 says that: *Abalienatio est eius rei quae mancipi est aut traditio alteri nexu aut in iure cessio inter quos ea iure civili fieri possunt. Traditio … nexu* here plainly means *mancipatio* (*cf* G. 2.27); there is no suggestion that *traditio* (in its legal sense) of *res mancipi* is involved.

[55] G. 2.25.

[56] Wills: M Nowak, 'Mancipatio and its life in Late Roman Law' (2011) 41 *The Journal of Juristic Papyrology* 103, 110 n 22. Slave sales: FIRA 130–32; discussion, eg, WAJ Watson, '*Apochatum pro uncis duabus*' in WAJ Watson, *Studies in Roman Private Law* (London, Hambledon, 1991) 185; T Sambrian, 'La *mancipatio* nei trittici della Transilvania' (2005) *Diritto@Storia: Rivista Internazionale di Scienza Giuridiche e Tradizione Romana*, available at: www.dirittoestoria.it/4/Tradizione-Romana/Sambrian-Mancipatio-trittici-Transilvania.htm.

[57] Nowak (n 56), 110–11 (wills), 112–13 (conveyances).

act, as was the case with stipulation,[58] this would add to the arguments above that the supposed inconvenience of *mancipatio* was not that great.

IV. Gaius's Pedagogic Choice

It follows that, if it were not for the testimony of G. 2.40–41, we would naturally conclude that the original development of the *in bonis* concept was connected with *bonorum venditio/emptio* and/or *bonorum possessio*. Both involve claimants in possession under court orders. *Bonorum venditio/emptio* is the slightly more likely candidate, since the bankruptcy context seems more likely to attract taking from the *bonorum emptor* and rapid transfer over of property by the bankrupt or his friends, giving rise to problems not soluble by the use of the interdicts, and the fictional action in this case seems, from its believed link to Rutilius Rufus, to be solidly attested as being early.[59]

The obstacle to this view is G. 2.40–41, already quoted.[60] How much weight should we place on the choice of this example in this place – given that Gaius tells us *elsewhere* that 'bonitary ownership' arises in *bonorum venditio/emptio* and in *bonorum possessio*? Other things being equal, quite a lot. In the first place, Gaius is our major source for 'bonitary ownership', for the reasons explained earlier. In the second place, his writing displays an unusual degree of interest in the history of the law.[61]

On the other hand, other things are *not* equal. Gaius's Institutes are structured around the acquisition and transfer of property and of rights – not their content. Book I on persons is mainly on change of status, not the incidents of particular statuses; Books II and III are organised by reference to modes of acquisition throughout: hence Gaius's silence at 2.14, 2.28–33 on the *nature and content* of praedial servitudes and usufruct; hence the comment at 2.191 that the discussion of legacies is in a sense a digression or out of order; and hence the classification of contracts by how they were formed, *re, verbis, litteris, consensu*.

Once we place G. 2.40–41 in this context, it is obvious that as a matter of *pedagogy* the natural example is the careless purchaser. The passage immediately succeeds discussion of *mancipatio, traditio* and *in iure cessio*. It is immediately

[58] Zimmermann (n 21), 80. *cf* also T Karlović, 'Propter celeritatem dirimendarum litium – Presumptions and Stipulatio in Roman Law' in CH van Rhee and A Uzelac (eds), *Truth and Efficiency in Civil Litigation: Fundamental Aspects of Fact-finding and Evidence-taking in a Comparative Context* (Cambridge, Intersentia, 2012) 375.

[59] ie, even if the link to Rutilius Rufus was not true (Gaius is tentative), it would not be plausible at all if the remedy did not go back to a late Republican date.

[60] G. 4.36, where Gaius's example formula for the *actio Publiciana* is on the case of *res mancipi* sold and delivered, cannot play the same role, since here *bonorum possessio* and *bonorum venditio/emptio* appear *first* in the list of actions with a fiction.

[61] O Stanojević, 'Gaius and Pomponius: Notes on David Pugsley' (1997) 44 *RIDA* 333 draws out the point relatively sharply.

followed by discussion of *usucapio*. To use any of the other cases of 'bonitary ownership' *at this point* would require a substantial digression to explain it. *Bonorum possessio* and *bonorum venditio/emptio* thus appear in the book where they belong, in the contexts of acquisition of inheritances and of actions, rather than at this point. It then follows that the prominence of the case of the careless purchaser in Gaius is to be explained by the pedagogic context and is not, as such, strong evidence for this being the central or original case of bonitary ownership.

V. The Post-Roman Reception of G. 2.40–41 and the Difficulty of Thinking Beyond this Text

It is possible that the role of *traditio* of *res mancipi* in G. 2.40–41 would be enough on its own to lead modern authors to focus on this issue and to disregard or marginalise the other places where Gaius discusses holding *in bonis* – in relation to the status of freedmen in 1.35 and 1.54, to legacies in 2.196, and to *bonorum possessio* and *bonorum emptio* in 3.80–81.

However, more than this is involved. As already indicated, Justinian's law abolishing 'nude Quiritary ownership' was transmitted in the *Code* and thus required some explanation from the medievals. The standard Accursian gloss was clearly at sea;[62] however, Jacques de Révigny (as referred to above) was able to give an explanation in terms of the careless purchaser, citing Boëthius. Cicero's *Topica* had adverted to the need for *mancipatio* or *in iure cessio* to convey *res mancipi*[63] and, to explain this passage, Boëthius, in his early sixth-century commentary on the *Topica*, quoted Gaius's descriptions of these two forms and referred to the fact that the recipient under an informal transfer had to usucape (G. 2.41). Boëthius's commentary was widely used in the middle ages.[64] Hence, this text shaped some later medieval discussions of *dominium bonitarium*.

Theophilus's *Paraphrase* was printed in 1534 and a Greek/Latin parallel text produced in 1536.[65] This added a little further information, and the idea that 'bonitary ownership' was 'natural ownership'; this influenced Jacques Cujas (1522–90) and later writers.[66]

[62] The *Glossa Ordinaria ad tit.* identifies only a point about differing statuses of freedmen. Le Conte adds a substantial explanation taken from Theophilus's *Paraphrasis* and Ps-Ulp LSR: A Le Conte (ed), *Corpus juris civilis glossatum ex recens. Dionys. Gothofredi*, vol IV (Lyon, 1604), cols 1635–36.

[63] Above, n 54.

[64] Latin text in J-P Migne (ed), *Patrologiae cursus completus*, vol 54, Series Latina (Paris, Migne, 1860) 1040, 1094–95; translation in Boethius, *Boethius's In Ciceronis Topica* (E Stump trans, Ithaca, Cornell University Press, 1988), 89–90. Widely used in the Middle Ages: ibid, 6–8. Known to medieval lawyers: D'Amelio (n 16), 49–58.

[65] JHA Lokin, R Meijering and BH Stolte (eds), *Theophili Antecessoris Paraphrasis institutionum* (AF Murison trans, Groningen, Chimaira, 2010), xxxvii–xxxviii.

[66] Theophilus: see above n 15. Cujas: cited in P Apathy, *Die publizianische Klage: das relative dingliche Recht des rechtmässigen Besitzers* (Vienna, Österreichische Staatsdruckerei, 1981), 20.

The overall result of this evolution is that, when the Verona palimpsest of Gaius was discovered, civil lawyers *already* had an idea of *dominium bonitarium* founded on G. 2.40–41, and this *existing* idea must have added to the emphasis on this text in interpreting the institution.

These deep roots have meant that the approach to 'bonitary ownership' starting with G. 2.40–41 has survived a variety of attempts to explore 'bonitary ownership' in more depth, as (for example) in Appleton's *Histoire de la propriété prétorienne et de l'action publicienne*, or to detach the *actio Publiciana* from the case of the careless purchaser, as in (for example) the (different) approaches of Wubbe, Kaser and Apathy.[67] Gaius 2.40–41 thus remains the dominant mode of explanation of the topic in Roman Law textbooks.

VI. 'Owner for All Practical Purposes'?

Was the 'bonitary owner' 'owner for all practical purposes'? Not quite. Our information is pretty limited but reasonably clear.

To begin with the positive. In the first place, as all the textbooks tell us, in the *actio Publiciana* the 'bonitary owner' had a remedy which was as good as the Quiritary owner's *vindicatio*. On some theories, it may even have been a better remedy.[68] Second, *bonorum venditio/emptio* and *bonorum possessio* caught assets which were *in bonis* of the bankrupt, or decedent – not those to which he had a nude Quiritary title but which were *in bonis* of someone else. This is obvious from the terminology, and indirectly confirmed from texts in relation to the creation of real securities.[69] The point is worth making because many cases in which we are concerned at the present day to establish who is owner (as opposed to considering obligations or the transmissibility of rights less than ownership) involve the death or insolvency of a person alleged to have been owner. Equally, slaves were in the *potestas* of the 'bonitary owner', not that of the Quiritary owner[70] – so that the 'bonitary owner' would be noxally (vicariously) liable for their delicts,[71] and their acquisitions would go to the 'bonitary owner'.[72] To this extent, the 'bonitary owner' does indeed look like owner.

On the other hand, the 'bonitary owner' was *not* in the same position as the Quiritary owner in three respects: the transmission of property by legacy; the

[67] Appleton (n 30); FBJ Wubbe, 'Quelques remarques sur la fonction et l'origine de l'action Publicienne' (1961) 8 *RIDA* 417 (summary of Dutch original, which I do not read); M Kaser, 'Nochmals zu *in bonis habere*' (1984) in M Kaser, *Römische Rechtsquellen und angewandte Juristenmethode* (Vienna, Böhlau, 1986) 346; Apathy (n 66), 12–22.

[68] Wubbe (n 67); but note the objections to this argument of G Diósdi, *Ownership in Ancient and Preclassical Roman Law* (Budapest, Akadémiai Kiadó, 1970), 154–65 and of Jolowicz and Nicholas (n 9), 266–67; cp Apathy (n 66), 13–18.

[69] Ankum and Pool (n 11), 16–29, especially at 22–23.

[70] G. 1.52.

[71] G. 4.77.

[72] Ps-Ulp, LSR 19.20.

emancipation of slaves; and liability to land tax. The first two were more important than they seem at first sight; the third only became important at the beginning of the fourth century CE.

A Roman testament in the classical period could include legacies in one of four ways: *per vindicationem*; *per damnationem*; *sinendi modo*; and *per praeceptionem*.[73] A legacy *per vindicationem*, as its name suggests, made the legatee Quiritary owner of the thing given.[74] A legacy *per damnationem* or *sinendi modo* imposed a personal obligation on the heir instituted by the will to pay or transfer the property, while a legacy *per praeceptionem*, according to Gaius originally and even in his time arguably, could only be made to an heir and thus affected only the division of the estate between co-heirs.[75] The 'bonitary owner', not being, technically, owner, could not create a legacy *per vindicationem*.[76] This might appear to be a pure technicality until we recollect that the Romans were highly litigious about issues of succession – as can be seen in the relatively very large volume of juristic commentary on these issues preserved both in Gaius's Institutes and in Justinian's Digest.[77] The 'bonitary owner' was thus in making a testament more dependent on the good faith of the person instituted as heir, and had less practical control of the destination of assets, than the Quiritary owner.

If a Quiritary owner manumitted slaves, he would normally by doing so make them Roman citizens. This was not true of the 'bonitary owner': if he manumitted slaves, he would give them the less advantageous status of 'Junian Latins'.[78] This is, of course, an issue strange to moderns, and again looks like a technicality. But Wallace-Hadrill argues forcibly in his 2011 book on Herculaneum that a list of names, probably a list of those entitled to vote, shows that at most a third of the citizen population of that smallish town at the time of its destruction in 79 CE were free-born.[79] It is thus clear that manumission leading to citizen status was an extremely important institution in the functioning of Roman slavery and society

[73] G. 2.192.

[74] G. 2.194.

[75] G. 2.204 (*per damnationem*), G. 2.213 (*sinendi modo*), G. 2.219–22 (*per praeceptionem*).

[76] G. 2.196 (but saved from total invalidity by conversion into legacy *per damnationem* by a senatus-consult in the time of Nero, G. 2.197); it seems that there were still difficulties in legacies of usufruct other than *per vindicationem* around 200 CE: Paul, *Manual* Book 1, in Fr.Vat. 47; the surrounding texts at Fr.Vat. 45–50 illustrate the complexities.

[77] G. 2.99–3.88, 143 pages of the total 516 pages of text and translation in Gordon and Robinson, or 27.7%; Digest, the large bulk of books 28–38, 226 pages out of 898 pages of text in the standard Mommsen/Krüger edition or 25.2% (some aspects of the topic are also here and there elsewhere in the Digest). *cf* also JM Kelly, *Studies in the Civil Judicature of the Roman Republic* (Oxford, Oxford University Press, 1976), ch 3, attempting to count more specifically 'real cases' in the *Digest* and *Code* and arriving at an even higher percentage of cases on succession. By way of comparison, in AA Burrows (ed), *English Private Law*, 2nd edn (Oxford, Oxford University Press, 2007), succession occupies 77 pages out of 1689 or 4.6%.

[78] G. 1.35.

[79] A Wallace-Hadrill, *Herculaneum: Past and Future* (London, Frances Lincoln, 2011), 138–45, the specific point on numbers at 145.

in the classical period.[80] The point is also worth flagging because of the *public* implications of ownership status: a Quiritary owner can make new citizens out of his slaves; a 'bonitary owner' cannot. Further, a 'bonitary owner' could not in the classical period both emancipate a slave and make him or her heir, since a Junian Latin could not be heir.[81]

Land tax liability fell on the (Quiritary) owner of the land. This was practically immaterial throughout the classical period, since Roman land ceased to be subject to the land tax in 167 BCE. By the time of Gaius, this exemption had been extended throughout Italy, and further to legally 'Italic' land elsewhere, and hence had produced an ideology in which provincial land was said to be owned by the state and land tax, therefore, 'rent'.[82] Diocletian as part of his general reform programme reimposed the land tax on Italy.[83] The result was that *traditio* of Italic land became a tax dodge: the vendor of land takes its capital value and walks away, probably untraceable by the local tax officials, while the purchaser gets two years free of land tax until *usucapio* has been completed. We know of the dodge through the reform introduced to deal with it, Constantine's law of 313 CE, which explicitly banned sale of land without its tax liability as well as superseding all other methods of land transfer on sale by *corporalis traditio*.[84]

It might at first sight seem odd that this problem was not simply solved by imposing the land tax on the *occupier*, rather than the owner, as modern English rates/council tax law does. But this would be both practically and conceptually problematic. Practically, as Jairus Banaji has argued, many occupiers in late antiquity were sharecroppers whose share amounted to little more than a subsistence wage, from whom it would be hard to extract any significant amount of tax.[85] Conceptually, liability to land tax had a deep-rooted connection with citizenship going back to the Republican census; the connection of ownership with citizenship was also visible in land allocations in *leges agrariae* and citizen colonies, and even in the formula *meum ex iure Quiritium*, mine by Roman-citizen right, which was

[80] *cf* also KR Bradley, *Slaves and Masters in the Roman Empire: A Study in Social Control* (Oxford, Oxford University Press, 1987), ch 4; WAJ Watson, *Roman Slave Law* (Baltimore, Johns Hopkins University Press, 1987), ch 2.

[81] Ps-Ulp LSR 22.3, 8.

[82] For the land tax see GP Burton, 'Tributum' in S Hornblower and A Spawforth (eds), *The Oxford Companion to Classical Civilization*, 2nd edn (Oxford, Oxford University Press, 2014) 814. Owned by the state – G. 2.7–8; displayed to be an ideology within Gaius's treatment by the circumstances that such land can be conveyed by *traditio* (G. 2.21) and servitudes over it can be created (G. 2.31); and *cf* Jones (n 5). Kantor argues that there were real differences between Italic and provincial ownerships, though not exactly corresponding to Gaius's formulation: G Kantor, 'Property in Land in Roman Provinces' in G Kantor, T Lambert and H Skoda (eds), *Legalism: Property and Ownership* (Oxford, Oxford University Press, 2017) 55.

[83] This statement simplifies a process begun under Diocletian and completed under Galerius with the census of 306 CE: B Leadbetter, *Galerius and the Will of Diocletian* (London, Routledge, 2009), 172–76.

[84] Honoré, 'Conveyances of Land and Professional Standards in the Later Empire' (n 26), 141–43; Voss (n 26), 140–48.

[85] J Banaji, *Agrarian Change in Late Antiquity: Gold, Labour, and Aristocratic Dominance* (Oxford, Oxford University Press, 2001), ch 8.

behind the conceptual problems which produced holding *in bonis* as a separate category.[86]

In other words, the differences between Quiritary ownership and holding *in bonis* reveal on the one hand the role of ownership (in the form of holding *in bonis* or *pleno iure*) in relation to *liability*; and on the other hand the connection between ownership (in the form of Quiritary ownership) and *public law and public status*, in the forms of the ability to make new citizens and of liability to tax.[87]

VII. Defining Ownership – And its Implications

It is notorious among Romanists that the Roman jurists made no attempt to define ownership – though some modern lawyers are prone to attribute to the Romans the late medieval or early modern definition of it as *usus, fructus, abusus* or *utendi, fruendi, abutendi*, (use, fruits and abuse) which was adopted by Robert Joseph Pothier (1699–1772) from François Hotman (1524–90). This definition is built – as the more elaborate version offered by Samuel von Pufendorf (1631–94) is – on distinguishing ownership as a *right* like *usufruct* and *usus*, but is more extensive.[88]

The more orthodox and widely used medieval and early modern civilian definition was Bartolus's, also in terms of rights: 'the right to freely dispose of the thing unless this is prohibited by the general law'.[89] This has the considerable advantage over *usus, fructus, abusus* of focusing more clearly on the right to *convey*, which addresses more clearly the common case where courts are forced to address the question of who *was* owner at times in the past when competing transfers were made from which titles in the present disputants are deduced.

[86] Census: S Northwood, 'Census and Tributum' in L de Ligt and S Northwood (eds), *People, Land, and Politics: Demographic Developments and the Transformation of Roman Italy 300 BC-AD 14* (Leiden, Brill, 2008) 257. Land grants: DJ Gargola, *Lands, Laws, & Gods: Magistrates and Ceremony in the Regulation of Public Lands in Republican Rome* (Chapel Hill, University of North Carolina Press, 1995).

[87] Wills also possibly fall (remotely) into the category of the 'public', having originally been made in the *comitia calata* or *in procinctu* (in the army, before battle), before these public methods were displaced by the fictional device of the mancipatory will: G. 2.101–03. I owe this point to Professor Joe Sampson, in discussion at the UCL Thomas Roman Law seminar.

[88] *Usus, fructus, abusus*: F Piccinelli, *Studi e ricerche intorno alla definizione «Dominium est ius utendi et abutendi re sua quatenus iuris rati patitur»*, repr edn (Naples, Joneve, 1980); RJ Pothier, *Traité du droit du domaine, de propriété*, vol 1 (Paris, Debure, 1772), 6. Pufendorf: S Pufendorf, *De Jure Naturae et Gentium Libri Octo*, repr edn (Oxford, Oxford University Press, 1934), 363–64 § 4.4.2; S Pufendorf, *Of the Law of Nature and Nations: Eight Books*, 4th edn (B Kennett trans, London, J Walthoe and others, 1729), 362–63.

[89] Bartolus, *Commentaries*, ad D. 41.2.17 (18), widely cited: the *ius, de re corporali, perfecte disponendi, nisi lege prohibeatur*. Subsequent authors elaborated on this by adding conditions and contracts as limits on freedom of disposition: For a mere couple of examples, see J Cowell, *Institutiones Iuris Anglicani* (Cambridge, Legat, 1605), 61: *disponendi aut vendicandi, nisi [lex] vel conventio obsistat* (citing Mynsinger); translated by W Gordon as 'the full and absolute right of disposing of or selling any thing corporeal, unless the law or any condition hinder' (1651 edn, 72); JG Heineccius, *Elementa Juris Civilis secundum ordinem Pandectarum*, vol I (Amsterdam, Jansson-Waesberge, 1740), 214: *ius in re corporali, ex quo facultas de re eiusque fructibus disponendi, eamque vindicandi, nascitur, nisi vel lex, vel conventio, vel testatoris voluntas obsistat.*

If classical jurists had been *forced* to define *dominium*, it is reasonably clear that they would also have wanted a definition which would exclude holding *in bonis*. Otherwise, they would have coined an expression like Theophilus's 'δεσπότης bonitarios' much earlier; and they did not. Even Gaius, though he says in 1.54 that *dominium* is *duplex*, double, and in 2.40 that *divisionem accepit dominium*, that it has become *divided*, in 1.36, 1.54 and 2.40 he uses *in bonis habere* for 'bonitary ownership'. There is some resemblance here to Paul's characterisation of usufruct as in some respects a *pars dominii*, a *fraction* of ownership, which does not in itself imply that usufruct is a *species* of ownership (unlike English 'tenancy for life', as much a 'tenancy' as 'tenancy in fee').[90]

Why? The answer we have already seen: the holder *in bonis* is not enough of an owner to make a legatee immediate owner *per vindicationem*; he does not have the public status as Quiritary (Roman-citizen) owner which would allow him to make slaves into citizens; and, when this was relevant, he does not have the public *obligation* of liability to land tax.

We might also observe a non-lawyer's point of view: the Christian apologist and rhetoric teacher Lactantius's *Divine Institutes*, written in the early 300s CE, has the following comment:

> When a man has a son whom he loves especially, and the son lives in the house, under the authority of his father, the father may grant son the name and power of owner (householder), but in civil law there is said to be only the one house and one householder (owner).[91]

When we say 'householder' in English, it is plain that we are not speaking only of rights, but also of status and of potential liabilities. So too of the linguistic link between *domus* and *dominus*, though this is routinely obscured in translation.

Approach the same issue from another angle. Possession is a fact. It may be completely unprotected by law or illegal, as, for example, in the case of possession of large quantities of heroin, and yet be the basis of market dealings. Of course, the law may attribute 'possession' to persons who are not in factual control; but the underlying *concept* remains one about factual control.[92]

Ownership, in contrast, is said by the textbooks, and by both Bartolus's definition and *usus, fructus, abusus* to be a right. What this 'right' statement means, if

[90] D. 7.1.4 (Paul. 2 *ad Ed.*); brief discussion, Thomas (n 7), 205–06.

[91] Lactant., *Div. inst.* iv.29.7 (*cum quis habet filium quem unice diligat, qui tamen sit in domo et in manu patris, licet ei nomen domini potestatem que concedat, ciuili tamen iure et domus una et unus dominus nominator*); Latin from *Corpus Scriptorum Ecclesiasticorum Latinorum* ix, s. Brandt, 1890, on *CETEDOC Library of Christian Latin texts* CD-ROM. The context of the example is the relation of the doctrine of the divinity of Christ to monotheism. An alternative translation, and the context, in Lactantius, *Lactantius: Divine Institutes* (A Bowen and P Garnsey trans, Liverpool, Liverpool University Press, 2003), 278. The lay character of the comment is illustrated by the use of *in manu* (translated here as 'under the authority of') where technically the son would be in potestate of the father.

[92] Here I follow the standard Roman law textbook accounts (derived ultimately from D. 41.2.12.1 (Ulp. 70 *ad Ed.*)) and F Pollock and RS Wright, *An Essay on Possession in the Common Law* (Oxford, Oxford University Press, 1888), 1–20 and ch 1, in preference to M Wonnacott, *Possession of Land* (Cambridge, Cambridge University Press, 2006), ch 1.

we unpack it into a world beyond academic discussion, is that it is regarded as legitimate to use force to enforce the 'right': whether this force is to be by way of self-help, or of the action of state officials.

Where does this right, the legitimacy of the use of force, come from *in relation to land*? We can, of course, amuse ourselves in the style of John Locke or Robert Nozick by imagining a state of nature in which there is a great deal of unoccupied land, *terra nullius*, which can be taken by *occupatio* or by first cultivation without injustice to any other person.[93] Elaborate moral objections were made to such arguments by Pierre-Joseph Proudhon and by Henry George.[94] But there is a shorter route out of these issues. In reality, as 'native title' cases should teach us, uncultivated so-called *terra nullius* is generally occupied by hunter-gatherers or pastoralists.[95] The work of archaeologists tells us that this has been true pretty much everywhere since the end of the last ice age. There is, therefore, no or negligible space in which either *occupatio*, or first cultivation, of land could *really* operate as an appropriation without injustice.

The real ultimate root of title to *land* in any, state or non-state, legal order is, in fact, given to us by Gaius – *Ea quoque quae ex hostibus capiuntur, naturali ratione nostra fiunt*, 'By natural reason we also become owners of things captured from enemies' (G. 2.69). It is conquest. *Within the state*, the Romans used *usucapio*, later *longi temporis praescriptio* and still later the 40-year, later reduced to 30-year, limitation period;[96] in England, we have the Limitation Acts. If the human rights objection to limitation in *Pye v UK*[97] had succeeded, it would be necessary on sale of land to trace title back to Domesday Book; it would not be possible even in theory to trace it further, because Domesday Book records land redistribution after a conquest: subsequent titles are necessarily under the conquerors' legal order.[98]

Land title ultimately rests on *taking from* foreigners – those outside the state or social group – by collective action. That it continues to rest on collective *holding from* potential adverse collective claimants is shown by the cases of 'facts on the ground' in the occupied territories in Israel–Palestine, of 'ethnic cleansing' in

[93] First cultivation, J Locke, *Two Treatises of Government* (first published 1689, P Laslett ed, Cambridge, Cambridge University Press, 1988), 285–302; *occupatio*, R Nozick, *Anarchy, State and Utopia* (Oxford, Blackwell, 1974), 174–82.

[94] P-J Proudhon, *What is Property?* (DR Kelley and BG Smith eds, Cambridge, Cambridge University Press, 1994); H George, *Progress and Poverty* (London, Reeves, 1884), book VII.

[95] See, in particular, *Mabo v Queensland [No 2]* (1992) 175 CLR 1 (HCA).

[96] Thomas (n 7), 157–65.

[97] *JA Pye (Oxford) Ltd v United Kingdom* (2008) 46 EHRR 45 (Grand Chamber), complaining of the decision in *JA Pye (Oxford) Ltd v Graham* [2002] UKHL 30; [2003] 1 AC 419 (HL(E)).

[98] I do not mean here to deny the rule of *antecessores tempore regis Edwardi* in Domesday or the fact that William did not formally and immediately expropriate all Anglo-Saxon landowners (see R Fleming, *Kings and Lords in Conquest England* (Cambridge, Cambridge University Press, 1991), especially ch 4), or William's propaganda use of a claim that he inherited from Edward the Confessor, with its reverberations in 12th century law (see G Garnett, *Conquered England: Kingship, Succession and Tenure, 1066–1166* (Oxford, Oxford University Press, 2007)). My point is that all rights-claims to land in England are necessarily *under the new regime*, even if this new regime *chose* to recognise and use some rights created by the old regime.

former Yugoslavia, and of 'sectarian purges' in post-invasion Iraq. It follows that land ownership necessarily involves an obligation to participate in the common defence against foreigners or enemies, whether by personal activity (for example, military service) or by contributing resources (for example, tax).

This obligation is expressed in the public quality of landownership: *meum ex iure Quiritium*. In non-state systems this may take the form of the restriction of land ownership to members of an ascribed ethnicity, as in pre-Conquest Welsh law, or in the case of Pakhtuns in the pre-colonial past of what became in colonial times the 'North-West Frontier' area.[99] In state systems, it involves a relationship of the landowner *to the state*.[100]

VIII. Conclusion

The 'standard narrative' of Quiritary ownership and 'bonitary ownership' tells us a story of excessive legal conservatism, mitigated by praetorian intervention, but persisting even after this intervention in the Roman jurists' fetishistic refusal to recognise a reality of divided ownership and of informal conveyancing.

If we de-centre this story in approaching the problem, a very different picture emerges: one which has something to tell us not only about *Roman* ownership, but about ownership of land *in general*, considered as the legal concept of a social practice. It may be that defining the ownership of land as a 'right' leads us to forget both its necessary *public* status, and the *liabilities* which are necessarily attached to it; and to think of it as more morally attractive than it would be if we recognised what these aspects tell us about its foundations.

[99] Welsh law: D Jenkins (ed), *The Law of Hywel Dda: Law Texts from Medieval Wales* (Llandysul, Gomer, 1986), 114–19 (in the fourth generation they can become proprietors). Pakhtuns: R Nichols, *Settling the Frontier: Land, Law and Society in the Peshawar Valley, 1500–1900* (Oxford, Oxford University Press, 2001), ch 1. In English law between late Middle Ages and 1870 the 'alien-born' could not own land: on the origins of this rule, see K Kim, *Aliens in Medieval Law: The Origins of Modern Citizenship* (Cambridge, Cambridge University Press, 2000); abolished by The Naturalization Act 1870, s 2.

[100] It may be objected that (as the textbooks tell us) developed Roman law allowed 'peregrine ownership'. But this is a rather remarkable entity. There is no direct support in the sources for Roman law 'peregrine ownership' at all, let alone 'peregrine ownership' of Italic land. The entire idea is a modern construct based on Gaius's description of remedies for theft, and under the *lex Aquilia* for wrongful damage to property, available to and against peregrines, which operated by including the fiction that the peregrine was a citizen (G. 4.37). Modern authors have then inferred the existence of 'peregrine ownership' by supposing that there must have been an analogous fictional *vindicatio* available to peregrines. But the analogy simply does not hold, and certainly does not hold in relation to claims to Italic land.

4

Explaining D. 41.1.36

JOE SAMPSON

I. Introduction

The language of *causa* is prominent in relation to acquiring *dominium* of a thing by *traditio* (delivery) and by *usucapio* (prescriptive acquisition). The term signifies the justificatory force for an individual's acquisition of a thing – it is the reason why *dominium* ought to vest. The term need not necessarily be understood in the same way in each mode of acquisition. The rationale for acquisition by derivative means is less controversial than for prescriptive acquisition. The former is fundamentally consensual and the latter fundamentally not. There is, however, a common language that has attached to *causa* across its contexts in the Anglophone textbook literature.[1] This language seeks to explain *causa* as either true (or real, meaning legally valid), or putative (meaning legally invalid but believed to be valid by the parties). The position invariably reached is that a true *causa* was always needed for *usucapio* but that, for at least some classical jurists, and certainly for Justinian, a putative *causa* sufficed for *traditio*.[2]

This chapter explores the way in which a framework for analysing *causa* in *traditio* and *usucapio* emerged in Roman law. Despite its title and its allusion to a pivotal text in the requirements for *traditio*, the chapter focuses on *usucapio* as presented in the Digest. In the context of *usucapio*, it is possible to see shifts in both the requirements and the function of *causa*. Initially, *causa* related to good faith, serving to explain when a party could legitimately believe they were entitled to a thing, so as to justify acquisition by *usucapio*. In essence, the question was whether good faith could only be founded on a legally valid *causa*, or whether an erroneous

[1] WW Buckland, *A Text-Book of Roman Law from Augustus to Justinian*, 3rd edn (PG Stein ed, Cambridge, Cambridge University Press, 1963), 228; JKBM Nicholas, *An Introduction to Roman Law* (Oxford, Oxford University Press, 1962), 117; JAC Thomas, *Textbook of Roman Law* (Amsterdam, North-Holland, 1976), 180; PJ du Plessis, *Borkowski's Textbook on Roman Law*, 5th edn (Oxford, Oxford University Press, 2015), 187–88.

[2] The lone voice defending the sufficiency of a putative *causa* in classical law is DF Pugsley, 'Was *justa causa* necessary for *traditio* in Roman law?' in DF Pugsley, *Americans Are Aliens: and other essays on Roman Law* (Exeter, University of Exeter, 1989) 27.

belief in such a *causa* could suffice – even if that would effectively collapse the requirements of *causa* and good faith.[3] Traces of this debate can be found in early juristic writing but its zenith was the early second century CE. By the middle of that century, jurists were beginning to separate distinct requirements of good faith and *causa*, and to insist that the *causa* be legally valid. This is the position that survives into high classical law, although traces of the contentious history of *causa* continue to be found in the writings of the jurists of the early third century CE.

It is within this chronology that the causal requirement in *traditio* needs to be contextualised. The texts that survive on this doctrinal point are few but inconsistent. The heart of the debate is a pair of texts by Julian and Ulpian that take diametrically opposed positions.[4] Julian appears to claim that *dominium* can pass by *traditio* even where there is no valid *causa*, while Ulpian explicitly rejects the opinion of Julian, and upholds the need for a true *causa*. A smattering of further Digest texts suggests support for Ulpian's position, although all are of later generations than Julian's.

How is this inconsistency to be explained? This chapter argues that the positions of Julian and Ulpian each evince a desire for uniformity. Writing at a time when a pervasive view about *usucapio* held that good faith could exist despite the absence of a true *causa*, Julian draws upon a small number of scenarios in which ownership might pass despite disagreement on the *causa* (bundling together disagreement about which *causa* is operative and disagreement that means no *causa* forms at all). In the first half of the second century CE, there is evidence that belief in acquisition was perceived to suffice for both modes of acquisition. However, a generation later, the requirements for *usucapio* had been more strenuously separated. The underlying *causa* and the presence of good faith were conceptually different requirements. Though there was clearly significant overlap in the scope and factual basis for each requirement, good faith in the absence of a true *causa* was now insufficient for *usucapio*. In *traditio*, this manifests in the need for a true underlying *causa*, in this later period.

At two distinct points in the narrative of *causa*, consistency between the modes of acquisition is perceived as valuable, though the outcomes pull in opposite directions in the conceptualisation of *causa*. This suggests that *causa* was subject to a degree of abstraction that detached it from its doctrinal context. While it is not obvious that *causa* should perform the same function in *traditio* and in *usucapio*, a principled desire for uniformity is revealed. Nevertheless, the historical treatment of certain test cases reveals the limits of the abstraction. Entrenched solutions had been reached that were incompatible with the proposed framework for understanding *causa*, forcing clumsy resort to ideas like 'utility' to explain the full scope of recognised doctrine. Abstractions have their limits as explanatory tools when mapped onto existing doctrinal frameworks, or else ill-fitting strands of doctrine must be jettisoned in the name of abstract purity.

[3] As, indeed, seems to have been the case in *longi temporis praescriptio*: C. 7.33.1 (Severus and Antoninus to Julianus, 202).

[4] D. 41.1.36 (Iul. 13 *Dig.*) and D. 12.1.18.pr (Ulp. 7 *Disp.*).

II. The Language of *Causa*

This chapter focuses on the role and juristic understanding of *causa* in classical law. The lynchpin controversy between Julian and Ulpian in relation to *traditio* has long been recognised, and has spawned an impressive literature.[5] Three adjectives are typically appended to *causa*, in order to describe different aspects of its ideal conceptualisation. The first is *iusta*. This term reflects the underlying normative function of *causa* within a given mode of acquisition, describing the range of justifications recognised as sufficient for the acquisition of *dominium*. It is obvious that not every act of delivery, for example, can suffice to pass ownership, without radically devaluing what ownership means. To take the most Oxford of examples, the passing of port around the table does not make each handler owner of the decanter or its contents. Delivery pursuant to a gift is a common basis for affording the act of handing over the item the legal effect of transferring ownership. Delivery pursuant to a sale and purchase is another. 'Gift' and 'purchase' are *iustae causae* – reasons underlying the transfer that are recognised by the law as sufficient to pass ownership. Letting someone borrow something in order to use it, in full expectation of its timely return (ie, a *commodatum* in Roman law), would not be expected to pass ownership to the borrower. Consequently, *commodatum* is not a *iusta causa*. The language of *iusta causa* is used to identify a restricted set of underlying justifications sufficient for the transfer of property.[6]

Every transaction in Roman law can be analysed in this way. It is important, however, to remember that the list of *iustae causae* need not be identical in different modes of acquisition. When considering the *causae* sufficient for *traditio*, our focus will be on consensual transactions, as our concern is with legal situations in which one party desires to transfer ownership of a thing to another, and that other desires to acquire it. Prescriptive acquisition by *usucapio* is different. Here, while the *dominus* of the property is unlikely to be involved in the events, there is still scope for *causae* based on consensus. A common fact pattern involves a consensual transaction by a non-owner, such as where X sells to Y a book belonging to Z. The sale and purchase between X and Y operates to explain why Y ought to be allowed to acquire the thing by *usucapio* (assuming all other conditions are met). However, there is scope for non-consensual *causae* in *usucapio*, as well. The clearest example is abandonment. Suppose X abandons Z's book. That act of abandonment does not render the book a *res nullius*, susceptible to acquisition by *occupatio* by the first

[5] The leading pieces on the language of *causa* as it relates to *traditio* are: M Kaser, 'Zur „iusta causa traditionis"' (1961) 34 *BIDR* 61; G Jahr, 'Zur iusta causa tradtitionis' (1963) 80 *ZRG RA* 141; R Evans-Jones and GD MacCormack, '*Iusta causa traditionis*' in PBH Birks (ed), *New Perspectives in the Roman Law of Property* (Oxford, Oxford University Press, 1989) 99; WM Gordon, *Studies in the Transfer of Property by Traditio* (Aberdeen, University of Aberdeen Press, 1970); WM Gordon, 'The Importance of the *iusta causa* of *traditio*' in PBH Birks (ed), *New Perspectives in the Roman Law of Property* (Oxford, Oxford University Press, 1989) 123.

[6] With reference to bare pacts, the point is made more succinctly (and authoritatively) in C. 2.3.20 (Valerian and Gallienus to Martial, 7 January 290).

taker, because abandonment is only effective if done by the *dominus*. However, when Y, having observed X's 'abandonment' of the book, takes possession of it, X's abandonment might explain why it is that Y is justified in acquiring the book by *usucapio*. Given the different rationales underlying the different modes of acquiring *dominium*, it stands to reason that the list of *causae* accepted as justifications may differ from mode to mode.

Supposing a *causa* is *iusta* – meaning that it is of the correct type for the relevant mode of acquisition – the two other qualifying adjectives relate to the features of that *causa*. One possibility is to focus on the validity, 'truth' or 'reality' of the *causa*. Each *causa* occupies a distinct legal category with requirements that determine validity. If the *causa* is sale and purchase, there needs to be agreement between the parties on the price, *res* and the nature of the transaction. The absence of any of these, or the presence of vitiating factors, means that the contract of sale and purchase is not validly formed. If the *causa* is abandonment, there must have been conduct by some party amounting to abandonment, accompanied by the requisite mental state. If cargo is thrown overboard to save a ship, the requisite mental state is absent, so there is no legally valid abandonment. Thus, we find references to the need for a 'real' *iusta causa* or a 'valid' *iusta causa* in *usucapio*, and perhaps classical *traditio*.[7] The use of 'true' and its synonyms is a reference to the legal efficacy of the underlying *causa*.

In contrast to a requirement for true *iusta causa* in this sense, there are arguments for the sufficiency of a belief in the existence of a *causa*. If the underlying sale and purchase is invalid, perhaps owing to a fundamental error, can *dominium* still pass, if the parties nonetheless genuinely want it to pass? If the abandonment is not legally effective but someone finding the jettisoned goods believes them to have been abandoned, can the finder acquire *dominium* by *usucapio*? This situation involves 'putative' or 'imagined' *causa*. The focus is not the actual existence of a legally valid *iusta causa* but, instead, a party's belief in, and desire for, a *causa* – one that, had it existed, would have been a *iusta causa* for the relevant mode of acquisition. It is perhaps obvious that ownership should not arise in the absence of a belief in a legally recognised basis for ownership but this forms part of the analysis behind arguments for the sufficiency of a putative *causa*.

In relation to *usucapio*, there is an additional wrinkle. *Usucapio* was a complex legal construct with several requirements, including possession of the right sort of *res*, pursuant to a *iusta causa*, and in good faith. The precise dynamic between these elements could shift, according to the *causa* behind the claim to prescriptive acquisition. Consequently, the treatment of *usucapio* in the Digest is organised by the underlying event: for example, *usucapio* 'as a purchaser' (*pro emptore*), 'as a donee' (*pro donato*) or 'of abandoned property' (*pro derelicto*). This instantiated approach to *usucapio* is also evident in the writings of the classical jurists, and has particular importance for the moment at which a potential acquirer needed to be in good faith.

[7] eg, Buckland, *Text-Book* (n 1), 228, 246.

This *causa*-based approach is also found in relation to possession, as is evident from the manner in which the Digest titles on *pro emptore* and its ilk unfold. In each title, the preliminary discussion considers when a person possesses – for instance, *pro emptore* – before turning to consider the consequent process of *usucapio*. Given the fundamental role possession plays in *usucapio*, this is hardly surprising. The difficulty comes in the obscure final title of book 41 of the Digest, which deals with possession and *usucapio* '*pro suo*'. It is a short title, of just five texts. The first two concern *possessio pro suo*. This appears to have been a ground of possession that arose out of the original modes of acquisition. The owner of a captured bird surely also possesses it but what is the *causa* for the possession? The simple fact that it is already his.[8] The same logic applies to things acquired as fruits, by *occupatio*, and even alluvion.[9] Ulpian goes a step further: this *causa* for possession applies whenever you own a thing.[10] So, if X takes delivery of a dog from its owner Y, having bought it from Y, X begins to possess the dog both 'as a purchaser' (*pro emptore*) and 'for himself' (*pro suo*). Though Ulpian's understanding of possession '*pro suo*' appears to be closer to possessing 'as owner' than 'for oneself', a final text makes it clear that *pro suo* applies even where not the owner: 'But if a thing be delivered to me on a lawful ground – say purchase – and I usucapt it, I begin to possess it for myself even before *usucapio*'.[11] The implication appears to be that, where a possessor needs to usucapt property that has been purchased, the purchaser begins to possess *pro suo* even before the completion of *usucapio*. This is coming close to saying that one possesses through the mere belief that one is the owner, whatever the reality, and that this belief replaced the need to think in terms of possessing pursuant to specific *causae*.[12] In relation to possession, the pertinent analytical question becomes whether or not the possessor's belief in entitlement is permissible. This collapsing of *causa* and belief in relation to possession had the potential to infect juristic treatment of *causa* and good faith in relation to *usucapio*.

III. Early *Usucapio*

The earliest identifiable texts on *causa* in *usucapio* date to the first century BCE. The first is attributed to Alfenus Varus, and shows a clear analytical focus on the

[8] D. 41.10.2 (Paul. 54 *ad Ed.*).

[9] ibid.

[10] D. 41.10.1.pr (Ulp. 15 *ad Ed.*).

[11] D. 41.10.1.1 (Ulp. 15 *ad Ed.*): *Sed si res mihi ex causa iusta puta emptionis tradita sit et usucapiam, incipio quidem et ante usucapionem pro meo possidere.*

[12] eg, L Vacca, '«Iusta causa» e «bona fides» nell'«usucapio» romana: A proposito del titolo «pro suo»' in V Giuffrè (ed), *Sodalitas: Scritti in Onore de Antonio Guarino*, vol 4 (Naples, Jovene, 1984) 1955; LC Winkel, '*Usucapio pro suo* and the Classification of the *causae usucapionis* by the Roman Jurists' in PBH Birks (ed), *New Perspectives in the Roman Law of Property: Essays for Barry Nicholas* (Oxford, Oxford University Press, 1989) 215; T Mayer-Maly, *Das Putativtitelproblem bei der usucapio* (Graz, Böhlau, 1962).

underlying *causa* for *usucapio*.[13] Discussing the situation where a slave sold an asset belonging to his *peculium* in circumstances where his *dominus* was unaware of the transaction, Alfenus holds that the purchaser was nevertheless able to acquire the thing by *usucapio pro emptore*. The heart of the text concerns the relevance of the ignorance of the *dominus*. Less clear is the point Alfenus seeks to make about *usucapio*, not least because the factual scenario feels incomplete. As it stands, the assertion that the possessor can usucapt in such a situation seems too simplistic to require stating. A slave was capable of alienating *peculium* assets as long as he was authorised to do so – that authorisation arising through the consent of the *dominus* to a particular transaction, generic authorisation for a range of transactions, or subsequent ratification.[14] If authorised, there would be a sale and purchase, and so, naturally, *usucapio pro emptore* would follow. The use of the verb *vendisset* suggests that there has been a sale (implying authorisation), and the straightforwardness of the point might just reflect initial doubts in the developing commercial position of slaves. It is conceivable that Alfenus is dealing with a more difficult point, such as the position of the possessor between agreement and ratification, or even where the slave is dealing without authorisation, but the surviving text does not suggest this. The text that is handed down is straightforward, and does not make overt reference to the good faith of the possessor, instead focusing squarely on the circumstances of the sale, the *causa* for the possible *usucapio*.

The second text consists of a view attributed to Trebatius, a jurist active in the first century BCE under both Julius Caesar and Augustus. His view is reported by Pomponius, who was writing in the middle of the second century CE:

> If you bought a stolen slave girl in good faith and, while with you, she conceived and gave birth to a child that you then possessed, if, within the period of *usucapio*, you discovered the child's mother was stolen, Trebatius in every case [*omni modo*] wrote that the child, because you possessed him in this way, was acquired by *usucapio* …[15]

The text continues with Pomponius's own view, addressed below. This is a significantly more complicated text than that of Alfenus, and shows a shift towards consideration of difficult questions involving the interplay of *causa* and good faith. The text concerns the *usucapio* of a child born to a stolen slave. The acquisition of the mother, a *res furtiva*, was barred by legislation,[16] leaving the child as the only possible focus of the text. It is significant that Trebatius does not approach the question

[13] D. 41.3.34 (Alf. 1 *Dig. a Paulo Epit.*): 'If a slave, without the knowledge of his master, sells property from his *peculium*, the buyer can acquire by *usucapio*' (*Si servus insciente domino rem peculiarem vendidisset, emptorem usucapere posse*).

[14] WW Buckland, *The Roman Law of Slavery: The Condition of the Slave in Private Law from Augustus to Justinian* (Cambridge, Cambridge University Press, 1908), 159.

[15] D. 41.10.4.pr (Pomp. 32 *ad Sab.*): *Si ancillam furtivam emisti fide bona ex ea natum et apud te conceptum est ita possedisti, ut intra constitutum usucapioni tempus cognosceres matrem eius furtivam esse, Trebatius omni modo, quod ita possessum esset, usucaptum esse* …

[16] There was a statutory bar on the *usucapio* of stolen property under the XII Tables and the *lex Atinia*: Inst. 2.6.2. Pomponius, the author of this text, elsewhere confirms that the statutory bar is absolute: D. 41.3.24.pr (Pomp. 24 *ad Q. Muc.*).

in terms of *causa*. Indeed, from this text alone, it is unclear what the *causa* for the possession of the child ought to be, though presumably it is acquisition as a fruit (leading to *usucapio pro suo*). Instead, Trebatius is concerned with good faith: if the possessor discovers the fact that the mother was stolen during the period of *usucapio* (and, by implication, was unaware at the moment *usucapio* began with the birth of the child), he can complete the process and become *dominus* of the child. In other words, so long as the process of *usucapio* began in good faith, subsequently learning that one is not entitled to the property being usucapted does not prevent completion of *usucapio*. It is also noteworthy that Pomponius emphasises that Trebatius took this position across multiple permutations of the scenario (*omni modo*), rather than viewing it as an isolated opinion. This has the appearance of an attempt by Pomponius to bolster the strength of Trebatius's opinion against anticipated opposition.

Although Trebatius's text is focused on the possessor's *bona fides*, the existence of an underlying *causa* for the purposes of possession is alluded to by the clause *quod ita possessum esset*. The text thus highlights Trebatius's emphasis on good faith but not to the exclusion of *causa*. Further evidence for the central role of *causa* in late Republican *usucapio* is provided by the praetor's promise of the *actio Publiciana*, which is expressly conditional on delivery for a *iusta causa*.[17] However, we ought not to attach too much significance to the link between *usucapio* and the *actio Publiciana*. Despite significant overlap, there is a modest disconnect between standing to bring the action and successful *usucapio*: according to Paul, it was possible to be in the process of *usucapio* without being protected by the *actio Publiciana*.[18] Such a case might be exceptional but it nevertheless highlights the absence of inevitable connection between the action and prescriptive acquisition: the *actio Publiciana* might have protected only a subset of *usucapio* possessors.

The Republican juristic evidence is slender but, even with only two texts, it is possible to discern different analytical emphases. Alfenus is concerned with the underlying *causa*, while Trebatius is principally interested in the *bona fides* of the acquirer. As we move into the early Empire, the textual evidence suggests a greater degree of indeterminacy surrounding the interplay between *causa* and *bona fides* in *usucapio*. This is alluded to in one of the earliest imperial jurists whose writings on *causa* are attested, Sabinus, whose view is reported by Paul:

> If a purchase is made subject to a condition, so long as that condition is unsatisfied, the purchaser does not acquire by use. The same is true if he thinks the condition has been satisfied when in fact it has not, which is similar to where he [only] thinks he has purchased. If, on the other hand, the condition has been fulfilled but the buyer is not aware of this, it can be said following Sabinus (for whom fact [*substantia*] was more important than belief [*opinio*]) that he acquires by *usucapio*.[19]

[17] D. 6.2.1.pr (Ulp. 16 *ad Ed.*).
[18] D. 41.4.2.16 (Paul. 54 *ad Ed.*).
[19] D. 41.4.2.2 (Paul. 54 *ad Ed.*): *Si sub condicione emptio facta sit, pendente condicione emptor usu non capiat. Idemque est et si putet condicionem extitisse, quae nondum exstitit: similis est enim ei, qui putat se emisse. Contra si exstitit et ignoret, potest dici secundum Sabinum, qui potius substantiam intuetur quam*

The presentation of the issue as a choice between what has actually happened (ie, the fact that the sale's condition has been fulfilled, rendering it true) and what the buyer believes to be the case neatly summarises the two sides of the debate that characterise the juristic treatment of *usucapio*. Paul suggests Sabinus would prioritise fact (true *iusta causa*) over belief (*bona fides* – tending to emphasise putative *causa*) but this view is not anchored to the scenario at hand, nor is it attested to elsewhere. Rather, it turns on Paul's ascribing to Sabinus an abstract position derived from his approach to other issues, which Paul thinks would hold true in the case under discussion. It is also noteworthy that Sabinus treats *bona fides* and *causa* as distinct elements. The *causa* can be satisfied, and can justify *usucapio*, even where the possessor is unaware of this. The *causa* is justifying the process of *usucapio* itself, rather than the possessor's *bona fides*. This approach is more typical of the Severan jurists, and might be attributable to Paul's interpretation.

The earliest texts in support of the need for a true *causa* that are not reported by an author of a later generation come from Javolenus. The issue is introduced with a factually ambiguous case: 'A thing delivered as a legacy will nevertheless be acquired by *usucapio pro legato* even though its owner is still alive'.[20] This scenario can be interpreted in two ways, with differing implications for the *causa* requirement in *usucapio*. In both interpretations, X is Y's legatee. On the first interpretation, X receives the subject of the legacy while Y still lives. On the second, Y dies, and Z's property is delivered to X in satisfaction of the legacy. The former would support the sufficiency of a X's belief in the existence of a non-existent *causa*, as there can be no valid legacy while the legator still lives; the latter would mean that the delivery of a third party's property pursuant to a valid legacy was sufficient for *usucapio*, as legacy constituted a valid *iusta causa*. The compilers continue Javolenus's text with an extract from Pomponius: 'if the recipient believes it the property of a dead person', suggesting that it is the *bona fides* of the recipient that matters, supporting the first interpretation, in which the testator still lives.[21] However, this is immediately contradicted by the next text in the sequence, in which Javolenus focuses on the need truly to be a legatee, in order to acquire by *usucapio pro legato*.[22] So, while superficially ambiguous, Javolenus (despite the interspliced opinion of Pomponius) appears to require a valid *iusta causa* for *usucapio pro legato*.

The text of Pomponius sandwiched between the pair from Javolenus emphasises the beliefs of the possessor in determining whether or not he is in the process of *usucapio* but Pomponius's views on *causa* are opaque. Further ambiguity stems from other texts of Pomponius. In relation to *usucapio pro herede*, he writes: 'Many have thought that, if I am an heir and think something is part of an inheritance

opinionem, usucapere eum. The text continues with Paul's explanation of the differences between the two scenarios.

[20] D. 41.8.5 (Iav. 7 *ex Cass.*): *Ea res, quae legati nomine tradita est, quamvis dominus eius vivat, legatorum tamen nomine usucapietur …*

[21] D. 41.8.6 (Pomp. 32 *ad Sab.*): … *si is, cui tradita est, mortui esse existimaverit.*

[22] D. 41.8.7 (Iav. 7 *ex Cass.*): *Nemo potest legatorum nomine usucapere nisi is, cum quo testamenti factio est, quia ea possessio ex iure testamenti proficiscitur.*

when it is not, I can acquire it by *usucapio*'.[23] Here, Pomponius does not expressly endorse any particular approach to *causa*. Instead, this text is interesting for its allusion to many supporters of the sufficiency of belief in *causa*. Celsus, a near contemporary of Pomponius, is reported by Ulpian as writing critically of the those who supported the sufficiency of a belief in *causa*, as if the view was still widely held in the reign of Hadrian, giving credence to Pomponius's reporting of the view's prevalence.[24]

A clearer idea of Pomponius's views comes in the latter half of the text reporting the opinion of Trebatius. In full, D. 41.10.4.pr reads:

> If you bought a stolen slave girl in good faith and, while with you, she conceived and gave birth to a child that you then possessed, if, within the period of *usucapio*, you discovered the child's mother was stolen, Trebatius in every case [*omni modo*] wrote that the child, because you possessed him in this way, was acquired by *usucapio*. I think that a distinction should be made: if during the statutory period you were unaware to whom she belonged, or if you did know but were unable to inform her owner, or if you could and did inform the owner, then you shall acquire by *usucapio*. However, if you knew to whom she belonged and were able to inform the owner but did not do so, then the opposite is true, for then you would seem to possess by secrecy [*clam*], and one person cannot possess both for himself [*pro suo*] and secretly [*clam*].[25]

Pomponius adopts a similar line of argument to Trebatius: the crucial question is whether or not the child can be acquired by *usucapio*. In answering that question, both focus on whether the mother was possessed in good faith at the time of conception and birth. Trebatius views the matter in generic terms: all that we need to ask is whether or not the possessor was in good faith. Pomponius goes a step further by explaining what considerations can lead to a determination of good faith. Good faith can persist even where the possessor knows that the mother is stolen, so long as it is beyond the possessor's ability to restore the mother to her owner. In adopting this stance, Pomponius's focus is firmly on the existence of possession *pro suo*, with *usucapio* viewed as the logical consequence of a finding of possession. Moreover, possession *pro suo* is divorced from a belief in entitlement. Ordinarily, *separatio* would mean that a *bona fide* possessor had a basis recognised by the law for regarding the child as his property. However, Pomponius goes further than that, treating as

[23] D. 41.5.3 (Pomp. 23 *ad Q. Muc.*): *Plerique putaverunt, si heres sim et putem rem aliquam ex hereditate esse quae non sit, posse me usucapere.*

[24] D. 41.3.27 (Ulp. 31 *ad Sab.*): 'Celsus, in his thirty-fourth book, describes as mistaken those who think that someone who obtained possession in good faith can usucapt *pro suo* and that it is irrelevant whether or not he bought the thing, or received it as a gift, so long as he believed he bought it or was gifted it. This is because no *usucapio* on the ground of legacy or gift or dowry has force if there is no gift, dowry or legacy'.

[25] D. 41.10.4.pr (Pomp. 32 *ad Sab.*): *Si ancillam furtivam emisti fide bona ex ea natum et apud te conceptum est ita possedisti, ut intra constitutum usucapioni tempus cognosceres matrem eius furtivam esse, Trebatius omni modo, quod ita possessum esset, usucaptum esse. Ego sic puto distinguendum, ut, si nescieris intra statutum tempus, cuius id mancipium esset, aut si scieris neque potueris certiorem dominum facere, aut si potueris quoque et feceris certiorem, usucaperes: sin vero, cum scires et posses, non feceris certiorem, contra esse: tum enim clam possedisse videberis, neque idem et pro suo et clam possidere potest.*

possessing *pro suo* the possessor who knows that the mother is stolen before the child is born, as long as the possessor takes steps to restore the mother to her master. Such possession, if found, is without a true justification but is permitted (and allowed to ripen into full ownership) based on nothing more than the possessor's state of mind – and perhaps good faith conduct, in attempting to restore the mother to her owner. That state of mind, for all that it evinces good faith, is something less than a belief in entitlement. It is this show of good behaviour that seems to explain the continued possibility of *usucapio*. With this, the combination of *bona fides* and the breadth of *pro suo* serves to remove the need for an underlying *causa*.

Other texts flesh out Pomponius's belief-based approach to justifying prescriptive acquisition. However, D. 41.10.4.pr is an outlier, insofar as it allows *usucapio* to proceed despite positive knowledge that there is no *causa*. In other texts, Pomponius's focus is on whether or not the acquirer believed there was a *causa*, such as in D. 41.10.3:

> You delivered to me a slave whom you wrongly believed was due to me under a *stipulatio*. If I know that nothing is due to me, I cannot acquire the slave by *usucapio*. But if I do not know that, the better view is that I can acquire him by *usucapio*, because the ground [*causa*] on which the slave is delivered, which I believe is true, is sufficient to make me possess that which is delivered for myself [*pro suo*]. This is the view of Neratius, and I think it is correct.[26]

The view is put in unambiguous terms by Neratius, with whom Pomponius concurs: belief in the underlying *causa* is sufficient for possession *pro suo*, and possession *pro suo* is sufficient for *usucapio*. The absorption of *causa* into *bona fides* in Neratius's and Pomponius's conception of *usucapio* is nearly total, though it does not go so far as D. 41.10.4.pr in allowing *usucapio* without a belief in *causa*. The final text of the Digest title on *pro suo* furnishes further evidence of Neratius's position. Here, Neratius lays down general principles about the plausibility of mistakes, and how far-fetched they need to be before a person cannot be said to possess (and so usucapt) *pro suo*.[27] As long as the error is *probabilis* – 'plausible' – the error will not bar *usucapio*, notwithstanding the absence of a recognised and validly constituted *causa*. This is also the approach of Marcellus, writing in the early second century CE. In a text on the *actio Publiciana*, he claims that a person who bought property from an insane seller could acquire that property by *usucapio* (and so bring the Publician action), as long as the buyer was unaware of the seller's mental state.[28] The lack of capacity on the part of the seller would mean the sale and purchase was void, unless made during a lucid interval (presumably not the case, if the example is to be more than trivial), and yet the failure of *causa* is salvaged by the *bona fides* of the purchaser.

[26] D. 41.10.3 (Pomp. 22 *ad Sab.*): *Hominem, quem ex stipulatione te mihi debere falso existimabas, tradidisti mihi: si scissem mihi nihil debere, usu eum non capiam: quod si nescio, verius est, ut usucapiam, quia ipsa traditio ex causa, quam veram esse existimo, sufficit ad efficiendum, ut id quod mihi traditum est pro meo possideam. Et ita Neratius scripsit idque verum puto.*

[27] D. 41.10.5.pr–1 (Ner. 5 *Memb.*).

[28] D. 6.2.7.2 (Ulp. 16 *ad Ed.*).

IV. Julian on *Usucapio* and *Traditio*

Neratius and Pomponius are Julian's contemporaries, and both appear to offer consistent and firm support for the sufficiency of a belief in *causa* in the context of *usucapio*, with a text of Pomponius's going even further, suggesting that *bona fides* might exist even without a belief in *causa*. Julian's texts on *usucapio* fit squarely with those examined thus far in focusing principally on the presence of good faith, rather than on *causa*.[29] Africanus, Julian's pupil, describes a view, taken to be that of his teacher,[30] that sees *causa* as pertinent not to *usucapio* itself but to good faith, with the language of *iusta causa* being invoked to describe the sufficiency of the mistake:

> It is commonly held that someone who believes he has bought something when in fact he has not cannot acquire by *usucapio pro emptore*. He [Julian] says this is true to the extent that the buyer has no good basis [*iusta causa*] for his mistake. But if a slave or procurator whom he had entrusted with the purchase of a thing persuaded him that they had indeed bought it, the better view is that he would usucapt.[31]

The common view to which Africanus alludes is significant for the development of *causa* after Julian, insofar as it marks a shift to thinking of *causa* as an external justificatory event rather than a basis for the possessor's *bona fides* – a shift considered below. For present purposes, it is the reported view in the second part of the text that is significant. The view, which Africanus endorses, is that the belief in the underlying sale and purchase is sufficient for *usucapio*, even when none actually occurred. The issue, echoing the view of Neratius at the end of the Digest title on *pro suo*, is whether or not there is a good reason for the possessor's belief that he is entitled to the thing. *Causa* becomes a basis for *bona fides*.

A further text, directly attributable to Julian, returns to the case of the stolen slave-woman's child discussed by Trebatius and Pomponius:

> Not only purchasers in good faith but anyone who possesses by a *causa* pursuant to which they are in the process of *usucapio* will acquire by *usucapio* the child of a stolen slave woman. I think this is admitted by the logic of the law [*ratione iuris*], for by whatever *causa* the slave woman would be acquired by *usucapio*, but for the Twelve Tables or the *lex Atinia* standing in the way, by that same *causa* the child must be usucapted, if it was conceived and born in his household at a time when he was ignorant that the mother had been stolen.[32]

[29] eg D. 41.4.7.5 (Iul. 44 *Dig.*): 'Someone who knowingly buys something from a person whom the praetor has forbidden from lessening an inheritance cannot usucapt' (*Qui sciens emit ab eo, quem praetor ut suspectum heredem deminuere vetuit, usu non capiet*).

[30] eg, F Schulz, *History of Roman Legal Science* (Oxford, Oxford University Press, 1946), 230.

[31] D. 41.4.11 (Afr. 7 *Quaest.*): *Quod volgo traditum est eum, qui existimat se quid emisse nec emerit, non posse pro emptore usucapere, hactenus verum esse ait, si nullam iustam causam eius erroris emptor habeat: nam si forte servus vel procurator, cui emendam rem mandasset, persuaserit ei se emisse atque ita tradiderit, magis esse, ut usucapio sequatur.*

[32] D. 41.3.33.pr (Iul. 44 *Dig.*): *Non solum bonae fidei emptores, sed et omnes, qui possident ex ea causa, quam usucapio sequi solet, partum ancillae furtivae usu suum faciunt, idque ratione iuris introductum arbitror: nam ex qua causa quis ancillam usucaperet, nisi lex duodecim tabularum vel Atinia obstaret, ex*

Previously Trebatius and Pomponius had been concerned with whether the child could be acquired by *usucapio*, and held that the child was possessed *pro suo* as long as the mother was possessed *pro suo*, thereby reducing the question to whether or not the possessor believed he was entitled to regard the slave woman as his own. Julian differs: the child is possessed on whatever *causa* the mother is possessed. Were it not for the statutory bar on the acquisition by *usucapio* of stolen property, here, the mother would be acquired by *usucapio pro emptore*. Consequently, 'admitted by the logic of the law', the same *causa* ought to apply to the child.

These two texts suggest that Julian is approaching *causa* in a slightly different manner from his contemporaries. He appears reluctant to make the same ready recourse to the bare idea of possessing *pro suo*, instead analysing a *pro suo* case so as to anchor possession to a transaction-based *causa*. However, his view of *causa* is inextricable from intention: the existence of a *causa* serves to justify the possessor's belief that the property is theirs. In the case of the stolen slave and child, the possessor thinks the slave his property because he has bought her. The slave then conceives a child. That child cannot be his *pro suo* because he does not own the mother: the underlying event (ie, the existence of ownership) has failed. However, he is entitled to regard the mother as his own by virtue of having purchased her, and so that same rationale applies to her child. As long as that belief persists until the child is born, the possessor can usucapt *pro emptore* that which he has not actually bought, as the statutory bar on usucapting stolen property does not apply to their offspring. The focus is consistently on the state of mind of the possessor and his continued good faith but the idea of *causa* is used to provide an objective basis for that state of mind.

It is this approach that characterises Julian's approach to *traditio* in D. 41.1.36, the earliest text on the causal requirements for *traditio* that survives in the Digest:

> When we agree on the physical thing [*corpus*] that is to be delivered but in fact disagree on the *causa*, I see no reason why the *traditio* should be ineffective. It is as where I deliver land to you thinking I am bound to do so by a will, while you think it is owed to you under a *stipulatio*. For instance, where I hand you coined money thinking it is a gift but you receive it as if it were a loan, it is agreed that our disagreement about the *causa* on which the coins are delivered is no barrier to ownership's passing to you.[33]

The text can be divided into three parts: a general rule followed by two illustrations. Taking the illustrations first, each establishes a different point. The first is most likely about a plurality of *causae*, where X is bound to deliver a plot of land to Y both on account of a direction in a will, and under a separate *stipulatio*.[34] If, at the time of delivery, X has in mind the testamentary direction and Y has in mind

ea causa necesse est partum usucapi, si apud eum conceptus et editus eo tempore fuerit, quo furtivam esse matrem eius ignorabat.

[33] D. 41.1.36 (Iul. 13 *Dig.*): *Cum in corpus quidem quod traditur consentiamus, in causis vero dissentiamus, non animadverto, cur inefficax sit traditio, veluti si ego credam me ex testamento tibi obligatum esse, ut fundum tradam, tu existimes ex stipulatu tibi eum deberi. Nam et si pecuniam numeratam tibi tradam donandi gratia, tu eam quasi creditam accipias, constat proprietatem ad te transire nec impedimento esse, quod circa causam dandi atque accipiendi dissenserimus.*

[34] Evans-Jones and MacCormack (n 5), 102–04.

the *stipulatio*, then ownership in the land will doubtless pass. Julian presents this as a situation where the two parties differ as to the underlying *causa*; however, this is a scenario that can readily be explained by those who would hold that *traditio* requires a valid *iusta causa*: there are in fact two such *iustae causae* here, and it does not particularly matter pursuant to which the land is delivered. Julian's point – that the delivery can be effective even if the parties have different *causae* in mind – does not deny the need for a validly constituted *causa*.

The second scenario is harder: coined money is handed over in the context of genuine *dissensus* as to the grounds of delivery. X believes it is a *mutuum*; Y believes it is a gift. Both *mutuum* and *donatio* require consensus and so, without agreement, neither *causa* validly comes into existence. Here, Julian claims it is already established that ownership of the coins will pass, so we have evidence of a situation in which *traditio* is effective despite the absence of a validly constituted *causa*. The shared intentions of the parties that ownership ought to pass is ostensibly sufficient.

Julian's choice of scenario is curious. Consider how students are introduced to the problem of *causa*. The jurist needs a problem that the two parties can conceivably misconstrue. Gift tends to be one half of the equation but a *mutuum* is a curious counterpoint. Why not the more quotidian sale and purchase? Of the various loans recognised in Roman law, why *mutuum*? The answer might lie in the typical subject matter of the transaction: money. Coined money – currency – is a unique asset, because of the heightened need for liquidity and certainty. For currency to circulate unimpeded, every transacting party needs to be confident that the coins in their hands are actually capable of fulfilling the function of money, without an additional requirement of probing the provenance of each coin to guarantee ownership – assuming proof of ownership could be humanly possible, as it would presumably require tracing its transactional history back to the moment of minting. Currency, as a guaranteed store of value, requires a special set of rules to ensure its liquidity is protected.

Julian presents the possibility of a *traditio* in such a case as 'established'. That claim is not entirely sound. While there is good textual evidence that Julian's contemporaries thought transfers of coined money were subject to different rules from ordinary cases of *traditio*, they do not go as far as Julian. Two texts from Javolenus and Pomponius illustrate the point. The first concerns the special rules that applied to mixed funds, compared with other mixtures:

> If a third party's coins are paid over, either without the knowledge or without the consent of their owner, they will remain his whose they were. If they should become mixed, such that is becomes impossible to tell to whom they belonged, it is written by Gaius [Cassius Longinus] that they become the property of the recipient but that the owner acquires an action for *furtum* against the man who paid them over.[35]

[35] D. 46.3.78 (Iav. 11 *ex Cass.*): *Si alieni nummi inscio vel invito domino soluti sunt, manent eius cuius fuerunt: si mixti essent, ita ut discerni non possent, eius fieri qui accepit in libris Gaii scriptum est, ita ut actio domino cum eo, qui dedisset, furti competeret*. The identification of Gaius with Gaius Cassius Longinus is taken from Watson's edition.

This is a text on the efficacy of a *traditio* by a non-owner. It begins with a straightforward statement of the *nemo dat* principle: as the transferor is not the owner of the coins, he cannot pass good title to the transferee. This much is perfectly orthodox. The twist comes in what follows, when the coins are mixed with those of another – ie, the transferee – in such a way that the ownership of each coin is no longer discernible. The ordinary practice in relation to separable but indistinguishable things mixed without the consent of both owners would be to apportion shares of the whole to each owner according to their representative contributions.[36] Conceptually, ownership of each ingredient remains unchanged but practicality demands an action to recover an equivalent portion, rather than the unidentifiable particular coins. Common ownership of the whole arises only where each owner consents to the mixture. Not so with money, however: Javolenus claims that the recipient with whose coins the disputed money has been mixed owns the entire mixture. This means the non-owner has effectively conveyed good title to those coins, circumventing the *nemo dat* restriction. The former owner of the coins is simply left with a claim in delict.

Pomponius provides a similar argument in D. 46.3.17:

> Cassius says that, if I gave money to another to pay to my creditor, and then he pays over the money in his own name, neither of us will be released. I am not released, because the money was not given in my name; and the other is not released, because he delivered another's property – though he will be bound on a mandate. However, if the creditor then uses up those coins without bad faith, the person in whose name they were delivered will be released, for otherwise the creditor would turn a profit.[37]

The scenario requires unpacking. X and Y both owe money to Z, as is implicit from the fact that neither party is said to be released when the coins are handed over. X gives money to Y, asking Y to give that money to Z in order to discharge X's debt to Z. The nefarious Y pays the money to Z but does so by way of discharging Y's own debt to Z, rather than the debt owed by X. The debt owed by Y is clearly not discharged: *nemo dat quod non habet*. The debt owed by X is not discharged either, 'because the money was not given in my name' (*quia non meo nomine data sit*).[38] The implication is that something more than delivery is needed in order to discharge an extant obligation: the coins have to be knowingly received in discharge of that precise obligation, providing further evidence of the importance of the *causa* to the efficacy of the *traditio*. However, it is the subsequent scenario that reveals the abnormalities of currency. Z, having received X's money from Y pursuant to a sham, is not the owner of those coins. However, if he goes on to spend them *sine dolo malo*, the *traditio* is retrospectively deemed effective, and title

[36] Inst. 2.1.28.

[37] D. 46.3.17 (Pomp. 19 *ad Sab.*): *Cassius ait, si cui pecuniam dedi, ut eam creditori meo solveret, si suo nomine dederit, neutrum liberari, me, quia non meo nomine data sit, illum, quia alienam dederit: ceterum mandati eum teneri. Sed si creditor eos nummos sine dolo malo consumpsisset, is, qui suo nomine eos solvisset, liberatur, ne, si aliter observaretur, creditor in lucro versaretur.*

[38] ibid.

passes to the ultimate recipient, releasing X from his debt in the process. Again, the importance of *nemo dat* is attenuated, to ensure that money can be spent in good faith without restriction.

The same tendency can be seen across these texts. Basic principles of property law apply to money as to any other property when dealing with a two-party scenario; but, once a third party is introduced, the rules fray. The failure of the transfer, whether because of lack of *causa* or lack of title on the part of the transferor, is, in other words, a problem that must be surmounted. So that the *bona fide* third-party recipient can make use of the coins, it is necessary for ownership to pass to him, even if it means ignoring foundational principles. This concern for liquidity explains Julian's choice of example. Julian's example in D. 41.1.36 does not involve a third party, and so it is not obvious that Javolenus and Pomponius would agree that it is 'established' that ownership in the coined money ought to pass.

Nevertheless, from these two scenarios – multiple *iustae causae* and money – Julian generalises. Whenever two parties agree that ownership in a thing ought to pass from transferor to transferee, Julian thinks ownership will pass. Using his two scenarios, this ought to be the case, both where the parties have different-but-valid *causae* in mind and also when, owing to dissensus, there cannot be a valid *causa*. It is the intentions of the parties that justify the transfer of *dominium*.

The general rule is not convincingly substantiated by the two examples, each of which is in some sense a special case. The verb with which Julian claims that there is no need for a valid *causa*, *animadverto*, is distinctly weak.[39] It smacks of tentative suggestion rather than confident claim. It is the verb used by the praetor when he exercises discretionary power after investigation.[40] In the same way, the verb perhaps indicates that this is Julian's own assessment of the right approach. This caginess contrasts sharply with Julian's tone in the *usucapio* texts, where he speaks in stronger language about the grounds for a novel conclusion – *ratione iuris introductum arbitror*.[41] It would appear that Julian is going out on a limb, building somewhat disingenuously from situations where ownership can pass notwithstanding the lack of clear agreement the underlying *causa* at the time of delivery to a general rule that it is just the intentions of the parties that are required for ownership to pass.

V. *Traditio* and *Usucapio* after Julian

Africanus, Julian's pupil, claims that 'it is commonly held that someone who believes he has bought something when in fact he has not cannot acquire by *usucapio pro*

[39] This weakness has been explained by the possibility that this is a *responsum*, although in doing so the author still acknowledged the peculiarity of Julian's use of *animadverto*: C Krampe, 'Julian im Dialog über *Mutuum*, *Traditio* und *Causa*' (2014) 20 *Fundamina* 489.

[40] eg, D. 4.4.1.1 (Ulp. 11 *ad Ed.*), D. 11.5.1.pr (Ulp. 23 *ad Ed.*).

[41] D. 41.3.33.pr (Iul. 44 *Dig.*).

emptore'.[42] This is an outright rejection of the sufficiency of good faith and the possibility of *usucapio pro suo*; Africanus instead affirms the need for a true *iusta causa* in *usucapio*. Moreover, the text – set out in full in section IV above – makes it clear that the transaction is disconnected from good faith. Africanus sees this as orthodox in his day, and the textual evidence suggests uniform support for this position from the middle of the second century CE onwards. Perhaps the most compelling evidence from the earlier part of classical law post-Julian is Gaius's Institutes. In a work aimed at instructing fledgling law students, Gaius claims that *traditio* is effective to transfer ownership if it occurs pursuant to a sale, gift or 'any other *causa*'.[43] Gaius's treatment of *traditio* contains no hint of the approach suggested by Julian but, instead, places emphasis entirely on whether or not an underlying transaction can be identified.

Clearer support for the need for a *iusta causa* in both *traditio* and *usucapio* is provided by jurists of the high classical period. Paul is unambiguous in the need for there to be a genuine purchase in order for *usucapio pro emptore* to begin: 'He possesses *pro emptore* who truly purchases a thing. It is not sufficient for him to possess in the belief that he is purchaser but, rather, there must be an underlying *causa* of purchase'.[44] The reason there truly needs to be a purchase in *usucapio pro emptore* is because, in this species of *usucapio*, the possessor needs to be in good faith both at the time of concluding the contract and at the time of delivery. If there is no contract, it is impossible for the possessor to adhere to the requirements of good faith. It stands to reason that there can be no *usucapio*. This does, however, leave open the possibility that there might not be a need for the *causa* to truly exist for *usucapio* pursuant to other *causae*.[45]

The clarity of Paul's position on *usucapio pro emptore* is slightly threatened by a pair of texts that raise issues of capacity. The first deals with a purchase from a *furiosus*, and claims that, in such a situation, *usucapio* can proceed.[46] *Furiosi* is the term used to describe those with intermittent bouts of mental incapacity.[47] During lucid intervals, they retain contractual capacity but, when affected by their condition, they are legally incapacitated. Paul's focus on *furiosi* rather than, for example, *insani* (who were entirely without contractual capacity) suggests he is concerned with the effect of the shift between having and not having capacity on the validity of the sale and purchase. Based on what Paul claims in text just examined, one might suspect that, as long as there is a valid sale and purchase (ie, the *furiosus* was in a lucid interval at the time of the sale), *usucapio pro emptore* can proceed, even if

[42] D. 41.4.11 (Afr. 7 *Quaest.*).

[43] G. 2.20: *Itaque si tibi vestem vel aurum vel argentum tradidero sive ex venditionis causa sive ex donationis sive quavis alia ex causa, statim tua fit ea res, si modo ego eius dominus sim.*

[44] D. 41.4.2.pr (Paul. 54 *ad Ed.*): *Pro emptore possidet, qui re vera emit, nec sufficit tantum in ea opinione esse eum, ut putet se pro emptore possidere, sed debet etiam subesse causa emptionis.*

[45] Indeed, this seems to be what Paul is suggesting in the case of *usucapio pro soluto* in the same text. However, D. 41.3.48 (Paul. 2 *Manual.*) suggests that *usucapio pro soluto* requires a meeting of the minds between the transferor and transferee as to the *causa* of the payment.

[46] D. 41.3.13.1 (Paul. 5 *ad Plaut.*).

[47] Buckland, *Text-Book* (n 1), 168.

the *furiosus* is without capacity at the time of delivery or later, within the *usucapio* window. However, in another text, Paul marks this scenario out as an exception:

> If I buy something from a *furiosus* whom I think is sane, then it is settled on grounds of utility [*utilitatis causa*] that I can usucapt, even though there is not a valid purchase and, as such, I will not have a claim if evicted, nor will I have the *actio Publiciana*, and I cannot benefit from *accessio possessionis*.[48]

It is significant that Paul regards this scenario as exceptional, and best explained 'on grounds of utility'. It would have been possible to say that the possession is in good faith, owing to the purchaser's belief in the seller's sanity, in a manner reminiscent of early texts on the relationship between *causa* and *bona fides*. Instead, Paul emphasises the requirement of a validly constituted *causa* but marks out the solution in this particular fact pattern as *sui generis*. In reality, this is an entrenched position that had been reached by earlier generations, and Paul's reconciliation reflects the difficulty of effecting a conceptual shift within a doctrine as fundamental to daily commercial life as *traditio*. This text should be understood as little more than a pragmatic concession by a jurist with a tendency towards abstraction.

Similarly difficult to reconcile with the requirement for a validly constituted *causa* is D. 41.4.2.15. The text explores two scenarios involving a sale by a pupil without authorisation from his *tutor*. Such a contract is legally invalid, as the role of the *tutor* was to supply capacity though his *auctoritas*.[49] What happens if the purchaser knows that the seller is a pupil but erroneously believes that pupils can transact without the *auctoritas* of their *tutor*? Here, Paul says that there can be no *usucapio*, as the pertinent error is one of law, and 'mistakes of law are never beneficial'.[50] Alternatively, what if the error is one of fact: the buyer is simply not aware that the seller is a pupil, owing to a mistaken belief as to his age? Here, *usucapio pro emptore* can proceed. Paul claims that this is because what has happened is more important than beliefs, a claim that accords with his account of Sabinus's approach to problems of *causa*.[51] The explanation may be that this is one of the handful of instances in which, though no legally valid contract arises, a natural obligation (*naturalis obligatio*) does.[52] As such, it is still possible to see the facts as giving rise to a recognised sale and purchase, albeit with legal enforceability suspended until the pupil acquires his own capacity.

Paul's texts are overwhelmingly focused on *usucapio* pursuant to purchase. In that context, it is apparent that there is a general requirement for a *iusta causa* – a valid sale and purchase – but also that there were exceptions. It is likely the presence of these exceptions that explains the concentration of Paul's texts on

[48] D. 41.4.2.16 (Paul. 54 *ad Ed.*): *Si a furioso, quem putem sanae mentis, emero, constitit usucapere utilitatis causa me posse, quamvis nulla esset emptio et ideo neque de evictione actio nascitur mihi nec Publiciana competit nec accessio possessionis.*

[49] Buckland, *Text-Book* (n 1), 158–59.

[50] D. 41.4.2.15 (Paul. 54 *ad Ed.*): *quia iuris error nulli prodest.*

[51] ibid: *hic plus sit in re quam in existimatione.*

[52] Buckland, *Text-Book* (n 1), 553.

this particular *causa*. The only other *causa* Paul discusses is legacy and, there, he is clear about the need for a *iusta causa*: 'If I possess something which I think has been left to me by legacy, when in truth it hasn't, then I cannot acquire it by *usucapio pro legato*'.[53] Furthermore, in the context of *traditio*, Paul is utterly unambiguous about the need for a valid *iusta causa*: 'Bare delivery can never transfer ownership unless sale or some other valid transaction [*iusta causa*] precedes it, on account of which *traditio* follows'.[54] This accords entirely with Paul's approach to *causa* in *usucapio*: his emphasis on the importance of the factual existence of a *causa* over a mere belief in *causa* is clear and consistent in relation to both modes of acquisition.

Ulpian's treatment is clearer still. In his analyses of *usucapio* and of *traditio*, Ulpian unambiguously requires a valid *iusta causa* and rejects earlier flirtations with putative *causa*. There are surprisingly few texts of Ulpian on *causa* in *usucapio* but the handful preserved in the Digest are straightforward and blunt. In relation to *usucapio pro legato*, he claims that this form of *usucapio* can never benefit anyone other than a legatee, ruling out any possibility of a putative legatee's acquiring the property on this ground.[55] So, too, in the case of *usucapio pro dote*, where, if the dowry fails because there was no marriage or because the marriage ends, *usucapio* will fail, precisely because the underlying *causa* fails.[56] In the contexts of sale and purchase and gift, as well as legacy, he cites the position of Celsus discussed above.[57] While he does not express an opinion on Celsus's insistence on there being a valid *causa* in all cases before *usucapio* can proceed, based on his views on specific instances of *causa*, it is safe to infer his approval.

Ulpian's text on *causa* in *traditio* is the second focal text in most accounts of the subject, and directly contradicts Julian's position:

> If I give you money as a gift but you accept it as a *mutuum*, Julian writes that it is not a gift; but it must be seen whether it is a *mutuum*. I think there isn't a *mutuum* either, and that the coins received do not become property of the recipient, since he received them with a different intention. If he uses up the coins, then a *condictio* can be brought against him, though he can use the *exceptio doli*, since it was in accordance with the will of the donor that the coins should be used up.[58]

[53] D. 41.8.2 (Paul. 54 *ad Ed.*): *Si possideam aliquam rem, quam putabam mihi legatam, cum non esset, pro legato non usucapiam …*

[54] D. 41.1.31.pr (Paul. 31 *ad Ed.): Numquam nuda traditio transfert dominium, sed ita, si venditio aut aliqua iusta causa praecesserit, propter quam traditio sequeretur.*

[55] D. 41.8.1 (Ulp. 6 *Disp.*).

[56] D. 41.9.1.3 (Ulp. 31 *ad Sab.*) deals with a marriage ending. D. 41.9.1.4 (Ulp. 31 *ad Sab.*) involves no marriage at all.

[57] D. 41.3.27 (Ulp. 31 *ad Sab.*); see n 24.

[58] D. 12.1.18.pr (Ulp. 7 *Disp.*): *Si ego pecuniam tibi quasi donaturus dedero, tu quasi mutuam accipias, Iulianus scribit donationem non esse: sed an mutua sit, videndum. Et puto nec mutuam esse magisque nummos accipientis non fieri, cum alia opinione acceperit. Quare si eos consumpserit, licet condictione teneatur, tamen doli exceptione uti poterit, quia secundum voluntatem dantis nummi sunt consumpti.*

This text is a pointed retort to Julian's position in D. 41.1.36. Ulpian takes one of Julian's chosen scenarios in that text, and gives a contrary position. Owing to the *dissensus* that exists between the parties, a *mutuum* cannot arise. As there is no *mutuum*, there is no justification for the transfer of ownership in the coins, and so the donor remains their owner. This is a direct contradiction of Julian's analysis of the same scenario, in which he asserted that it was 'settled law' that the transferee would become owner of the coins. As shown above, the weight of the evidence even among Julian's contemporaries – including several who were satisfied as to the sufficiency of a belief in *causa* in the context of *usucapio* – supports Ulpian's view that ownership would not pass until the transferee uses up the coins, at which point the proper claim becomes a *condictio* (ownership in the coins having passed from the transferor to the third party). Until that point, however, the *traditio* is ineffective, owing to the failure of *causa*.

Between Julian and Ulpian, there is a fundamental change in how *causa* is analysed in *usucapio*. At least some of Julian's contemporaries were willing to consider that prescriptive acquisition was justified by *bona fides*, and viewed *causa* as the foundation for that justificatory concept. Their focus was on whether a failure of *causa* was inherently fatal to *bona fides*, and they generally arrived at the conclusion that it was not: as long as the party believed their acquisition rested on a *iusta causa*, they retained *bona fides*, and *usucapio* could proceed. Pomponius appears to have gone even further than this, countenancing *usucapio* by a possessor who behaved honourably despite knowing that there was no underlying *causa*. However, based on the evidence in the Digest, this is the most extreme incarnation of the belief-centric approach to *usucapio*. It is against this background that we must understand Julian's text on *traditio*. It is tentative in tone, and rests on ostensibly unsound doctrinal pillars, but it reflects an attempt to give a common reading to *causa* in both modes of acquisition. If a belief in *causa* is what justifies prescriptive acquisition, why should not a shared desire for the transfer of ownership carry the same justificatory force in the context of consensual delivery? By the time of Ulpian, *causa* in *usucapio* had been separated from *bona fides*. It was a distinct requirement and, but for a handful of exceptional cases – themselves the product of historical doctrinal accretion, the demand was uniformly for a validly constituted *causa*. Bare *bona fides*, or a belief in entitlement, was insufficient justification for prescriptive acquisition. It is thus no surprise that Ulpian emphatically rejects Julian's account of *traditio* and, equally emphatically, affirms the need for a validly constituted *causa*.

VI. The Significance of the Debate

The role of *causa* in *traditio* is a peculiar topic. Even within the voluminous treatment of doctrinal disputes in classical Roman law, few points have attracted as much attention as the conflict between Julian in D. 41.1.36 and Ulpian in

D. 12.1.18.pr.[59] This stands in stark contrast to the treatment of the subject by the jurists themselves, with remarkably few texts on the causal requirements for a valid *traditio* to be found in the Digest. To some extent, this reflects the banality of the subject: in pragmatic terms, it really did not matter. Take a straightforward fact-pattern: A delivers a book to B. A believes the book has been sold to B, while B receives it as a gift. Neither belief is true, owing to the absence of consensus. On Ulpian's view, the failure of *causa* means that ownership of the book remains with A. As owner, he can recover his book by *vindicatio*. On Julian's view, the shared belief that ownership should pass is effective, and B becomes owner. If A realises his mistake and decides he wants what was once 'his' book back, he will have to bring a different action, the *condictio indebiti*: the book was delivered by mistake, and so needs to be returned.

In practical terms, the primary significance of the debate is the boundary between the *vindicatio* and the *condictio indebiti*. The former but not the latter could be brought against third parties, so, on Julian's view of *traditio*, the owner's claim to his former property would cease to be effective once the transferor alienated the thing. Otherwise, the practical differences between the two views boil down to which action is brought. Ulpian's view of *traditio* confines the *condictio indebiti* to cases involving coined money, as it is only coined money that can pass into the ownership of other without a valid *causa*. Julian's view, by contrast, makes the *condictio indebiti* akin to a personal *vindicatio*, allowing the claimant to recover any sort of property delivered by mistake to the transferee-defendant but incapable of application against the defendant's successors in title. The focus of the Digest title on the *condictio indebiti* makes it clear that the dominant focus of the *condictio indebiti* aligns with Ulpian's presentation of *traditio*: the vast majority of texts concerns either coined money or funds (*peculia*, legacies, etc).[60]

Julian's rationale in D. 41.1.36 appears to be motivated by abstract principle – the desire for a coherent interpretation of *causa* across the modes of acquiring *dominium*. While there are pragmatic consequences to his argument – chiefly the limitation of claims by former owners against third parties – the basis of his argument is essentially an appeal to consistency. Julian seems to select his examples according to the idea he wishes to show. Based on two examples where (he claims) ownership can pass despite disagreement on the underlying *causa*, he leads the reader to his conclusion: if *causa* is not essential in these two cases, why should it be essential in any other case? This attempt at legal logic carries the same sense of

[59] Evans-Jones and MacCormack (n 5), 99 fn 1 provides references to both the earlier literature and contemporary literature, as of 1989. To this can be added D Schanbacher, 'Zur Bedeutung der Leistungszweckbestimmung bei der Übereignung durch *Traditio* und beim Leistungsversprechen durch *Stipulatio*' (1999) 60 *Leg Hist Rev* 1 and JD Harke, *Si error aliquis intervenit – Irrtum im klassischen römischen Vertragsrecht* (Berlin, Duncker & Humblot, 2005), though there are many more pieces touching on cognate questions, such as the nature of *donatio* and *solutio* in classical Roman law. My thanks to Professor Wolfgang Ernst in identifying relevant literature in German.

[60] As can be seen throughout the title D. 12.6.

ratio iuris found in other Julian texts.[61] Implicit in Julian's conclusion is an appeal to the value of consistency within an area of law. Julian's position only makes sense if he and the reader both consider it anomalous that the requirements for *traditio* differ based on the object being delivered.

Ulpian, in contrast, works through citation and refutation. Honoré estimated that Ulpian referred to earlier jurists at 'five or six times the rate of his predecessors', with references to Julian counting more than double those of his second most regularly cited source.[62] Like Julian, Ulpian does not shy away from presenting his own opinion, albeit in far more resolute language.[63] In doing so, however, Ulpian goes no further than refuting the earlier position. Digest 12.1.18.pr simply states that Julian incorrectly reasoned his way through one of his chosen scenarios. The implications of that refutation are left to the reader. The logical consequence of Ulpian's position is that an effective *traditio* requires a valid *iusta causa*. Owing to the inability of the transferor and transferee to agree on whether the transfer was pursuant to a gift or a *mutuum*, neither *causa* came into existence, as both require consensus. As neither existed, ownership does not pass. However, all of this is left unstated: Ulpian is content to make the pointed doctrinal argument.

Ulpian's approach to such doctrinal problems is not universal. Paul, for instance, operates at a more abstract level in his *causa* texts. Although he, like Julian and Ulpian, approaches the issue through concrete scenarios, he is far readier to appeal to overarching ideas to justify his conclusions. Across half a dozen texts, we find a conclusion being justified on grounds of convenience (*causa utilitatis*), alongside two general principles: that 'mistakes of law are never beneficial' and that, following Sabinus (with whom he agrees), fact (*substantia*) was more important than belief (*opinio*).[64] The last of these is particularly telling: in order to be forceful, Paul does not merely rely on the names of earlier jurists but extracts and articulates an abstract principle applicable to the scenario under discussion. This stands in sharp contrast to earlier generations, who were content simply to rely on the weight attached to the names of their predecessors.[65]

The conclusions that can be reached based on this analysis are far from novel. First, the narrative highlights the importance of avoiding conceptualising classical Roman law as a monolithic entity based on its presentation in the Digest. It should come as no surprise that doctrines and concepts could develop, sometimes radically, over the course of a couple of centuries. Thinking of either Julian's or Ulpian's view on *traditio* as 'dominant' or 'prevailing', in the manner that some of the leading Anglophone textbooks of Roman law do, risks distorting the dynamic

[61] eg, D. 41.3.33.pr (Iul. 44 *Dig.*).

[62] AM Honoré, *Ulpian: Pioneer of Human Rights*, 2nd edn (Oxford, Oxford University Press, 2002), 129–30.

[63] Ulpian says 'I think' (*puto*) in D. 12.1.18.pr, whereas Julian opted for 'I see no reason' (*non animadverto*) in D. 41.1.36.

[64] D. 41.4.2.15 (Paul. 54 *ad Ed.*); D. 41.4.2.2 (Paul. 54 *ad Ed.*).

[65] See Africanus on Julian in D. 41.4.11 (Afr. 7 *Quaest.*) and Pomponius on Trebatius in D. 41.10.4.pr (Pomp. 32 *ad Sab.*) and on Neratius in D. 41.10.3 (Pomp. 22 *ad Sab.*).

by which the doctrines of Roman law developed. Second, it highlights the importance of approaching jurists as individuals. By examining their approaches to a single doctrinal issue, a range of methods comes into view. The jurists all face the same difficulties in adequately explaining the material but they approach their endeavour in markedly different ways. Paul and Julian are more willing to link doctrine to underlying principles, whereas Ulpian, like many of Julian's contemporaries, works methodically through scenarios, adopting a pragmatic, fact- and context-sensitive approach to explain discrete situations. The implications of those solutions are left to the reader, though evidently jurists using this method were working from ideas as to what the 'correct' answer ought to be. These methods, which emphasise principle and pragmatism in different ways, are not linked to particular generations of classical jurists but reflect a rich diversity of approaches in every era.

5

The Place of Rhetoric in Late Republican Law: Some Thoughts on *Pietas* and the *Querela Inofficiosi Testamenti*

GRAEME CUNNINGHAM

The general understanding of modern scholarship on Roman law concludes that the discipline is based on scientific principle.[1] This perspective informs not only our understanding of how Roman law operated among the ancients, but also modern interaction with the subject, not least in its application to contemporary domestic laws.[2] Among Romanists, there has been enthusiasm for asserting scientific principle as the fundamental basis of the discipline. This is derived from an adherence to two connected historical narratives created in nineteenth-century Germany and adopted with vigour by subsequent scholars.[3] The first narrative is that of continuity. It asserts that law has undergone a progressive process since the decline of the Roman Empire in the West, by which it has moved in stages toward a recapturing of the scientific accomplishments of the Romans.[4] The second narrative is that of science. It asserts that, during the later Republic period, under the guidance of professionalised jurists such as Quintus Mucius Scaevola *pontifex*, and after a singular injection of Greek categorical thought, Roman law became an autonomous, scientific system, free from extra-legal considerations, such as the social and the economic.[5] The achievement of

[1] DJ Osler, 'The Myth of European Legal History' (1997) 16 *Rechtshistorisches Journal* 393.

[2] R Zimmermann, *Roman Law, Contemporary Law, European Law: The Civilian Tradition Today* (Oxford, Oxford University Press, 2001); R Zimmermann, 'Roman Law in the Modern World' in DEL Johnston (ed), *The Cambridge Companion to Roman Law* (New York, Cambridge University Press, 2015) 452, 453–58.

[3] F Schulz, *History of Roman Legal Science*, (Oxford, Oxford University Press, 1946).

[4] MP Gilmore, *Argument from Roman Law in Political Thought, 1200-1600* (Cambridge, Cambridge University Press, 1941), 3; F Wieacker, *A History of Private Law in Europe* (AD Weir trans, Oxford, Oxford University Press, 1995), 27; JQ Whitman, *The Legacy of Roman Law in the German Romantic Era* (Princeton, Princeton University Press, 1990), 29; K Tuori, *Ancient Roman Lawyers and Modern Legal Ideals: Studies on the Impact of Contemporary Concerns in the Interpretation of Ancient Roman Legal History*, 2nd, corrected edn (Frankfurt am Main, Vittorio Klostermann, 2007).

[5] Twentieth-century adherents to this view include but are not limited to F Schulz, *Principles of Roman Law* (M Wolff trans, Oxford, Oxford University Press, 1936), 33–37; WAJ Watson, *The Law*

science is the *summum bonum* and end-point of the teleological trajectory of legal continuity.

It is my intention to cast some doubt on this foundational myth of a scientific revolution in Roman law in the late Republic, and, by extension, on the narratives of continuity and science that rely upon its supposition.[6] In order to do so, I will examine the extent to which legal change in the later Republic, the period of the theoretical inception of legal science, was decisively reliant upon extra-legal considerations. In particular, I intend to argue that rhetoric was used in order to assert the existence of the socially understood normative value of *pietas* in the relationship between testators and potential heirs, and that a rhetorical proof of such a relationship was the postulate, or *locus*, upon which a change in the law was based.

To this end, the first point I will examine is the development and operation of the *querela inofficiosi testamenti*. The second point I raise will examine how *pietas*, as a socially understood concept within Roman culture, informed decision-making in succession disputes. This will require a twofold examination of the social understanding of the concept of *pietas* in the later Republic, alongside a study of its direct application in law.

I. The Development and Operation of the *Querela Inofficiosi Testamenti*

The *querela inofficiosi testamenti* came into use in the mid-first century BCE, a later addition to Roman succession law than the praetorian innovation *bonorum possessio*. The *querela* provided protection to expectant heirs against a testator who, for reasons beholden unto himself, had disinherited them through a will. Reasons for disinheriting expectant heirs are several and varied, some more rational than others. Roman law had been satisfied as a matter of general principle to afford to a testator the broad discretion to disinherit almost whomsoever he pleased: prodigal sons, wayward daughters, and inattentive spouses could all effectively be disinherited by testament. Some restrictions existed – not least the formal requirement

of Succession in the Later Roman Republic (Oxford, Oxford University Press, 1971), 155; A Schiavone, *Nascita della giurisprudenza: Cultura aristocratica e pensiero giuridico nella Roma tardo repubblicana* (Roma, Laterza, 1976), 95–110; A Schiavone, 'Forme normative e generi letterari. La cristallizzazione del ius civile e dell'editto fra tarda repubblica e primo principato' in E Dovere (ed), *La codificazione del diritto dall'antico al moderno* (Naples, Editoriale Scientifica, 1998) 51; BW Frier, *The Rise of the Roman Jurists. Studies in Cicero's pro Caecina* (Princeton, Princeton University Press, 1985), 159–63.

[6] Recent work has been done in a similar vein: OE Tellegen-Couperus, *Quintilian and the Law: The Art of Persuasion in Law and Politics* (Leuven, Leuven University Press, 2003); JW Cairns and PJ du Plessis (eds), *Beyond Dogmatics: Law and Society in the Roman World* (Edinburgh, Edinburgh University Press, 2007); PJ du Plessis (ed), *New Frontiers: Law and Society in the Roman World* (Edinburgh, Edinburgh University Press, 2013); PJ du Plessis (ed), *Cicero's Law: Rethinking Roman Law of the Late Republic* (Edinburgh, Edinburgh University Press, 2016); PJ du Plessis, C Ando and K Tuori (eds), *The Oxford Handbook of Roman Law and Society* (Oxford, Oxford University Press, 2016).

in law to adhere to valid testamentary form.[7] *Bonorum possessio* came to form a post-death restriction upon the realisation of the will of the testator but, as the operation of a claim was necessarily *post mortem*, its relationship to the writing of a testament takes on a different hue from measures designed to offer protection to expectant heirs during a testator's lifetime. Some protection for expectant heirs was provided through *praeteritio*.[8] This rule set out that a testator had a duty by which he ought either expressly to institute as heirs those to whom in intestacy the property would pass, or, conversely, ought expressly to disinherit them. If no mention of such people was made in the will, they took on the title of *praeteriti* and the whole will could be undermined and property passed on under the civil law rules of intestacy.[9] The protection afforded by *praeteritio*, as Leage cogently argues, is the lingering trace of the ancient idea that property was vested in the family and not the individual *paterfamilias*.[10] This view is rooted in the idea that *sui heredes* were regarded in their father's lifetime as something approaching family property, socially if not legally. The result was that, for instance, in the *ius civile*, a son in *potestas* could be disinherited either by being named in the testament as disinherited or by an expression making it clear by identification that the intention of the testator is to disinherit him. Failure to do so could result in the will becoming void on challenge and falling into intestacy. *Praeteritio* therefore offered some protection to the family of the testator, insofar as the disinheritance of *sui heredes* must be explicitly expressed and formally enshrined in order to be free from challenge. *Praeteritio*, though providing some solace to a child fearful of the intentions of a disgruntled parent, was far from a perfect protection of his expected birth right. A testator with the determination to disinherit his disaffected kin need only, perhaps with some legal advice, construct a formally valid testament which identified those potential *praeteriti* whom he wished to divest. The ancient *ius civile*, in this respect, very much favoured the testator over the dispossessed potential heir, and allowed for disinheritance as long as it was explicitly expressed.

The *querela* developed as an attempted perfection of the protection afforded by *praeteritio*. It exceeded its antecedent in the protection it afforded to expectant heirs, and instituted a nascent philosophical change as to whom the law favoured – the expectant heir could now truly expect the ability to challenge if disinherited unduly. As Johnston outlines:

> Only with the evolution of the *querela inofficiosi testamenti* did Roman law arrive toward the end of the Republic at the principle that descendants (or ascendants) of a testator actually had a legitimate expectation of acquiring a share of his estate, by virtue of law rather than the testator's own fancy.[11]

[7] D. 31.88.17 (Scaev. 3 *Resp.*).

[8] AM Prichard, *Leage's Roman Private Law*, 3rd edn (London, Macmillan, 1961), 146.

[9] Exceptions existed to this principle: women were under no obligation to disinherit as they had no *sui heredes*.

[10] Prichard (n 8), 246.

[11] DEL Johnston, *The Roman Law of Trusts* (Oxford, Oxford University Press, 1988), 3.

The reasoning behind 'the evolution' of this change in the principle of protection of expectant heirs remains obscure. The most convincing explanation for its development is that it was rooted in the idea that a *paterfamilias* owed a duty to those in his power to provide for them after his death, especially to those with ties of close kinship.[12] While the *querela* offered improved protection against the total arbitrariness of a testator, it was nevertheless far from a complete revision of the general principle of the freedom to testate which underpinned Roman succession law.[13]

The first, early justification given for hearing a challenge was based on the sanity of the testator when the will was made. The sources belie the authenticity of insanity as the actual cause for action, as the wide scope of what was meant by insane is perceptibly disingenuous, as can be seen in the jurist Marcian's definition:

> The proposition on which an action for undutious will is raised is that the testators were of unsound mind when making the will. And by this is meant not that the testator was truly insane or incapacitated but that the will was properly formed but without a necessary concern for natural claims; for if he were really insane or incapacitated, the will is void.[14]

A worryingly low bar for insanity, indeed. Yet, as Marcian points out, true insanity would render any will void *ab initio* as the testator would be *furiosus*. A will is considered *iniustum* if a testator lacks the capacity, *testamenti factio*, when making it.[15] A generally insane person, therefore, could make a will, but only if he was lucid at the time the will was made; a person who was insane without lucid intervals was lacking in capacity and therefore could not make a valid will.[16] Wills made before the onset of insanity remained valid despite a later decline in the mental health of the testator. So, given that a will made by a person who was insane at the time of making it was void *ab initio*, it is clearly outside the boundaries of logic to assume that a challenge via the *querela* could reasonably be based on an insane testator, as there would, in fact, be no legally valid will to challenge at all. Rather, as du Plessis argues, the juristic conversation of insanity was a 'pretence as it is clear that insanity was not really the issue'.[17] What, then, was really at issue in a challenge for an undutiful will?

The fundamental criterion which ought to be fulfilled was that the testator had been 'undutiful' in the making of his will. This terminology is not brimming with clarity, yet it seems fair to suppose that the basic scenario is when the testator acts in a manner which is unjust towards the claimant. The issue, then, is not so much

[12] Prichard (n 8), 252. Further on Roman patronage, see RP Saller, *Personal Patronage under the Early Empire* (Cambridge, Cambridge University Press, 1982).

[13] The extension of *legitimi* to expectant heirs only began to take shape in the late fourth century CE before the reign of Theodosius II.

[14] D. 5.2.2 (Marc. 4 *Inst.*).

[15] D. 28.1.4 (Gai. 2 *Inst.*).

[16] D. 28.1.2 (Lab. 1 *post. a Iav. Epit.*).

[17] PJ du Plessis, *Borkowski's Textbook on Roman Law*, 5th edn (Oxford, Oxford University Press, 2015), 234.

insanity as inequity. Yet, this realisation does little to aid our understanding of the exact circumstances in which a claim may be brought, or in what way the court of the *centumviri* exercised its discretion to allow these cases to be heard with any consistency.

One of the reasons the juristic sources identify as an underlying cause for challenge to a will was a misunderstanding between the testator and the claimant resulting in an undutiful disinheritance, as the jurist Marcellus writes:

> To state that a will is undutious is to argue that one ought not to have been disinherited or overlooked. In general, this happens when parents disinherit or overlook their children from a misunderstanding.[18]

This falls outside what could be reasonably termed grounds of challenge by insanity, as misunderstandings are not the same as madness on the part of the testator. The pretence of insanity was a ruse to justify disregarding the testator's right to choose his heirs. It was also used as a reason for disregarding the civil law of succession. Inequity takes centre stage in considerations of when the *querela* could be brought, as Gaius tells us:

> For parents ought not to be unjust to their children in wills. In general, they do this, making a poor judgement on their own offspring, when their opinion has been altered by the flatteries or machinations of stepmothers.[19]

Here, we are given clear evidence that injustice and inequity is at the heart of what constitutes an undutiful will. Gaius goes on to provide an example of when a misunderstanding between a testator and prospective heir can lead to an unjust and undutiful disinheritance: a child passed over by a father as a result of the intrigues of a begrudging stepmother. This example reveals that, rather than insanity of the testator being the reason for the use of the *querela*, an intuition of injustice is the pivotal factor in the challenge. However, this raises further issues. It is still not clear where the limitations of a potential challenge lie; moreover, it is even less clear how consistency could be attained where an intuition of injustice underpins a challenge. It is not incredible to envisage a situation in which every child feels unjustly cheated by every disinheritance, leading to the use of the *querela* with overzealous abandon. Restriction existed as to the degree of familial separation by which claims could be challenged, alongside other limitations, such as a personal bar through acquiescence to other terms in the will. Even so, a claim of pure dutifulness still made complaints under the *querela* relatively common. According to Ulpian:

> It should be noted that claims against the undutiful are made often. It is possible for everyone to claim a lack of duty, parents as well as children. Yet one's cognates beyond the degree of brother would be better not concerning themselves with needless cost as they are not in a position to win.[20]

[18] D. 5.2.3 (Marc. 4 *Inst.*).
[19] D. 5.2.4 (Gai. *ad leg. Glitiam*).
[20] D. 5.2.1 (Ulp. 14 *ad Ed.*).

Challenges to the will as set out were reasonably common; those who were not sufficiently close to the deceased did not frequently press a challenge, however, as their degree of separation made them unable to succeed in a claim. As the *querela* could only be brought by those who would have inherited had the testator died intestate, the claims which succeeded were limited to those made by descendants, ascendants, brothers and sisters.[21]

The key phrase in Marcian's description of when the *querela* was applicable is when the will was regarded as being *non ex officio pietatis*.[22] That is, without regard to the *pietas* that is required of a particular office, or relationship. The interplay between these two concepts is of prime significance in the reason for deciding the worthiness of a challenge. First, the relationship between the testator and the aggrieved claimant is of central importance to the merit of the claim, insofar as the status assigned to the parties – that is, how the interpersonal relationship is viewed institutionally – is the basis upon which the law itself assigns property transfers in the *ius civile*.

II. *Pietas* in Roman Society and Law

The *Oxford Classical Dictionary* defines *pietas* as, 'the typical Roman attitude of dutiful respect towards gods, fatherland, and parents and other kinsmen'.[23] Wagenvoort provides a good encapsulation of its general meaning, by outlining that the man who possesses *pietas* 'performed all his duties towards the deity and his fellow human beings fully and in every respect'.[24] In its broad sense, *pietas* was a pervasive, philosophical concept, entrenched in the mindset of the Roman and more broadly in Roman society. The nature of the concept is necessarily hierarchical, insofar as it was always a factor in a relative relationship, as Saller points out:

> First, the emphasis is on duty rather than affection or compassion. Secondly, it is a virtue displayed primarily toward a high power, whether it be the gods, the fatherland, or parents.[25]

This is reflected in the cultural value attached to it in art and literature, particularly in Virgil.[26] There is also evidence in inscription which stresses the virtue of *pietas*.[27] Moreover, it is made clear in the reverence shown to it within the law.

[21] Later law changed the scope of claims under the *querela*.

[22] D. 5.2.2 (Marc. 4 *Inst.*).

[23] NGL Hammond and HH Scullard (eds), *The Oxford Classical Dictionary*, 2nd edn (Oxford, Oxford University Press, 1970), 833.

[24] H Wagenvoort, *Pietas: Selected Studies in Roman Religion* (Leiden, Brill, 1980), 7.

[25] Saller (n 12), 105.

[26] For an overview of Virgil's concept of *pietas*, see Wagenvoort (n 24); J Farrell and MCJ Putnam (eds), *A Companion to Vergil's Aeneid and its Tradition* (Chichester, Wiley-Blackwell, 2010).

[27] A striking example is the *Laudatio Turiae*. See *CIL* VI 1572, 10–12; 31–33. For a brief but informative sketch, see S Dixon, *The Roman Family* (Baltimore, John Hopkins University Press, 1992), 27–28.

The virtue of *pietas* was in turn subdivided into three forms: in regard to parents; in regard to fatherland; and concerning divinity.[28] *Pietas* has a religious undertone, rooting itself in a natural order. Its realisation, as Wissowa alludes to, is all-encompassing, a complete fulfilment of what is expected in duty from the individual to his surrounding world. Specific types of *pietas* for other relationships were also acknowledged, such as fraternal *pietas*.[29] All forms were reliant upon the acknowledgement of an institutional status – that is, upon the realisation that the status of individuals in relation to each other changed their interaction at an institutional level. Therefore, the relationship between father and son, for instance, takes two forms, the true relationship of everyday life and the institutional relationship of status which is imposed in various social, moral and legal ways. Gardner draws the important distinction that 'in real life the Romans lived in families … *familia*, being a legal construct'.[30] The *familia* is a legal concept subject to institutional convention and in this way the *pietas* between parents and children was both real, insofar as it was based on natural affinity, but also social, insofar as it was enforced by the relationship of social status. The duality of *pietas* between social order and familial affection is well accounted for in Dixon's description of 'a strong sentimental ideal of family feeling … overlapped with and supplemented (by) the traditional sense of obligation'.[31]

Key examples of *pietas* are related in Latin literature. Valerius Maximus, who is fundamentally concerned with parental *pietas*, provides seven examples, under the title *de pietate erga parentes et fratres et patriam*.[32] Most striking of these is the account of a young woman breastfeeding her imprisoned mother to sustain her life.[33]

Valerius Maximus sets this up as the archetypal example of *pietas*, a notion evidently held in some consensus, by the fact the Romans raised a temple to *pietas* at the site where the event took place. Three key points can be taken from this anecdote. First, we can see clearly that *pietas* was not strictly limited to fathers and sons but is dependent upon duty towards a kind of relationship, mother and daughter included.[34] Second, we can see that acknowledgement of duty resulting from a hierarchy is essential to its function. The daughter exemplifies *pietas* through her loving devotion (*deligere*) to her mother, the affection born out of devotional duty, more so than sentimental affection.[35] Third, that *obsequium* (deference) is a significant characteristic of the duty owed as part of *pietas*.[36] The expression of this duty is provided by Valerius Maximus in a series of *exempla* which focus on

[28] This classification is set out in reference to Cicero's statement in *Inv. rhet.* 2.22.66.

[29] For a full study on fraternal *pietas* see CJ Bannon, *The Brothers of Romulus: Fraternal Pietas in Roman Law, Literature, and Society* (Princeton, Princeton University Press, 1997).

[30] JF Gardner, *Family and Familia in Roman Law and Life* (Oxford, Oxford University Press, 1998), 1.

[31] Dixon (n 27), 30.

[32] Val. Max. 5.4. ('Concerning *Pietas* with Regard to Parents, Brothers and the Fatherland').

[33] Val. Max. 5.4.7.

[34] Saller (n 12), 108.

[35] ibid, 105: 'the emphasis is on duty rather than affection'.

[36] JPVD Balsdon, *Romans and Aliens* (Chapel Hill, University of North Carolina Press, 1979), 18.

paternal *pietas*: Coriolanus ceasing hostilities at his mother's behest;[37] Scipio Africanus being driven by *pietas* towards his father's memory to defeat Hannibal;[38] Lucius Manlius Torquatus's son threatening the tribune Pomponius to persuade the official to drop charges against his horrible father, despite the hardship he had endured in his father's power;[39] Marcus Cotta, on taking the *toga virilis*, accusing his father's prosecutor;[40] the tribune Gaius Flaminus coming down from the *rosta* at his father's orders out of respect for *auctoritas patria*;[41] and the vestal virgin Claudia using her prestige to stop a tribune preventing her father's triumph.[42] These examples from Valerius Maximus are generally seen in terms of *exempla* of good moral behaviour, a form which is usually attributed to rhetoric. As Saller suggests, 'in Roman society the experts at the invocation of the conventional values illustrated by Valerius Maximus were the rhetoricians, for whom *exempla* were the tools of persuasion'.[43] This is the established practice of rhetoricians in setting out moral goods with reference to social norms. Saller, however, takes these examples to be essentially fictionalised and detached from any purposive reality:

> The rhetoricians' manipulation of virtues in debates over imaginary conflicts provides insights into the meanings and associations of moral values. The fact that these rhetorical exercises are fictitious and highly contrived does not diminish their value as evidence for the meanings of virtue and the logic of the Roman moral system.[44]

Certainly, some rhetorical debates were contrived and used explicitly for academic purposes but Saller, in my view, underplays the important practical role of rhetorical *exempla*, and the very evident fact that Valerius Maximus takes his examples of *pietas* from reality, not imagination. The *exempla* provided reveal that *pietas* was not the construction of a manipulated virtue but, rather, an extant, socially understood value, widely acknowledged within Roman society.

Pietas in the modern legal scholarship is confined to a simpler and less sophisticated notion of filial obedience. Schulz provides a good example of this limitation, where he only discusses *pietas* in relation to children obeying parents. For Schulz, the only legal impact of *pietas* was that it imposed a duty towards parental authority and therefore *pietatis ratio* was simply *obsequium* toward parents.[45] In legal practice, this did not impose or create any obligations but, rather, meant that there was an obligation not to abuse parents. This is manifest in following what Schulz labels 'three legal rules': a child must not summon a parent to court without the permission of the praetor; a child must not bring *actiones famosae* against parents; and a

[37] Val. Max. 5.4.1.
[38] Val. Max. 5.4.2.
[39] Val. Max. 5.4.3.
[40] Val. Max. 5.4.4.
[41] Val. Max. 5.4.5.
[42] Val. Max. 5.4.6.
[43] Saller (n 12), 109.
[44] ibid, 110.
[45] Schulz's argument is founded on the Digest title D. 37.15.

child must not effect execution against his parents.[46] Schulz's view places the stress of parental relationships on the *auctoritas* of the father as a signifier of the creation of certain legal effects: that is, the effects of coming under the *patria potestas*.[47] The focus is very legalistic and does not examine the relationship of parents and children in closer detail; it has scant regard to the operation of relationships within either the actual family or the legal *familia*. In this understanding, *pietas* is reduced to a broad notion of filial obedience, rather than the more nuanced interpretation that we derived from Valerius Maximus.

The narrow view of *pietas* as filial obedience and of its legal effect as a proscription on abusing parents is not displayed in the juristic sources. In social terms, the central theme of *patria potestas* was its characterisation by *pietas*. Rather than strict adherence to *obsequium* as subjection of the child to the whims of the father, the *patria potestas* of the *paterfamilias* was underpinned by an aversion to *atrocitas*, or the harsh and rigid imposition of authority.[48] It is my view that to understand *pietas* merely as *obsequium* and to conflate *obsequium* with filial obligation is to misstep. This is shown in the literary sources, where, although the duty of *obsequium* is outlined as a defining theme, the affection of a real family bond is also present in *pietas* as a concept. Schulz's narrowing of the concept is not in keeping with these sources. Nor is it in keeping with the legal sources; for instance, in the Digest, we find the following:

> It is said that when during a hunt a certain man killed his son, who had been committing adultery with his stepmother, the deified Hadrian banished him to an island [because he acted] more as a bandit in killing him than as [someone] with a father's right; for paternal power should be contingent on compassion, not brutality.[49]

Here, we are provided with a clear example of the law recognising that *pietas* constitutes more than the recognition of an obligation to filial obedience through *obsequium*; it restrains the father from exercising his rights to the letter of the law, lest he behave in such a way as to endanger the reciprocal feeling of *pietas* that ought to exist between father and son. This shows that Schulz's narrow interpretation does not represent the whole understanding of *pietas* in the Roman mind; *pietas*, rather than simply setting out three restrictions on the basis of parental deference, can, in fact, require a father not to act in the way ascribed by law to his *patria potestas*. The law in its strictest, literal interpretation is circumvented by an appeal to a conceptual idea, which outranks it, an unwritten obligation to behave with *pietas* which is here legally enshrined by imperial proclamation. This section is sufficient to show the narrowness of the limitation but does not reveal to us the means by which the Emperor Hadrian felt it incumbent upon himself to rule as he did. For this, other examples of *pietas* in the legal sources are illuminating.

[46] F Schulz, *Classical Roman Law* (Oxford, Oxford University Press, 1951), 160.
[47] ibid, 140–61.
[48] Dixon (n 27), 47.
[49] D. 48.9.5 (Marc. 14 *Inst.*).

The jurists were more than happy to modify or circumvent the law in such a way as to consider *pietas* as a directly and implementable factor in construing legal rules. An example is found in the case where relatives provide *alimenta* for a fatherless child (*pupillus*) out of *pietas*. This personally bars them from recovery of that cost from the child's estate under the normal rules of unauthorised administration:

> I replied that, if Titus supported his sister's daughter from a sense of duty [*pietatis*], he did not have an action against her on this account.[50]

We can clearly see that *pietas* is noted as directly affecting juristic argument. Nevertheless, we are left without much of an explanation as to what Modestinus meant when he employed the term. What can be seen, however, is that Schulz's limited view that *pietas* in legal terms is synonymous with filial obedience through *obsequium* is insufficient. The circumvention of the usual rules of unauthorised administration is not achieved by reference to the kind of relationships Schulz discusses but appears to be based on an appeal to the kind of *pietas* seen in Valerius Maximus. Indeed, supporting a sister's daughter out of pious duty is more akin to the actions described in Valerius Maximus 5.6.7 than it is to the prescriptive obligations outlined by Schulz. This is not an isolated example. Other passages from the Digest show the jurists circumventing standard legal rules by reference to the kind of broader 'social' *pietas* of the *exempla* in Pliny and Valerius Maximus, rather than to Schulz's narrower 'legal' *pietas*. For instance, the general rules of law applied to dowry can again be disregarded in favour of an appeal to *pietas*:

> If a woman labours under the notion that she is required to give a dowry, she cannot recuperate anything given on that account; for underneath there remains the moral bond [*pietatis*], and a payment based on that reason cannot be recuperated.[51]

Again, this is not obviously limited to filial obedience. In fact, it has little to do with *obsequium* to parents. The stress here is on the fulfilment of the moral obligation arising out of a relationship, in this case, with her husband. I would suggest that this is more akin to the *pietas* of Valerius Maximus than it is to pure deference to authority. The *pietas* of the *exempla* circumvents or modifies the law, and fits no narrow legalistic interpretation of the term.

Further examples abound, where *pietas* is central to modifying the rules on untrustworthy tutors and curators:

> Furthermore, even women are admitted, but only those who take this step under the compulsion of duty [*pietate*] and necessity, as for example, a mother. A nurse also and a grandmother can bring a charge. So can a sister; for in a case of a sister, there even exists a rescript of the deified Severus; and if there is any other woman whose deliberate sense of duty [*pietatem*] is perceived by the praetor although she does not go beyond

[50] D. 3.5.26.1 (Mod. 2 *Resp.*).
[51] D. 12.6.32.2 (Iul. 10 *Dig.*).

> the modesty of her sex, but was induced by her sense of duty [*pietate*] not to conceal the wrong beyond the *pupilli*, the praetor should allow her to make an accusation.[52]

Once more, the *pietas* in question here is not simple filial deference but depends, rather, on an appreciation of the broader notion. It is analogous to several of the examples provided in Valerius Maximus. Once more, the jurists commit to modification of the law based on arguments rooted in the broad 'social' understanding of *pietas*, and not a limited 'legalistic' one. A similar example makes the point clear:

> But moreover, when it is a mother who appeals concerning the property of her son being ruined by a judgment, she should be granted a hearing out of reverence to family piety, and if she prefers to take on the preparation of the lawsuit, she is not regarded as bringing a disruptive action, even if initially she cannot defend the case.[53]

The concession made by law to *pietas* has ostensibly no link to authority here but, rather, to a mutual relationship of affection and duty. This mutuality is a symmetrical appreciation of the role of duty regarding *pietas* but it is not truly synallagmatic: there is no obligatory reciprocity but a unilateral moral obligation which is mirrored but non-dependent on particular action. Nor is there a determined obligation in the form of a legal imposition of particular action, as we see from our example. A mother can, and indeed *ought*, to protect her son's property by raising an action, based on the social practice of *pietas*. The interesting thing for present purposes is that the law gives way to this social demand, and the civil law is modified in favour of this social – not legal – reasoning.

One more example shows this social understanding of *pietas* being used directly to modify law:

> But if the freedman has given his daughter a dowry, he does not appear to have defrauded his patron in respect of the amount of the dowry, because a father's duty [*pietas*] is not to be the cause of condemnation.[54]

Justinian's Institutes recall that the origin of Roman law may lie outwith written statement.[55] Contained within the very fabric of the law is an appreciation of the unwritten nature of determinative socially understood values as important sources of law. The silence of the text on the nature of these unwritten laws goes beyond a mere tradition of customary acceptance of particular modes of behaviour, extending to the cultural appreciation of the underlying values which cause that behaviour. It is in this way that *pietas*, as a socially understood value, operates as the basis for law.

We find further discussion of *pietas* in the *Rhetorica ad Herennium*. Here the Auctor brings up *pietas* in his discussion of the division (*partes*) of law (*ius*). Of the six divisions of law – nature, statute, custom, precedent, equity and agreement[56] – which

[52] D. 26.10.1.7 (Ulp. 35 *ad Ed.*).
[53] D. 49.5.1.1 (Ulp. 29 *ad Ed.*).
[54] D. 38.5.1.10 (Ulp. 44 *ad Ed.*).
[55] Inst. 1.2.3.
[56] *Rhet. Her.* 2.13.19.

the Auctor sets out, he provides a specific example of each, except for nature, where he raises *pietas*.[57] The provision given by the Auctor of natural law is the bond of children and parents:

> Natural law is seen in the relationships formed from the reason of *pietas*; it is by this law that parents are nurtured by children and children by parents.[58]

Pietas is presented to us by the Auctor as a principle which is directly related to natural law, not only as a result of natural law but rather as an integral part of it, as a concept which is inherent to natural law. The ascription of *pietas* to natural law is made with little explanation, other than a simple assertion that it is an observable inference. The sentiment replicates that of Valerius Maximus in his assessment of the virtue of *pietas*. The difficulty here lies in our understanding of law, because the nurturing of children is not law in the same sense as property rights or delictual liability. Natural law provides an overarching superstructure to which man-made law is often referential and to which it is sometimes inextricably bound. That said, natural law is not enforceable in the same direct sense as man-made law. Therefore, its enforceability takes the form of social normativity and not legal obligation. Ill-treatment of children by parents then – the failure to nourish – is a social and moral breach, rather than a legal one, in terms of how society enforces its standards.

Honoré's distinction between appeals to particular types of argument put forward by the Romans in providing reasons for decision-making is of use here in formulating this thought, between what he calls 'appeals to rules of law', 'open arguments' (*topoi* or principles), 'the facts', and '*argumenta ex auctoritate*' (specifically juristic authority).[59] In the instance where *pietas* governs the relationship between parents and children, in order to give not only a social–moral but also a legal dimension to that relationship based on natural law, the argument is principled or open, it concerns a *topos*. Winkel argues that the lack of a coherent hierarchy of sources was the cause of the need for open, topical arguments in decision-making.[60] Winkel's classification is correct, insofar as the diversity of rationality for decision-making is less well defined than it is in modern civilian legal systems. However, although it engages a broad interpretation in decision-making, it does not provide us with an answer as to how open reasoning behind decisions in a case exists within a system which purportedly had developed a nascent scientific tendency. What is of more interest in the example with which we are presented here is how the open-argumentation (that is, topical rhetoric) is a cornerstone of legal argumentation, necessary for the creation of legal obligations.

In *De oratore*, Cicero, in the voice of his interlocutor Crassus, acknowledges the needs of the orator to make pronouncements on a variety of subjects.[61] Among

[57] *cf* Cic., *Inv. rhet.* 2.21.62–68.

[58] *Rhet. Her.* 2.13.19.

[59] AM Honoré, 'Legal Reasoning in Rome and Today' (1973) 4 *Cambrian Law Review* 58, 84. The idea that Roman legal decision-making involved a plethora of approaches is worth bearing in mind.

[60] LC Winkel 'L'histore du droit, exemple d'une science interdisciplinaire' (1996) 9 *Sartoniana* 125.

[61] Cic., *De or.* I.55. It is worth reiterating that the nature of the dialogue means that neither Crassus nor Antonius can be conclusively regarded as the 'mouthpiece' of Cicero, that and some caveat must be

these topics with which the orator must deal is *pietas*.[62] Cicero points out that the orator's dabbling in more specialised topics results in some disgruntlement among the specialists:

> All the academies and schools of philosophy will, I do believe, raise the cry that all these matters are their exclusive province, and in no way whatever the concern of the orator.[63]

On issues of philosophy and law, the technical specialisation of these topics makes knowledge of the subject an essential for informed speech. Apart from these more discrete topics, Cicero also includes friendship, harmony, equity and virtue. These subjects are less obviously accounted for than law and philosophy, which have easily understood parameters. The answer to their inclusion comes from the contention – made by Crassus later in the same interaction with Scaevola – that the expertise of the orator lies in the broader theme of 'human life and conduct'.[64] This statement – that the true province of the orator lies in human life and conduct – is revealing; and it is contested, in its fundamental terms, by neither Scaevola nor Antonius in Cicero's text. The implication is that the orator – through the technical process by which he acquires his argument, rhetoric – is properly to be understood first and foremost as an expert in human social interaction: human life and conduct. The orator, therefore, in making his pleadings, has a particular social expertise, from which he can draw the *loci* of his arguments.

Turning to the issue of the *loci* of arguments for the conclusion of equitable remedies, Cicero, in his *Topica*, points out the need to distinguish three types of speech in constructing an argument from particular places. Judicial speeches, which appeal to equity, concern different rhetorical origins from deliberative or encomiastic speeches, which deal in advantage and honour. Cicero explains the *locus* for arguments in judicial speeches.[65] He argues that each of these three forms of argumentation has, through the practice and theory of oratory and rhetoric, developed stylistic differences. In judicial argumentation (*iuridicalis*), the purpose of equitable remedy is to distinguish right from wrong.

The actual application of this kind of argumentation is outlined in the case of the will of a soldier in *De oratore*. At first impression, it appears that the decision here is made on legal grounds, specifically on a question of the civil law: does a son have a right to a legitimate share of his father's estate by virtue of being a son not explicitly named as disinherited? However, in reality, Cicero attributes the award of the estate to the rhetorical arguments of *pietas* used by Lucius Licinius Crassus in the course of the argument.[66] Cicero's attribution reveals how the socially understood value of *pietas* has an actual application in legal decision-making.

given to claims made by either interlocutor as definitively the opinion of Cicero himself; see CEW Steel, *Roman Oratory* (Cambridge, Cambridge University Press, 2006), 73.

[62] Cic., *De or.* I.56.

[63] Cic., *De or.* I.56.

[64] Cic., *De or.* I.68.

[65] Cic., *Top.* XXIII, 91.

[66] Cic., *De or.* I.245.

III. Later Evidence for the Application of *Pietas* in the *Querela Inofficiosi Testamenti*

It is right to say that, apart from the attestation of Valerius Maximus, the Auctor of the *Rhetorica ad Herennium* and Cicero, there is little evidence for the actual application of *pietas* as the ratio decidendi for decisions made in challenges under *querela* during the later Republican period. Nonetheless, we can be sure that it was applied as a key factor in the decision-making process. The jurists, as outlined, give verification of this fact. However, our source material is dishearteningly limited in providing us with an insight as to the exact mechanisms by which the *querela* was dependent on *pietas* as the decisive factor by which the *centumviri* were persuaded. Furthermore, the justification for the reasoning behind *pietas* overriding the civil law as a basis for decision-making remains shrouded in uncertainty. This uncertainty is behind the rise of the prevailing idea that a separation occurred between the law as set out by jurists in the first phase of a challenge, and an extra-legal second phase which began in pleadings before the centumviral court, where rhetoric was applied with little relation to the preceding legal phase. Despite this lack of sources from the late Republic, legal literature from later periods provides us with a discernible insight as to how *pietas* operated in relation to law in challenges for undutiful wills. In particular, the *Codex Iustinianus* provides a series of imperial rescripts which, though written at a much later period than that of the inception of the *querela* – and, as such, subject to the social and legal differences which the intervening centuries imply – mention claims of undutiful wills in their historical context, either directly, or as an analogous legal form through which other issues could be solved. These texts are useful, though it must be stressed imperfect, in providing us with evidence of the actual, practical relationship between law and rhetoric in the centumviral court in the period of the later Republic.

Before undertaking this examination, some consideration must be given to the substantive changes in succession law which occurred in the intervening time, which have a direct impact on the cases presented. First, obvious institutional changes separate the Republic from the Empire: the introduction of specific legal instruments with regard to succession law must be borne in mind to properly contextualise the law according to period. Second is the *senatus consultum Orphitianum* of 178 CE, during the reign of Marcus Aurelius. This made provision for children to make first claim on their mother's estate as *legitimi* under the praetorian rules of succession. This prevented fathers from limiting emancipated daughters from making wills through guardianship and also afforded children the same priority in inheritance from mothers' wills as they were due under fathers' wills, changing the dimension of the order of succession.[67] Third,

[67] For a useful outline of the implications of the *senatus consultum Orphitianum*, see Gardner (n 30), 231–33. For a more doctrinal analysis see WW Buckland, *A Manual of Roman Private Law*, 2nd edn (Cambridge, Cambridge University Press, 1953), 373–74. Juristic references: D. 38.17; PS 4.8; Reg.Ulp. 26.7; Inst. 3.4.

the edictal category of *unde liberi* was not conclusively in existence by the 50s BCE and therefore is of dubious application in regard to development of the *querela* in the mid-first century BCE.[68] These changes to the law caused divergence in terms of substantive legal points but did not undermine the general integrity of the form of challenge for undutiful wills.

The first of the related rescripts found in the *Codex Iustinianus* is given by the Emperor Philip the Arab to a certain Nicanor and Papiniana, and deals directly with the *querela*, dating from 245 CE. The case concerns a mother offering gifts to strangers and certain children in order to deprive other children of their legal portion:

> If, as you allege, your mother, in order to frustrate a complaint seeking to have her will set aside as undutiful, during her lifetime almost exhausted all her property by making gifts either to certain of her children or to strangers, and afterwards made you heirs to two-twelfths of her property and wanted to reduce that to nothing through legacies and testamentary requests, you do not unjustly desire to be aided by the provisions of the constitutions made concerning undutiful wills, as not having received your legal portion.[69]

The text provides us with a clear case of a challenge based on a mother neglecting her supposed duty to make provision in her will for her children. As the text dates from after 178 CE, the *senatus consultum Orphitianum* applies. Given that there is a use of legacies and testamentary requests (ie, *fideicomissa*) to delimit what was actually inherited to below a quarter of the estate, an immediate issue arises, as this is a reduction to below the value which ought to be apportioned to heirs under the *lex Falcidia* of 40 BCE. A quarter of the estate is recoverable for apportionment between named heirs on this ground alone, and combats legacy provisions which reduce the inheritance to nothing.[70] However, the deliberate exhaustion of the estate through a series of gifts given to strangers and other children still frustrates the claimants from attaining an equitable amount in the will. Phillip the Arab, on noting this, points out that a remedy can be sought for the mother's cynical attempt to manipulate her property away from Nicanor and Papiniana, and can be redressed by a challenge under the *querela*. The challenge for an undutiful will is due, as such a claim would not be unjust in relation to the constitutions regarding the assignment of the legal portion. The text provides us with clear evidence that

[68] Watson (n 5), 83 points to the testament of Val. Max. 7.8.4 to deduce that had the category been in existence then *bonorum possessio* would have provided a more obvious remedy than the claim under *querela inofficiosi testament*. D. 2.2.23 is also of interest, insofar as it states that an emancipated son could claim under *bonorum possessio contra tabulas* but not bring the *querela inofficiosi testamenti* if disinherited, the implication being that before *unde liberi* was introduced, that is, before this text, only *sui heredes* had to be expressly named to be disinherited or instituted. Gardner (n 30), 3–8 points to some evidence of the existence of *unde liberi* and *unde cognati* by 66 BCE based on Val. Max. 7.7.2 but the documentary evidence remains inconclusive.

[69] C. 3.29.1 (Philip to Nicanor and Papiana, 19 August 245).

[70] Not only is the *lex Falcidia* a protection against the reduction of the estate to nothing, but also a *senatusconsultum* of a date between Hadrian and Vespasian. See D. 39.6.15 (Iul. 27 *Dig.*).

the *querela* had survived in a discernible form to the third century CE. Moreover, it reveals that it is applied in scenarios where an injustice has occurred, due to non-receipt of the prescribed legal portion. Other than that, this injustice presents us with a viable challenge; the text does not go further to reveal the bases on which an action would be successful. Nevertheless, the text frames the use of the *querela* in a similar vein to earlier juristic texts, and allows us to understand with confidence that claims for undutiful wills were made in circumstances similar to those set out by the classical jurists. The question in law here is whether the exhaustion of the property by the mother was done to frustrate a duty to provide for the legal portion to the claimant children. If the dispersal of gifts was designed to do this, the fact that the claim is made under provisions for undutious wills is indicative of the existence of a relationship of duty between mother and children beyond the provision for the remaining *hereditas* under the quarter apportionment rule of the *lex Falcidia*. The inference is that some portion of the gifts *mortis causa* can be recovered under a challenge of an undutiful will by aggrieved child heirs. The implication is that the duty by which that inheritance is owed is more akin to *pietas* than it is to the kind of apportionment set out in positive law. An examination of other rescripts sheds further light on this.

The rescript of Emperors Valerian and Gallien to Aetia from 256 CE is of great interest in establishing the operation of the *querela* by reference to rhetorical conceptions and arguments. The scenario is typical of a claim for undutiful will: a daughter, Aetia, does not receive the allotted quarter portion as a child on the death of her father, due to the 'extravagant generosity' with which the father gave all his property to his son prior to his death. The decision is dependent on whether the son was emancipated or not, and the emperors' rescript makes provision for both circumstances:

> If your father, by some whim of excessive kindness, gave all his belongings to his son, the latter either stayed in the power of his father, in which case, in an action to divide, it suits the judge to split the property in such a way that you entirely inherit the quarter of the share due on intestacy; or the son is emancipated, in which case, since a gift requires no outside assistance but is supported by its own strength, that is, no confirmation is required, the governor will, according to the constitutions, extend equitable relief following the pattern of a complaint to set a will aside as undutiful.[71]

The first permutation refers to the apportionment of wills under the *lex Falcidia*. Where the son – presumably Aetia's brother – to whom Aetia's father so generously granted all of his property so extravagantly, is not emancipated but still in the power of his father, Aetia ought to receive the legal portion which is legally owed to her: that is, the quarter share which would be due on intestacy. The remedy attested to here is well attested. It shares a factual and legal theme with the rescript of Philip

[71] C. 3.29.2 (Valerian and Gallien to Aetia, 27 July 256). In reading this, it is worth bearing in mind that gifts to unemancipated sons were generally invalid: C. 8.53.11 (Diocletian and Maximian to Septimius Dabinianus, 30 April 293). Gifts to emancipated sons were valid: C. 8.53.17 (Diocletian and Maximian to Hermia, 27 December 293).

the Arab to Nicanor and Papiniana. Where a legal portion of an inheritance has been taken away from a child in order to benefit another child, the law offers the *querela* as a standard remedy for the recovery of the legal portion. The reasoning behind the exercise of a challenge of undutiful will goes no further than allowing a remedy for a recovery of an amount that ought to be inherited by prescription of positive law. The more significant scenario is that outlined in the case where the son is emancipated and beyond the scope of *patria potestas*.

In the second situation presented in the rescript, consideration is given to Aetia's position where the son to whom her father gave so generously is emancipated. The son's emancipation changes the complexion of the problem. If the son is emancipated, the gift remains legally valid. No direct legal remedy is offered to Aetia, and the gift of the father to his son stands in law. However, the imperial rescript does not leave Aetia without redress. Rather, we are told that the provincial magistrate is able to hear a challenge to assignment of the property. Although the gift is able to stand on its own strength (*suis viribus*), the constitutions (*iuxta constitutiones*) made provision for equitable relief to be sought by analogy to the *querela* (*ad similitudinem inofficiosi querellae auxilium tibi aequitas impertiet*). This is interesting for two reasons: first, despite a valid gift existing in law, the emperor is still willing to attempt to find Aetia a remedy on the grounds of equity (*aequitas*) through the constitutions; second, the argument is made by analogy to the q*uerela*, indicating that the decision reached upon equitable grounds against a legally valid gift in order to redress an unfairness in inheritance law shares the conceptual and mechanistic qualities of the *querela* itself.

The fact that the emperor felt comfortable making an analogy to the *querela inofficiosi testamenti* in this instance is not an isolated case. Later examples show that actions against 'undutious gifts' were introduced to the law by analogy to the *querela*. The interesting feature is the means by which the emperor frames the resolution of the issue: by following the solution provided by equitable remedy in extension from cases of challenges for undutious wills.

On what basis is the challenge made? We see that, by this stage, the pretence of insanity as the ground for a claim has long since evaporated. Aetia's case is clear that the father's motivation for favouring gifts is extravagant generosity (*immensae liberalitatis*), which, though unwise, is not insane. Accordingly, the development of a claim analogous to the *querela* need not dwell on the sanity of the testator – nor, in fact, did the challenge of undutiful will itself. The solution provided is born out of a feeling of equitability. This might seem a vague and insufficient method for solving the problem presented, were it not for the fact that, as we have seen, *aequitas* was a definable and understood concept in Roman society. This was the same for *pietas*. Rather than an appeal to woolly and esoteric ideals, these terms had social and legal meaning. Both of them relate to Aetia's case and to the decision of the emperors to allow a challenge to the apportionment of her father's estate based on the constitutions, despite the legal validity of the will at civil law.

We have seen that *pietas* forms the foundation for a claim under the *querela*. Aside from the requirements of status which entitle a claimant, *pietas* is the concept which asserts itself as the principal consideration in the *ratio decidendi*. *Pietas* is itself dependent on status and relationship. The form of *pietas erga parentes* is the definitive factor in establishing a moral and social duty, which, though not symmetrical, nevertheless creates reciprocal social and moral duties upon parents and children. The challenge to undutiful wills is the transformation of moral and social duty into legal obligation. That transformation is provided through the enforcement of the challenge in the centumviral court. That *pietas* and *aequitas* are used as tools of legal reasoning is also a transformation. These ideas change from moral and social virtues to legal concepts. Legal concepts can authoritatively decide legal remedies, and here we find that Aetia is provided with a challenge based on the legal authority of *pietas* and *aequitas*, as is done in a challenge for undutiful will, to provide her with legal redress.

A further example is provided in a rescript of the Emperors Diocletian and Maximian to a certain Calpurnia Aristaeneta, who sought a remedy for a prodigal son lavishing gifts unreasonably to the detriment of the familial property. Yet again, the redress is provided by analogy to a claim for undutiful will:

> If your son used up his property through profligate and wasteful generosity, you may seek aid from the governor; and if on examination of the root of truth he judges that you, through your son, should have restitution of your rights as to the excessively large gifts, he will help you by rescinding the wrongful acts. Hence, for the purpose of setting the excessive gifts aside, you need no action similar to that of setting a will aside as undutiful.[72]

The extension of the criteria of a claim for undutiful will to a claim for undutiful gifts is telling, on two points. First, it indicated that the emperor, in making these rescripts, was not averse to the application of analogy in legal reasoning. This, in itself, reveals the scope for rhetorical figures in the expansion of legal concepts, as dutiful gifts are viewed, *ex similitudine*, to share a fundamental essence with undutiful wills. The logic was that property divested unreasonably, whether *inter vivos*, or on death through testament, is challengeable on the grounds that it breaches a duty. The establishment of that duty, we can infer, is through the maternal relationship shared between Calpurnia Aristaeneta and her profligate son, the duty of *pietas erga parentes*. Second, based on this first inference, we can state with reasonable confidence that the reasoning which underpins a claim for undutiful wills is the same as that used for undutious gifts. The importance of this observation is that we can directly see the law expanding, purely on the basis of rhetorical reasoning: wills are challengeable when a duty of *pietas* is breached; undutiful wills are analogous to undutiful gifts, insofar as they both amount to the transfer of family property unreasonably against a duty of *pietas* to a relative; on the basis of this analogy, the remedy for the two ought to be the same. On the basis of this argument, therefore, a remedy similar to the *querela inofficiosi testamenti* is provided for undutiful gifts. This demonstrates not only that rhetoric provided the underlying

[72] C. 3.29.4 (Diocletian and Maximian to Calpurnia Aristaeneta, 10 February 286).

ratio decidendi for decisions on undutiful gifts, insofar as it followed the pattern of undutiful wills in using breaches of *pietas erga parentes* as the definitional breach in allowing for a challenge, but also that rhetorical reasoning, through the use of analogy, was central to legal development, in expanding the scope of the remedy from challenges to wills to challenges to donations *inter vivos*.

The rescript to Calpurnia Aristaeneta is not an isolated case. Further rescripts follow a similar theme, addressing undutiful gifts by analogy to the remedy for undutiful wills. Examples of these are readily available: Cottabaeus was informed by Diocletian and Maximian that gifts given to emancipated sons which were 'extravagant and generous' are recoverable by children seeking 'the amount legally due to them' by analogy to the *querela*;[73] the same emperors informed a certain Demetriana that she was entitled to recover for extravagant gifts made to her brother by her father 'following the pattern of a complaint for setting undutiful wills aside';[74] Ammianus was told by the same *Augusti* that, if his mother 'dissipated her property and bled her resources dry through extravagant generosity' to his younger brother, such gifts could be set aside following the logic 'from a complaint to set a will aside as undutiful';[75] the Emperor Constantius wrote to a certain Olybrius that

> there is no doubt that the action concerning immoderate gifts has been introduced into the laws following the pattern of laws regarding undutiful wills, and in this respect both actions must be deemed as one or similar, both as to time and conditions.[76]

The use of a version of the challenge to undutiful gifts formulated on the basis of the challenge to undutiful wills is well established. The same logic is also extended, though with less evidence, to claims for undutiful dowry gifts, *de inofficiosis dotibus*.[77]

The reasoning which underpins these points is consistent with that used in the decision in the case of Calpurnia Aristaeneta. The fundamental points are as follows: first, undutiful gifts are analogous to undutiful wills and therefore the same remedy following the same criteria is a reasonable resolution to claims; second, the reason that these claims are analogous is that they fundamentally invoke *pietas* as the ratio decidendi.

IV. Concluding Remarks

The idea of a scientific revolution in the later Republic has influenced scholarly interaction with Roman law to the present day. However, during the period in

[73] C. 3.29.5 (Diocletian and Maximian to Cottabeus, 28 February 286).
[74] C. 3.29.6 (Diocletian and Maximian to Demetriana, 26 April 286).
[75] C. 3.29.7 (Diocletian and Maximian to Ammianus, 10 May 286).
[76] C. 3.29.9 (Constantine to Olybrius, 19 May 361).
[77] C. 3.30.1 (Constantine to Maximus, 19 December 358).

which Roman law is thought to have attained scientific qualities, legal decision-makers relied on social, cultural and economic concepts to inform their judgments, rather than isolating themselves in a gapless system of law. In showing the impact of *pietas* on the development of the *querela inofficiosi testamenti*, I hope to have presented a nascent challenge to the narrative of Roman legal science, and widened the scope of enquiry to consider law within the society in which it functions.

6

Writing, Speaking and the Roman *Stipulatio*

DAVID IBBETSON

Most textbooks of Roman law, at least those written in English, focus on the formal law, found primarily in Justinian's *Corpus Iuris* and typically grounded in the Institutes. Historical development is not totally ignored, of course, but it is rarely allowed to take centre stage. The way in which the law actually worked is similarly relegated to a background role. Yet law is, and was, a social phenomenon; its formal legal rules can only properly be understood in the context of their practical application. This textbook bias towards formal rules is true of many legal systems but it is particularly problematic for Roman law, because the preponderance of formal juristic literature tells only part of the story. The purpose of this chapter is largely pedagogical; its aim is to take a well-known institution of Roman law, the *stipulatio*, and show how it was, in practice, adjusted to social reality.

The orthodox story is told in all the standard modern textbooks: in origin, the *stipulatio* was a purely oral formal agreement, dependent simply on the use of the correct verbal form; in the course of the Empire, it was transformed from being an agreement stemming from the parties' speaking to one that was fundamentally written.[1] It probably remained in theory an oral agreement – but

[1] WW Buckland, *A Text-Book of Roman Law from Augustus to Justinian*, 3rd edn (PG Stein ed, Cambridge, Cambridge University Press, 1963), 434–37; JAC Thomas, *Textbook of Roman Law* (Amsterdam, North-Holland, 1976), 259–62; PJ du Plessis, *Borkowski's Textbook on Roman Law*, 5th edn (Oxford, Oxford University Press, 2015), 298–300; PBH Birks, *The Roman Law of Obligations* (E Descheemaeker ed, Oxford, Oxford University Press, 2014), 49–51; R Zimmermann, *The Law of Obligations: Roman Foundations of the Civilian Tradition* (Oxford, Oxford University Press, 1996), 68–72, 78–82; HF Jolowicz and JKBM Nicholas, *An Historical Introduction to the Study of Roman Law*, 3rd edn (Cambridge, Cambridge University Press, 1972), 418–20. There is an abundant monographic and periodical literature. See in particular, with different emphases, S Riccobono, *Stipulation and the Theory of Contract* (B Beinart and J Kerr-Wylie eds and trans, Amsterdam, Balkema, 1957); JKBM Nicholas, 'The Form of the Stipulation in Roman Law II' (1953) 69 *LQR* 233; JC van Oven, 'La Stipulation a-t-elle dégénéré' (1958) 26 *Legal Hist Rev* 409; R Feenstra, 'L'"Epistula" comme preuve d'une stipulation' in *Studi in onore di Emilio Betti*, vol 2 (Milan, Giuffrè, 1962) 405; EA Meyer, *Legitimacy and Law in the Roman World: Tabulae in Roman Belief and Practice* (Cambridge, Cambridge University Press, 2004). A recent study, with abundant references, is N Coch Roura, *La forma estipulatoria: Una aproximación al estudio del lenguaje directo en el Digesto* (Madrid, Dykinson, 2017).

one increasingly evidenced by writing.[2] Approaching the subject from a more practice-based point of view, it could be said that, by the late Republic, both speech and writing were central to the *stipulatio*.[3] The range of positions that have been taken in describing its evolution brings out the problematic dual (or indeed multifaceted) nature of the *stipulatio* in theory and in practice. The point of this chapter is simply this: we fail to capture the essence of the original form of the *stipulatio* if we think of it purely as an oral agreement, and we misrepresent its later history if we accept too easily that writing came completely to supplant speaking in post-classical law.

The basic nature of the *stipulatio*, from as early as we can confidently say anything about it right up to the time of Justinian, is described in Gaius's Institutes:

> *Verbis obligatio fit ex interrogatione et responsione, velut DARI SPONDES? SPONDEO; DABIS? DABO; PROMITTIS? PROMITTO; FIDEPROMITTIS? FIDEPROMITTO; FIDEIUBES? FIDEIUBEO; FACIES? FACIAM.*
>
> An obligation is created by words, for example: DO YOU SWEAR TO GIVE? I SWEAR; WILL YOU GIVE? I WILL GIVE; DO YOU PROMISE? I PROMISE; DO YOU PROMISE BY YOUR FAITH? I PROMISE BY MY FAITH; DO YOU GUARANTEE BY YOUR FAITH? I GUARANTEE BY MY FAITH; WILL YOU DO? I WILL DO.[4]

The obligation is created by words, when one person puts to another a question and receives from the other a reply using the same verb that was used in the question. This is, however, only an idealised form. Meyer rightly speaks of it as being designed to express the essence of the *stipulatio* – but no more than this; it is likely that no Roman would ever have recognised this statement as a complete description of what a *stipulatio* involved.

This leads us to ask two questions. First, what more might we have to say if we want to approach more closely what a Roman – lawyer or layperson – would have recognised as a *stipulatio*; and, second, why is it that Gaius's definition, and all the other definitions that we find, focus so heavily on this narrow core of the institution, and make no mention of the other aspects?

We should begin in the Roman Republic, around 100 BCE. At this time, we can think of Roman law as being in a pre-juristic stage. Although there are some formal rules – such as those of the XII Tables and other *leges publicae* of the Comitia, and the *plebiscita* of the *consilium plebis* – for the most part, Roman law was essentially indistinguishable from social practice. It was only after the rise of juristic science, something we might place in the years around 100 BCE, that law becomes a discrete object of knowledge and enquiry, with its own rules and techniques of analysis. At

[2] Nicholas (n 1) is perhaps the clearest expression of this.
[3] Compare Meyer (n 1), 41–43, 117–19.
[4] G. 3.92.

this early period, it is pointless to look for a legal definition of the *stipulatio*; all we can properly do is try, as well as we can, to identify the components of the social practice that made up the *stipulatio* at the time.

It is likely that it involved, from the start, an exchange of question and answer. This is the form taken by a *stipulatio* in the *Pseudolus* of Plautus around 200 BCE:[5]

> *Dabisne argenti mi hodie viginti minas?*
>
> *Dabo.*[6]
>
> Will you give me twenty *minas* of silver today?
>
> I will give.

The form of the dialogue is not coincidental. Immediately before this exchange, the promisor, who has taken the initiative, says to the promisee, 'Ask me' – *Roga me*. Moreover, later in the play, this form is referred to as a *stipulatio*. Even if we had no such early evidence, this would still very likely have been the original form of the *stipulatio*, for it is otherwise difficult to see how the essentialist definition of Gaius could have arisen.

It is abundantly probable that the *stipulatio* originally involved some sort of ritual. Aside from the prevalence of ritual in early Roman law – typified by *mancipatio* as a means of transferring things – there are two strong reasons for this. First, it has long been recognised that the principal formal words associated with the *stipulatio* – *spondere*, *promittere*, *fidepromittere*, *fideiubere* – have a dimension associable with symbolic gestures.[7] The first word in Gaius's list, and the word that seems most commonly to have been used, *spondere*, is etymologically linked to the Greek word referring to the making of a libation; when we discover that, in some early legal cultures, the practice was to make formal agreements by sharing a drink,[8] it is tempting to guess that the Romans, too, might have concluded contracts in something like this way. The verbs *promittere*, *fidepromittere* and *fideiubere* point to a different type of ritualised gesture. The origin of *promittere* in the sense of promise may derive from its conjunction with

[5] For the stipulatio in Plautus, see E Costa, *Il Diritto Privato Roman nelle Comedie di Plauto* (Turin, Bocca, 1890), 274–75; WAJ Watson, *Roman Private Law around 200 BC* (Edinburgh, Edinburgh University Press, 1971), 117–18; VI Mazhuga, 'Сцены стипуляции в комедиях Плавта' (1997) 3 *Hyperboreus* 10 (Russian with French summary).

[6] Plaut., *Pseud.*, 117–18; compare 1076–77, referring to it as a *stipulatio* created by the *verba concepta*.

[7] Meyer (n 1), 117, with further references. This was once thought to reflect a belief in the magical force of formal words or acts. For an important corrective, see GD MacCormack, 'Formalism, Symbolism and Magic in Early Roman Law' (1969) 37 *Leg Hist Rev* 439.

[8] Tac., *Ann.*, 12.47; Hdt., *Histories*, 4.70; S Greengus, 'Old Babylonian Marriage Ceremonies and Rites' (1966) 20 *Journal of Cuneiform Studies* 55, 62–66. The Hebrew *berith*, commonly translated as 'covenant', is similar: M Weinfeld, 'בְּרִית *b^e^rîth*' in GJ Botterweck and H Ringgren (eds), *Theological Dictionary of the Old Testament*, vol II, rev edn (JT Willis trans, Grand Rapids, William B Eerdmans, 1975) 253.

the noun *manus*, hand: *manum promittere* would, literally, mean holding out one's hand. Given the strong link between the Roman concept of *fides* and the right hand, we can be fairly confident that the other two words – *fidepromittere* and *fideiubere* – were also associated with some form of hand gesture.[9] Whether it was the shaking of hands, the promisor's holding up his hand, or perhaps his placing it on relics or some other sacred thing cannot be told. There is nothing to prevent its having been any or all of these. Right across Europe in the early Middle Ages, we can see contracts being finalised by sharing a drink or shaking hands – to some extent, it is still the case today – and it may be that the earliest form of the *stipulatio* foreshadowed this later practice. Another early medieval form of contract-making, known as *fides facta*, involved one party's handing a small stick to the other party, who took it and broke it in two. The stick was known as a *stipula*, and Isidore of Seville suggested that this was the derivation of the word *stipulatio*.[10] We cannot, of course, know whether this is right; but it is certainly plausible, and it is quite possible that, in some places, this type of formality was already used in the early Roman period to signal the making of a serious contract.

Second, already by the time of Plautus in the mid-Republic, the verb *dare* – give – could be used in the first person singular future tense.[11] Without something accompanying the spoken words, it would have been quite impossible to distinguish between predictions, statements of intention, and formally created obligations.[12] It is possible, of course, that the question–answer form was sufficiently distinctive, though the absence of a straightforward Latin word for 'yes' suggests that this was probably not the case. The connotations of the four formal words in Gaius' list – excluding *dare* and *facere* – make it altogether more likely that there was an accompanying gesture or ritual of some sort.

Equally important, there must have been an interpretative aspect to the judge's determination whether or not there had been a *stipulatio*: in the absence of any legal definition at this stage in the history of Roman law, the only question that could have been asked was whether the words and conduct of the parties amounted to a *stipulatio*. We may reach the same point from a different angle, if we imagine how a judge would react to an action brought on a *stipulatio* that had occurred in the course of acting in a play. It is impossible to believe that this would be enforced outside the context of the play; even if all the formalities had been properly replicated, as a matter of interpretation, we would have to say simply that this was not a *stipulatio* in real life. We might even say the same of an apparent *stipulatio* entered into under the threat of force. It was not until 80 BCE (or perhaps much later) that the threat of force grounded a formal defence to an action, by means of the *exceptio*

[9] P Boyancé, 'La Main de Fides' (1964) 70 *Collection Latomus* 101.

[10] Isidore of Saville, *Etymologiae*, 5.24.30.

[11] Plaut., *Pseud.*, 117–18.

[12] For the importance of the tense, see JL Austin, 'Performative Utterances' in JO Urmson and GJ Warnock (eds), JL Austin, *Philosophical Papers* (Oxford, Oxford University Press, 1979) 233, 241–42.

metus.[13] Before this, we might well suppose that a judge, faced with incontrovertible evidence that the promise had been extorted by the threat of violence, would simply say that the words and acts, though on the face of it sufficient for a *stipulatio*, nonetheless did not amount to a *stipulatio*. Again, if this is right, it is the judges' role in interpreting social practice that would have made this possible.

Sometime around 100 BCE, we seem to see a change. Although we cannot rule out the possibility that the change is merely apparent – the result of our having a great deal more evidence of forensic practice, once we have the works of Cicero and the beginnings of juristic writing – there is good reason to believe that the change was genuine. This change had two features: the increasing use of writing, and the process of essentialisation associated with juristic science.

Unless the surviving evidence from the first century BCE deceives us, there was a very substantial increase in the use of writing in Rome, in all sorts of contexts. We know that writing was used to record evidence of the making of stipulations. Simple evidence that writing might be used does not show how common this was but a passing observation in Cicero's *Topica* suggests that it was very common:

> *Iam hoc perspicuum est, non magis in legibus, quam in testamentis, in stipulationibus, in reliquis rebus quae ex scripto aguntur, posse controversias easdem exsistere.*
>
> Now this is abundantly clear, no more in laws than in wills, in stipulations and in other things which are done in writing, that ambiguities can exist.[14]

Problems of interpreting words arose in a range of situations in which there was writing: in legislation as much as in wills and in stipulations. For Cicero, therefore, we might conclude that a *stipulatio* could be understood as a written instrument, just as a *lex* or a will might be. In each case, there was some act behind the document – legislation, for example, required a resolution of a *comitia*, not simply an inscribed piece of bronze – but where that act had been put in written form, as it commonly would have been, the judges' role was largely to decide what the words meant. By this time, too, we find quite complex common forms of stipulatory clause, such as this one, which Varro records in the sale of sheep in the first century BCE:

> That these sheep with which we are dealing are thoroughly sound, according to the standard of a thoroughly sound flock, excluding any that is one-eyed, deaf or smooth-bellied, and that they do not come from sickly stock, and that I am free to possess them without disturbance – do you solemnly warrant these matters? [*haec sic recte fieri spondesne?*][15]

While there is nothing impossible about the development of complex standard-form clauses in the context of oral agreements, they are more likely to emerge when writing was more widely used. This strengthens the conclusion to be

[13] WAJ Watson, *The Law of Obligations in the Later Roman Republic* (Oxford, Oxford University Press, 1965), 257–58.

[14] Cic., *Top.*, 26.96. See also: Cic., *Part. or.*, 37.130; and, at about the same time, *Rhet. Her.* II.IX.13–14.

[15] Varro, *Rust.*, 2.2.6.

drawn from Cicero that the late-Republican *stipulatio* would commonly – or at least not uncommonly – be recorded in writing. To stress the point still further, in the late Republic, we begin to find the written evidence of the *stipulatio*, the *cautio*, being expressly mentioned in formal legal texts – as, for example, in the edictal requirement that a usufructuary should give a *cautio* promising that he or she would look after the usufruct property with the care of a diligent *paterfamilias*.[16]

The second factor in the development of the *stipulatio* around 100 BCE is the rise of juristic science. Roman law ceased to be mere social practice, as the emergent class of jurists began to elucidate legal concepts and institutions. 'What *was* a *stipulatio*?' became a question of definition, rather than just a question of identification. How would a jurist go about defining a *stipulatio*? What was important was to identify the feature common to all instances of making a *stipulatio*, and not to worry about features that might or might not be used. The *stipulatio* might normally have involved a mixture of words and gestures but the gestures were as fluid as the words were fixed. Some people might have shared a drink, others shaken hands, others broken sticks, some produced a written document; some, no doubt, simply spoke the words. The common core of the *stipulatio* was to be found in the question and answer, in the words used. Hence, it was this that constituted the essence of the *stipulatio* in Gaius's definition.

There was no requirement of writing, however frequent its use might have been, but this does not mean that writing was irrelevant. Quintilian, for example, tells us that it was very hard to argue against written *tabulae* produced in evidence.[17] The increased use of writing would have significantly diminished the interpretative role of the judge: though he might still have to determine what the words meant, he would rarely have to decide whether there had in fact been a *stipulatio*. If a document said there had been, that would surely have been strong evidence of the fact.[18] I suspect that it was this that gave rise to the introduction of the *exceptio metus*. Whereas it would once have been possible for the judge to say that a *stipulatio* entered into under the threat of force was not a *stipulatio* at all, it would be almost impossible for him to do so when an apparently proper written document was produced as evidence. If the defendant was to go behind the document, he had to say not that there had been no *stipulatio* at all but, rather, that the *stipulatio*, which had admittedly taken place, was legally invalid.

From the end of the Republic to the beginning of the third century CE, through the whole of the classical period of Roman law, there was a tension in the conception of the *stipulatio*: on the one hand, it was an oral transaction; on the other, it increasingly consisted of a written document. As a matter of legal theory, though,

[16] O Lenel, *Das Edictum Perpetuum*, 3rd rev edn (Leipzig, Tauchnitz, 1927), 368.
[17] Quint., *Inst.*, 5.5.
[18] Nicholas (n 1), 235.

its oral nature dominated. Pomponius, at about the time of Gaius, put it in these terms, probably adopting a definition of the early imperial jurist Sabinus:

> *Stipulatio autem est verborum conceptio, quibus is qui interrogatur daturum facturumve se quod interrogatus est responderit.*
>
> A stipulation is a formulation in words, in which he who is asked replies that he will give or do what he has been asked.[19]

Although there is no absolutely explicit statement that the *stipulatio* was a spoken agreement, this is surely implicit in the description of the question and the answer. A few decades later, in his *Commentary on Sabinus*, Ulpian seems to allow no compromise in the description of the *stipulatio* as an oral transaction. His discussion[20] begins with a stark statement, again probably taken from Sabinus:

> *Stipulatio non potest confici nisi utroque loquente …*
>
> A stipulation cannot be made unless both parties speak …

It followed that a dumb person could not himself make a *stipulatio*; nor, more problematically, could a deaf person; nor could an *infans*, a child as yet too young to be able to talk; nor could people who were not present together:

> *… et ideo neque mutus neque surdus neque infans stipulationem contrahere possunt: nec absens quidem, quoniam exaudire invicem debent.*
>
> … and hence neither a deaf nor a dumb person nor an infant can contract a stipulation; nor indeed an absent person, since they should be able to hear each other.

It did not follow, though, that such people could not become parties to stipulations – only that they could not make them for themselves. There was nothing to prevent a slave's entering into a *stipulatio* for such a person, obtaining the benefit of the transaction for the *dominus*, or acting in such a way that the *dominus* became bound by it:

> *Si quis igitur ex his vult stipulari, per servum praesentem stipuletur, et adquiret ei ex stipulatu actionem. Item si quis obligari velit, iubeat et erit quod iussu obligatus.*
>
> Therefore, if any of these wishes to stipulate, let him stipulate through a slave who is present and through him acquire an action *ex stipulatu*; and if any wishes to become obliged he will instruct [a slave] and be obliged [by an *actio*] *quod iussu*.

Ulpian goes on to insist on the unity of the transaction, stating that the answer must follow more or less immediately after the question:

> *Qui praesens interrogavit, si antequam sibi responderetur discessit, inutilem efficit stipulationem: sin vero praesens interrogavit, mox discessit et reverso responsum est, obligat: intervallum enim medium non vitiavit obligationem.*

[19] D. 45.1.5.1 (Pomp. 26 *ad Sab.*).
[20] D. 45.1.1.pr (Ulp. 48 *ad Sab.*).

> A person asks a question in the presence of the other party: if he goes away before he is answered, the stipulation is ineffective; but truly, if he asks a question, goes away directly afterwards and, after he has returned, is answered, it obliges, for the short interval did not vitiate the obligation.[21]

Venuleius had earlier referred to the same requirement in a slightly different form, saying that the question and answer had to take the form of one continuous act, so that, if one of the parties had started to do something else between the asking of the question and the giving of the answer, this would not be a valid *stipulatio*.[22] We might surmise that it was accepted that the transaction needed to constitute a single, unitary act, and that, insofar as there was juristic disagreement, it concerned what exactly amounted to a unitary act. If this was still worth arguing about at the time of Ulpian, we may be fairly sure that the *stipulatio* was conceived of as an oral transaction.

Ulpian's next text seems to be exploring the boundary between oral and non-oral transactions:

> *Si quis ita interroget 'dabis?' responderit 'quid ni?', et is utique in ea causa est, ut obligetur: contra si sine verbis adnuisset. Non tantum autem civiliter, sed nec naturaliter obligatur, qui ita adnuit: et ideo recte dictum est non obligari pro eo nec fideiussorem quidem.*
>
> If someone should ask, 'Will you give?' and he respond 'Why not?', he is in the same position as being obliged; it is otherwise, if he nods without words. The person who so nods is not only not civilly obliged but neither is he naturally obliged; and so it is rightly said that he is not obliged in himself and neither is a guarantor obliged on his behalf.[23]

This text can be criticised if it is suggesting that replying *Quidni?* – 'Why not?' – to a stipulatory question was sufficient; all other texts follow the model of Gaius in using the same verb in the answer as in the question. I have no doubt that it has been substantially mutilated by the compilers but whatever point Ulpian was trying to make must have involved some contrast between the spoken *Quidni?* and the non-spoken nod of the head; and such a point could only have been worth making in the context of discussing the making of the *stipulatio* if the oral nature of the transaction were in some way important. The nod of the head might have been just as clear evidence of the promisor's agreement as his saying *spondeo* but, in the absence of speech, it was not enough to create a legal obligation.

The remainder of Ulpian's texts from Book 48 *ad Sabinum* preserved in the first fragment of D. 45.1 point in the same direction. The failure of the answer to correspond precisely to the question – dealt with in D. 45.1.1.4 and D. 45.1.1.5 – points to a problem arising in a genuinely oral exchange, rather than in the written record of an agreement; so, too, does the issue discussed in D. 45.1.1.6, whether the question might be put in one language and answered in another. This is not really

[21] D. 45.1.1.1 (Ulp. 48 *ad Sab.*).
[22] D. 45.1.137 (Ven. 1 *Stip.*).
[23] D. 45.1.1.2 (Ulp. 48 *ad Sab.*).

a point that could arise in dealing with written documents, unless we suppose that the scribe changed languages halfway through, but it could have been a real issue if parties of different nationality were speaking to each other.

Ulpian's treatment of the *stipulatio*, therefore, was closely based on its oral nature, however common the use of documents might have been in practice. If the *stipulatio* was drawn up in documentary form, it was only evidence of the oral agreement; it was written in the past tense, and described an event that had already occurred; to use what was described by Ulpian as the standard clause, *rogavit Titius, spopondit Maevius* – 'Titius asked, Maevius swore'.[24]

That Ulpian seems to have conceptualised the *stipulatio* as an oral transaction does not necessarily mean that its form was oral in practice. If, as Quintilian says, the written *tabula* was effectively conclusive proof that the *stipulatio* had been entered into,[25] it should mean that there was no need in practice for the oral exchange actually to have taken place, as long as the document said that it had occurred. Gaius is perhaps wrestling with this difficulty in his Institutes. Following his analysis of the *stipulatio*, he immediately moves on to the contract *litteris*, whose written nature must be contrasted with what has just gone before:

> *Litteris obligatio fit veluti in nominibus transscripticiis.*
>
> An obligation is made by writing: for example, by transcriptive entries.[26]

After describing the different modes of transcriptive entries that might generate legal liability, he ends his treatment by underlining the restrictive range of situations in which writing itself operated as the source of liability:

> *Praeterea litterarum obligatio fieri videtur chirografis et syngrafis, id est, si quis debere se aut daturum se scribat, ita scilicet, si eo nomine stipulatio non fiat. Quod genus obligationis proprium peregrinorum est.*
>
> Moreover, an obligation seems to be created by writing by chirographs and syngraphs; that is, if someone writes that he owes or will give, if there has not been a stipulation. This type of obligation is peculiar to peregrines.[27]

We should note the concessive sense of *videtur* here: an obligation 'seems' to arise from writing in the case of chirographs and syngraphs – but these only apply to foreigners, *peregrini*. The contrast with the Roman *stipulatio* is therefore made very firm: however common writing was as evidence of the *stipulatio*, it was not the source of the obligation.

The same tension between orality and writing at this time is well brought out by a rescript of Antoninus Pius:

> *Si interrogatione praecedente promissio usurarum recte facta probetur, licet instrumento conscripta non sit, tamen iure optimo debentur.*

[24] D. 2.14.7.12 (Ulp. 4 *ad Ed.*).
[25] Quint., *Inst.*, 5.5.
[26] G. 3.128.
[27] G. 3.134.

> If, after a preceding question, a promise of interest is proved to have been properly made, although it is not written in the instrument, nonetheless, by the best law it is owed.[28]

Money has been lent; the borrower has made a stipulatory promise to repay the money with interest but either no documentary proof has been drawn up, or there is a document but it makes no reference to the interest (*licet instrumento conscripta non sit* could have either meaning). Nonetheless, says Antoninus Pius, an action can be brought on the promise to pay the interest. The text brings out two points of significance. The first is that someone saw fit to raise the question at all and that it was sufficiently interesting that the answer was worth recording. If it was worth asking in the middle of the second century CE whether the oral *stipulatio* itself generated rights, it must have been a plausible view that, if the promise to pay interest were not embodied in the written document, it could not be enforced. Second, there is the obvious point embodied in the rescript itself, that the oral agreement was, in itself, sufficient. If the true sense of the text is that there had been a written document but that it only referred to the repayment of the loan itself and not to the payment of the interest, then the point of the text would be that, in the case of conflict between the oral agreement and the written document, the oral agreement would prevail – provided, that is, that it could be proved. This point is made by Cervidius Scaevola:

> *Si librarius in transscribendis stipulationis verbis errasset, nihil nocere, quo minus et reus et fideiussor teneretur.*
>
> If a book-keeper makes an error in transcribing the words of a stipulation, it does not destroy the fact that the defendant and the guarantor are bound.[29]

The book-keeper has made an error in transcribing the *stipulatio*; nonetheless, the promisor and his guarantor are still liable. While we cannot be certain that there had been a full oral *stipulatio* here, it may be significant that the words of the *stipulatio* are said to have been erroneously *transcribed* by the book-keeper, not erroneously *written*. If the book-keeper's function was to draw up a document embodying a *stipulatio* that had not in fact already taken place – that is, if the document itself was the source of the *stipulatio* – then we might expect to read *scribendis* rather than *transscribendis*: *transcriptio* requires that stipulatory words already existed, and they could not have done, unless there had been a *stipulatio* before the document was drawn up.

These texts all point to the primacy of the oral agreement over the written text in late classical law. Nonetheless, the cynical Western lawyer of the twenty-first century might still wonder whether there really was any need for an oral exchange. If the document was such strong evidence that the *stipulatio* had in fact taken place, why should the parties not simply write that it had happened? For example, we know that a contract of sale could be made *inter absentes*, through a *nuntius* or by letter,[30] but also that the seller could be required to give a stipulatory promise to compensate the

[28] C. 4.32.1 (Antoninus Pius to Aurelius, undated).
[29] D. 50.17.92 (Scaev. 5 *Resp.*).
[30] G. 3.136; D. 18.1.1.2 (Paul. 33 *ad Ed.*).

buyer in case of eviction by the true owner of the property.[31] If the *stipulatio* could only be made orally and *inter praesentes*, then it is hard to see how the contract of sale and purchase could be made at a distance, if the seller had to make the stipulatory promise. At some point the promise came to be implied[32] but it is hard not to suppose that, before this, a document saying that there had been a stipulatory promise would have been treated as sufficient. We are nowhere told that the deaf or dumb could not buy or sell – and it would be a very odd legal and social system that so held – yet this would seem to be the effect of a rule requiring the inclusion of a *stipulatio* that had to be made orally – unless, perhaps, a person who was deaf or dumb could not shop without taking a slave who could take the necessary *stipulatio* on his or her behalf. What of usufructuaries? They had to make a stipulatory promise to look after the property as a careful *paterfamilias*[33] but, if the deaf and dumb were precluded from making stipulatory promises, it would seem that they could only take the benefit of the usufruct if they could find a slave whom they could instruct to make the promise on their behalf. It is altogether more attractive to suppose that a document would be drafted saying that the stipulatory question had been put and the promissory answer given. Moreover, we cannot ignore the fact that the texts expressly refer to the making of a *cautio* – a written record of a transaction – rather than to the making of a promise.

Another situation perhaps reveals a way through the thicket. A small child's father dies, and a *tutor* has to be appointed to look after his interests; the *tutor* is required to make a stipulatory promise that he will take good care of the property of the *pupillus*. To achieve this, the *pupillus* should formally put to the prospective *tutor* the question whether he promises to take due care, and the *tutor* should formally respond that he promises to do so. But what if the *pupillus* is too young to speak? The cynical lawyer might say that this did not matter in practice: provided that a document was drawn up saying that the *pupillus* or his slave had stipulated and the *tutor* had promised, this would effectively be *conclusive*, and the tutor would be liable if he failed to look after the property. But this is emphatically not Ulpian's approach:

> *Exigere autem cautionem magistratus sic oportet, ut pupilli servus aut ipse pupillus, si fari potest et in praesentiarum est, stipuletur a tutoribus, item fideiussoribus eorum rem salvam fore: aut, si nemo est qui stipuletur, servus publicus stipulari debet rem salvam fore pupillo, aut certe ipse magistratus.*
>
> *Plane ubi servus publicus vel ipse magistratus stipulatur, dicendum est utilem actionem pupillo dandam.*
>
> And the magistrate should demand a *cautio* thus: a slave of the pupil or the pupil himself, if he is able to speak and is present, should stipulate from the tutors and their guarantors that the property will be safe; or if there is none who will stipulate, a public slave should stipulate that the property will be safe, or even the magistrate himself.
>
> Clearly if a public slave or the magistrate himself stipulates it has to be said that an *utilis actio* is given to the pupil.[34]

[31] D. 19.1.11.8 (Ulp. 32 *ad Ed.*, citing Neratius).
[32] D. 19.1.30.1 (Afr. 8 *Quaest.*); C. 8.44.6 (Alexander to Octavius, 8 March 222).
[33] D. 7.9.1.pr–1 (Ulp. 79 *ad Ed.*).
[34] D. 27.8.1.15–16 (Ulp. 36 *ad Ed.*).

We should note especially the final point. If necessary, the magistrate could put the question on behalf of the pupil, despite the fact that, following the normal rules of Roman law, the pupil, as a stranger to the agreement, would not have any right to enforce it. If the promise were to have any value, some remedy was obviously necessary; and Ulpian finds this by moving out of the normal rules of law and saying that an *actio utilis* – not, it should be noted, a regular *actio ex stipulatu* – should be granted.

Around 200 CE, though, at the time of Ulpian and Paul, we do begin to find a shift in the focus of the texts, putting greater weight on the written evidence than the oral exchange of question and promise. We may sense this clearly in a passing reference of Ulpian when dealing with the question of simple pacts:

> *Quod fere novissima parte pactorum ita solet inseri 'rogavit Titius, spopondit Maevius', haec verba non tantum pactionis loco accipiuntur, sed etiam stipulationis: ideoque ex stipulatu nascitur actio, nisi contrarium specialiter adprobetur, quod non animo stipulantium hoc factum est, sed tantum paciscentium.*
>
> In almost the newest part of pacts it is common to insert 'Titius asked, Maevius swore', these words are not only accepted as part of a pact but also of a stipulation: and so an *actio ex stipulatu* arises, unless the contrary is specially proved, that this was not done with the intent of stipulating but of making a pact.[35]

The modern practice is to insert – *inseri* – into a pact a clause that Titius asked the question and Maevius promised; the normal effect of this would be to turn the pact into an enforceable *stipulatio*. There is no hint here that the words of stipulation had to be spoken; Ulpian's focus is simply on the insertion of this clause into the document. Paul is more explicit:

> *Non figura litterarum, sed oratione, quam exprimunt litterae, obligamur, quatenus placuit non minus valere, quod scriptura, quam quod vocibus lingua figuratis significaretur.*
>
> We are obliged not by the form of the letters but by the meaning that the letters express, since it has been accepted that there is no less worth in writing than in what is signified by words formed by the tongue.[36]

It is not the external form of the letters that matters but the *oratio* – the meaning – that lies behind them. The important point for us is the suggestion that writing is just as good as speaking to express this meaning. The oral transaction may still be the central case but the written form can have the same effect.

In the light of this, we can turn to three texts of this period, all of which concern the interpretation of documents that seem on their face to evidence an ineffective *stipulatio*. All, I think, are dealing with the same situation: where there has been a

[35] D. 2.14.7.12. The final clause may be a post-classical addition.
[36] D. 44.7.38 (Paul. 3 *ad Ed.*).

promise by one person and a guarantee by another. Clearest is a text of Ulpian in D. 45.1.30:

> *Sciendum est generaliter, quod si quis se scripserit fideiussisse, videri omnia sollemniter acta.*
>
> It is to be known that, in general, if anyone should write that he has guaranteed, it is understood that everything has been solemnly done.[37]

The guarantor has written that he has guaranteed the debt of another; it is to be presumed that everything has been done in due form. We are, perhaps, dealing with a document incorporating a clause in something like this form: *Rogavit Titius; spopondit Maevius; fideiussit Seius.*[38] This would point to a valid *stipulatio* between Titius and Maevius, constituted by the question and answer between them; but Seius's promise of guarantee seems to lack any antecedent question, and was therefore in principle defective. Ulpian's presumption that everything had been done in due form avoids this problem.

A text of Paul – D. 45.1.134.2 – though not quite so explicit, seems to make the same point:

> *Idem respondit, cum Septicius litteris suis praestaturum se caverit pecuniam et usuras eius semisses, quae apud Sempronium depositae sint: si inter praesentes actum est, intellegendum etiam a parte Lucii Titii praecessisse verba stipulationis.*
>
> The same man replied when Septicius by his letters undertook that he would pay money that had been deposited with Sempronius with six percent interest; if it was done between parties who were present, it must be understood that it had been preceded by words of stipulation on the part of Lucius Titius.[39]

Septicius has made a *cautio*, presumably one referring to a stipulatory promise, that he will repay with interest money deposited with Sempronius. We are told that it must be understood as if Lucius Titius had earlier put the stipulatory question to Septicius. The facts behind the text are not quite clear but the most likely situation is that Septicius is guarantor to Lucius Titius for a loan of some sort made to Sempronius; I suspect it is a *depositum irregulare* made to a banker but it does not matter. If the text is concerned with a guarantee, then the situation is probably the same as that dealt with by Ulpian in D. 45.1.30: a document testifying to a question put by Lucius Titius to Sempronius, a promise by Sempronius, and a guarantee by Septicius. The fact that there is no reference to a question put by Lucius Titius to Septicius does not invalidate the guarantee. We should note that, in one respect, Paul's text seems to point to a more conservative approach than does Ulpian's: for Paul, the presumption operates only if the parties were actually present at the time.

[37] D. 45.1.30 (Ulp. 47 *ad Sab.*).
[38] D. 2.14.7.12 (Ulp. 4 *ad Ed.*).
[39] D. 45.1.134.2 (Paul. 15 *Resp.*).

Digest 45.1.134.2 has to be interpreted alongside a rescript of Severus and Antoninus preserved in the *Codex Justinianus*:

> *Licet epistulae, quam libello inseruisti, additum non sit 'stipulatum esse eum, cui cavebatur', tamen si res inter praesentes gesta est, credendum est praecedente stipulatione vocem spondentis secutam.*
>
> Although it was not added in the letter which you inserted in your petition, 'that it had been stipulated by him to whom it was undertaken', nonetheless, if it had been done by parties who were present, it is to be supposed that the word of the promisor followed a preceding stipulation.[40]

Although this rescript makes no reference to a guarantee, it may be that it refers to exactly the same case as D. 45.1.134.2. Paul was probably on the *consilium* of Severus, and would have known of rescripts issuing from it; he might even have been responsible for drafting the text. It is telling that the same qualification is made as in Paul's text in the Digest, that the presumption of a preceding question applies only if the parties were present together – *si inter praesentes gesta est*.

Another phenomenon begins to be observed at about this time. A shift becomes visible in the wording of stipulatory documents, moving from a formulation in the past tense to a formulation in the present. A good example of this is the letter discussed by Paul in D. 24.1.57:

> '*quae summa mihi numerata est … daturam restituturam me sine ulla dilatione: spondeo*'.
>
> 'I swear to give and restore without delay the sum which has been paid to me'.[41]

We need not concern ourselves with the rest of the text; all that needs to be noted is the verb *spondeo*, in the first-person present tense, replacing the orthodox *spopondit*. This is not a *cautio* purporting to describe an event that has happened but a document purporting to embody the promise in itself. It is likely that this use of the present tense reflects the form of Greek chirographs, where, as we have seen, the writing was recognised as the source of the obligation, a form superseded in the papyri from around 221 CE by a stipulatory clause in the perfect tense, in accordance with the Romans' formal requirements.[42]

It would be good to be able to say that tension between oral and written formulations of the *stipulatio* was dissolved after the time of Ulpian and Paul but the evidence suggests that it was not. It is still plainly visible in the *Sententiae Pauli*, the little teaching manual of the early fourth century wishfully attributed to Paul:

> *Verborum obligatio inter praesentes, non etiam inter absentes contrahitur. Quod si scriptum fuerit instrumento promisisse aliquem, perinde habetur, atque si interrogatione praecedente responsum sit.*

[40] C. 8.37.1 (Severus and Antoninus to Secundus, 15 April 200).

[41] D. 24.1.57 (Paul. 7 *Resp.*).

[42] V Arangio-Ruiz, 'L'application du droit romain en Égypte après la constitution antoninienne' (1948) 29 *Bulletin de l'Institut d'Égypte* 83, 122.

> An obligation by words is contracted between those who are present, not those who are absent. So that if it was written in the instrument that someone had promised, it is taken to have been an answer to a preceding question.[43]

While there is no formal incompatibility between the two sentences, the requirement of the presence of the parties contained in the first sentence looks back to the need for an oral exchange, while the second sentence is clearly concerned with the interpretation of a superficially defective written document, reproducing in a generalised form the rule found in the rescript of Severus and Antoninus. We should not try to interpret too dogmatically any text drawn from the *Sententiae* but it may be that we can see here a distinction between legal theory and practice: as a legal construct, the *stipulatio* was an oral agreement made between parties who were present together but, in practice, the documentary form saying that someone had promised was treated as proof that there had been an oral question and answer.

A century later, I think it is fairly clear that there was just such a separation between the law as taught in the law schools and the law as enforced in the courts. So far as the former is concerned, it is likely that the basic text used was still the Institutes of Gaius, pointing towards the *stipulatio* as an oral agreement, and stating expressly that its validity stems from the form of words used. The practice, though, is reflected in the well-known constitution of the Emperor Leo:

> *Omnes stipulationes, etiamsi non sollemnibus vel directis sed quibuscumque verbis consensu contrahentium compositae sint, legibus cognitae suam habeant firmitatem.*

This is a text that has been frequently commented upon but a literal translation makes its direction obvious:

> All stipulations recognised by the law shall have full force, even if they are not drawn up in solemn or direct words, so long as they are in words that reveal the consent of the parties.[44]

It is sometimes suggested that the effect of this is to make all agreements into stipulations, provided that the consent of the parties is revealed, but this must be wrong. Its opening words make it clear that it is only concerned with stipulations – in whatever form they are drawn up – that are *compositae*. Clearly, it presupposes that we can know that we have a *stipulatio*, independently of the verbal form. The use of *compositae* strongly suggests that we know this from the fact that it is contained in a written document bearing some mark that it is meant to be a *stipulatio* – and it should be noted that, in other constitutions of this year, Leo was concerned with the operation of written documents.[45] Assuming this is so, the constitution has to be interpreted as a further step in the process of generalisation of the rescript of

[43] PS 5.7.2.
[44] C. 8.37.10 (Leo to Erythrius, 1 January 472).
[45] eg, C. 2.4.42 (Leo and Anthemius to Erythrius, 1 July 472), C. 8.17.11 (Leo to Erythrius, 1 July 472). I am grateful to Mike Macnair for this point.

Severus and Antoninus: saying that, whatever words are used in the written *stipulatio*, it will be enforced as such.

I shall not delve at any length into model of the *stipulatio* found in Justinian's Institutes;[46] that would require a paper of its own. Two points need to be made, though. First is that Justinian's Institutes bring together, unsuccessfully in my view, the law in theory and the law in practice. In English translation:

> A verbal obligation is contracted by question and answer, as where we stipulate that something will be given to or done for us ... Formerly, the words used in making this kind of contract were as follows:
>
> Do you engage yourself? [*Spondes*?] I do engage myself. [*Spondeo.*]
>
> Do you promise? [*Promittis*?] I do promise. [*Promitto.*]
>
> Do you promise on your good faith? [*Fidepromittis*?] I do promise on my good faith. [*Fidepromitto.*]
>
> Do you make yourself *fideiussor*? [*Fideiubes*?] I do make myself *fideiussor*. [*Fideiubeo.*]
>
> Will you give? [*Dabis*?] I will give. [*Dabo.*]
>
> Will you do? [*Facies*?] I will do. [*Faciam.*]
>
> ...
>
> ... Anciently indeed it was necessary to use the formal words just mentioned, but the constitution of Leo was afterwards enacted, which, removing formalities of expression, requires only that the parties understand one another and mean the same thing, no matter what words they use.[47]

Leo's constitution in C. 8.37.10, originally applicable only to the interpretation of documents evidencing stipulations, is now taken across into the very definition of the *stipulatio*, producing a sharp conflict between the requirement of oral question and answer found at the beginning of the text and the loose acceptance of any words whatsoever at the end of the text. Moreover, in removing the rule of C. 8.37.10 from its original context, there is now no distinction to be drawn between the theoretical requirement of orality and the practical sufficiency of writing. Hence:

> A verbal obligation made between absent persons is also void. But, as this doctrine afforded matter of strife to contentious men, who alleged, after some time had elapsed, that either they or their adversaries were not present, we issued a constitution addressed to the advocates of Caesarea, in order to provide for the speedy determination of such suits. By this we have enacted that written acts which declare that the contracting parties were present shall be considered as indisputable evidence of the fact, unless the party who has recourse to such shameless allegations makes it evident, by the most manifest proofs, either by writing or by credible witnesses, that either he or his adversary was in some other place during the whole day in which the instrument was made.[48]

[46] GD MacCormack, 'The Oral and Written Stipulations in the Institutes' in PG Stein and ADE Lewis (eds), *Studies in Justinian's Institutes in memory of J. A. C. Thomas* (London, Sweet & Maxwell, 1983) 96.

[47] Inst 3.15.pr–1.

[48] Inst 3.19.12.

It is impossible to ignore the attempt here to hold together the reality of the written document and the primacy of the oral exchange. The contract requires, as in classical law, an oral exchange of question and answer; but to deny the truth of a document that refers to this is 'shameless' – *turpis* – and a person who has recourse to such an allegation must prove conclusively – *manifestissimis probationibus* – that the parties could not possibly have met on the day on which the agreement was written to have occurred.[49]

I should conclude by making a general point, applicable to modern legal systems as much as to Roman law. Social practices are complex, and attempts to encapsulate them in legal rules are always in some way inadequate. The legal rule, as we see very clearly through the history of the *stipulatio*, is always the result of a process of essentialisation, identifying its minimum core and ignoring its peripheral aspects. This minimum core may be so tightly bound that it can remain in place despite very significant changes in practice; so long as these changes can be assigned to the periphery of the institution, perhaps treated as evidence rather than as matters of substance, there is no need to rethink the core of the rule. Once the rule has become embedded in the system, it becomes increasingly difficult to remove it; even when the practical changes become so significant that they cannot simply be marginalised, the rule can nonetheless retain its original form by the use of fictions and presumptions that simultaneously shore it up and undermine its practical import.

[49] Compare C. 8.37.14.2 (Justinian to John PP, 1 November 531), making it even clearer: the parties must have been in different cities for the whole of the day in question.

7

Principle and Practice in the *Pacta Adiecta*

BOUDEWIJN SIRKS

I.

A principle is a concept that serves as a basis for other concepts, or for practice, or for explanation.[1] In law, principle can refer to a basic rule but it can also designate a concept – a free-standing notion or idea – used in the application of rules, as part of juristic method. In this sense of juristic concept, the principle I explore in this chapter is the condition in contract. As the pragmatic antithesis of this principle, I focus on the interpretation of contracts by close textual analysis of their content; when applying this method, the outcome depends on the way in which the contract was phrased, rather than on any independent concept of a condition. As subject matter, I take the three more or less standardised ancillary agreements (*pacta adiecta*) in the contract of sale and purchase.[2] These are the *pactum displicentiae* (sale on approval), the *in diem addictio* (sale subject to a better offer) and the *lex commissoria* (sale subject to forfeiture in default of payment on the due date). The reason for selecting these three *pacta adiecta* is that they reveal a tension between applying the concept of a condition and applying the textual explanation of what the parties agreed; the very validity of the contract depends on this tension. As ancillary agreements (*pacta*), they derive their force from the contract of sale and purchase, if they were agreed concurrently with it; they can be seen as integral parts of the sale and purchase contract, or as parallel agreements (*conventiones*). The contract of sale and purchase with which we are dealing is the

[1] 'Prinzip' in J Ritter and K Gründer (eds), *Historisches Wörterbuch der Philosophie*, vol 7: P–Q (Darmstadt, Wissenschaftliche Buchhandlung, 1971) col 1336.

[2] There are, of course, other examples of conditions in contracts: eg, D. 19.2.9.3 (Ulp. 32 *ad Ed.*) has a *lex locationis* (condition in a lease of land); and D. 19.2.13.10 (Ulp. 32 *ad Ed.*) a *lex operis locandi* (condition in the placing out of work to be done). The contracts are in force regardless of these conditions. It is different with testaments but, first, these are – in modern terms – unilateral expressions of the testator's will and, second, the circumstances of a testament require a definitive disposition.

consensual form, rather than the alternative concluded by two stipulations. The condition itself can be seen as suspensive or resolutive: that is, either the contract does not become operative until the condition is fulfilled (suspensive), or the contract is operative upon agreement but later annulled when the condition is fulfilled (resolutive).

II.

Before proceeding further, we have to examine the place and evolution of the condition in Roman jurisprudence. Jurists like Servius Sulpicius and Quintus Mucius Scaevola, of the first century BCE, engaged with this concept; Scaevola even designed the *cautio Muciana* to solve the problem of testamentary conditions that heirs or legatees *not* do something.[3] Unfortunately, there is no indication of what might have influenced the thinking of these early jurists. Rhetorical influence is possible but we find no clear discussion of this in Quintilian's *Institutio Oratoria*. There is an obvious connection with causality: depending on the condition, a cause has, or does not have, a particular effect. With regard to causation, we are in Aristotelian and Stoic territory, with the arrival of Greek teachers of philosophy in Rome in the second century BCE. However, those philosophers – such as Chrysippus, cited by Cicero – dealt with conditions in the context of logic.[4] Accordingly, they did not deal with the question whether a condition is suspensive or resolutive. The older jurists, of the late Republic, preferred to keep to textual interpretation, and refrained from reasoning based on categorising a term as a condition. However, the Roman jurists of the early Principate were well prepared to address conditions in the context of the law.

A condition was for them a future event, the occurrence or non-occurrence of which was unknown, and upon which a legal effect depended. There are two titles in the Digest where conditions are discussed intensively. One is the title on conditions: D. 35.1 *De conditionibus et demonstrationibus et causis et modis eorum quae in testamento scribuntur* ('On conditions and case descriptions and reasons and the ways they are written down in testaments'). As the rubric indicates, it is in the context of testamentary dispositions that the matter is extensively treated. The question whether a condition is suspensive or resolutive is important here, since the deceased often wanted to provide for unforeseen circumstances, yet the inheritance – including conditional manumissions – has to be wound up, in one way or another. Hence the distinctions 'certain or uncertain whether' (*certum* or *incertum an*) and 'certain or uncertain when' (*certum*

[3] D. 35.1.7.pr (Ulp. 18 *ad Sab.*). See D. 35.1.1 (Pomp. 3 *ad Q. Muc.*); D. 35.1.6.1 (Pomp. 3 *ad Sab.*), mentioning Servius.

[4] See, eg, S Bobzien, 'Stoic Logic' in B Inwood (ed), *The Cambridge Companion to the Stoics* (Cambridge, Cambridge University Press, 2003) 85, 94 on conditionals in logic, mentioning Chrysippus. The philosophers do not discuss the suspensive or resolutive effect of conditions.

or *incertum quando*). If it the event was impossible – 'if I shall touch the sky with my finger' (*si digito caelum attigero*)[5] – the condition would make the whole disposition void. Conversely, if it was certain that the event would take place, the effect was immediately valid – 'if I shall not touch the sky with my finger' (*si digito caelum non attigero*). In the other title, D. 45.1 *De stipulationibus* ('On formal promises'), the condition is also extensively discussed, because often the validity of the promise depended on it. For example, a stipulation was not valid if it depended on the will of the promising person.[6] Hence, it is not possible to formulate the *pactum displicentiae* in the form of a stipulation ('Do you promise me to pay the price for the horse if it is acceptable to you after three days?'). Was it effective to embed in a consensual sale the term, 'We agree that you buy the horse for ten if it is acceptable to you after three days'? We shall return to this; it probably it had to be formulated differently. Another matter discussed in D. 45.1 is how to formulate conditions for doing or not doing something. What if a promise depended on the act of an unknown person – for example, 'If somebody will ascend the Capitoline Hill, do you promise to give me ten?' This was considered valid.[7] This is, in fact, the kind of condition we see in the *in diem addictio*. Promises with the condition of a time limit did not take effect until the time had elapsed. This is the kind of condition present in the *lex commissoria*. It was also possible for a condition to depend on the person who would benefit by its effect.

Regarding the nature of these conditions, the Romans interpreted a condition either as suspensive,[8] or as resolutive.[9] Where a condition was seen as suspensive, there was, in theory, no legal effect until the condition was satisfied. Nevertheless, the suspension casts its shadow over other legal dealings; for example, a slave sold conditionally cannot be manumitted.[10] If the condition was seen as resolutive, the legal act was valid immediately but the occurrence of the condition annulled it. In relation to obligations that were considered *stricti iuris* and to acts concerning legal status – such as manumission, grant of ownership, or institution as heir – resolutive conditions were plainly unacceptable.[11]

Thus, there was considerable discussion among the jurists about the nature and structure of conditions as prerequisites for the validity of legal dispositions. The issues were primarily discussed in the context of testaments and stipulations but also elsewhere. Once difficulties arose in particular cases, did the jurists stick to the principles elaborated, or did they make concessions to practicality? The case of the *pacta adiecta* is a good touchstone.

[5] An example borrowed from G. 3.98 and Inst. 3.19.11 on *stipulatio*.

[6] D. 45.1.17 (Ulp. 28 *ad Sab.*); D. 45.1.46.3 (Paul. 12 *ad Sab.*).

[7] D. 45.1.108.pr (Iav. 10 *Epist.*).

[8] D. 35.1.79.pr (Pap. 1 *Def.*); D. 40.4.44 (Mod. 10 *Resp.*).

[9] D. 18.1.3 (Ulp. 28 *ad Sab.*).

[10] D. 33.5.14 (Iav. 2 *ex Cass.*); D. 40.9.29.1 (Gai. 1 *de Manumiss.*).

[11] D. 40.4.33 (Paul. 12 *Quaest.*); D. 28.5.89 (Gai. l.s. *de Casib.*). See M Kaser, *Das römische Privatrecht*, 2nd rev edn (Munich, Beck, 1971), 252–58.

III.

First, the *pactum displicentiae*, where the buyer could trial the object sold. Paul states that, if it was agreed that if the thing sold displeased the buyer within a certain time, it could be returned, and that an *actio empti* would be available according to Sabinus, or else an *actio in factum* close to an *actio empti*, for the buyer to force the seller to take it back.[12] The condition was formulated as: 'if the thing that is sold displeases within a certain time, it should be returned' (*ut res quae venit, si intra certum tempus displicuisset, redderetur*). We should note, first, that whether or not the condition is realised depends on the buyer; theoretically the agreement should, therefore, be void. Second, there is a time limit: after the period has ended, the agreement is valid, unless the primary condition had been realised. On the first point, let us say that the (prospective) buyer replies within the time limit that the thing displeases him. The question is whether there is an action available for the no-longer buyer to insist that the no-longer seller take back the thing. For Sabinus, the contract still exists, so he allows the action on purchase (*actio empti*). However, we can also consider that the entire agreement is (retrospectively) void *ab initio* once the condition is realised, and thus an action on the case close to the action on purchase (*actio proxima empti in factum*) is necessary – this is Paul's view. Paul adheres to the theory that there had been a contract of sale and purchase (*res quae venit*) but that it had subsequently been voided. For Sabinus, it was different: he most likely considered that the *pactum* could be enforced though the actions of the principal contract.

We see similar dissent between older and younger jurists with Ulpian at D. 19.5.20.1. Mela poses the question: If mules are sold with the *pactum displicentiae* and with the term that, if they did not please, rent should be paid for each day, and the mules are stolen within that period, what may be claimed? Price and rent, or only rent?[13] For Mela, it depends on the words: 'If I shall give you mules so that you may try them and if they please you, you shall buy them; if they do not please you, you shall give me something for every day' (*si mulas tibi dedero ut experiaris et si placuissent emeres si displicuissent ut in dies singulos aliquid praestares*). If a purchase has been concluded (*emptio iam erat contracta*) the price can be claimed. The condition can no longer be fulfilled, in the sense that the buyer can no longer renounce and return within the period set. Mela applies here the theory – the

[12] D. 18.5.6 (Paul. 2 *ad Ed.*): *Si convenit, ut res quae venit, si intra certum tempus displicuisset, redderetur, ex empto actio est, ut Sabinus putat, aut proxima empti in factum datur.* See also D. 41.4.2.5 (Paul. 54 *ad Ed.*): *Sed et illa emptio pura est, ubi convenit, ut, si displicuerit intra diem certum, inempta sit.*

[13] D. 19.5.20.1 (Ulp. 32 *ad Ed.*): *Item apud Melam quaeritur, si mulas tibi dedero ut experiaris et, si placuissent, emeres, si displicuissent, ut in dies singulos aliquid praestares, deinde mulae a grassatoribus fuerint ablatae intra dies experimenti, quid esset praestandum, utrum pretium et merces an merces tantum. Et ait Mela interesse, utrum emptio iam erat contracta an futura, ut, si facta, pretium petatur, si futura, merces petatur: sed non exprimit de actionibus. Puto autem, si quidem perfecta fuit emptio, competere ex vendito actionem, si vero nondum perfecta esset, actionem talem qualem adversus desultorem dari.*

principle of a condition – and, thus, the *actio venditi* is available. However, if the wording is read differently, as a mere agreement to test, with a conditional sale and purchase postponed until after the test (*emptio iam erat ... futura*), the owner can claim only the rent. Mela does not say anything about the action but Ulpian thinks the action on sale (*actio venditi*) applies if the sale was concluded, and otherwise an action on the case (*actio praescriptis verbis* – an *actio in factum* in Mela's time), because it was not a contract of hire but an innominate contract (to use later terminology). Mela and Ulpian leave it to the wording – the facts and circumstances – to determine whether there is a contract of sale and purchase with a resolutive condition, or an innominate contract with a suspensive condition.

In D. 18.5.6, Paul interprets the condition as resolutive. He says the same in D. 41.4.2.5 about the condition 'if it will have displeased within a day, it will be unsold'.[14] Ulpian in another text takes the same view: 'If a thing is sold in this way, on terms that if it displeases it is unsold, it is a fact that it is not sold under a condition but that the sale is resolved under a condition'.[15] The words 'will be returned' (*redderetur*) and 'will be unsold' (*inempta esset*) have the same effect. The kind of condition that applies depends, therefore, on the text of the agreement. One might argue that, as long as the prospective buyer has not yet decided that the thing handed over is what he wanted, the condition is suspensive: the object of the sale is not yet certain. Perhaps the risk of loss (*periculum*) was the reason for preferring the resolutive interpretation.

In D. 19.5.20.pr, Labeo proposes the case where horses are on trial for three days (*si in triduo displicuissent, redderes*) and the prospective buyer uses them to win a race, after which he has no use for the horses and does not want to buy them.[16] Does the putative seller have an action? Ulpian does not think that he has the action on sale (*actio venditi*) but rather an action on the case (*actio praescriptis verbis*): 'because between us this had been transacted: that you would accept a free trial, not that you would run a race' (*nam inter nos hoc actum ut experimentum gratuitam acciperes non ut etiam certares*). The wording is essentially the same as in D. 18.5.6, yet Ulpian opts for this construction. How might Labeo have replied? Judging from Ulpian's rejection (*et puto verius*), Labeo allows the action on sale (*actio venditi*). Perhaps Labeo's view is that the horses did not displease the prospective buyer – or else he would not have used them; using them for a race was probably more than just testing. Accordingly, the suspensive condition is not fulfilled, and the seller has an action under the contract. In contrast, Ulpian perhaps focuses on the words 'you did not want to buy' (*emere nolueris*); in this case, it can be understood as a situation like D. 19.5.20.1 – an innominate contract with a suspensive condition to buy.

[14] D. 41.4.2.5 (Paul. 54 *ad Ed.*): *Sed et illa emptio pura est, ubi convenit, ut, si displicuerit intra diem certum, inempta sit.*

[15] D. 18.1.3 (Ulp. 23 *ad Sab.*): *Si res ita distracta sit, ut si displicuisset inempta esset, constat non esse sub condicione distractam, sed resolvi emptionem sub condicione.*

[16] D. 19.5.20.pr (Ulp. 32 *ad Ed.*).

IV.

A similar pattern can be discerned with the *in diem addictio*. This is a *pactum adiectum* used to enlarge the number of interested buyers, by extending the period in which an offer may be made. It is used predominantly in sales of land – both private and at state auction – because the amount of capital required is often not easily available or raised, and thus interested buyers cannot react quickly. The sale is made subject to the condition of a better offer's being received within one, two, or more years. If a better offer is received, the first buyer may bid again, or else the new buyer pays him the original purchase price and pays the seller the surplus as *adiectio*. Here, it is not possible to assume an innominate contract with a suspensive condition for sale: in an auction there is, once an offer is accepted, sale and purchase. What, then, is the effect of the *in diem addictio* condition? Paul gives a formulation, perhaps a standard one in state auctions: 'That estate is bought for you for 100, unless if someone will have offered better terms before the next Kalends of January, by which the object leaves the owner'.[17] The first part recalls words of the *mancipatio*, and could indicate the claim of civil ownership, which is what we might expect at a state auction. It is also clear that the offer – combined with the acceptance, we may assume – of better terms suffices to displace that claim. To all appearances, we have here a resolutive condition that has a direct effect in property law. However, Ulpian says that two interpretations of the *in diem addictio* are possible, depending on the wording of the agreement: 'whether it is a pure purchase but one resolved under a condition, or really rather a conditional sale, is the question' (*utrum pura emptio est, sed sub condicione resolvitur, an vero condicionalis sit magis emptio, quaestionis est*). He replies: 'To me it seems that what has been done matters more' (*mihi videtur verius interesse, quid actum sit*).[18] Evidently, Paul's example was not standard. The key is in the formulation. If it is said: 'it is sold but, when better terms are offered, it is a pure sale that will be annulled subject to a condition' (*ut meliore allata condicione discedatur, erit pura emptio, quae sub condicione resolvitur*). Alternatively: 'if it is sold unless better terms are offered, it is a conditional purchase' (*ut perficiatur emptio, nisi melior condicio offeratur*). For Ulpian, purchase subject to the suspensive condition is a conditional purchase, whereas purchase subject to the resolutive condition is a 'pure' purchase. It seems to depend, for example, on use of words like 'to make perfect, conclude' (*perficere*) and 'to withdraw' (*discedere*), as opposed to words like 'to dissolve' (*resolvere*); the above use of 'leaves the owner' (*a domino abeat*) is definitively in the category of withdrawing (*discedere*). The reason for the terminological

[17] D. 18.2.1 (Paul. 5 *ad Sab.*): *In diem addictio ita fit: 'ille fundus centum esto tibi emptus, nisi si quis intra kalendas Ianuarias proximas meliorem condicionem fecerit, quo res a domino abeat'.*

[18] D. 18.2.2.pr (Ulp. 28 *ad Sab.*): *Quotiens fundus in diem addicitur, utrum pura emptio est, sed sub condicione resolvitur, an vero condicionalis sit magis emptio, quaestionis est. Et mihi videtur verius interesse, quid actum sit: nam si quidem hoc actum est, ut meliore allata condicione discedatur, erit pura emptio, quae sub condicione resolvitur: sin autem hoc actum est, ut perficiatur emptio, nisi melior condicio offeratur, erit emptio condicionalis.*

distinction is this, for which Ulpian cites Julian: in a pure – we might say 'outright' – purchase, the buyer begins to usucapt, is entitled to the revenues, and bears the risk of accidental loss of the object (*periculum*).[19] Why is this? Paul gives the answer in the succeeding text: once the object is lost, better terms can no longer be offered.[20]

Clearly, reality imposes itself on theory and confines conditionality to the area where it cannot do any harm. The construction of the *in diem addictio* necessitated, on one hand, treating the first buyer as lawful possessor immediately (with, at least in state auctions, protection against claims of third parties) and recognising his concomitant right to enjoy the fruits, and, on the other hand, treating the second buyer in the same fashion. If the sale were suspensive, the second buyer would retrospectively be entitled to all past fruits, which the first buyer then had to surrender. What about fruits where the object itself had been lost in the interim? Fruits such as the offspring of a slave woman might be interesting enough for a second buyer to bid.[21] Julian denied this possibility: you actually bid for the fruits, not the object itself; as a bid for something else, this was not a better offer for the thing sold.[22] For Julian (and Ulpian), this follows from the *pura emptio* view. We do not know what Pomponius would have said. If a sale and purchase under *in diem addictio* was suspensive, he denied the possibility to usucapt or enjoy the revenues.[23] The cases in the Digest title are all examples of pure purchase (*emptio pura*), except probably D. 18.2.16, where the first buyer has to restore to the seller the fruits of the *domus* sold.

An example of what Ulpian defines as a conditional purchase (*emptio condicionalis*) is found with Paul in D. 41.4.2.4: 'unless if someone offers better terms, the purchase is perfect' (*nisi si quis meliorem condicionem attulerit, perfectam esse emptionem*). Paul cites Julian, who thinks the buyer in this case can usucapt and is entitled to the fruits.[24] That contradicts Ulpian and Neratius in D. 18.2.4.pr and, indeed, other jurists considered this a conditional sale.[25] However, Julian interpreted the condition here as resolutive. The solution may be slightly disingenuous,

[19] D. 18.2.2.1 (Ulp. 28 *ad Sab.*): *Ubi igitur secundum quod distinximus pura venditio est, Iulianus scribit hunc, cui res in diem addicta est, et usucapere posse et fructus et accessiones lucrari et periculum ad eum pertinere, si res interierit …*

[20] D. 18.2.3 (Paulus 5 *ad Sab.*): *Quoniam post interitum rei iam nec adferri possit melior condicio.*

[21] This may seem strange but a better-drafted term would express precisely what would constitute a better offer: apart from a greater price, there might be less onerous conditions, quicker payment, better surety, etc, even if the price were lower; see D. 18.2.4.6 (Ulp. 28 *ad Sab.*) *in fine*. That could be the case here. See also D. 18.3.5 (Ner. 5 *Membr.*).

[22] D. 18.2.4.1 (Ulp. 28 *ad Sab.*): *Idem Iulianus libro quinto decimo quaerit, si res in diem addicta interciderit vel ancilla decesserit, an partus vel fructus eius nomine adiectio admitti possit. Et negat admittendam adiectionem, quia alterius rei quam eius quae distracta est non solet adiectio admitti.*

[23] D. 18.2.4.pr (Ulp. 28 *ad Sab.*): *Ubi autem condicionalis venditio est, negat Pomponius usucapere eum posse nec fructus ad eum pertinere.*

[24] D. 41.4.2.4 (Paul. 54 *ad Ed.*): *Si in diem addictio facta sit, id est nisi si quis meliorem condicionem attulerit, perfectam esse emptionem et fructus emptoris effici et usucapionem procedere Iulianus putabat: alii et hanc sub condicione esse contractam, ille non contrahi, sed resolvi dicebat, quae sententia vera est.*

[25] Whereas Ulpian uses the language of pure and conditional purchase (*pura emptio, condicionalis emptio*) in D. 18.2.2.pr, his references to Julian (D. 18.2.2.1) and Pomponius (D. 18.2.4.pr) use the language of pure sale (*pura venditio*) and conditional sale (*condicionalis venditio*), respectively.

perhaps inspired by the wish to avoid all the trouble of a suspensive sale. Contrary to the *pactum displicentiae*, which did not last more than a few days, the *in diem addictio* could last for years in the case of estates and land, and the longer period made the occurrence of problems more likely. Julian's interpretation solved problems if the *in diem addictio* stretched over, say, three years, and the buyer had in the meantime harvested fruits or the land had deteriorated. On Julian's solution, the fruits were the buyer's, as was the risk.

Thus, according to Ulpian, whether the *in diem addictio* condition was suspensive or resolutive depended on the text of the agreement. For reasons of practicality, however, there was a definite preference for the resolutive interpretation; so strong was this preference that the purchase subject to a resolutive condition was called pure rather than conditional, whereas the purchase subject to a suspensive condition was called conditional (*condicionalis*). Notwithstanding that practice, the pure purchase (*emptio pura*) was, in truth, also conditional.

V.

Turning to the *lex commissoria*, our point of departure is Sabinus's opinion in D. 41.4.2.3, mere exegesis of the terms of the pact: 'if it is bought in this way that, unless the price has been paid within a certain period, the thing will become unbought; he will not usucapt unless the price is paid'.[26] This is, in my opinion, an interpretation based on a close reading of the text of the agreement. Paul and Ulpian, on the other hand, discuss the problem in more abstract terms, contrasting agreement (*conventio*) and condition (*condicio*). Paul's reaction to Sabinus is: 'but let us see, whether this is a condition or an agreement' (*sed videamus, utrum condicio sit hoc an conventio: si conventio est, magis resolvetur quam implebitur*). Thus, if it is interpreted as a condition, it is a suspensive condition. If it is interpreted as an agreement, it is an agreement to dissolve the sale if the price is not paid in time. Paul casts the agreement (*conventio*) here as a *pactum adiectum* to the contract, which becomes effective if the condition is realised. In effect, it is a resolutive condition.

We find Ulpian's statement in D. 18.3.1: 'If an estate has been sold under a *lex commissoria*, it is rather the case that the purchase is dissolved under a condition than that the contract is entered under a condition'.[27] The word 'rather' (*magis*) indicates a debate – but what debate? It is a debate about the nature of the condition. It could be interpreted as the resolutive condition providing that, if the buyer does not pay in time, the sale is off, because the seller has set a limit to his line of credit. Alternatively, it could be interpreted as the suspensive condition that, if the

[26] D. 41.4.2.3 (Paul. 54 *ad Ed.*): *Sabinus, si sic empta sit, ut, nisi pecunia intra diem certum soluta esset, inempta res fieret, non usucapturum nisi persoluta pecunia. Sed videamus, utrum condicio sit hoc an conventio: si conventio est, magis resolvetur quam implebitur.*

[27] D. 18.3.1 (Ulp. 28 *ad Sab.*): *Si fundus commissoria lege venierit, magis est, ut sub condicione resolvi emptio quam sub condicione contrahi videatur.*

buyer pays in time, the sale is operative, since a sale is only substantively perfect when the price is paid. Since the *lex commissoria* could stretch over years – land was costly and the buyer had to find the money – questions about fruits and risk arise, just as with the *in diem addictio*.

The buyer should not do something by which his ability to pay on the due date would be frustrated; he could not use the *lex* in this way. The *lex* was for the benefit of the seller. The seller could, on the *dies solvendi*, declare that he waived the *lex*. He had to do this *statim*;[28] this precluded waiver at a later time. Digest 18.3.7, a text of Hermogenian, nevertheless puts it differently: 'If the seller claims the price after the last day of the *lex commissoria*, he cannot change his mind and come back to the *lex*'.[29] All the same, this text (like D. 18.3.6.2) refers to acts after the due date (*dies solvendi*); such acts do not necessarily imply that the seller still had the option to exercise the *lex commissoria* – or that he did not. The ancillary agreement comes into force upon the due date; the seller might not immediately reclaim the thing sold. Claiming or accepting money afterwards can be seen as a waiver of his right under the *lex* to reclaim his property. Claiming money would imply unilateral revival of the contract, which goes against the requirement for *consensus* in sale and purchase. In contrast, accepting money would imply the continuing wish of the buyer to buy and to offer payment; in that case, a new contract would be concluded.

A different problem is encountered in D. 44.3.6.1. A slave is sold subject to a *lex commissoria*; the price is not paid; and the slave is returned. The question is which of the buyer and the seller should have the benefit of the buyer's time in possession: since the *usucapio* period for a slave was one year, this was an important point.[30] It is treated akin to the return of performances where a sale and purchase is annulled (*redhibitio*): the seller who has regained the sold slave may add the buyer's time in possession to his own for the purposes of usucapion. Again, we see that the condition was not treated as resolutive or as suspensive: an analogy with *redhibitio* was used to solve the problem. If it had really been resolutive, the slave should have been considered as having been in the seller's possession all along. Apparently, the buyer's possession was too much of a fact to be set aside for the sake of theory; however, the sale was not treated as subject to a suspensive condition, either.

VI.

The *lex commissoria* presented additional problems in practice. A famous example is Rutiliana's case in D. 4.4.38.pr.[31] Aemilius Larianus bought the Rutilian estate from

[28] See D. 18.3.4.2 (Ulp. 32 *ad Ed.*), quoting Papinian and also D. 18.3.6.2 (Scaev. 2 *Resp.*).

[29] D. 18.3.7 (Hermog. 2 *Iuris Epit.*): *Post diem commissoriae legi praestitutum si venditor pretium petat, legi commissoriae renuntiatum videtur, nec variare et ad hanc redire potest.*

[30] D. 44.3.6.1 (Afr. 9 *Quaest.*).

[31] This famous case has been discussed by many scholars, including, most recently: ES Daalder, *De rechtspraakverzamelingen van Julius Paulus: Recht en rechtvaardigheid in de rechterlijke uitspraken van keizer Septimius Severus* (The Hague, Boom Juridisch, 2018). For a discussion of the case, see AJB Sirks, 'The causa Rutiliana' (forthcoming).

Ovinius, subject to a *lex commissoria*: paying part of the price now, he would pay half of the remainder within two months, and the other half within the two months after that, or else the sale would be off. Larianus died within the first two months, and was succeeded by his daughter Rutiliana, whose guardians did not pay at all; they were later replaced by new guardians. Having several times admonished the guardians to pay, Ovinius sold a year later to Claudius Telemachus. Rutiliana (through her guardians) requested restoration to the former situation (*in integrum restitutio*), which was denied at first instance. Emperor Septimius Severus, however, granted Rutiliana her request, on the basis that the *lex* took effect – that is, the due date fell – when she was under guardianship. Paul thought it should have been granted on the ground that Ovinius had forfeited his right to the *lex* by admonishing the buyer to pay.[32]

Paul's initial stance was the same as that taken at first instance by the praetor and the Urban Prefect: the first instalment had not been paid in time; the contract of sale and purchase was annulled; the *lex* was resolutive. Paul's second position was different. The realisation of the condition had annulled the contract but, by admonishing the guardians for payment, Ovinius had waived his right under the *lex commissoria* and revived the sale. How Paul viewed the condition doctrinally is obscure. The best explanation appears to be that he extended the rule about accepting payment after the ultimate due date (*dies solvendi*) and interpreted admonishments, which would normally count as advice or recommendations, as amounting to waiver of the *lex*. However, this would mean that Ovinius, having declared the *lex* applicable (else he could not waive it), could then waive its effect and validate the contract – unilaterally and retrospectively. That goes against the basis of consensual agreements: agreement between parties. Apparently, Paul assumes that the buyer is still willing to contract – but where is the evidence for this? True, the *lex* operates for the benefit of the seller alone; but, if a buyer cannot pay in time and the seller applies the *lex*, why should evidence of the buyer's continuing willingness to be bound be admitted, apart from his offering payment? The situation is different where the buyer, regretting the annulment, later offers the money: in this case, acceptance by the seller constitutes a new sale at that moment, on the same conditions; but that was not the case here.

[32] D. 4.4.38.pr (Paul. 1 *Decr.*): *Aemilius Larianus ab Ovinio fundum Rutilianum lege commissoria emerat data parte pecuniae, ita ut si intra duos menses ab emptione reliqui pretii partem dimidiam non solvisset, inemptus esset, item si intra alios duos menses reliquum pretium non numerasset, similiter esset inemptus. Intra priores duos menses Lariano defuncto Rutiliana pupillaris aetatis successerat, cuius tutores in solutione cessaverunt. Venditor denuntiationibus tutoribus saepe datis post annum eandem possessionem Claudio Telemacho vendiderat. Pupilla in integrum restitui desiderabat: victa tam apud praetorem quam apud praefectum urbi provocaverat. Putabam bene iudicatum, quod pater eius, non ipsa contraxerat: imperator autem motus est, quod dies committendi in tempus pupillae incidisset eaque effecisset, ne pareretur legi venditionis. Dicebam posse magis ea ratione restitui eam, quod venditor denuntiando post diem, quo placuerat esse commissum, et pretium petendo recessisse a lege sua videretur: non me moveri quod dies postea transisset, non magis quam si creditor pignus distraxisset, post mortem debitoris die solutionis finita. Quia tamen lex commissoria displicebat ei, pronuntiavit in integrum restituendam. Movit etiam illud imperatorem, quod priores tutores, qui non restitui desiderassent, suspecti pronuntiati erant.*

It is no wonder that the emperor was disgusted with the *lex commissoria.* In view of these problematic examples, the best that may be said about the *lex commissoria* is that any principle of condition here is lost.

VII.

The principle of a condition, with its effect being either suspensive or resolutive, was well known in the late Republic and frequently applied in the interpretation of testamentary clauses. It differed in the area of agreements. In the late Republic, interpretation of the three standard ancillary agreements (*pacta adiecta*) to sale and purchase is determined by reference to close examination of the text of the agreements. Interpretation determined by reference to the principle or concept of a condition arises in the early Principate, with allowances made for practical reasons. The *pactum displicentiae* is basically a suspensive condition; the *in diem addictio* a resolutive one. The *lex commissoria* is read as a side agreement and interpreted textually according to circumstances – here, the practice of the parties reigns, rather than abstract principle.

Regarding the principle of the condition as a prerequisite for the validity of legal dispositions, the case of the three *pacta adiecta* demonstrates that in contracts, too, the principle was known and referred to but that, in practice, the old technique of simply interpreting the text of the agreement was strong, particularly in relation to the *lex commissoria*, in view of the many complications it entailed.

8

Plato, Principle and Pragmatism: Market Regulation in D. 50.11.2

CONSTANTIN WILLEMS

I. The Starting Point: D. 50.11.2 (Call. 3 *Cogn.*)

In the Digest title 'On Markets' (*de Nundinis*), a very peculiar fragment, D. 50.11.2 (Call. 3 *Cogn.*), has been passed down, which appears to be of economic more than legal relevance. The author of this text is Callistratus, a jurist from the Greek-speaking east of the Roman Empire who lived during the reign of Emperor Septimius Severus (second to third century CE)[1] and authored at least five works attested to in the Digest.[2] The text is extracted from the third book of Callistratus's monograph on *Cognitiones*. We are relatively well-informed about these *Libri de cognitionibus*, Callistratus's six books on 'judicial examinations'[3] pertaining to special legal proceedings,[4] as a total of 53 fragments are passed down through the Digest. Callistratus's linguistic and cultural background becomes apparent from four Greek quotations from imperial rescripts of the Emperors Hadrian, Antoninus Pius and his co-regent Lucius Verus, and Pertinax, which can be found in the *Libri de cognitionibus*.[5] In contrast to these sources,

[1] On Callistratus, see D Liebs, 'Römische Provinzialjurisprudenz' in H Temporini (ed), *Aufstieg und Niedergang der römischen Welt*, vol II.15 (Berlin, De Gruyter, 1976) 288, 310–12; D Liebs, 'Compte rendu: Roberto Bonini, I libri de cognitionibus di Callistrato, Ricerche sull'elaborazione giurisprudenziale della cognitio extra ordinem, vol 1, Giuffrè, Milano, 1964' (1966) 34 *Leg Hist Rev* 254, 256.

[2] Namely *de Cognitionibus Libri Sex, ad Edictum Monitorium Libri Sex, Institutitionum Libri Tres, de Iure Fisci et Populi Libri Quatuor, and Quaestionum Libri Duo*; see O Lenel, *Palingenesia Iuris Civilis*, vol 1 (Leipzig, Tauchnitz, 1889), cols 81–106.

[3] MH Crawford, trans of D. 50.11.2 in WAJ Watson (ed), *The Digest of Justinian*, vol 4 (Philadelphia, University of Pennsylvania Press, 1985), 440.

[4] O Behrends and others (eds), *Corpus Iuris Civilis. Text und Übersetzung*, vol 2 (Heidelberg, CF Müller, 1995), 24: 'außerordentliche Gerichtsverfahren'. On the *cognitio* process in Roman private law see T Rüfner, 'Imperial *Cognitio* Process' in C Ando, PJ du Plessis, and K Tuori (eds), *The Oxford Handbook of Roman Law and Society* (Oxford, Oxford University Press, 2016), 257 and C Willems, 'Kognitionsprozess' in U Babusiaux and others (eds), *Handbuch des Römischen Privatrechts* (Tübingen, Mohr Siebeck, 2020) § 15 (forthcoming).

[5] See D. 50.6.6.2 (Call. 1 *Cogn.*) (Greek rescript by Emperor Pertinax to Silvius Candidus); D. 50.6.6.6 (Call. 1 *Cogn.*) (Greek rescript by the *divi fratres*); D. 8.3.16 (Call. 3 *Cogn.*) (Greek rescript by Emperor Antoninus Pius); D. 5.1.37 (Call. 5 *Cogn.*) (Greek rescript by Emperor Hadrian). On these, see A Plisecka, 'The Use of Greek by Roman Jurists' in L Beck Varela, P Gutiérrez Vega and A Spinosa

the fifth source in which Callistratus quotes Greek at length, D. 50.11.2, stands out. One reason for the peculiar character of this source is that the fragment does not give an explicit account of an imperial decision but quotes another illustrious authority verbatim, namely the philosopher Plato:[6]

> Should someone order crop farmers or fishers to carry their *utensilia* to town in order to sell them themselves, the supply of victuals would become destitute as the farmers are called off their work: They shall, as soon as they have given the wares to sale, transfer them and return to their work. Indeed, among the Greeks, Plato, of supreme wisdom and authority, while establishing the ways in which a state can be inhabited in a good and blessed way, in the first place deemed those merchants to be necessary. As he speaks in his second book on the *Republic*: 'In fact, one needs many farmers and other workers and others who take care of import and export; those, however, are the merchants. If, on the other hand, a farmer, say, produced something and carried it to the market, or another one of the workers, but did not arrive at the same time as those who came with the intention to get something from him in exchange, would he leave his work behind and sit idle on the market? – "Not at all," he said, "but there are people who see this and place themselves at disposal for this work."'[7]

II. Callistratus and His 'aderenza alla realtà economica e sociale'

To use Salvatore Pulliatti's words, the text shows Callistratus's 'aderenza alla realtà economica e sociale', his eye for the socio-economic relations in legal life.[8] Callistratus calls for famers and fishers to return to their work immediately after

(eds), *Crossing Legal Cultures* (Frankfurt am Main, Peter Lang, 2009) 59, 70 f; G Bortolucci, 'Index verborum Graecorum quae in Institutionibus et Digestis occurrunt' (1906) 76 *Archivio giuridico Filippo Serafini* 353, 355 f.

[6] On the Roman jurists' explicit borrowings from Greek philosophy, see J Giltaij, 'Greek Philosophy and Classical Roman Law: A Brief Overview' in PJ du Plessis, C Ando and K Tuori (eds), *The Oxford Handbook of Roman Law and Society* (Oxford, Oxford University Press, 2016) 188, especially 194; U Babusiaux, '*Quod Graeci … vocant* – Emblematischer Codewechsel in den Juristenschriften' in J Hallebeek and others (eds), *Inter cives necnon peregrinos: Essays in honour of Boudewijn Sirks* (Göttingen Vandenhoeck & Ruprecht, 2014) 35, 36–42; LC Winkel, 'Le droit romain et la philosophie grecque, quelques problèmes de méthode' (1997) 65 *Leg Hist Rev* 373, 377. A list of cases in which the jurists quote *ex auctoribus Graecis* is given by Bortolucci (n 5), 354 f.

[7] D. 50.11.2 (Call. 3 *Cogn.*): *Si quis ipsos cultores agrorum vel piscatores deferre utensilia in civitatem iusserit, ut ipsi ea distrahant, destituetur annonae praebitio, cum avocentur ab opere rustici: qui confestim ubi detulerint mercem, tradere eam et ad opera sua reverti debeant. Denique summae prudentiae et auctoritatis apud Graecos Plato cum institueret, quemadmodum civitas bene beate habitari possit, in primis istos negotiatores necessarios duxit. Sic enim libro secundo politeias ait*: δεῖ γὰρ πλειόνων ἄρα γεωργῶν τε καὶ τῶν ἄλλων δημιουργῶν καὶ τῶν ἄλλων διακόνων τῶν γε εἰσαξόντων καὶ ἐξαξόντων ἕκαστα· οὗτοι δέ εἰσιν ἔμποροι. κομίσας δὲ ὁ γεωργὸς εἰς τὴν ἀγοράν τι ὧν ποιεῖ ἤ τις ἄλλος τῶν δημιουργῶν μὴ εἰς τὸν αὐτὸν χρόνον ἥκῃ τοῖς δεομένοις τὰ παρ' αὐτοῦ ἀνταλλὰξασθαι, ἀργήσει τῆς αὐτοῦ δημιουργίας καθήμενος ἐν ἀγορᾷ; οὐδαμῶς, ἦ δ' ὅς, ἀλλ' εἰσὶν οἵ τοῦτο ὁρῶντες ἑαυτοὺς ἐπὶ τὴν διακονίαν τάττουσι ταύτην.

[8] S Puliatti, *Il de iure fisci di Callistrato e il processo fiscale in età severiana* (Milan, Giuffrè, 1992), 48.

having passed on their *utensilia*, ie their crop or catch,[9] to a merchant. The source refers to the need for specialisation and division of labour in economic life[10] and to the losses of efficiency which would occur outside an economy of divided labour.[11] Should fishers and farmers put their crop on the market themselves, first production would suffer,[12] as finally would the *annonae praebitio*.

On the one hand, *annonae praebitio* could mean only the publicly procured supply of corn.[13] On the other hand, especially as not only farmers (*cultores agrorum*) but also fishermen (*piscatores*) are mentioned in the text, this could mean the general market supply.[14] The notion of *annona* has the basic meaning of the annual revenue from agricultural cultivation, but could – as shown by Evenlyn Höbenreich – encompass not only grain, oil and wine, but also fish and fish sauce (*garum*).[15] Such adverse effects on the market supply for food would in the first place affect arable crops for which cultivation and monetisation depend on the rhythm of the agricultural

[9] On this sense of *utensilia* see the Gloss in Ioannis Fehius (ed), *Corpus Iuris Civilis Iustinianei*, vol 3 (Lyons, 1627), col 1772 n s: 'Utensilia. *id est frumentum, & gallinas, & pisces*'. See also KE Georges, '*utensilis*' in KE Georges, *Ausführliches lateinisch-deutsches Handwörterbuch*, vol 2, 11th edn (H Georges ed, Hannover, Hahn, 1962) col 3330: 'subst., ūtēnsilia, ium, n., brauchbare Dinge, bes. zur Wirtschaft (Lebensmittel, Geräte)'. Forms of *utensilia* only occur in three instances in the *Corpus Iuris*. HG Heumann and E Seckel, '*utensilia*' in *Handlexikon zu den Quellen des römischen Rechts*, 10th edn (A Thon ed, Graz, Akademische Druck- und Verlagsanstalt, 1958) 607 only mentions D. 33.7.12.28 (Ulp. 20 *ad Sab.*) where the word is used in the context of a *fundus instructus* and indeed means 'instruments' or 'utensils'. The other two instances are both from Callistratus's *Libri de cognitionibus*, namely D. 50.2.12 (Call. 6 *Cogn.*) (*Eos, qui utensilia negotiantur et vendunt*) and our text, D. 50.11.2 (Call. 3 *Cogn.*). In both texts, *utensilia* seems to have the broader sense of 'commodities' mentioned above, see GC Treitschke, trans of D. 50.2.12 and of D. 50.11.2 in CE Otto, B Schilling and CFF Sintenis (eds), *Das Corpus Juris Civilis in's Deutsche übersetzt*, vol 4 (Leipzig, Carl Focke, 1832), 1161 and 1197: both times 'Waaren'. More cautiously Crawford (n 3), 424 and 440: 'objects of daily use' and 'things' respectively.

[10] See Puliatti (n 8), 35: 'necessità dell'ordinato apporto degli operatori economici e dei produttori di beni per l'esistenza di una bene istituita e felicemente "vivibile" città'; R Bonini, *I libri de cognitionibus di Callistrato: Ricerche sull'elaborazione giurisprudenziale della cognitio extra ordinem*, vol 1 (Milan, Giuffrè, 1964), 75: 'l'esigenza di un ordinato svolgimento della produzione e dello scambio, attraverso la creazione di precisi meccanismi d'incontro tra le varie categorie, rurali e cittadine'; C Rodríguez and MJ Azaustre Fernández, 'Algunas consideraciones sobre las ferias y los mercados en Derecho Romano y su recepción en Derecho Español' (2016) 17 *Revista Internacional de Derecho Romano* 145, 181: 'división de funciones'; J Andreau, 'Concepts économiques dans les œuvres des juristes romains' in E Lo Cascio and D Mantovani (eds), *Diritto Romano e economia. Due modi di pensare e organizzare il mondo (nei primi tre secoli dell'Impero)* (Pavia, Pavia University Press, 2018) 223, 237: 'division du travail'. MC Besta, 'Pesca e pescatori nell'Egitto greco-romano' (1921) 2 *Aegyptus* 67, 69 f and 72 reproduces evidence from papyri found in Egypt which attests a coexistence of fishers (ἁλιεῖς) and fishmongers (ἰχθυοπῶλαι).

[11] *cf* M Silver, 'In Dubious Battle: An Economic Analysis of Emperor Hadrian's Fish and Olive Oil Laws' (2011) 7 *Roman Legal Tradition* 1, 7: 'Callistratus recognises that productive resources were being wasted by an attempt to "cut out the middleman"'.

[12] See L de Ligt, 'The Nundinae of L. Bellicius Sollers' in H Sancisi-Weerdenburg (ed), *De agricultura: in memoriam Pieter Willem de Neeve (1945–1990)* (Amsterdam, Gieben, 1993) 238, 259: 'agricultural production will be adversely affected'.

[13] See Crawford (n 3) 440: 'supply of corn'.

[14] See de Ligt, 'The Nundinae of L. Bellicius Sollers' (n 12), 259: 'food supply'; S Günther, '(K)einer neuen Theorie wert? Neues zur Antiken Wirtschaftsgeschichte anhand Dig. 50,11,2 (Callist. 3 cognit.)' (2017) 124 *Gymnasium: Zeitschrift für Kultur der Antike und Humanistische Bildung* 131, 137: 'Versorgungsangebot'; Andreau (n 10), 237: 'ravitaillement'.

[15] See E Höbenreich, *Annona: juristische Aspekte der stadtrömischen Lebensmittelversorgung im Prinzipat* (Graz, Leykam, 1997), 24.

calendar.[16] At harvest time, the farmers are tied to their fields and so cannot simultaneously procure the distribution of their crop at a permanent market.[17]

III. Possible Historical Background: IGII/III^2 (1.2) 1103

Callistratus discusses fishermen alongside farmers. Fishing, especially in the Mediterranean Sea, should be less dependent on the seasons. Therefore, the mention of fishers is, at least at first sight, astonishing. This is all the more striking as Strabo reported that, to take just one example, fish were caught in the Black Sea even in winter, in frozen bodies of water.[18]

Therefore, the economic historian Morris Silver assumed that Callistratus's reference to fishing might allude to a legislative measure taken by Emperor Hadrian in 124/125 CE, aiming at the regulation of the local fish market around Athens.[19] In the *Inscriptiones Graecae* we find the following text, which, unfortunately, is only passed down to us in a very fragmentary way,[20] especially in the first lines:

IGII/III^2 (1.2) 1103

... Λ. ει μετρη[σ ???]

δὲ τὴν διοβελίαν [... c.11 ....]α μηδὲ [....c.14 ....τοῖς]

δὲ ἐν'Ελευσεῖνι ἁλιεῦσιν ἀτέλειαν ἰχθύ[ων εἶναι ὅταν ἐν'Ελευ-]

σεῖνι ἐν τῆι ἀγορᾶι πιπράσκωσιν, ὡς μένῃ [.c.6. ἵνα τὸ διὰ τὰ][21]

εἰσαγώγια ὄφελος εἰς μέγα τι ἀπαντήσῃ· τ[οὺς δὲ ... c.10 ...][22]

[16] K Ruffing, 'Auctions and Markets in the Roman Empire' in M Frass (ed), *Kauf, Konsum und Märkte. Wirtschaftswelten im Fokus – Von der römischen Antike bis zur Gegenwart* (Wiesbaden, Harrassowitz, 2013) 213, 219: 'In a world in which production mainly is based on agriculture ... production and monetarization of crops to a high degree are governed by the rhythms of the agricultural calendar'.

[17] Another way out – not mentioned in the source – would be an auction of the crop; on this alternative to permanent markets, resulting in lower transaction cost: ibid, 215–20.

[18] *cf* D Bohlen, *Die Bedeutung der Fischerei für die antike Wirtschaft* (Hamburg, Diss U Hamburg, 1937), 18 fn 42, referring to Strabo, *Geographica* VII.307: ὀρυκτοί τέ εἰσιν ἰχθύες οἱ ἀποληφθέντες5 ἐν τῷ κρυστάλλῳ τῇ προσαγορευομένῃ γαγγάμῃ – 'And fish that become caught in the ice are obtained by digging with an implement called the "gangame"' (Strabo, *Geography*, vol III: Books 6–7 (HL Jones trans, Cambridge, Harvard University Press, 1924), 225).

[19] Silver (n 11) 1 and 3.

[20] First attempts of a reconstruction have been made, eg, by C Curtius, 'Mittheilungen aus Athen und dem Piraeus' (1870) 29 *Philologus* 691, 693–95. On the finding history, see JH Oliver, *Greek Constitutions of Early Roman Emperors from Inscriptions and Papyri* (Philadelphia, American Philosophical Society, 1989), 193 and JM Cortés Copete, 'Adriano y la regulación de los mercados cívicos: una nueva lectura de IG II^2 1103' (2015) 46 *Habis* 239, 240.

[21] Reconstruction proposed by P Graindor, *Athènes sous Hadrien* (Cairo, Imprimerie Nationale, 1934), 127: μὲν ᾖ [εὐθενία, τὸ δὲ διὰ τὰ]; likewise E Lytle, 'Fishless mysteries or high prices at Athens? Re-examining IG II 1103' (2007) 64 *Museum Helveticum* 100, 101. On these lines, see Cortés Copete, 'Adriano y la regulación de los mercados cívicos' (n 20) 243–46.

[22] Reconstruction proposed by A Wilhelm, 'Inschriften aus Erythrai und Chios' (1909) 12 *Jahreshefte des österreichischen archäologischen Instituts in Wien* 126, 147: *ἰχθυοπώλας*; likewise HW Pleket in *SEG* 21-502. Different proposal by Graindor (n 21), 127: καπήλους; likewise Lytle (n 21), 101. On the reconstruction of this and the following line, see Cortés Copete, 'Adriano y la regulación de los mercados cívicos' (n 20), 246–50.

καὶ τοὺς πάλιν καπηλεύοντας πεπαῦσθ[αι … … .c.18 … … .][23]
βούλομαι ἢ ἔνδειξιν αὐτῶν γείνεσθαι πρ[ὸς τ]ὸν κ[ή]ρυκα τῆς ἐξ Ἀ-
ρείου πάγου βουλῆς· τὸν δὲ εἰσάγειν εἰς το[ὺς Ἀ]ρεοπαγείτας, τοὺς δὲ
τειμᾶν ὅτι χρὴ παθεῖν ἢ ἀποτεῖσαι· πιπρασκέ[τω]σαν δὲ πάντα ἢ αὐτοὶ οἱ
κομίζοντες ἢ οἱ πρῶτοι παρ' αὐτῶν ὠνού[με]νοι· τὸ δὲ καὶ τρίτους ὠ-
νητὰς γεινομένους τῶν αὐτῶν ὠνίων με[τα]πιπράσκειν ἐπιτείνει
τὰς τειμάς. ταύτην τὴν ἐπιστολὴν στήλῃ ἐ[γ]γράψαντες ἐν Πειραεῖ
στήσατε πρὸ τοῦ δείγματος. εὐτυχεῖτε.
ἐπιμελητεύοντος τῆς πόλεως Τ'Ιουλίου'Ηρωδιαν[οῦ] Κολλυτέως.

… If you measure […] but the fee of two obols […] but not [… for those] who fish in Eleusis, that there is exemption of tax for fish if they sell in Eleusis on this market, so that on the one hand [a good market offer] exists [and on the other hand the] revenue from import tax is significant concerning its amount: However, We want to prevent the [(fish) merchants] and the re-sellers [from avarice], and that there should be a denunciation against them before the herald of the council meeting on the Areopagus. Indeed, the latter should introduce proceedings before the members of the Areopagus, who, in fact, stipulate what will be announced to be suffered or paid. Indeed, either those who acquired it themselves, or the first ones to purchase it from them should sell everything, as if also the purchasers of the same wares, standing third in line, resell them, this increases the prices. Put this letter, engraved into a stele, in the Piraeus in front of the Deigma. Fare well!

Under the epimelete of the city Titius Iulius Herodianus, from Collytus.[24]

With this inscription, Emperor Hadrian[25] firstly grants a tax exemption (ἀτέλεια)[26] for the local fishermen[27] on the market in Eleusis,[28] a place of worship dedicated to the fertility goddesses Demeter and Kore, situated next to ancient Athens, in the modern urban district of Athens called Elefsina. It remains, however, unclear which tax the fishermen are exempted from[29] and whether this tax exemption was

[23] Reconstruction proposed by Wilhelm (n 22), 147: τῆς αἰσχροκερδείας; likewise Pleket (n 22) and Lytle (n 21), 101.

[24] For another English translation see Oliver (n 20), 194.

[25] See the since then undisputed statement by Wilhelm (n 22), 147: 'Der Schrift nach gehört der Stein in die Zeit Hadrians'.

[26] On this, see Höbenreich (n 15), 278.

[27] With reference to the fragmentary nature of the beginning of the inscription, some authors opine that what we call the 'fish law' was directed to commodities in general: J Day, *An Economic History of Athens under Roman Domination* (New York, Columbia University Press, 1942), 192 f. Others remain sceptical, as FF Abbott and AC Johnson, *Municipal Administration in the Roman Empire* (New York, Russell & Russell, 1968), 414.

[28] On the town, see K Clinton, 'The Eleusinian Mysteries: Roman Initiates and Benefactors, Second Century B.C. to A.D. 267' in W Haase (ed), *Aufstieg und Niedergang der Römischen Welt*, vol II.18.2 (Berlin, De Gruyter, 1989) 1499; O Kern, 'Eleusis 1' in A Pauly and others (eds), *Paulys Realencyclopädie der classischen Altertumswissenschaft*, vol V.2 (Stuttgart, JB Metzler, 1905) col 2336.

[29] Wilhelm (n 22), 147 presumes that Hadrian exempts the fishermen of Eleusis from a 'sales tax' in the amount of two obols which they would have to pay when selling their catch in the Piraeus. From the first century CE onwards, there were several instances of such 'sales taxes' of 0.5% to 1% in the

only granted during the Eleusinian 'mysteries',[30] a religious festival honouring both goddesses.[31] Second, the imperial decree is addressed to 're-sellers' (τοὺς πάλιν καπηλεύοντας): fish shall only be sold by those who caught it (αὐτοὶ οἱ κομίζοντες) or by those who purchased it immediately from the fishers (οἱ πρῶτοι παρ' αὐτῶν ὠνού[με]νοι) – there shall be no further trade levels,[32] as the longer the supply chain becomes via the insertion of third persons (τρίτοι), the higher the purchase price gets (ἐπιτείνει τὰς τειμάς).

Adolf Wilhelm, professor of Greek antiquity and epigraphy in Vienna, wrote in 1909 that the imperial decree was based on a desire to restrict intermediate trade.[33] Modern economic historians also view Hadrian's 'fish law' as based on an intent 'to suppress', 'to curb', or 'to cut out the middleman'.[34]

In the case at hand, this objective could, on economic and political grounds, aim at strengthening the fish market in the coastal village of Eleusis, while at the same time prohibiting the transport of fish via the port of Athens, the Piraeus, to Athens itself by intermediaries and their sale there at an excessive price.[35]

Roman Empire, the so-called *centesima rerum venalium* (Tac., *Ann.* 1.78.2), *ducentesima auctionum* (Suet., *Calig.* 16.3), or *vectigal venalium rerum* (D. 50.16.17.1 (Ulp. 10 *ad Ed.*)), see S Günther, *Vectigalia nervos esse rei publicae. Die indirekten Steuern in der Römischen Kaiserzeit von Augustus bis Diokletian* (Wiesbaden, Harrassowitz, 2008), 127–48, especially 133 f, and G Vivenza, 'Roman Economic Thought' in W Scheidel (ed), *The Cambridge Companion to the Roman Economy* (Cambridge, Cambridge University Press, 2012) 25, 29. Another possibility would be related to harbour taxes; on these, see C Adams, 'Transport' in W Scheidel (ed), *The Cambridge Companion to the Roman Economy* (Cambridge, Cambridge University Press, 2012) 218, 232 f; on incentives to lower them see AI Wilson, 'A Forum on Trade' in W Scheidel (ed), *The Cambridge Companion to the Roman Economy* (Cambridge, Cambridge University Press, 2012) 287, 289. On the other hand, Höbenreich (n 15), 278 fn 270 refers to the evidence from other provinces that fishermen were obliged to pay a certain tax for the concession of the right to fish, see eg, for Egypt, Besta (n 10), 69 and 71.

[30] No connection to the mysteries is drawn by Wilhelm (n 22), 146–8. Advocating a connection with the mysteries: K Harter-Uibopuu, 'Hadrian and the Athenian Oil Law' in R Alston and O van Nief (eds), *Feeding the Ancient Greek City* (Louvain, Peeters, 2008) 127, 138; L de Ligt, *Fairs and Markets in the Roman Empire. Economic and Social Aspects of Periodic Trade in a Pre-Industrial Society* (Amsterdam, Gieben, 1993), 233; Oliver (n 20), 194; Day (n 27), 193; Graindor (n 21), 128 f. The same might be true for the fixed fish prices known from a third century BCE inscription from the Boiotian town of Akraiphia; it is suspected that the fish prices were fixed on the occasion of the *Ptoia*, a quinquennial festival honouring Apollo Ptoios, to prevent visitors being taken advantage of by local merchants; see C Vatin, 'Le tarif des poissons d'Akraiphia' in F Salviat and C Vatin (eds), *Inscriptions de Grèce centrale* (Paris, De Boccard, 1971) 95, 109; de Ligt, *Fairs and Markets in the Roman Empire* (n 30), 222 65; C Willems, 'Markt und Recht in der Spätantike' in K Droß-Krüpe and K Ruffing (eds), *Market(s) – Market Buildings – Market Squares* (Wiesbaden, Harrassowitz, 2020) (forthcoming).

[31] See Clinton (n 28), 1499–539; O Kern, 'Mysterien (eleusinische Weihen)' in A Pauly and others (eds), *Paulys Realencyclopädie der classischen Altertumswissenschaft*, vol XVI.2 (Stuttgart, Alfred Druckenmüller Verlag, 1935), col 1211.

[32] See de Ligt, *Fairs and Markets in the Roman Empire* (n 30), 214.

[33] Wilhelm (n 22), 146: 'Absicht der Beschränkung des Zwischenhandels'. See also Cortés Copete, 'Adriano y la regulación de los mercados cívicos' (n 20), 256: 'la lucha contra los intermediarios'.

[34] Silver (n 11), 3 and 5; Abbott and Johnson (n 27), 414; Day (n 27), 192. This view is approved by JM Cortés Copete, 'Koinoi Nomoi: Hadrian and the Harmonization of Local Laws' in O Hekster and K Verboven (eds), *The Impact of Justice on the Roman Empire. Proceedings of the Thirteenth Workshop of the International Network Impact of Empire (Gent, June 21–24, 2017)* (Leiden, Brill, 2019) 105, 117.

[35] Lytle (n 21), 105; Höbenreich (n 15), 278: the measure should be an incentive to fishers to sell on the local agora ('den Fischern den Verkauf auf der örtlichen agora schmackhaft machen'); Oliver (n 20), 195.

The fishmongers of the Greek cities were noted for their exorbitant prices.[36] For instance, Apuleius's *Metamorphoses*, written in the second century CE,[37] tell the story of a foreigner to the city of Hypata who bargained with a local fishmonger and managed to negotiate a fairly decent price reduction of 80 per cent, a price that the local Aedile still considered excessive.

By striving to expand the market offer in Eleusis,[38] Hadrian intensified the 'market thickness'[39] in the small coastal town and tried to counter-steer the artificial price increase for staple food[40] in the market in Athens. The decreed position of the inscription[41] advocates for the fact that a regulation of the market price in Athens was intended as well; at least the copy found was not supposed to be erected in Eleusis but in the port of Athens, the Piraeus, in front of the Deigma, the market hall where the merchants showed samples of their goods to prospective customers before selling them *en gros ou en détail*.[42]

Silver opposes Hadrian's conclusions that the use of middlemen results in increased prices for consumers.[43] He considers the exclusion of intermediate trade to raise the total cost of production, as the producer is kept from producing while spending time at the market – in this case, the producer may not be forced to share his profits but, at the same time, might realise less profit compared with the situation in which he is able to focus fully on his expertise by delegating the marketing to a specialised third party.[44] It is in this context that Silver mentions the text from the Digest, written by Callistratus.[45] He argues that Callistratus – unlike Hadrian – realised that productive resources would be wasted by cutting out the middleman.[46]

[36] See – with many examples from the sources – C Wachsmuth, *Die Stadt Athen im Alterthum*, vol 2.1 (Leipzig, Teubner, 1890), 464–74.

[37] Apul., *Met.* 1.24–25; see Wilhelm (n 22), 148; H Graßl, 'Marktorganisation und Preisbildung in der römischen Kaiserzeit' in R Rollinger and C Ulf (eds), *Commerce and Monetary Systems in the Ancient World: Means of Transmission and Cultural Interaction* (Stuttgart, Steiner, 2004) 352, 353; Lytle (n 21), 105; L de Ligt, 'Roman Law, Markets and Market Prices' in PJ du Plessis, C Ando, and K Tuori (eds), *The Oxford Handbook of Roman Law and Society* (Oxford, Oxford University Press, 2016) 660, 665.

[38] Höbenreich (n 15), 214 fn 36, 231 fns 101 and 278.

[39] On this concept A Roth, *Who Gets What – and Why: The New Economics of Matchmaking and Market Design* (Boston, Houghton Mifflin Harcourt, 2015), 8.

[40] Höbenreich (n 15) 214 fn 36: 'artifizielle Preissteigerungen von Grundnahrungsmitteln'.

[41] On this, see Cortés Copete, 'Adriano y la regulación de los mercados cívicos' (n 20), 261 and Oliver (n 20), 194 f.

[42] On this place and its function Höbenreich (n 15), 278 fn 269; Oliver (n 20), 195; Wachsmuth (n 36), 103 and 106–109; E Szanto, 'Δεῖγμα' in A Pauly and others (eds), *Paulys Realencyclopädie der classischen Altertumswissenschaft*, vol IV.2 (Stuttgart, JB Metzler, 1901) col 2383.

[43] Silver (n 11), 4: 'Hadrian's peculiar policy for Eleusis clearly implements a belief that sales to and by middlemen are unproductive – that is, repeated sales serve only to raise consumer prices'.

[44] ibid, 5: 'The individual who "cuts out" the middleman will typically raise his total cost because he is a relatively high-cost producer of middleman-type processes and/or because he is diverting his time from productive (or even consumptive) processes in which he has a comparative advantage – ie, is a relatively low-cost producer. Total costs will surely rise when rulers prevent transactors from utilizing the services of market makers'.

[45] ibid, 6 f.

[46] ibid, 7: 'Callistratus recognizes that productive resources were being wasted by an attempt to "cut out the middleman"'.

In fact, transporting merchandise from Eleusis to Athens would entail considerable cost: according to 'Google Maps for Ancient Historians', the *Orbis* database of the University of Stanford, created by Walther Scheidel and Elijah Meeks,[47] transport over land from Eleusis to Athens covered 20 km and would have taken 0.7 days, making a day trip there and back impossible. A fisher who went to the market himself would consequently lose two working days selling his wares. The sea route, spanning 31 km, would take 0.2 days, which is why – dependent on daylight – the feat of fishing, sailing to Athens, and returning the same day could have been possible in theory. However, sea transport is fraught with risk and it remains doubtful whether the same ships that could be used for fishing could also be used for a longer transport over the open sea.

Silver therefore concludes that Hadrian's measure was counterproductive and led to unproductiveness and inflation on the fish market.[48] However, against this it must be noted that Hadrian does not advocate for direct marketing to be performed by the fishermen. Not only should those who caught the fish be entitled to sell it, but also the first buyers (πρῶτοι) who obtained it directly from the fishermen. Consequently, Hadrian accepts introducing a second person as a seller, and only the extension of the chain of distribution via the introduction of third persons (τρίτοι) shall be prohibited. Therefore, the argument of unproductivity must be rebutted and Silver's hypothesis cannot stand.

IV. Hadrian as the Agent Addressed by Callistratus?

One of the merits of Silver's paper is the way in which he stresses the possible connection between Hadrian's inscription and Callistratus's text from the *Libri de cognitionibus*. Indeed, earlier works have mentioned both sources side by side, but – as far as I can see – neither a direct connection between the sources nor a reference to Hadrian's measure by Callistratus has been suggested.

Twenty-six fragments contained in the Digest testify to the fact that Callistratus was familiar with the rescripts issued by Hadrian. In these fragments, the jurist quotes rescripts or other legal measures of this very emperor, mostly verbatim.[49]

[47] Available online at: orbis.stanford.edu.

[48] Silver (n 11), 5.

[49] Call. 5 *Cogn.* D. 5.1.37 (Call. 5 *Cogn.*) (*divus Hadrianus* τῷ κοινῷ τῶν Θεσσαλῶν *Graece rescripsit*); D. 5.1.47 (Call. 1 *Quaest.*) (*divus Hadrianus rescripsit*); D. 22.5.3.1 (Call. 4 *Cogn.*) (*divus Hadrianus Vibio Varo legato provinciae Ciliciae rescripsit*); D. 22.5.3.3 (Call. 4 *Cogn.*) (*divus Hadrianus Iunio Rufino proconsuli Macedoniae rescripsit*); D. 22.5.3.6 (Call. 4 *Cogn.*) (*divus Hadrianus rescripsit*); D. 42.1.33 (Call. 5 *Cogn.*) (*divus Hadrianus, aditus per libellum a Iulio Tarentino ... rescripsit*); D. 47.9.7 (Call. 2 *Quaest.*) (*divus Hadrianus edicto praecepit*); D. 47.21.2 (Call 3 *Cogn.*) (*divus Hadrianus in haec verba rescripsit*); D. 48.2.19.1 (Call. 5 *Cogn.*) (*divus Hadrianus rescripsit*); D. 48.3.12.pr (Call. 5 *Cogn.*) (*divus Hadrianus Statilio Secundo legato rescripsit*); D. 48.8.14 (Call. 6 *Cogn.*) (*divus Hadrianus in haec verba rescripsit*); D. 48.15.6.pr (Call. 6 *Cogn.*) (*divus Hadrianus in haec verba rescripsit*); D. 48.19.28.6 (Call. 6 *Cogn.*) (*divus Hadrianus in haec verba rescripsit*); D. 48.19.28.13 (Call. 6 *Cogn.*) (*edicto divi Hadriani*); D. 48.19.35 (Call. 1 *Quaest.*) (*divus Hadrianus rescripsit*); D. 48.20.2 (Call. 6 *Cogn.*) (*divus Hadrianus*

Accordingly, D. 50.11.2 could also contain a reference – at least indirectly – to the Hadrianic legislation.

Should this be the case, it would be very important to ascertain the agent Callistratus addresses in the fragment at hand. The fragment concerns the person, (*ali-*)*quis*, giving out the order (*iusserit*) to the farmers and fishermen to sell their crop and catch directly. Luuk de Ligt suspects that the source addresses an owner of slaves or land and, consequently, that there was a *iussum* in the technical sense of Roman law.[50] Valerio Marotta, on the other hand, proposes that the person giving this order was one of the magistrates entrusted with the administration of the *annona* and with the regulation of the exchange of goods.[51] Additionally, a possible addressee of Callistratus's statement could be the legislator regulating the whole body of the economy. In this later case, *iubere* would not refer to the order of a slave owner or a minor magistrate but to the person empowered to legislate.[52] Putting the fragment in the context of Hadrian's 'fish law', Callistratus could have addressed not only the 'ideal' legislator but also the historical one. In fact, Callistratus might be accusing the emperor of a failure in economic and legal policy. If this were the case, the seemingly unimposing fragment would harbour a highly explosive force in the field of legal policy.

V. The Reference to the *Politeia* and Callistratus's 'Plato Collage'

While Emperor Hadrian is quoted at most indirectly as (*ali-*)*quis*, another authority is quoted directly in the source. Callistratus reinforces his statement with a quotation from Plato's *Politeia*: merchants (ἔμποροι) are necessary, as otherwise the producer would have to sit idle at the market and wait for customers while at the same time he would be kept from further production.[53]

rescripsit); D. 49.14.2.1 (Call. 2 *de Iure Fisci*) (*divus Hadrianus Flavio Arriano in haec verba rescripsit*); D. 49.14.2.4 (Call. 2 *de Iure Fisci*) (*divus Hadrianus rescripsit*); D. 49.14.3.1 (Call. 3 *de Iure Fisci*) (*divus Hadrianus rescripsit*); D. 49.14.3.6 (Call. 3 *de Iure Fisci*) (*divus etiam Hadrianus in haec verba rescripsit*); D. 49.14.3.9 (Call. 3 *de Iure Fisci*) (*divus Hadrianus Flavio Proculo rescripsit*); D. 50.1.37.pr (Call. 1 *Cogn.*) (*divus Hadrianus rescripsit*); D. 50.4.14.6 (Call. 1 *Cogn.*) (*divus etiam Hadrianus ... rescripsit in haec verba*); D. 50.6.6.5 (Call. 1 *Cogn.*) (*divus Hadrianus rescripsit*); D. 50.6.6.8 (Call. 1 *Cogn.*) (*epistula divi Hadriani scripta est*); D. 50.9.5 (Call. 2 *Cogn.*) (*divus Hadrianus Nicomedensibus rescripsit*).

[50] See de Ligt, *Fairs and Markets in the Roman Empire* (n 30), 221; de Ligt, 'The Nundinae of L. Bellicius Sollers' (n 12), 260.

[51] V Marotta, 'I giuristi romani come "intellettuali": la cultura di Callistrato' (1992) 1 *Ostraka* 287, 289: 'sarebbe ancor meglio percepibile se i destinatari del discorso del giurista potessero essere identificati con quei magistrati (*si quis ... iusserit*) su cui gravava, nelle diverse *civitates*, il compito di disciplinare l'annona e il regolare afflusso dei beni di uso commune'. This was already the understanding of the Gloss, see Fehius (n 9), col 1772 n r: 'Si quis: *scilicet magistratus*'.

[52] On both meanings of this word, see HG Heumann and E Seckel, '*iubere*' in *Handlexikon zu den Quellen des römischen Rechts*, 10th edn (A Thon ed, Graz, Akademische Druck- und Verlagsanstalt, 1958) 290.

[53] P Cerami and A Petrucci, *Diritto commerciale romano. Profilo storico*, 3rd edn (Torino, Giappichelli, 2010), 33 stress the role of the merchants as 'intermediatori fra città e campagna'.

With a view to this inefficiency, a division of labour[54] is obviously desirable: 'there are people who see this [the desirability of allowing fishermen to focus on productivity] and place themselves at disposal for this work', namely the sale of the goods.[55]

In 2017, Sven Günther, an ancient historian from Changchun University, dug deeper into the roots of the quotation from Plato's work by Callistratus. In doing so, he showed how this quotation is pieced together out of snippets from chapters 11 and 12 of the second book of Plato's *Politeia*.[56] This 'Plato collage' obscures what Plato was originally putting forward concerning merchants.

Plato himself deemed trade as something necessary but had serious doubts concerning the integrity of the persons involved in everyday market practice.[57] In the original source, Plato distinguishes between two different kinds of sellers: on the one hand 'merchants' (ἔμποροι), who are also involved in overseas trade, and on the other, 'retailers' (κάπηλοι), who engage in market transactions within the cities. In Callistratus's reproduction of the quote, the κάπηλοι are left out and only the ἔμποροι are mentioned.

Günther considers that the changes in the quotation could have occurred as a result of a conscious interference by the jurist Callistratus[58] or subsequently as an interpolation by the compilers of the Digest.[59] In addition to these possibilities, one could also think of an unconscious interference, for instance if Callistratus had merely possessed a corrupted copy of Plato's work, or if a scribe left out aspects of the Greek text. According to the principle of *lectio difficilior*, however, one should assume a conscious interference with the Platonic original text. In both instances considered by Günther, the question of why the source has been mutilated and interfered with must be raised.

[54] See S Föllinger, *Ökonomie bei Platon* (Berlin, De Gruyter, 2016), 34 f; S Föllinger and E Korn, 'Glück und Ökonomie – ein interdisziplinäres Projekt zur Bedeutung von Institutionen bei Platon' in V Mammitzsch and others (eds), *Die Marburger Gelehrten-Gesellschaft: Universitas litterarum nach 1968* (Berlin, De Gruyter, 2016) 337, 344; S Föllinger, 'Anthropologie und Ökonomie bei Platon' in W Enkelmann and B Priddat (eds), *Was ist? Wirtschaftsphilosophische Erkundungen. Definitonen, Ansätze, Methoden, Erkenntnisse, Wirkungen* (Marburg, Metropolis, 2015) 413, 416 f. On the impact and significance of division of labour in Plato's model state, see A Becker, *Platons Politeia. Ein systematischer Kommentar* (Ditzingen, Reclam, 2017), 75; M Schofield, 'Plato on the economy' in M Hansen (ed), *The Ancient Greek City-state: Symposium on the Occasion of the 250th Anniversary of the Royal Danish Academy of Sciences and Letters, July, 1–4, 1992* (Copenhagen, Det Kongelige Danske Videnskabernes Selskab, 1993) 183, 190 f.

[55] This emphasises the importance of social networks and the socio-economic regulatory framework in which the single market participants are automatically embedded; see Günther, '(K)einer neuen Theorie wert? (n 14), 144. On the 'embeddedness' of the market participants in social networks see Ruffing (n 16), 220 and 224 f.

[56] Günther, '(K)einer neuen Theorie wert? (n 14), 140–42. It remains unclear whether Winkel (n 6), 377 also states that the fragment is a corrupted quotation or that the fragment addresses the problem of *corruptio*, when he writes: 'Dans D. 50,11,2 on trouve un renvoi à Platon en matière de corruption'.

[57] See Föllinger, *Ökonomie bei Platon* (n 54), 36–38 and 143; Föllinger, 'Anthropologie und Ökonomie bei Platon' (n 54), 417 and 420.

[58] Günther, '(K)einer neuen Theorie wert? (n 14), 142.

[59] ibid, 141 fn 26.

VI. Callistratus's Position on the Models Proposed by Plato and Hadrian

In the sources at hand, we are confronted with three different models or conceptions of how production and trade should be organised in principle. It might therefore be appropriate to first give a short overview of the different economic models presented, before turning to the question of why Callistratus might have altered the quotation from Plato's *Politeia*.

In the pertinent section from the second book of the *Politeia*,[60] Plato initially stresses the need for farmers (γεωργοί) producing for the local market as well as trading with foreigners. In addition, there must be merchants (ἔμποροι) for the import and export business, namely persons travelling to other cities (πολεῖς). Finally, there is a need for retailers (κάπηλοι) for the common market trade. These should be the weakest in bodily strength, who are not fit for any other business and so are who ought to sit at the market and procure the market transactions.[61]

According to Hadrian's 'fish law', production shall be geared to the local market. Any further link in the retail chain via third persons (τρίτοι) would lead to an increase in prices and shall therefore be prohibited,[62] while a marketing of the catch by the first salespersons (πρῶτοι) who acquired the fish from the fishers themselves shall be allowed.[63]

Callistratus, on the other hand, proposes first that producers shall focus on production, in order to maintain the *annonae praebitio*, and second that *negotiatores* shall take the crop to town.[64] Callistratus tries to emphasise this with the use of his 'Plato collage' on the role of the ἔμποροι in market sales.

Having set out the differences concerning these accounts, culminating in Callistratus's synthesis, the question must be raised how the economic models

[60] Pl., *Rep.* 2.11–12, 371a–371d.

[61] Pl., *Rep.* 2.12, 371d: ἢ οὐ καπήλους καλοῦμεν τοὺς πρὸς ὠνήν τε καὶ πρᾶσιν διακονοῦντας ἱδρυμένους ἐν ἀγορᾷ, τοὺς δὲ πλανήτας ἐπὶ τὰς πόλεις ἐμπόρους … – 'Don't we call "retailers" those who are of use concerning buying and selling and who sit on the market, those, however, who roam around to the cities, "merchants"?' On this, see Föllinger, 'Anthropologie und Ökonomie bei Platon' (n 54), 417.

[62] See also Cortés Copete, 'Koinoi Nomoi' (n 34), 117, who also stresses the closeness to the 'edict against speculators' (τοὺς πληστηρ[ιάζοντας]), of which a fragmentary copy (*TAM* IV 1.3) has been found in Nicomedia. On possible ties between both edicts, see also Cortés Copete, 'Adriano y la regulación de los mercados cívicos' (n 20), 256–59. On the 'edict against speculators', see also Oliver (n 20), 239 f.

[63] Interestingly, M Rostovtzeff, *The Social and Economic History of the Roman Empire*, vol 2, 2nd edn (Oxford, Oxford University Press, 1957), 700 argues that 'the letter of Hadrian drew its inspiration from some laws in the spirit of Plato, Leg. Xi, p. 817, B–C' and does not refer to the pertinent part in the *Politeia*, but to an excerpt from Plato's *Nomoi* on price stability – no merchant may lower or raise the market price of the goods he is selling in the course of one single day (ὁ πωλῶν ὁτιοῦν ἐν ἀγορᾷ μηδέποτε δύο εἴπῃ τιμὰς ὧν ἂν πωλῇ, ἁπλῆν δὲ εἰπών, ἂν μὴ τυγχάνῃ ταύτης, ἀποφέρων ὀρθῶς ἂν ἀποφέροι πάλιν).

[64] In this sense, also de Ligt, *Fairs and Markets in the Roman Empire* (n 30), 222 states that the 'purport of this text is thus the very antithesis of the "fight against middlemen" that is such an important feature of the food policies of later-medieval towns'.

presented relate to one another. First, one must ask why Callistratus is quoting Plato, albeit in a mutilated way, while Hadrian is not mentioned at all. A possible answer to this question poses the idea that Callistratus was looking at the problem from a different perspective from that of the emperor, and therefore prioritised a different economic interest.

Hadrian can be seen as being driven by two motives.[65] He wants to secure the possession of enough fish for the inhabitants of the coastal region while at the same time prohibiting price-rigging in the market at Athens as well. This serves to illustrate that there are two hearts beating in Hadrian's chest: Hadrian was, on the one hand, a 'lover of Athens', who used to be *archon* of the city before he became the emperor.[66] On the other hand, Hadrian had – to use Kevin Clinton's words – an 'extraordinary interest in Eleusis'.[67] He visited the local Mysteries more than once when he was emperor, for instance in 124 CE,[68] which is shortly before the supposed enactment of the 'fish law'.

Callistratus, quoting Plato, claims that it would be unproductive for fishermen to take care of the marketing of their catch themselves and calls for local retailers of the kind even Hadrian does not want to suppress. However, Callistratus describes these retailers that are deemed to be necessary as 'merchants', ἔμποροι. While, of course, this could merely be intended as some kind of generalisation,[69] it could also constitute a conscious modification. In this context, it should be noted that in fact there was a spatial separation between merchants and retailers in the city of Athens. Höbenreich underlines that retail trade (καπηλεία) took place on the Agora, ie within the city centre of Athens, while the importing merchant's activities (ἐμπορία) were conducted on the Emporium in the port of the Piraeus,[70] to which the Deigma belonged.[71] So even in practice there was a difference between ἔμποροι and κάπηλοι. With that in view, the modification of the Plato quotation could be founded on a different perspective taken by Callistratus or, perhaps more accurately, reflects a different result envisaged by the latter: Callistratus might be primarily taking the market in Athens into consideration and trying to increase the offer of fish in that particular place. To sustain this argument, it should be noted that Callistratus mentions the crop which is supposed to be carried *in civitatem* at the very beginning of the fragment. Such a *deferre in civitatem* implies a considerable act of transport, different from selling the crop at the market in the fishing village itself. It seems possible that *civitas* alludes to the very city of Athens, in a similar way to that in which *urbs* traditionally means the city

[65] For a double motive, see also Oliver (n 20), 195: 'The epistle both encouraged fishermen to take their fish directly to Eleusis at the time of the festival and warned off the wholesale merchants from trying to get the business as middlemen'.

[66] See Clinton (n 28), 1517.

[67] ibid, 1519.

[68] ibid, 1516; Kern, 'Eleusis 1' (n 31), col 1255.

[69] In this sense Treitschke (n 9), 1197 n 225.

[70] Höbenreich (n 15), 279 fn 276: 'der Kleinhandel (καπηλεία) [wird] auf der Agora, der Großhandel (ἐμπορία) auf dem Emporium im Hafen Piräus abgewickelt'.

[71] Wachsmuth (n 36), 106.

of Rome[72] – even Justinian's Institutes expressly mention the *civitas Atheniensium*.[73] If one accepted this, Callistratus's approach would differ from Hadrian's insofar as Callistratus only focuses on the market *in civitate*, while Hadrian has an eye to the fishing village and to the city at the same time.

VII. The Rationale Behind the Mutilated Quotation from Plato's Work

The final question concerns the rationale behind the mutilated quotation from Plato's work. The lines above suggest that the reference to Plato's *Politeia* in this position is not – as in other places[74] – only decorative. In this regard, Roberto Bonini stressed that the quotation takes 'un ruolo non esclusivamente ornamentale'.[75]

Rather, Callistratus is, on the one hand, looking for an authority which is capable of outweighing that of the emperor when he stresses that Plato is of *summa prudentia et auctoritas*. On the other hand, he is using a specific authority by someone who knows the very *polis* of Athens – this is underlined by the addition *apud Graecos*. While Salvatore Puliatti argues that the expression *apud Graecos* should be of limiting character – 'delimita l'area d'influenza del pensiero di Platone'[76] – I would argue that, taking into account the esteem and relevance of Plato, the expression is rather of a localising nature.

However, as Plato's position does not exactly fit that which Callistratus is positing, the latter modifies the quotation from the *Politeia* in such way that it suits his opinion: the explicit differentiation between ἔμποροι and κάπηλοι is taken out and instead, the importance of independent market traders on the market *in civitate* is evoked, while the pejorative attitude towards these retailers taken by Plato is effaced as well. This appears to be a quite pragmatic way of dealing with authorities in a matter that is fundamentally one of principle.

VIII. Conclusion

In Justinian's Digest, D. 50.11.2 appears to state a matter of principle, namely that the division of labour between producers and marketers is generally economically

[72] At least in ancient Greek ἄστυ means the (capital) city, and is often to be understood as referring to Athens; *cf* W Gemoll and K Vretska, 'ἄστυ' in *Griechisch-deutsches Schul- und Handwörterbuch*, 10th edn (Munich, Oldenbourg, 2012) 140.

[73] See Inst. 1.2.2 and Inst. 1.2.10.

[74] In this regard, the source at hand does not fit into the system for *Graeca* in the Digest sketched by H Troje, *Graeca leguntur* (Cologne, Böhlau, 1971), 12–18, especially 13, according to which quotations of the Greek classics from Homer to Plutarch feature as mere decoration ('in der Regel bloße Dekoration').

[75] Bonini (n 10), 75 f.

[76] Puliatti (n 8), 11: 'l'espressione *apud Graecos* … delimita l'area d'influenza del pensiero di Platone'.

beneficial. However, this chapter aims to show that it is plausible that Callistratus's text in its original context takes as its focus in approaching this question of principle a concrete case, that of Hadrian's 'fish law' from 124/125 CE, and aims at a rather pragmatic solution. The fact that the jurist does not mention Hadrian in the passage handed down to us while at the same time assembling a 'Plato collage' could support the theory that Callistratus agreed with Hadrian only in the starting point, namely that fishers should focus on their business and catch fish, while he was of a different opinion as to the question whose *annonae praebitio* should be secured. While Hadrian (also) wanted to secure the offer of fish in the coastal village of Eleusis, Callistratus wanted to raise market thickness *in civitate*, in the city of Athens. To justify this, he first refers to Plato's work on how an ideal state should be constituted in principle and stresses Plato's authority *apud Graecos* but then proceeds to mutilate Plato's quotation so as to make it support the result he thinks right himself – a quite pragmatic approach.

Both texts, D. 50.11.2 and IGII/III^2 (1.2) 1103, are examples of a market regulation in Roman law, trying to find a solution between the theoretical approach of how the economy should work (namely the division of labour and the question of specialisation versus direct marketing, alongside the desirable length of the supply chain and its implication for prices) and practical aspects, concerning the question of who exactly shall profit from a certain economic policy and at which place market thickness shall be increased. In that, both texts exemplify the balancing act Roman jurists and legislators had to perform between principle and pragmatism.

9

Limits of Juristic Argument in the Exercitorian Edict

PETER CANDY

I. Introduction

This volume follows quickly on the passing of Alan Watson and Hans Ankum, two of the foremost Romanists of their generation. Each offered profound insight into the development of Roman juristic thought. In an influential essay published in 1968, Ankum put forward the proposition that 'from the beginning of the first century AD until the end of the classical period, especially Papinian, Ulpian and Paul used rather often in their works *utilitas* as a reason to explain the acceptance of a dogmatically indefensible solution or as an argument, invoked to defend a similar solution'.[1] He also argued that, where there was 'contradiction between the necessities of practice and the results of logical reasoning … [the] Roman lawyers very often gave victory to practical life and … set aside theoretical objections'.[2] This, Ankum concluded, was a consequence of their 'casuistic, processualistic and practical' approach, by which he meant:

> Casuistic: their greatness is in finding the law in concrete cases of daily life, it is not in making general rules; their work is not very systematic. Processualistic, not substantial: they ask nearly always: Is an *actio* or an *exceptio* or an interdict applicable; is it possible that A sues B and that B opposes an *exceptio*? Practical, pragmatical: their interest is to find good answers to concrete legal questions, to find solutions that are suitable for practical life. They do not like to make theoretical considerations and often they refuse to suffer decisions in legal disputes to depend only on dogmatic and logical reasonings.[3]

[1] JA Ankum, '*Utilitatis causa receptum*, On the Pragmatical Methods of the Roman Lawyers' in JA Ankum, R Feenstra and WF Leemans (eds), *Symbolae iuridicae et historicae Martino David dedicatae* (Leiden, Brill, 1968) 1, 28. Ankum translated *utilitas* as 'the necessities of practical life': ibid, 3. For the argument, see: ibid, 28–31; JA Ankum, 'The Functions of Expressions with *Utilitatis Causa* in the Works of the Classical Roman Lawyers' (2010) 16 *Fundamina* 5, 6.

[2] Ankum, '*Utilitatis causa receptum*' (n 1), 2–3.

[3] ibid 2.

Ankum's view, however, did not extend to the Republican lawyers, whom he considered 'more dogmatical' than their classical counterparts.[4] 'On the three mentioned points', he concluded, 'British lawyers are much nearer to the Romans than lawyers on the Continent; they are also more casuistic, processualistic, and surely more pragmatical'.[5]

One year later, in his inaugural lecture from the Chair of Civil Law at the University of Edinburgh, Watson responded by arguing that the Republican lawyers were not so bound by strict legal thinking as was commonly supposed, and 'were prepared to be ruthless and make original and extreme interpretations' when the outcome was socially desirable.[6] Though they differed on points, both scholars placed new emphasis on the propensity of jurists to rely upon pragmatic arguments to justify positions that were untenable in principle.

This chapter examines three texts drawn from the Digest title on the exercitorian action (D. 14.1) that contain the views of lawyers from the late Republican, high classical and late classical periods.[7] Two of these are generally considered to be examples of a 'wide' or pragmatic approach to interpretation by the Roman jurists. In my view, a close reading of these fragments shows that the approach taken by the jurist in each case was narrower and more principled than is usually supposed. This, however, should not be taken to indicate that these jurists were generally more principled than Watson or even Ankum was prepared to admit. Rather, their cautious pragmatism was likely a consequence of the exercitorian edict's special context, in which the praetor's equitable response to the limitations of the civil law required interpretation with an eye to the unique and specialised environment of maritime trade. This, ultimately, makes it hard to generalise from the approach taken by the jurists to the problems raised in these texts: much depends on the precise interpretation of each jurist's opinion, and on the context in which his arguments were advanced.

II. The Exercitorian Edict

Before turning to the interpretation of the edict, it is necessary to make some remarks about the legal and socio-economic context of its introduction. To the Roman mind,

[4] Ankum, '*Utilitatis causa receptum*' (n 1), 6.

[5] ibid. This echoes Buckland and McNair's observation that 'It may be a paradox, but it seems to be the truth that there is more affinity between the Roman jurist and the common lawyer than there is between the Roman jurist and his modern civilian successor': WW Buckland and AD McNair, *Roman Law and Common Law*, 2nd edn (FH Lawson ed, Cambridge, Cambridge University Press, 1952), xvi. See also PG Stein, 'Roman Law, Common Law, and Civil Law' (1992) 66 *Tulane Law Review* 1591, 1591–2; though *cf* the detailed discussion of the relationship between Roman law and common law in J Gordley, *The Jurists: A Critical History* (Oxford, Oxford University Press, 2013), 21–27.

[6] WAJ Watson, *Limits of Juristic Decision in the Later Roman Republic*, Inaugural Lecture No 36 (Edinburgh, University of Edinburgh, 1969), 14. See also WAJ Watson, 'Narrow, Rigid and Literal Interpretation in the Later Roman Republic' (1969) 37 *Leg Hist Rev* 351, 367–68.

[7] For a study concerning some other aspects of the relationship of principle and pragmatism in the exercitorian context, see DEL Johnston, 'Suing the *Paterfamilias*: Theory and Practice' in JW Cairns and

the fundamental legal relation between persons was the *obligatio*, which Justinian defined as a 'tie of law [*vinculum iuris*], whereby we are constrained by the necessity of paying some thing, according to the laws of our *civitas*'.[8] Though this definition was included in the Institutes, and therefore lacks attribution, it was probably drawn from a classical or immediately post-classical work (possibly by Gaius or Papinian). This would explain the residual characterisation of the concept as one that – according to the classical understanding – was only appropriate to relationships arising under the *ius civile*. *Obligationes* were intimately associated with contract, so that they were said to arise, among other things, *ex contractu*; and, in most cases, where an *obligatio* arose, an action lay.[9] As Gaius states, an action raised on the strength of an *obligatio* was *in personam*, which is to say that the claim was that the defendant (who was specifically identified) ought, at civil law, to give or do something for the claimant (also specifically named).[10]

One consequence of the strictly personal quality of the *obligatio* was that direct agency was excluded as a matter of principle. Although the effects of this rule were mitigated to some extent by the possibility of acquiring rights through those in power, it remained the case that – as Ulpian remarked in the context of stipulation – *alteri stipulari nemo potest* ('no-one can stipulate on behalf of another').[11] Against a backdrop of intensifying commercial activity following Rome's triumph in the Carthaginian wars, the practical consequences of this position must have been thrown into sharp relief.[12] This would have been no more evident than in the context of maritime trade, which shipwreck evidence shows increased quite spectacularly in volume in the western Mediterranean between the mid-second and mid-first centuries BCE.[13] Although shipping enterprises were both expensive and risky, their potential to generate vast profits made them attractive to the Roman elite. For social and political reasons, however, wealthy landowners preferred to profit from maritime ventures at arm's length, operating through the agency of dependants and freedmen.[14] Several business structures were possible.[15]

PJ du Plessis (eds), *Beyond Dogmatics: Law and Society in the Roman World* (Edinburgh, Edinburgh University Press, 2007) 173, 179–83.

[8] DJ Ibbetson, '*Obligatio* in Roman Law and Society' in PJ du Plessis, C Ando and K Tuori (eds), *The Oxford Handbook of Roman Law and Society* (Oxford, Oxford University Press, 2016) 569, 573.

[9] Exceptionally, no *actio* arose from 'natural obligations' (*obligationes naturales*).

[10] G. 4.2; see Ibbetson (n 8), 576–77.

[11] D. 45.1.38.17 (Ulp. 49 *ad Sab.*); see also Inst. 3.19.19. See R Zimmermann, *The Law of Obligations: Roman Foundations of the Civilian Tradition* (Oxford, Oxford University Press, 1996), 47–54.

[12] For an economic perspective on this issue, see DP Kehoe, 'Contracts, Agency, and Transaction Costs in the Roman Economy' in DP Kehoe, DM Ratzan and U Yiftach (eds), *Law and Transaction Costs in the Ancient Economy* (Ann Arbor, University of Michigan Press, 2015) 231.

[13] AI Wilson, 'Developments in Mediterranean shipping and maritime trade from the Hellenistic period to AD 1000' in D Robinson and AI Wilson (eds), *Maritime Archaeology and Ancient Trade in the Mediterranean* (Oxford, Oxford Centre for Maritime Archaeology, 2011) 33, 33–39.

[14] JH D'Arms, *Commerce and Social Standing in Ancient Rome* (Cambridge, Harvard University Press, 1981), 44–45; A Tchernia, *The Romans and Trade* (J Grieve and E Minchin trans, Oxford, Oxford University Press, 2016), 23–32.

[15] See A Földi, 'Remarks on the legal structure of enterprises in Roman law' (1996) 43 *RIDA* 179, 192.

In one structure, the *paterfamilias* appointed a dependant or freedman to oversee the commercial operation of a vessel directly, as a shipmaster (*magister navis*). In another, he authorised one of his dependants to run a shipping business out of their *peculium*, which would empower them to appoint a shipmaster themselves. In both cases, the person who appointed the shipmaster and to whom the revenues of the business accrued was termed the *exercitor*.[16] Whichever structure was preferred, it was perfectly possible for persons not in the *potestas* of the *exercitor*, or of his or her *paterfamilias*, to be appointed shipmasters – that is, persons who were slaves of another, or else free(d)men. A range of epigraphic, archaeological and textual evidence suggests that freedmen were commonly involved in shipping ventures;[17] although only a handful of (mostly servile) *magistri* are attested to in the epigraphic sources, it is likely that freedmen were sometimes appointed by their patrons to this role.[18]

Since the *magister navis* was responsible for the commercial operation of the vessel, he was the person with whom merchants contracted for the purpose of, for example, arranging carriage of their goods.[19] In this context, the rule against direct agency was obviously a serious impediment to trade. If the *magister navis* was a dependant, then all was not lost: the merchant could at least sue on the *peculium*. If, however, the *magister* was a freedman, then he was both *sui iuris* and *extraneus*, with the result that any actions available to the merchant lay exclusively against the *magister*, not the *exercitor*. With large sums at stake, this was clearly unsatisfactory: not only were merchants confined to a suit against the shipmaster (who was likely a person of modest financial means) but the *exercitor* (or his *paterfamilias*) – the person benefiting most from the enterprise – was shielded from liability.

It is therefore little surprise that the praetor intervened by issuing an edict, probably at some point during the latter half of the second century or the first quarter of the first century BCE.[20] The classical version of the edict consisted of two parts, the first of which ran as follows:

> *Quod cum magistro navis gestum erit eius rei nomine, cui ibi praepositus fuerit, in eum, qui eam navem exercuerit, iudicium dabo.*
>
> Where business is conducted with a shipmaster, in connection with those matters for which he was appointed, I will grant a *iudicium* against the person exploiting the ship.[21]

[16] D. 14.1.1.15 (Ulp. 28 *ad Ed.*); see also G. 4.71; Inst. 4.7.2.

[17] H Mouritsen, *The Freedman in the Roman World* (Cambridge, Cambridge University Press, 2011), 215; *cf* W Broekaert, 'Freedmen and Agency in Roman Business' in AI Wilson and M Flohr (eds), *Urban Craftsmen and Traders in the Roman World* (Oxford, Oxford University Press, 2016) 222, 243–44.

[18] See J-J Aubert, 'Les *institores* et le commerce maritime dans l'Empire romain' (1999) 9 *Topoi* 145, 155–64; W Broekaert, *Navicularii et Negotiantes: A Prosopographical study of Roman merchants and shippers* (Rahden, Marie Leidorf, 2013).

[19] D. 14.1.1.1 (Ulp. 28 *ad Ed.*); D. 14.1.1.3 (Ulp. 28 *ad Ed.*).

[20] For debates surrounding the dating of the edict, see P Candy, 'Parallel Developments in Roman Law and Maritime Trade during the Late Republic and Early Principate' (2020) 33 *Journal of Roman Archaeology* (forthcoming).

[21] O Lenel, *Das Edictum Perpetuum*, 3rd rev edn (Leipzig, Tauchnitz, 1927), 257–58.

By the first half of the second century CE, the edict had been expanded to cover the situation in which a *paterfamilias* had authorised a dependant to run a shipping business out of their *peculium*. In these circumstances, the praetor made the additional promise that:

> *Si is, qui navem exercuerit, in aliena potestate erit eiusque voluntate navem exercuerit, quod cum magistro eius gestum erit, in eum, in cuius potestate is erit qui navem exercuerit, iudicium dabo.*
>
> If the person exploiting the vessel is in the power of another and is acting according to their will, where business is conducted with a shipmaster, I will grant a *iudicium* against the person in whose power the person exploiting the ship is.[22]

The edict had two outstanding features. The first, as Gaius noted, was that the *exercitor*'s liability was unlimited (that is, *in solidum*); the second was that it was available not only for contracts entered into with those in the *exercitor*'s power but also with 'outsiders' (*extranei*).[23] Both features were justified by reference to the appointment (*praepositio*). The crucial point was that, in making the appointment, the *exercitor* demonstrated his will (*voluntas*) that the *magister* should enter into transactions in pursuit of the business. In the words of Gaius, it was therefore 'most equitable' (*aequissimum*) that the *exercitor* should be fully accountable.[24] From this it followed that: (i) the material relationship between the *exercitor* and the shipmaster for the purpose of the edict was founded on the *praepositio*, rather than, for example, on *potestas*; and (ii) the only limit on the extent of the *exercitor*'s liability was the scope of the appointment. Naturally, the *exercitor* was entitled to limit the appointment's scope by publicising explicit restrictions (*proscriptiones*) on the transactions he was willing to authorise (for example, by prohibiting certain sailing routes or specifying that the vessel was a passenger- or cargo-ship); but, in the absence of restrictions, he would be liable in full for any contract ordinarily entered into in the course of a shipping business.[25]

The procedural mechanism by which the edict was likely given effect was quite ingenious: if a person brought an action, the *formula* of which was *in ius concepta* (as would be the case if the action were brought on the strength of an *obligatio* arising *ex contractu*), then the name of the *exercitor* (or their *paterfamilias*) was simply transposed into the *condemnatio* in place of the name of the shipmaster.[26]

[22] See D. 14.1.1.19 (Ulp. 28 *ad Ed.*). Ulpian's text is exactly the same as that of the edict, except for the substitution of *dabo* for *datur*: P Huvelin, *Études d'histoire du droit commercial romain (histoire externe – droit maritime)* (H Lévy-Bruhl ed, Paris, Sirey, 1929), 162; Lenel (n 21), 258.

[23] G. 4.71; *cf* Inst. 4.7.2–2a.

[24] G. 4.71.

[25] See, eg, the discussion in D. 14.1.1.12 (Ulp. 28 ad Ed.); see also J-J Aubert, *Business Managers in Ancient Rome: A Social and Economic Study of Institores, 200 B.C. – A.D. 250* (Leiden, Brill, 1994), 9–16.

[26] The whole question is controversial. The account preferred here was first proposed in FL Keller, *Ueber Litis Contestation und Urtheil nach classischem Römischem Recht* (Zurich, Gessner, 1827), 431–33 and defended in Lenel (n 21), 264–70. For a different account, in which the exercitorian edict created a personal and direct liability in the *praeponens*, see M Miceli, *Studi sulla «rappresentanza» nel diritto romano* (Milan, Giuffrè, 2008), 44–48; and, generally, M Miceli, *Sulla struttura formulare delle 'actiones adiecticiae qualitatis'* (Turin, Giappichelli, 2001).

In other words, though the praetor allowed the suit to proceed on the ordinary basis that an *obligatio* had arisen between the merchant and the shipmaster (the latter being named in the *intentio* as the person who ought to give or do some thing at civil law); he gave effect to the edict by instructing the judge to condemn not the *magister* but the person by whom he had been appointed (or the appointer's *paterfamilias*). By this procedural sleight-of-hand, the praetor preserved the foundation of the claim *in ius* – that is, the underlying contractual relationship remained unaffected – but exercised his *imperium* to order the judge to condemn or absolve someone other than the person whose legal duty it was to perform. This, as it happens, was only possible because the praetor's instruction to the judge was not to order performance but, rather, to assess damages and make a pecuniary award (according to the principle *omnis condemnatio pecuniaria*[27]).

III. Juristic Interpretation of the Edict

The Digest title on the exercitorian action consists principally of an extended extract taken from the twenty-eighth book of Ulpian's commentary *ad Edictum*, together with some additional fragments by Paul and Africanus. The focus here will be the interpretation of two different aspects of the edict: (i) the meaning of the word *magister*; and (ii) the question as to which transactions counted as 'in connection with the matter' for which the shipmaster had been appointed. Both lines of discourse share a common theme in the tension that arose between the preservation of the equitable principle that sustained the edict – the idea that the *exercitor*'s liability flowed from the *praepositio* – and the protection of third parties who transacted with the *magister* in good faith, in circumstances where the strict logical application of the equitable principle would exclude an exercitorian remedy. This tension was not confined to the exercitorian context: in mandate, for example, Gaius held that, if a mandatary fulfilled the mandate after the mandator's death – an event that ended the contract – the mandatary's *iusta et probabilis ignorantia* justified the view that the *actio mandati contraria* lay against the heirs for costs *utilitatis causa*.[28] In this case, Gaius was moved by practical considerations to protect the third party, who ought not to be penalised for continuing to honour the contract under the justifiable misapprehension that the mandator was still alive. However, the situation under the exercitorian edict was more delicate, for the praetor's words already represented a departure from the orthodox position at civil law. To adopt a broad interpretation of its terms, or to depart from them altogether, was therefore to find oneself two steps removed from the position at law: first, from the civil law principle that precluded direct agency; and, second, from the equitable principle that justified the departure from that rule. For this reason,

[27] See G. 4.48; G. 4.51.
[28] G. 3.160, on which see Ankum, '*Utilitatis causa receptum*' (n 1), 19.

though expediency on occasion provided a powerful justification for stretching the interpretation of the edict, the jurists were generally not inclined to stray too far from the equitable principle upon which it was founded.

A. The Interpretation of *Magister*

The praetor said he would grant an action 'Where business is conducted with a shipmaster'. In what circumstances could the *exercitor* be held accountable for contracts entered into by sub-appointees? The issue was considered by Ulpian:

> We take '*magister*' to include not only a person appointed by the *exercitor* but also one appointed by a shipmaster: this was Julian's response when he was consulted in a case concerning an *exercitor* who was unaware [that the sub-appointment had been made]. Besides, if he knew about and permitted the person to discharge the office of shipmaster on board, he appears to have made the appointment himself. This opinion appears reasonable to me: for if I have appointed a shipmaster, I am bound to stand by whatever he does, otherwise those making contracts will be let down – and for pragmatic reasons this is to be more readily admitted in the case of shipmasters than business managers [*institores*]. What, though, if the *exercitor* appointed a shipmaster who was not allowed to appoint someone else? Should Julian's opinion still hold? Suppose that he prohibited the appointment of a specific person, on terms such as 'You are not to employ Titius as shipmaster'. Even here, it must be said that the interests of those involved in shipping must prevail.[29]

The core of this text is Ulpian's report of a *responsum* issued by Julian, apparently in reply to the question whether an *exercitor* was liable for the contracts of a person whom his shipmaster had appointed as *magister* without his knowledge. Julian's response was that the *exercitor* was liable because the word *magister* was taken to include sub-appointees, adding that, once he had discovered and continued to permit the sub-appointee to discharge his duties, he was considered to have made the appointment himself. Ulpian approved the opinion, for the practical reason that to hold otherwise would be to let down people who entered into contracts with the sub-appointee. The question that arose was whether Julian's *sententia* extended to those appointed contrary to an express prohibition by the *exercitor*. Even here, the interests of those engaged in travel by sea compelled Ulpian to say that it should.

What was the precise scope of Julian's opinion? The *sententia* – at least insofar as it has been reported – extends from the beginning of the extract to Ulpian's comment that the reply appeared reasonable to him (that is, from *magistrum autem*

[29] D. 14.1.1.5 (Ulp. 28 *ad Ed.*): *Magistrum autem accipimus non solum, quem exercitor praeposuit, sed et eum, quem magister: et hoc consultus Iulianus in ignorante exercitore respondit: ceterum si scit et passus est eum in nave magisterio fungi, ipse eum imposuisse videtur. Quae sententia mihi videtur probabilis: omnia enim facta magistri debeo praestare qui eum praeposui, alioquin contrahentes decipientur: et facilius hoc in magistro quam institore admittendum propter utilitatem. Quid tamen si sic magistrum praeposuit, ne alium ei liceret praeponere? An adhuc Iuliani sententiam admittimus, videndum est: finge enim et nominatim eum prohibuisse, ne Titio magistro utaris. Dicendum tamen erit eo usque producendam utilitatem navigantium.*

to *imposuisse videtur*). The starting point is to recognise that the opinion consists of two statements:[30] first, that sub-appointees also counted as shipmasters for the purpose of the edict; and, second, that, if an *exercitor* knew about and permitted a sub-appointee to discharge the duties of the shipmaster (*in nave magisterio fungi*), he appeared to have made the appointment himself. In the clause interposed between these two statements, Ulpian says that the first statement was given in response to a case *in ignorante exercitore*. At this point, there are two possibilities. The first is that *in ignorante exercitore* sets out the circumstances in which the sub-appointee was held to be within the meaning of *magister* – that is, if the *exercitor* was ignorant that the appointment was made. *Ceterum* would then introduce an alternative set of circumstances, in which a sub-appointee would also fall under the edict's terms – namely, if the *exercitor* both knew about and permitted the appointment. On this reading, Julian's view was that sub-appointees fell within the scope of the edict, and that this applied to *exercitores* who either: (i) knew about and permitted; or (ii) were unaware of the appointment.[31] The second possibility is that *in ignorante exercitore* refers to the circumstances of the case about which Julian was consulted. *Ceterum* may then be treated as an adverb,[32] so that the *exercitor*'s acquiescence in the sub-appointee's discharge of the office also constitutes part of the context of Julian's reply. On this interpretation, Julian's opinion was that an *exercitor* who was unaware of the sub-appointment at the time it was made was liable if he came to know about and permitted the person to continue in the role.

In my view, the second of these interpretations is the more likely. On this reading, Julian's opinion was narrower than is usually supposed: he was not saying that an *exercitor* who was unaware (*ignorans*) of a sub-appointment was liable in all circumstances but that he was liable only if – presumably at the time the contract was concluded – he was both aware (*sciens*) and permissive (*patiens*) of the sub-appointee's continuing discharge of the shipmaster's duties. It was, after all, perfectly possible that the *exercitor* could be ignorant of the sub-appointment at the time it was made, only to discover at a later time that someone other than the original *praepositus* was acting as *magister*. If he acquiesced in this state of affairs, Julian's view was that he ought to be accountable, because 'he appeared to have put the person there himself'.

Ulpian's approval of Julian's view makes easy sense in this light. Once it is accepted that an *exercitor* who knows and permits the sub-appointee to continue operating appears to have made the appointment himself, it follows that he is bound to stand by everything the (new) shipmaster (that is, the sub-appointee) does, in the ordinary way. What is more, this narrow interpretation of Julian's opinion makes Ulpian's position at the conclusion of the text markedly less problematic. In the account given earlier, Ulpian's view was that, even if an *exercitor* prohibited the sub-appointment

[30] Ankum supposed that Ulpian omitted part of Julian's response in an interval conjectured between *respondit* and *ceterum*: '*Utilitatis causa receptum*' (n 1), 20 fn 1.

[31] See, eg, A Kirschenbaum, *Sons, Slaves and Freedmen in Roman Commerce* (Jerusalem, Magnes, 1987), 101–04; Aubert, *Business Managers in Ancient Rome* (n 25), 60–61.

[32] With the meaning of 'besides', 'moreover', or 'what is more'. See E Seckel, 'Ceterus' in *Heumanns Handlexikon zu den Quellen des römischen Rechts*, 9th edn (Jena, Fischer, 1926) 67.

of a certain person as *magister*, he would nevertheless be liable for contracts entered into by that person if he were sub-appointed to the role. Unsurprisingly, the apparent radicalness of this position has prompted allegations of interpolation.[33] However, if the proposed interpretation of Julian's opinion is accepted, the scope of Ulpian's opinion narrows considerably: now, as in the case of the *exercitor* who was unaware that the sub-appointment was made, the *exercitor* who prohibited the appointment of a certain person would only be liable if he came to know about and permitted that person to continue acting as the shipmaster.

The opinions developed in this text demonstrate the challenges the jurists faced in striking a balance between the demands of principle and the demands of expediency. On the side of principle, both recognised that the *exercitor*'s *voluntas*, entailed by the *praepositio*, was the source of the edict's *aequitas*. Moreover, preserving the principle that the *exercitor*'s liability flowed from his *voluntas* was crucial, because the edict already cut across another principle – the principle of privity that precluded the possibility of direct agency. It was, therefore, only the *voluntas* of the *exercitor* that justified the departure from the ordinary rule. The problem both Julian and Ulpian confronted, however, was that, if this equitable principle were strictly preserved – to exclude the *exercitor*'s liability in cases where he had not made the appointment directly – it would mean that 'those making contracts would be let down' (*alioquin contrahentes decipientur*). In these circumstances, to borrow Gaius's words, the contracting party's ignorance that the *exercitor* had not made the appointment (and had not therefore demonstrated his *voluntas*) was *iusta et probabilis*; and penalising them for a justifiable error of fact would run counter to the idea that parties who entered into contracts in good faith ought to be protected. After all, as Ulpian noted in his *laudatio edicti*, it was seldom possible to conduct a thorough investigation into the standing and character of the shipmaster in the hectic environment of maritime trade.[34] The extension was modest and casuistic: even if the *exercitor* was ignorant of, or had prohibited, the making of the sub-appointment, if he later acquiesced in the sub-appointee's fulfilling the role, he was liable, because to the outside world he appeared to have made the appointment himself.

B. The Interpretation of *Eius Rei Nomine, Cui Ibi Praepositus Fuerit*

A second issue that arose concerned the transactions for which the *exercitor* could be held accountable. According to Ulpian, the praetor did not state that he would give an action on every ground (*ex omni causa*) but only 'in connection with those

[33] For an overview of the history of the criticism of the text, see A Petrucci, 'Ulteriori osservazioni sulla protezione dei contraenti con gli *institores* ed i *magistri navis* nel diritto romano dell'età commerciale' (2002) 53 *IVRA* 17, 51.

[34] D. 14.1.1.pr (Ulp. 28 *ad Ed.*).

matters for which [the *magister*] was appointed'.[35] Loans presented a particular problem, because, on a literal interpretation, they were not directly connected to the matter in hand:

> 8. If [the shipmaster] borrows money, does this appear to be done 'on account of those matters' [for which he was appointed]? Pegasus considers that, if the money was borrowed for the furtherance of a matter for which he was appointed, an action will lie. I think that this opinion is right: for what if money was borrowed to fit out or equip the ship or to provision the crew?
>
> 9. Here Ofilius asks whether an action lies against the *exercitor* if [the shipmaster] borrowed the money for the purpose of repairing the ship, and then turned the funds to his own use. And he says that, if [the shipmaster] took the money with the explicit agreement that it would be spent on the ship but soon after changed his mind, the *exercitor* is liable and has only himself to blame for appointing such a man; but that, if he had it in his mind to defraud the creditor from the start and specifically did not say that he was taking the money for purposes connected with the ship, then the opposite is the case – and this distinction is approved by Pedius.[36]

First, Ulpian approved Pegasus's view that an exercitorian action would lie if the proceeds of a loan were put towards a purpose for which the shipmaster had been appointed. This was relatively unproblematic: if the money had been applied to a matter within the scope of the shipmaster's appointment, then the loan was factually connected to the matter at hand, and therefore fell within the terms of the edict. The question that arose was whether the *exercitor* would still be liable if the shipmaster borrowed money to repair the ship but then turned the funds to his own use – that is, did not put them towards the matter at hand. According to Ulpian, the late Republican jurist Ofilius distinguished two cases: the first, in which the *magister* had expressly agreed to use the money on the ship and then changed his mind (*mox mutavit voluntatem*); and the second, in which he had always intended to use the money for his own ends, and had specially avoided giving an undertaking that he would put the loan towards the vessel. He concluded that the *exercitor* ought to be held accountable in the first case but not in the second.

Identifying the precise content of Ofilius's distinction has proved controversial. At the height of the search for interpolations during the first half of the last century, considerable alteration of the fragment was suspected.[37] Beseler, for example,

[35] D. 14.1.1.7 (Ulp. 28 *ad Ed.*).

[36] D. 14.1.1.8–9 (Ulp. 28 *ad Ed.*): 8. *Quid si mutuam pecuniam sumpserit, an eius rei nomine videatur gestum? Et Pegasus existimat, si ad usum eius rei, in quam praepositus est, fuerit mutuatus, dandam actionem, quam sententiam puto veram: quid enim si ad armandam instruendamve navem vel nautas exhibendos mutuatus est?*

9. *Unde quaerit Ofilius, si ad reficiendam navem mutuatus nummos in suos usus converterit, an in exercitorem detur actio. Et ait, si hac lege accepit quasi in navem impensurus, mox mutavit voluntatem, teneri exercitorem imputaturum sibi, cur talem praeposuerit: quod si ab initio consilium cepit fraudandi creditoris et hoc specialiter non expresserit, quod ad navis causam accipit, contra esse: quam distinctionem Pedius probat.*

[37] These are canvassed in WAJ Watson, *The Law of Obligations in the Later Roman Republic* (Oxford, Oxford University Press, 1965), 190–91.

doubted the phrases *mox mutavit voluntatem* and *consilium fraudandi creditoris*.[38] Pringsheim, following Beseler, excised *mox mutavit voluntatem*, removed *imputaturum ... esse*, and substituted *sententiam* for *distinctionem*, to reflect the reality of what remained.[39] Eisele, too, supposed that *et hoc ... accipit* was a later addition, and also doubted the authenticity of *imputaturum ... praeposuerit*.[40]

Certainly, the justification for the *exercitor*'s liability in the first case is suspect (that is, *imputaturum ... praeposuerit*), not least because the *cur* construction is typical of the compilers. Even if this is an addition, however, its removal does not affect the interpretation of the rest of the passage. Further, I agree with Watson – for both the reasons given by him and those elaborated below – that the arguments that all or part of the section *quod si ... esse* is interpolated are not strong enough to warrant regarding it as inauthentic.[41] This leaves the phrase *mox mutavit voluntatem*. According to Beseler, the words *ad reficiendam navem* ('for the purpose of repairing the ship') are ambiguous, in the sense that they could refer either to a purpose that had been agreed upon by the parties or to one intended privately by the borrower. The words *hac lege* ('with the express agreement that'), he continued, can only refer to an agreed purpose; and since the expression *mox mutavit voluntatem* implies that *hac lege* carries both meanings, it cannot have been written by Ofilius.[42] Miceli, however, has argued that the expression is genuine.[43] According to her, the shipmaster's intentions are not considered separately from the fact of any agreement but, rather, together with it. Thus, in the first case, the *magister*'s change of mind is mentioned to underline the fact that the sums were not spent as stated in the *lex*; and, in the second, his fraudulent intent is provided as justification for his decision not to state what the funds would be used for.

Both interpretations lead to the conclusion that, for Ofilius, the only relevant consideration was whether the *magister* had expressly agreed to put the proceeds of the loan towards a purpose in connection with his appointment. Thus, according to Watson, 'when a *magister navis* borrows money expressly for the purposes of the ship, the *exercitor* is liable even if the *magister* is completely fraudulent'.[44] I do not

[38] G Beseler, *Beiträge zur Kritik der römischen Rechtsquellen*, vol 2 (Tübingen, Mohr, 1911), 125.

[39] FR Pringsheim, *Gesammelte Abhandlungen*, vol 1 (Heidelberg, Carl Winter, 1961), 406–07.

[40] F Eisele, 'Beiträge zur Erkenntniss der Digesteninterpolationen' (1897) 18 *ZRG RA* 1, 20; see also F De Martino, 'Studii sull'actio exercitoria' (1941) 7 *Rivista del Diritto della Navigazione* 7, 10; G Longo, 'Actio exercitoria – Actio institoria – Actio quasi institoria' in G Grosso (ed), *Studi in onore di Gaetano Scherillo*, vol II (Milan, Cisalpino-La Goliardica 1972) 581, 591–92.

[41] In my view, Watson's critique of these arguments, which shall not be repeated here, is convincing: Watson, *The Law of Obligations in the Later Roman Republic* (n 37), 190–91.

[42] Beseler's argument is quoted by Pringsheim as follows: '*ad reficiendum navem* ist undeutlich; kann „der Abrede nach zu dem Zwecke" oder „der wirklichen Absicht nach zu dem Zwecke" bedeuten. Ofilius ersetzt in seiner Antwort, um den zweiten Begriff auszuschließen, jenen Ausdruck durch *hac lege*. *Mox mutavit voluntatem* tut so, als bedeute *hac lege* „der Abrede nach und auch in Wirklichkeit zu dem Zwecke", folglich ist es nicht von Ofilius': Pringsheim (n 39), 406. Watson considered the argument 'very strong': Watson, *The Law of Obligations in the Later Roman Republic* (n 37), 190.

[43] Miceli, *Sulla struttura formulare* (n 26), 195–96, n 17.

[44] Watson, *The Law of Obligations in the Later Roman Republic* (n 37), 191; see also G Pugliese, 'In tema di «actio exercitoria»' (1957) 3 *Labeo* 308, 317. *cf* Miceli, who reaches the same conclusion, though

find this interpretation convincing. Rather, it is my opinion that the likely content of Ofilius's distinction can be established by placing the text alongside a response reported by Africanus, a jurist who flourished about the middle part of the second century CE:

> pr. Stichus, whom Lucius Titius had appointed as shipmaster, borrowed money and gave an explicit acknowledgment that he had received the money for the purpose of repairing the ship. The question that arose was whether Titius was only liable under an exercitorian action if the creditor proved that the money was spent on the ship's repairs. Our authority replied that the creditor could effectively sue, if the ship in question required the repairs at the time the money was lent. For, while the creditor ought not to be bound to the necessity of taking the repairs upon himself and conducting the owner's business (which would certainly be the result if he had to show that the money had been paid out for the work), it must be required that he know he is lending in connection with a purpose for which the shipmaster was appointed, which certainly cannot be the case unless he also knows that the money is needed for repairs. It follows that, even if the ship in question was in need of repair, if a much greater sum was lent than was required for that purpose, an action for the full amount ought not to be given against the owner of the ship.
>
> 1. Sometimes it must also be determined whether the thing on account of which the money was lent can be acquired in the place where the loan was made. For what, our authority says, if money was lent for the purchase of a sail on an island where none could be acquired? In short, the creditor is bound to show some care in the matter.[45]

In this hypothetical, a *magister* (likely a slave – Stichus) had taken a loan and provided an undertaking as to the purpose.[46] The question was whether the

by a different route: *Sulla struttura formulare* (n 26), 195–98. This is also the implication of Cerami's argument that the basis for the *exercitor*'s liability was the inclusion of an 'appropriation clause' (*clausola di destinazione*) in the loan contract by the *magister*: P Cerami, '"*Mutua pecunia a magistro 'navis reficiendae causa' sumpta*" e "*praepositio exercitoris*": Profilo storico-comparatistici' (2000) 46 *AUPA* 133, 135–36; see also P Cerami and A Petrucci, *Diritto commerciale romano: Profilo storico*, 3rd edn, (Turin, Giappichelli, 2010), 278–81.

[45] D. 14.1.7.pr–1 (Afr. 8 *Quaest.*): pr. *Lucius Titius Stichum magistrum navis praeposuit: is pecuniam mutuatus cavit se in refectionem navis eam accepisse: quaesitum est, an non aliter Titius exercitoria teneretur, quam si creditor probaret pecuniam in refectionem navis esse consumptam. Respondit creditorem utiliter acturum, si, cum pecunia crederetur, navis in ea causa fuisset, ut refici deberet: etenim ut non oportet creditorem ad hoc adstringi, ut ipse reficiendae navis curam suscipiat et negotium domini gerat (quod certe futurum sit, si necesse habeat probare pecuniam in refectionem erogatam esse), ita illud exigendum, ut sciat in hoc se credere, cui rei magister quis sit praepositus, quod certe aliter fieri non potest, quam si illud quoque scierit necessariam refectioni pecuniam esse: quare etsi in ea causa fuerit navis, ut refici deberet, multo tamen maior pecunia credita fuerit, quam ad eam rem esset necessaria, non debere in solidum adversus dominum navis actionem dari.*

1. *Interdum etiam illud aestimandum, an in eo loco pecunia credita sit, in quo id, propter quod credebatur, comparari potuerit: quid enim, inquit, si ad velum emendum in eiusmodi insula pecuniam quis crediderit, in qua omnino velum comparari non potest? Et in summa aliquam diligentiam in ea creditorem debere praestare.*

[46] De Martino very plausibly proposed that *cavit* was intended to indicate that the agreement was executed as a *stipulatio* recorded in a *cautio*: De Martino, 'Studii sull'actio exercitoria' (n 40), 12; F De Martino, 'Ancora sull'«actio exercitoria»' (1958) 4 *Labeo* 274, 283–86. If this is right, the author

creditor had to prove that the money had been correctly applied. The answer – which was probably supplied by Julian (Africanus's mentor)[47] – was that he did not, for the (pragmatic) reason that this would effectively compel him to oversee the work. On the other hand, the creditor was required to know that he was lending for a purpose within the scope of the shipmaster's appointment, which necessarily involved knowing that the money was actually required for the purposes of the ship. A loan would therefore only fall within the terms of the edict to the extent that there was in reality a matter (*res*) to which it was connected.[48] In other words, if there was no factual basis for the agreed purpose of the loan, the act of borrowing the money could not be said to be 'in connection with a matter' for which the shipmaster was appointed. It followed that the creditor could only sue the *exercitor* for as much as was required to carry out the purpose, and that it was the creditor's responsibility, for example, to establish whether articles that the shipmaster wanted to acquire with the money were actually available at the location in question. Lenders were therefore well advised to undertake 'due diligence' before entering into the transaction, to ensure that the credit they extended was fully recoverable from the *exercitor*.[49]

Returning to Ofilius, the significance of the expression *mox mutavit voluntatem* is therefore not just its attribution of an initial intention to the shipmaster to spend the loan on repairs for the ship but, crucially, its implication that there was actually a real purpose towards which the money could have been put. The starting point for Ofilius is therefore the same as that taken by Julian in the Africanus text: in each case, a *magister* took a loan and agreed to put it towards a purpose that was both within the scope of his appointment and actually existing at the time of receipt. The Republican jurist's distinction was therefore between a *magister* who had borrowed money both intending and agreeing to put it towards repairs that were actually required – but who subsequently turned the funds to his own use – and one who, in the context of the need for repairs, neither intended nor agreed to spend the money on repairs.

The thought here is that, when both the loan and the *res* were present but the money had been applied to some other purpose, the question as to whether the

may well have had in mind a *chirographum* of the kind preserved in the archive of the Sulpicii. See, eg, TPSulp. 50–59 in G Camodeca (ed), *Tabulae Pompeianae Sulpiciorum*, vol I (Rome, Quasar, 1999), 133–50. *cf* Pugliese, who suggested *cavit* should be interpreted more broadly in light of the *lex* referred to by Ofilius in D. 14.1.1.9 (Ulp. 28 *ad Ed.*) (ie, as though the shipmaster had not so much formally committed to spending the money towards a specific purpose as stated that he had received it to that end): Pugliese (n 44), 318–19 n 23; see also Cerami (n 44), 135 n 7; Cerami and Petrucci (n 44), 278–81; Miceli, *Sulla struttura formulare* (n 26), 197 n 19; and *Studi* (n 26), 74–76.

[47] Cerami (n 44), 138; see also P Lazo, 'La interpretación de la cláusula *eius rei nomine* de los edictos *de exercitoria* y *de institoria actione*' (2016) 43 *Revista Chilena de Derecho* 1081, 1094–95.

[48] See the reading by DEL Johnston, 'Limiting Liability: Roman Law and the Civil Law Tradition' (1995) 70 *Chicago-Kent Law Review* 1515, 1520.

[49] Valiño suggested that the appropriate action to raise against an *exercitor* whose shipmaster had borrowed money was a *condictio exercitoria*: E Valiño, 'Las relaciones básicas de las acciones adyecticias' (1968) 38 *Anuario de Historia del Derecho Español* 377, 420.

magister had undertaken to put the funds towards the *res* became decisive. In the first case, there was – at least initially – a loan, a *res* and an undertaking that provided a connection between them. This being the case, the edict applied – in my view, because the obligation *ex re* generated by the paying over of the loan was connected to the matter at hand by means of a second obligation arising from, for example, a stipulation.[50] In the second case, though there was still a loan and a *res*, the money had not been applied to the *res* and the undertaking that provided the connection between them in the first instance was absent. Even though the shipmaster was in bad faith from the start, the absence of the connective undertaking meant that the transaction was not 'in connection with a matter' for which the shipmaster had been appointed. Though the shipmaster was still accountable to the creditor *ex re*, to hold that the edict ought to apply, so as to permit an action against the *exercitor*, would be to stretch the *exercitor*'s implied *voluntas* to encompass transactions that were not legally or factually connected to the appointment.

In light of this analysis, Julian's reasoning in the Africanus case also becomes apparent: (i) a shipmaster who received a loan was bound *ex re* to the creditor; (ii) the edict made the *exercitor* fully liable if the transaction was 'in connection with a matter' for which the shipmaster was appointed; (iii) a loan was only 'connected' if the shipmaster had undertaken (probably formally) that the money would be applied to one of these matters; and (iv) if the matter did not exist, the undertaking was incapable of performance – and since, as Celsus remarked,[51] *impossibilium nulla obligatio est* – the absence of the *obligatio* left a logical gap between the *res* and the loan. Hence the observation, for example, that the *exercitor* could not be held accountable under the edict for money that was borrowed to acquire a sail when there was none available for purchase on the island. For Africanus and Julian, then, there were limits to the protection of creditors who lent money in good faith on the strength of an undertaking to apply the funds in a certain way: though they were not required to ensure that the loan was correctly applied, the onus was on them to exercise *diligentia*, by establishing the substance of the matter in hand.

IV. Conclusion

A recurring tension in the interpretation of the edict was between respecting the equitable principle that the *exercitor*'s liability flowed from the *praepositio* and protecting third parties who transacted with the *magister* in good faith. The issue was complicated by the recognition that the edict already represented a departure from the civil law principle of privity that precluded the possibility of direct

[50] This is likely the significance of the *lex* and the verb *cavere* in the respective texts: a pact was probably not sufficient to bridge the gap, since it could not give rise to an *actio* or be relied upon in a *condictio*, for want of a clause *ex fide bona*.

[51] D. 50.17.185 (Cels. 8 *Dig.*): 'There is no obligation to do the impossible'.

agency. One problem that arose was whether sub-appointees fell within the meaning of the term *magister*. When asked about an *exercitor* who was ignorant of the sub-appointment but acquiesced in the sub-appointee's continuation in the role, Julian took the view that, because the *exercitor*'s *scientia* and *patientia* gave the impression that he had made the appointment himself, this would overcome his initial lack of *voluntas*. Ulpian approved the opinion, and extended it to cases in which the *exercitor* had prohibited the sub-appointee *nominatim*. Though the position was dogmatically indefensible – the *exercitor*'s *voluntas* was explicitly excluded – it was tenable on the grounds that the interests of those engaged in sea travel required it.

A second problem involved identifying the circumstances in which loans would count as 'in connection with a matter' for which the shipmaster had been appointed. Again, the broader the interpretation, the more strained the proposition that the *exercitor*'s liability flowed from the *praepositio*. Ofilius established that, even if there was no factual connection between the loan and the matter in hand – for instance, because the shipmaster turned the funds to his own use – a legal connection would suffice. This preserved the link between the loan and the matter for which the shipmaster had been appointed, while protecting the third party who had transacted with the shipmaster in good faith. Later, Julian tested the limits of this proposition, by demonstrating that a legal connection was necessary but not sufficient: there actually had to be a *res* to which the loan was connected, otherwise the undertaking would be incapable of giving rise to a 'legal tie' between the two. These texts – originally by Ofilius and Africanus (possibly reporting Julian) – reveal a balanced approach that maintained the requirement for a connection (whether factual or legal) between the transaction and the edict, while at the same time protecting third parties who exercised *diligentia* in their dealings.

The three fragments addressed in this chapter represent the dawn, noon and dusk of the classical period of Roman jurisprudence. Two of the extracts – those attributed to the twenty-eighth book of Ulpian's commentary *ad Edictum* – were given wide interpretations by Ankum and Watson.[52] Both scholars went on to develop arguments that the Republican and classical lawyers were less dogmatic in their approach than was commonly admitted by their forebears. While I agree with these propositions in outline, some nuance is also possible. Since we have examined only three fragments, only narrow conclusions may be drawn – though sometimes a closer reading of only a few texts reveals important details that a wider survey might miss. Schulz characterised the (Roman) question of law as 'which of the two interpretations, the literal or the equitable, ought to prevail'.[53] The subtlety in the exercitorian edict was that the literal and equitable interpretations were one and the same. In my view, this explains the relatively cautious approach to interpreting

[52] Ankum, '*Utilitatis causa receptum*' (n 1), 20; for D. 14.1.1.9 (Ulp. 28 *ad Ed.*), see Watson, *The Law of Obligations in the Later Roman Republic* (n 37), 190–91.

[53] F Schulz, *History of Roman Legal Science* (Oxford, Oxford University Press, 1946) 76.

the edict, which admitted incremental extension of its terms only where a strictly literal reading would disadvantage a third party who had acted diligently and in good faith. On those occasions where the jurists were caught squarely between preserving the edict's *aequitas* and protecting the interests of the third party acting in good faith, they did not abandon principle lightly. Rather, their casuistic style enabled them to take pragmatic positions that were narrowly circumscribed by specific factual contexts. This allowed for modest extension and easy distinction.

10

Insulam Exurere: Reading Collatio 12.7.1–3 Closely

WOLFGANG ERNST

I. Coll. 12.7.1–3 in Context

Collatio 12.7.1–3 is taken from book 18 of Ulpian's commentary on the urban praetor's edict. This book is devoted to the *lex Aquilia*, the passage here at stake dealing with cases of arson under chapter III of the *lex*.[1] The same Ulpianic text, or a version of the same text, also appears in Justinian's Digest. There, it is split up, and features partly in the title *De lege Aquilia* (9.2) and partly in the title *Ad legem Corneliam de sicariis et veneficis* (48.8). The two texts, derived from the same Ulpianic original, differ. These differences have been taken to be cosmetic or incidental in nature, so that, in essence, Coll. 12.7.1–3 and D. 9.2.27.7–8 with D. 48.8.10 are seen as witnesses to one and the same legal statement, which can be attributed to Ulpian. On the basis of the *confronto* set out below, this view will be challenged: reading closely, we find that the compilers of the Digest fundamentally altered the case discussed by Ulpian, and changed the legal content of the passage accordingly.

Regarding the Collatio, the analysis in this chapter is not based on – nor does it aim at – an innovative understanding of the history of the text; for this, the reader can be referred to other recent contributions.[2] In line with the prevailing view,

[1] For a brief overview of our knowledge of the *lex* and the Roman jurisprudence that developed on its basis, see JW Sampson, '*lex Aquilia* on wrongful damage to property' in *Oxford Classical Dictionary* (Oxford, 2018) DOI: 10.1093/acrefore/9780199381135.013.8261.

[2] AM Rabello, 'Collatio Legum Mosaicarum et Romanarum' in F Skolnik and M Berenbaum (eds), *Encyclopaedia Judaica*, vol 5, 2nd edn (Farmington Hills, Macmillan, 2007); F Lucrezi, 'Ancora sulla data della "Collatio"' in F Sturm and others (eds), *Liber Amicorum Guido Tsuno* (Frankfurt, Vico, 2013) 193; S Corcoran, 'Collatio legum Mosaicarum et Romanarum' in RS Bagnall and others (eds), *The Encyclopaedia of Ancient History* (Blackwell, 2012) DOI:10.1002/9781444338386.wbeah13050; RM Frakes, *Compiling the Collatio Legum Mosaicarum et Romanarum in Late Antiquity* (Oxford, Oxford University Press, 2011); U Manthe, 'Die Collatio: Inhalt, Textkritik und Verfasserfrage' in U Manthe, S Nishimura

the working hypothesis here employed is that:[3] the Collatio uses or reproduces Ulpian's commentary, as available to the author of the Collatio. The reproduction is not altogether reliable, as the manuscript basis for the Collatio itself is rather difficult, and the specific copy of Ulpian's commentary used by the author may already have been marred by deteriorations that could have befallen the text in the course of its transmission between the 220s CE and the compilation of the Collatio. On the bright side, the text of the Collatio shows us a text without the intervention of Justinian's compilers. For reasons of brevity, the Collatio text is here equated with Ulpian's text, even though this may only be an approximation.

Collatio 12.7.1–10 is a continuous discussion of liabilities triggered by the use – or abuse – of fire.[4] The predominant – but not the exclusive – interest is Aquilian liability, not only regarding the third chapter but perhaps also the first, since Coll. 12.7.7 encompasses the loss of a slave. The whole passage is artfully structured. Collatio 12.7.1–5 deal with the use of fire on or against farmland and buildings in town and in the countryside. Collatio 12.7.6 stays on this topic and introduces a Severan constitution (with slight variations owing to the specificities of the imperially decided case); this is also the topic in Coll. 12.7.7 and Coll. 12.7.9. Collatio 12.7.8 addresses a problem regarding the object damaged, namely a hearth that is part of a common wall; here, the *cautio damni infecti* comes into view. Collatio 12.7.7–9 bring in additional layers of complexity: first, in that slaves are the handling the fire (Coll. 12.7.7 and 9); and, second, in that a hearth is part of a common wall, and causation can be seen as based on omission. The discussion culminates in the well-known report on the controversial treatment of the burning out of someone else's bees (Coll. 12.7.10). The easy thread of topics, interwoven so that one topic flows into another, is characteristic of Ulpian's (as of others') edictal commentaries.

and M Igimi (eds), *Aus der Werkstatt römischer Juristen: Vorträge der Europäisch-Ostasiatischen Tagung 2013 Fukuoka* (Berlin, Duncker & Humblot, 2016) 197; U Manthe, 'Dubletten im Text der Collatio als Spuren der Redaktionstätigkeit' in K Muscheler (ed), *Römische Jurisprudenz – Dogmatik, Überlieferung, Rezeption: Festschrift für Detlef Liebs zum 75. Geburtstag* (Berlin, Duncker & Humblot, 2011) 395; U Manthe, 'Collatio 6,7 pr. isdem adstipulantibus' in M Avenarius, R Meyer-Pritzl and C Möller (eds), *Ars Iuris: Festschrift für Okko Behrends zum 70. Geburtstag* (Göttingen, Wallstein, 2009) 351; ME Montemayor Aceves, *Comparación de Leyes Mosaicas y Romanas*, 2nd edn (México City, Universidad Nacional Autónoma de México, 2006), XV–XXVII; R Pilipow, 'The Jeweled Jurist: Late Roman Legal Aesthetics' (2020) 4 *Studies in Late Antiquity* 185.

[3] Frakes (n 2), 121–23.

[4] See Pilipow (n 2), 191–96 (on our text, at 195); F Lucrezi, *Il procurato incendio in diritto ebraico e romano* (Turin, Giappichelli, 2012), 11–30; WAJ Watson, 'Two Studies in Textual History' in WAJ Watson, *Studies in Roman Private Law* (London, Hambledon Press, 1991) 345; PJ du Plessis, 'Notes on a fire' in F Sturm and others (eds), *Liber Amicorum Guido Tsuno* (Frankfurt, Vico, 2013) 309, mentioning our text in passing at 314.

II. *Confronto*

A. The Two Texts

Coll. 12.7[5]	Digest
1. […] *Item si insulam meam adusseris vel incenderis Aquiliae actionem habebo idemque est et si arbustum meum vel villam meam*	D. 9.2.27.7 *Item si arbustum meum vel villam meam incenderis Aquiliae actionem habebo.*
2. *Quod si dolo quis insulam exusserit etiam capitis poena plectitur quasi incendiarius*	D. 48.8.10: *Si quis dolo insulam meam exusserit capitis poena plectetur quasi incendiarius.*
3. *Item si quis insulam voluerit exurere et ignis etiam ad vicini insulam pervenerit Aquilia tenebitur lege vicino etiam non minus inquilinis ob res eorum exustas et ita Labeo libro XV responsorum refert*	D. 9.2.27.8 *Si quis insulam voluerit meam exurere et ignis etiam ad vicini(s?) insulam pervenerit Aquilia tenebitur etiam vicino non minus etiam inquilinis tenebitur ob res eorum exustas.*
1. […] If you have singed my tenement-house, or set it on fire, I shall have an Aquilian action; this also applies [if done] to my tree-planation or my villa.	D. 9.2.27.7 Moreover, if you set fire to my tree-plantation, or to my villa, I shall have an Aquilian action.
2. But if someone has maliciously burnt out a tenement-house, he is also capitally punished as if an incendiary.	D. 48.8.10 If someone has maliciously burnt out my tenement-house, he is also capitally punished as if an incendiary.
3. Moreover, if someone should intend to burn out a tenement-house, and the fire has spread to the neighbour's tenement house, he will be liable to the neighbour according to the *Lex Aquilia*, no less so than to the tenants on account of their burnt-out belongings as well; and thus Labeo holds in the Fifteenth Book of his *Responses*.	D. 9.2.27.8 If someone should intend to burn out my tenement-house, and the fire has spread also to the neighbour's tenement house, he will be liable also to the neighbour according to the *Aquilia*; no less will he be liable, also, to the tenants on account of their burnt out belongings.

These are the differences that can be spotted between each pair:

- From Coll. 12.7.1 to D. 9.2.27.7 – The object named first, *insula*, is omitted. The two objects that the Collatio states can be handled like the *insula*, the *arbustum* and *villa*, have become the objects dealt with. Of the two verbs, *adurere* and *incendere*, only *incendere* is retained.
- From Coll. 12.7.2 to D. 48.8.10 – The *quod* at the beginning is omitted. The *insula*, the target of the arsonist, is qualified as *mea*. The *etiam* is cut out.

[5] Both texts are here reproduced without punctuation.

- From Coll. 12.7.3 to D. 9.2.27.8 – The information that the case has been the subject of a *responsum* of Labeo is cut out. The *insula*, the target of the arsonist, is qualified as *mea*. An *etiam* is so placed that it refers to the *vicinus*. An *etiam* is added so as to refer to the inhabitants and their movables. The *tenebitur* is doubled, now expressly referring to the neighbour and to the inhabitants, respectively.

B. Coll. 12.7.1 – D. 9.2.27.7

Insula is the object dealt with by Ulpian throughout Coll. 12.7.1–3, with the *arbustum* and the *villa* only mentioned in passing. The whole text is about arson relating to *insulae*.[6] By contrast, the Digest deals with the arson directed against *villa* and *arbustum* on the one hand, and *insula* on the other, in neat separation. We shall return to the reason for the compilers' elimination of *insula* in this first sentence a little later.

Two acts, directed against an *insula*, are said to trigger liability under the *lex Aquilia*: *adurere* and *incendere*. *Adurere* is the term needed to explain the direct applicability of chapter III, which uses the term *urere*. The verb *incendere* works as a bridge to criminal liability, since this is the verb used to describe the delict of arson (*incendium*). The *vel* in my view signals synonymity: *adurere* and *incendere* here describe the very same action, alerting the reader to a potentially two-fold relevance of both Aquilian and criminal liability.

The clause *et si arbustum meum vel villam meam* has been severely criticised as superfluous.[7] The Roman law of arson, however, did make a distinction between arson in the city and in the countryside, in that only *incendium in oppidum* met with capital punishment.[8] For Aquilian liability, it made no difference.

C. Coll. 12.7.2 – D. 48.8.10

The object remains the same – an *insula* – but the act is now described as *exurere*. From here on, the text mainly uses this verb, with varying objects. The objects

[6] For *insulae* in Roman law, see JM Rainer, 'Zur *insula* im Römischen Recht' in MJ Schermaier, JM Rainer and LC Winkel (eds), *Iurisprudentia universalis: Festschrift für Theo Mayer-Maly zum 70. Geburtstag* (Cologne, Böhlau, 2002) 609; on the landlord–tenant relationship, see PJ du Plessis, *Letting and Hiring in Roman Legal Thought: 27 BCE—284 CE* (Leiden, Brill, 2012), 161 ff and passim; PJ du Plessis, 'Urban Landlords and Tenants' in PJ du Plessis, C Ando and K Tuori (eds), *The Oxford Handbook of Roman Law and Society* (Oxford, Oxford University Press, 2016) 635; on leasing practices in Rome, see C Willems, '„Urbanes" Mietrecht? Der römische Wohnungsmarkt zwischen Preismechanismus und Intervention' (2019) 136 *ZRG RA* 233.

[7] Watson (n 4) 359, following F Wieacker, *Textstufen klassischer Juristen* (Göttingen, Vandenhoeck & Ruprecht, 1960), 238.

[8] Coll. 12.2.1, 12.4, 12.5.1; *cf* T Mommsen, *Römisches Strafrecht* (Leipzig, Duncker & Humblot, 1899), 841.

are: *insula* (Coll. 12.7.2, 3 and 9); *praedium* (Coll. 12.7.4–5); *villa* (Coll. 12.7.7, 9); tenants' movable property (Coll. 12.7.3); and bees (Coll. 12.7.10). In a non-legal context, *exurere* often refers to the use of fire as a tool of war: *oppida, villas, classem exurere*.[9] By contrast, Ulpian describes damaging agricultural land by fire as *adurere/incendere* (Coll. 12.7.1) and *depopulare* (Coll. 12.7.6). *Exurere* refers to intentional destruction by fire and/or smoke, with a connotation that the fire affects, or is even directed at, objects that are inhabited, thus indirectly targeting the users or inhabitants.

Why is the wrongdoer here punished *quasi incendiarius*?[10] The Roman jurists' use of *quasi* has been the subject of extensive research.[11] It is perhaps a fair summary to say that *quasi* signals two matters: first, the case at hand can ultimately be dealt with by the statute (or action) in question but, second, this appears prima facie doubtful and it is only by liberal interpretation that the statutory rule can be applied. What is the cause of doubt in our case? The Digest inserts a *meam*. This insertion removes the possibility that the arsonist is the owner of the *insula*; this, in fact, is its only function. If the insertion of *meam* is a response to an ambivalence, the original must have invited, or at least allowed, the understanding that the arson was undertaken by the owner himself. This would have been a good reason to doubt the applicability of the *lex Cornelia de sicariis et veneficis*: the perpetrator is only *quasi incendiarius*, since he endangers or damages not another's but his own property, targeting his own tenants. No other reason for the *quasi* presents itself. All this has been set out, in wonderful detail, by Luciano Minieri,[12] who has thus also paved the way for a new understanding of Coll. 12.7.3. If the original text addressed the case of an *insula*-owner who burnt out his own urban *insula*, the initial *quod* would be an appropriate preposition, because the text would change from an arsonist-versus-owner situation in Coll. 12.7.1 to cases where the arsonist is the owner.

It is a requirement for *incendium* that the perpetrator act with a sinister purpose (*dolo*);[13] the standard case was probably the intent to use the mayhem for theft: 'An incendiary, one guilty of arson (*incendium*) … was punished with the death penalty (by burning) when he willfully had set fire to another's property within the city, either for reasons of enmity or for the purpose of committing a robbery'.[14] If

[9] 'exūrō' in PGW Glare (ed), *Oxford Latin Dictionary*, vol I (A–L), 2nd edn (Oxford, University Press, 2012) 728.

[10] On this question, see L Minieri, *Exurere, adurere, incendere: Studi sul procurato incendio in diritto romano* (Naples, Satura, 2012), 79–101; the relevant chapter has been re-published: 'Sul *quasi incendiarius*' in F Sturm and others (eds), *Liber Amicorum Guido Tsuno* (Frankfurt, Vico, 2013) 251.

[11] On Ulpian's use of *quasi*, see B Spagnolo, below, ch 11. To cite just one other contribution: G Wesener, 'Zur Denkform des "quasi" in der römischen Jurisprudenz' in Università di Parma Facoltà di giurisprudenza (ed), *Studi in memoria di Guido Donatuti*, vol 3 (Milan, Cisalpino-La goliardica, 1973) 1387.

[12] Minieri, 'Sul *quasi incendiarius*' (n 10).

[13] Mommsen (n 8), 841; OF Robinson, *The Criminal Law of Ancient Rome* (London, Duckworth, 1995), 35–36.

[14] A Berger, 'Incendiarius', in *Encyclopedic Dictionary of Roman Law* (Philadelphia, The American Philosophical Society, 1953), 497.

someone burns out his own tenement-house, the sinister purpose will presumably involve the targeting, or at least endangering, of his *insularii*.

Last but not least, the Digest has also cut out the *etiam*. The *etiam* must refer to another liability falling upon the arsonist. The most natural reading is to understand this as referring to the liability for compensation, based on the *lex Aquilia*; the victims claiming compensation would be the tenants. In the context of D. 48.8, there was no reason to retain this reference in the text.

D. Coll. 12.7.3 – D. 9.2.27.8

We learn that the case here addressed was the subject of a *responsum* of Labeo. In all likelihood, Labeo's *responsum* was given in respect of a real-life case. Ideally, it would be possible to identify the parties to the dispute, which led one of them, or both, to consult the famous jurist. More likely than not, it would have been a case of some economic import, although it is possible, in theory, that the jurist was consulted over *minima*, about which a *praetor* would hardly care.

The Ulpianic text in Coll. 12.7.3 has no *ego* and no *tu*, whereas these juxtapose the owner and the arsonist in Coll. 12.7.1; all parties in Coll. 12.7.3 are referred to as 'he'. By contrast, *ego* features as one of the victims in the parallel text in D. 9.2.27.8, by virtue of the inserted *meam* (but the arsonist is not morphed into a 'you' again). The number of victims is thus increased: the Collatio only expressly mentions the neighbour and the tenants, while the Digest encompasses, in plain terms, (1) *ego*, the owner of the house set on fire, (2) the neighbour, and (3) the tenants. The Digest text entails surgical linguistic changes that reinforce this three-victim scenario, namely the addition of one *etiam* and the rearrangement of yet another *etiam*. The *etiam* shifted in front of *vicino* implies that, apart from the neighbour, there is a more obvious victim, which can only be the owner of the house set on fire in the first place. The *etiam non minus*, which, as a clause could freely be translated as 'no less than to the tenants' (*inquilinis* is an ablative of comparison), is by an inversion of *etiam* and *non minus* turned into '[and] also no less' to the tenants. This last change is reinforced by the doubling of *tenebitur*: while the liability vis-à-vis the tenants in the Collatio was but the reference point (to the neighbour 'no less liable than to the tenants'), it now becomes a regular sub-clause, which rounds up the overall legal analysis ('and, not to forget, the arsonist becomes liable to the tenants, too'). *Inquilinis* is now in the dative case, the object of the immediately subsequent *tenebitur*.

The real-life dispute, if we assume that Labeo's *responsum* was written for such, must have been between the neighbour and the *insula*-owner, who set fire to his own *insula*.[15] Hence the liability towards the tenants came in, for Ulpian as for

[15] Another case of an owner who sets fire to his own *insula* is dealt with by Paul in D. 4.3.18.2 (Paul. 11 *ad Ed.*). Here, the arsonist's objective may have been to extinguish a *ususfructus* that restricted his use of his property.

Labeo, as a side aspect, albeit one that supports holding the owner-arsonist liable to the neighbour. This argument only works if the tenants are taken to be the tenants of the house targeted by the wrongdoer. If compensation for the neighbour's tenants' property had been at stake, a problem of remoteness would have arisen; their damage seems even more remote than the damage to the neighbour's building. However, since both liabilities mentioned seem to be based uncontroversially on an *actio directa*, Ulpian cannot have seen any serious remoteness problem, which would have called for a discussion of an *actio in factum*. Bruce Frier aptly asked, with regard to both the neighbour and the tenants: 'Why can they bring a statutory rather than an *in factum* lawsuit? Is it … because [the] act of arson was intentional?'[16]

Unfortunately, modern editions of the Collatio support the three-victim scenario: they place a comma between *etiam* and *non minus*,[17] thereby suggesting and supporting the idea that the arsonist becomes liable to three victims, namely – tacitly – to the owner of the first house he set on fire, to the owner of the adjacent house, and to the tenants (with regard to their belongings).

Coming back to Coll. 12.7.1 and D. 9.2.27.7, we can now understand the surgical cut-out of the *insula*. In the Ulpianic text, the *insula* is dealt with first, as the target of an extraneous arsonist in Coll. 12.7.1, whereas Coll. 12.7.2–3 then tackle the *insula*-owner who targets his own property. Since the Digest turns the latter passage into an *extraneus*-arsonist-case, the same case turning on an *insula* would feature twice; redundancy was averted by taking the *insula* out of D. 9.2.27.7, leaving as objects only the *villa* and *arbustum*.

This, then, is the real-life case that emerges: a landlord tries to get rid of his tenants – they are his target – and he uses fire to drive them out; in doing so, the neighbouring house catches fire. The parties to the real-life dispute, for whom Labeo's *responsum* elucidated the legal situation, were the arsonist and his neighbour, as claimant. A considerable compensation claim may have been at stake. As Ulpian did not give a more elaborate explanation of the situation, one may assume that his readers could be expected to understand *insulam exurere* as referring to the landlord's targeting his tenants.

III. *Insulam Exurere*: Evicting Tenants *Dolo Malo* with Fire

This is the gist of Ulpian's text: if an arsonist sets fire to someone else's *insula*, he is liable under the *lex Aquilia* for damage to that property. Should someone burn out

[16] BW Frier, *A Casebook on the Roman Law of Delict* (Atlanta, Scholars Press, 1989), 75.

[17] Frakes (n 2), 185; M Hyamson (ed), *Mosaicarum et Romanarum Legum Collatio* (London, Oxford University Press, 1913), 118; PF Girard and F Senn, *Textes de droit romain*, vol I, 7th edn (Dalloz, Paris, 1967), 576. The one edition that pointed in the right direction was PE Huschke, *Iurisprudentiae Anteiustinianae quae svpersvnt* (Leipzig, Teubner, 1861), 570: *Si quis insulam (suam) uoluerit exurere, et ignis etiam ad uicini insulam peruenerit, Aquilia tenebitur lege uicino: non minus etiam inquilinis ob res*

his own tenement-house for a sinister purpose, he will be punished as if he were an arsonist, on the basis of an extensive (liberal) interpretation of the *lex Cornelia de sicariis et veneficis*, to say nothing of his liability to pay compensation for the damage. Further, if the fire should spread to his neighbour's *insula*, he will become liable, under the *lex Aquilia*, to the neighbour for the damage to or destruction of his *insula*, and he will of course also be liable under the *lex Aquilia* for the damage done to the tenants' properties.

There might be several reasons why a landlord would try illegally to evict tenants by means of fire. He may want to get rid of these specific tenants, perhaps because they cannot come up with the rent, or perhaps he intends to demolish and rebuild the tenement block in a more profitable manner. It is a practice that survives into our time. In the *The Times* obituary of Toni Morrison, one reads: 'She was two when the family's landlord set fire to their house because her parents were unable to pay the rent'.[18] This happened 1931 in Lorain, Ohio, a steel-manufacturing town near Cleveland.

It is worth briefly looking at the link to the subsequent passages, Coll. 12.7.4 and D. 9.2.27.8, respectively. The case dealt with in Coll. 12.7.4 differs from the one resolved in Coll. 12.7.3 in two respects. First, we turn to a country setting (*extra oppidum*) and, second, the defendant is not an arsonist but a farmer undertaking the age-old agricultural practice of burning stubble in his own field. If we take it that, in Coll. 12.7.3, it was the owner who targeted his own tenants, the cases share a similarity, since in Coll. 12.7.4–6 it is also the owner who employs fire on his own property.

The deliberation in Coll. 12.7.4 is related to the preceding sentence by a *sed*. Indeed, the cases of Coll. 12.7.3 and Coll. 12.7.4 are disposed of in an antithetical fashion. Why is the direct applicability of the *lex Aquilia* a problem here, but not in the case of Coll. 12.7.3? The answer is given in Celsus's words, *quia non principaliter hic excussit*: the wrongdoer in Coll. 12.7.3 has the intention to burn out a (one) house, so he can be held liable also for the destruction of (or damage to) the neighbour's house. He is undoubtedly liable in any event and on the strength of a direct action, to the (his) tenants; it is a small step, therefore, to hold him liable to the neighbour as well. However, the burning of stubble on one's own field is a neutral activity, which does not, as such, entail a wrong. It does not imply *dolus malus*. The effect on the neighbouring *praedium* is the result of negligence (as suggested in the rescript referred to in Coll. 12.7.6). By contrast, the nasty landlord in Coll. 12.7.3 has overstepped the boundaries of the law by setting fire to his *insula*, and, as he faces both criminal and delictual liability (towards his tenants), there is no reason not to hold him liable to the neighbour, too.

eorum exustas. Et ita Labeo libro 'xv. responsorum refert. Huschke assumed that the loss of *suam* was due to a scribal slip, induced by the haplography *insulam/suam*. He further saw the word *lege* after *tenebitur* switched for *etiam*.

[18] Obituaries, 'Toni Morrison' *The Times* (7 August 2019) 47.

IV. Collatio and Digest

The Collatio has always been used as fertile ground for research focused on pre-Justinianic changes in the textual transmission of the classical jurists' writings.[19] It was once assumed that, along the way, some of these texts had been considerably reworked here and there, and that Justinian's compilers in these instances could only rely on already deteriorated material (so-called 'post-classical editions'). The idea was launched by Fritz Schulz.[20] In his footsteps, in 1949 Hans Julius Wolff scrutinised select passages from 'Ulpian XVIII ad edictum' in the Collatio.[21] He saw Coll. 12.7.3 (which was not among the texts he analysed closely) as proving that Justinian's compilers and the author of the Collatio did not use identical copies of Ulpian's commentary; Wolff tried to show that the compilers had a relatively better text at their disposal. Here, however, he found the variances 'very minor':[22]

> The Digest version does not run any more smoothly than the Collatio, so that the deviations in the former can hardly be laid to a desire of the compilers to improve on the style of their source. In particular, I can see no reason other than a difference of their respective copies for the fact that the Digest adds *meam* where the Collatio omits it …

Franz Wieacker, who built on Schulz's ideas in presenting his own hypotheses to the German-speaking Roman law community,[23] diligently noted all textual variants.[24] Like Wolff, he thought that the omission of the Labeo reference was in line with the general editing policies of the compilers.[25] *Item* had to be cut out, since, in the Digest, the text does not link to the previous sentence. The only other variation of substance was the omission of *meam*. Here, Wieacker assumed that the author of the Collatio took *meam* out of the Ulpianic original. He realised that the loss of *meam* takes out the information that the arsonist was someone else ('Fremdbrandstiftung'). This, he thought, would be a massive interpolation (by the author of the Collatio), unless it were incidental. Alan Watson also saw – but discarded – the possibility of reading the Collatio as dealing with the owner of a tenement-house, who sets his own property on fire:

[19] See the literature in n 2.

[20] F Schulz, *History of Roman Legal Science* (Oxford, Oxford University Press, 1946), 141–44. Schulz had sketched his view in earlier publications.

[21] HJ Wolff, 'Ulpian XVIII ad edictum in collatio and digest and the problem of postclassical editions of classical works' in Università cattolica del Sacro Cuore (ed), *Scritti in onore di Contardo Ferrini*, vol 4 (Milan, Vita e pensiero, 1949) 64.

[22] ibid, 81.

[23] Schulz's book had initially been written in German but a German edition came out only in 1961, so that, in a German arena, one might assume that Wieacker could claim priority. For a recent critique of Wieacker's approach, see D Liebs, 'Wenn Fachliteratur Gesetz wird: Inwieweit wurden römische Juristenschriften im Lauf der Jahrhunderte überarbeitet' (2018) 135 *ZRG RA* 395.

[24] Wieacker (n 7), 238–39.

[25] Wieacker contradicted Wolff, in that he thought that the compilers had a copy of Ulpian's commentary that in principle suffered from the same corruptions as the one used by the author of the Collatio.

> The sole flaw in this Collatio text is the absence of *meam* which, almost certainly wrongly, gives the impression that the tenement was set on fire by the owner. This lack, which is not reproduced in the Digest should be attributed to a scribal slip.[26]

> Much more likely [than the 'extreme interpretation' of the owner's burning his own tenement], *meam* which appears in D. 9.2.27.8 has been omitted and this is a case of arson by a third party.[27]

The main thrust of Watson's piece was to push back against the idea of an intensive and substantial reworking of the classical jurists' texts in a pre-Justinianic period.

It was unfortunate that these authors dismissed most of the variations as incidental and unimportant. The various changes are all linked to one another, in a purposive reworking of the text. The overarching purpose of all of these changes is expressly to re-stylise the case, so that the arsonist cannot be taken to be the landlord/owner. This change can only be attributed to Justinian's compilers. It is impossible that, in a reverse scenario, the text used by Justinian's compilers could be truer to Ulpian's original, while the author of the Collatio doctored an essentially identical text so as to let ambiguities creep in, ambiguities that – unlike Ulpian's putative original – would have invited identifying the arsonist as the owner of the *insula*. The changes are simply too elaborate and too artful to originate from anyone but the high-calibre professionals compiling the Digest.[28] Given the coherence of the multitude of coordinated textual changes, the classification of *meam* as a 'scribal slip' (Watson, following Wieacker) is out of the question. The compilers' canny interpolation remained somewhat imperfect. Above all, they overlooked that, for the re-stylised case, the arsonist's liability to the neighbour and tenants needed to be based on an *actio in factum*, whereas a direct action could be granted to the house-owner.

Why did Justinian's compilers so fundamentally change the case? As with most, if not all, interpolations not accompanied, or backed up, by one of Justinian's *Quinquaginta decisiones*,[29] this interpolation did not change the law. Omitting the reference to Labeo's *responsum* seems to streamline the text for its use as 'statute law'. The compilers must then have realised that Ulpian's text could (or should) be read as dealing with the horrid landlord, and we can deduce that they did not want such a text for the Digest. If it had been otherwise – if they were just anxious that Ulpian's text not be ambivalent – they could easily have inserted a clarifying *suam*

[26] Watson (n 4), 360 (footnotes omitted).

[27] ibid, 348 fn 10.

[28] On the working of Justinian's compilers, see the contributions to M Avenarius and others (eds), *Gradenwitz, Riccobono und die Entwicklung der Interpolationenkritik: Methodentransfer unter europäischen Juristen im späten 19. Jahrhundert = Gradenwitz, Riccobono e gli sviluppi della critica interpolazionistica: Circolazione di modelli e metodi fra giuristi europei nel tardo Ottocento* (Tübingen, Mohr Siebeck, 2018), as well as JHA Lokin, 'The End of an Epoch: Epilegomena to a Century of Interpolation Criticism' in R Feenstra and others (eds), *Collatio Iuris Romani*, vol I (Amsterdam, Gieben, 1995) 261, FJ Andrés Santos, 'Brevissima storia della critica interpolazionistica nelle fonti giuridiche romane' (2011) 23 *Revista de estudios histórico-jurídicos* 65.

[29] Lokin (n 28), 267.

after *insulam*. Could it be that the evil practice of evicting one's undesirable tenants by fire, which may have been notorious in Rome in the first and second centuries CE, was uncommon or unknown in sixth-century Constantinople and other cities of the Byzantine Empire?

This humble enquiry is not meant to be a contribution to the general debate about the respective places of the Collatio and the Digest in the grand scheme of the transmission of the Roman jurists' writings. Suffice it to say that credit for the differences between the Digest and Collatio must here go to Justinian's compilers. This is, of course, not to say that the text of Ulpian's commentary that the author of the Collatio used was a perfect reproduction of an 'original' copy from Ulpian's times.

11

Quasi and *(Cor)ruptio*

BENJAMIN SPAGNOLO

The notion of *corruptio* arises in diverse contexts in Roman public and private law. It is named in the *actio de albo corrupto* and *actio servi corrupti*, and famously subsumes *ruptio* as a controlling concept in an *actio damni iniuriae* under chapter III of the *lex Aquilia*. In the context of damage to property, disagreement between the third-century jurist Ulpian and some of his predecessors has been discerned on the question whether *corruptio* requires a physical change to the *res*. This chapter reveals an 'antiphonal' structure in Ulpian's edictal commentary on the Aquilian verbs *rumpere* and *corrumpere*: it argues that the Severan jurist repeatedly pairs a text affirming a principle about *ruptio* or *corruptio* with an 'answering' text illustrating pragmatic attenuation of that principle – an extension of liability that is economically, socially or politically useful, though not strictly logical. In particular, this chapter argues that Ulpian employs the adverb *quasi* in the answering text of each pair to signal this pragmatic, analogical extension. Understanding this stylistic marker and the broader structure in which it is employed facilitates more nuanced reflection on Ulpian's overall argument and on his approach to the works of his predecessors.

I. Ulpian 18 *ad Edictum*

Commentary on the Aquilian verbs *rumpere* and *corrumpere* is excerpted from book 18 of Ulpian's *ad Edictum* in the continuous run from D. 9.2.27.13 to 28. In his reconstruction of *ad Edictum*, Lenel retains the sequence of texts but tentatively inserts D. 47.10.25, about *stuprum* of a female slave, between 17 and 18.[1] Having regard to the link between 17 and 18 identified below,[2] Lenel's suggested interposition should be resisted.[3] Lenel considers that Ulpian's commentary on *ruperit* ends at 24.[4] Rodger differs; he would include 25–28 on *ruperit*, identifying 29–33

[1] O Lenel, *Palingenesia Iuris Civilis*, vol 2 (Leipzig, Tauchnitz, 1889), cols 529–30.
[2] Below, section VIII.
[3] Birks also resists Lenel's suggestion, placing D. 47.10.25 after D. 9.2.28, for other reasons: PBH Birks, 'Other Men's Meat: Aquilian Liability for Proper Use' (1981) 16 *Irish Jurist* 141, 151.
[4] Lenel (n 1), col 530 §624.

as commentary on *fregerit*.[5] Subject to impacts of possible interpolation, Rodger's palingenesia is preferable, for two reasons. First, in the approach to *rumpere* set out at 17, Ulpian includes *damnum* as a limit on what count as *ruptiones*; 25–28 explore that limit in a coherent fashion, in a plausible sequence following the discussion of other aspects of *ruperit* at 17–24. Second, in light of Rodger's compelling reconstruction of the sequence up to 13 as a commentary on *urere* and the sequence after 28 as a commentary on *fregerit*, 25–28 is better understood as continuing the commentary on *ruperit* commenced at 13 than as part of the commentary on *damnum faxit ... iniuria*.

It is usually contended that the passage 13–28 reveals juristic disagreement: Celsus, writing in the earlier second century CE, holds that *rumpere*, interpreted as *corrumpere*, required some change to the *res*; Ulpian, writing about a century later, seems to suggest there is *corruptio*, with or without change to the thing, as long as there was functional or economic deterioration.[6] To appreciate properly Ulpian's ultimate position, it is necessary to discern the granular structure of his argument and, in particular, the significance of a pattern texts introduced by *quasi*.

II. *Quasi*

The adverb *quasi* 'is one of those elastic expressions'[7] that has several meanings. Preceding an indicative verb, *quasi* often means 'as'. However, in some juristic texts, *quasi* means 'as if'[8] – it signifies an extension by 'simile'[9] or, broadly speaking,[10] by

[5] AF Rodger, 'The Palingenesia of the Commentaries Relating to the Lex Aquilia' (2007) 124 *ZRG RA* 145, 196.

[6] FH Lawson, *Negligence in the Civil Law* (Oxford, Oxford University Press, 1950), 23; R Zimmermann, *The Law of Obligations: Roman Foundations of the Civilian Tradition* (Oxford, Oxford University Press, 1996), 986–87.

[7] A Berger, 'quasi' in *Encyclopedic Dictionary of Roman Law* (Philadelphia, The American Philosophical Society, 1953) 665.

[8] D Nörr, *Causa mortis: auf den Spuren einer Redewendung* (Munich, Beck, 1986), 130; U Von Lübtow, *Untersuchungen zur lex Aquilia de damno iniuria dato* (Berlin, Duncker & Humblot, 1971), 112–13; F Musumeci, '*«Quasi ruperit», «quasi rupto»*. In tema di applicazione concreta del terzo capitolo della lex Aquilia' in C Russo Ruggeri (ed), *Studi in onore di Antonino Metro*, vol IV (Milan, Giuffrè, 2010) 347, 350–51.

[9] E Bund, *Untersuchungen zur Methode Julians* (Cologne, Böhlau, 1965), 126. The term 'analogy' is used here, ignoring Bund's technical distinctions (124–26) between phenomena including analogies, fictions, presumptions and hypothetical cases – distinctions that are in any case unclear in the Roman juristic context: M Kaser, *Römische Rechtsquellen und angewandte Juristenmethode* (Vienna, Böhlau, 1986), 263–66. See also D Nörr, 'Book Review: Wolfram Kerber, Die Quasi-Institute als Methode der römischen Rechtsfindung' (1973) 90 *ZRG RA* 421, 423; K Hackl, 'Sulla finzione nel diritto privato' in F Pastori (ed), *Studi in onore di Arnaldo Biscardi*, vol I (Milan, Cisalpino–La Goliardica, 1982) 245; K Hackl, 'Vom „quasi“ in römischen zum „als ob“ im modernen Recht' in R Zimmermann, R Knütel and JP Meincke (eds), *Rechtsgeschichte und Privatrechtsdogmatik* (Heidelberg, CF Müller, 1999) 117, 122–25; and, on 'comparaisons associatives', T Giaro, 'L'Art de comparer les cas' (1994) 60 *SDHI* 522.

[10] G Wesener, 'Zur Denkform des "quasi" in der römischen Jurisprudenz' in Università di Parma Facoltà di giurisprudenza (ed), *Studi in memoria di Guido Donatuti*, vol 3 (Milan, Cisalpino-La goliardica, 1973) 1387, 1413–14.

> analogy or resemblance ... it negatives the notion of an identity between [two conceptions]; but it points out that they are sufficiently similar for one to be classed as the sequel to the other ... and employed without violent straining in the statement of rules which would otherwise be imperfectly expressed.[11]

Quasi signals the admissibility of treating equally situations that are relevantly distinguishable but also relevantly similar,[12] having regard to practical effects[13] and underlying reasons.[14] The tool allows the jurists 'to attain indirectly ends that could not be attained directly, while keeping intact, and respecting, the fundamental principles of the system'.[15] While classical jurists tend to apply *quasi* to verbs,[16] Byzantine texts further stretch the adverb's creative potential, to generate substantives such as *quasi ususfructus*, *quasi possessio* and *quasi castrense*.[17]

Ulpian uses *quasi* in over 580 surviving instances.[18] Often, he employs *quasi* to mean 'as' – the sense of explanation or exemplification.[19] However, Ulpian also frequently deploys *quasi* analogically, signifying extension to a situation contrary to established fact or legal principle; as in D. 11.7.16, where funeral expenses are to be paid 'as if' from deceased wives' dowries – *quasi de patrimoniis suis* – although the dowry was never in the *patrimonium* of the wife but always that of her husband or father.[20] All eight instances in which Ulpian writes *quasi de* are arguably counterfactual, though sometimes only the weak counterfactual 'on the imagined basis that' is intended.[21] Ulpian uses *quasi* before a verb in 11 texts in

[11] HJS Maine, *Ancient Law*, repr edn (first published 1861, London, Oxford University Press, 1954), 286.

[12] Kaser, *Römische Rechtsquellen und angewandte Juristenmethode* (n 9), 262; S Riccobono, 'Analisi delle decisioni di Paolo in confronto alle riforme giustinianee: Appendice III: Analogia, assimilazione, approssimazione nell'opera dei giuristi romani ed in particolare dell'uso dell'avverbio "quasi"' (1917) 3–4 *AUPA* 697, 699.

[13] A Carcaterra, *Il possesso dei diritti nel diritto romano* (Milan, Giuffrè, 1942), 136.

[14] A Lovato, *Studi sulle Disputationes di Ulpiano* (Bari, Cacucci, 2003), 276.

[15] S Riccobono, 'Studi critici sulle fonte del diritto romano' (1895) 8 *BIDR* 169, 179 ('raggiungere per vie oblique quei fini, che non si potevano con le dirette, pur tenendo fermi e rispettando i principi fondamentali del sistema'). See also S Riccobono, 'La Giurisprudenza classica come fattore di evoluzione nel diritto romano' in GG Archi (ed), *Scritti di diritto romano in onore di Contardo Ferrini* (Milan, Hoepli, 1946) 18, 54.

[16] Wesener (n 10), 1394. On Ulpian's use of *quasi* preceding a noun, see: ibid, 1398–406, 1409–11.

[17] For a detailed survey of Byzantine and classical sources for *quasi*, see ibid.

[18] Search conducted using G Rosenblaum and P Riedlberger's *Amanuensis* program (v 3, 2017); Riccobono suggests 700 instances: Riccobono, 'Analogia, assimilazione, approssimazione' (n 12), 698.

[19] eg, D. 9.2.5.3: Musumeci, '*«Quasi ruperit», «quasi rupto»*' (n 8), 349; or D. 3.4.2 (Ulp. 8 *ad Ed.*): A Guzmán Brito, 'El significado de "quasi" en el vocabulario de los juristas romanos' (2016) 38 *Revista de estudios histórico-jurídicos* 79, 83. See also L Pellecchi, 'L'Azione in ripetizione e le qualificazioni del *dare* in Paul. 17 *ad Plaut.* D. 12.6.65: Contributo allo studio della *condictio*' (1998) 64 *SDHI* 69, 144 fn 19.

[20] On *quasi* in another case of legal impossibility, D. 12.7.2 (Ulp. 32 *ad Ed.*), see A Saccoccio, *Si certum petetur: Dalla condictio dei veteres alle condictiones giustinianee* (Milan, Giuffrè, 2002), 219–20.

[21] See D. 2.15.1, D. 9.2.15.1, D. 9.4.21.6, D. 11.7.16, D. 16.3.1.33 and D. 28.3.6.8; on D. 9.2.27.20, see below, section IX. Given Ulpian's use of *quasi de* in various other contexts, Hausmaninger's suggestion that Ulpian may have taken the formulation *quasi de corrupto* in D. 9.2.27.20 from Julian seems unlikely: H Hausmaninger, 'Zur Gesetzesinterpretation des Celsus' in *Studi in onore di Giuseppe Grosso*, vol V (Turin, Giappichelli, 1972) 243, 268–69. In relation to D. 9.2.15.1 (*quasi de vulnerato* and *quasi de occiso*), Ernst suggests a link between *quasi* and production in court: *quasi* may signal the admissibility

book 18 *ad Edictum*. Digest 4.9.7.6 appears to be a weak counterfactual about the scope or specificity of a master's or father's undertaking of liability for his slave's or son's management of a ship, inn or stable. In D. 9.4.2.1, a counterfactual – or at least hypothetical – quality is imported by Ulpian's disagreement with Celsus about noxal liability under the XII Tables and under the *lex Aquilia*.

More relevant are the other nine instances of *quasi* in book 18 *ad Edictum*, all excerpted in Digest 9.2 – five relating to chapter I verbs and four relating to chapter III verbs. The five chapter I instances concern liability in cases of cumulative causes (or evidentiary insufficiency), in D. 9.2.11.2, and multiple sufficient causes, in D. 9.2.11.3. *Quasi* is probably used in the descriptive, explanatory sense in these cases – 'held liable for slaying' or 'held liable for wounding'. However, counterfactual use also fits the context of at least those instances where several are 'held liable as if they slew' when it was unclear who struck the fatal blow and where a prior assailant who struck a fatal blow is only 'held liable as if for wounding', because a subsequent assailant, who struck the blow from which the victim perished, is 'held liable as if for slaying'.

This chapter scrutinises in detail the four chapter III instances: D. 9.2.27.18, 20, 22 and 24. Ulpian's use of *quasi* in these texts has been noticed;[22] the striking feature that is explored in this chapter is the 'antiphonal' pattern in Ulpian's argument: no *quasi* in 17, 19, 21 or 23 but *quasi* in 18, 20, 22 and 24.[23] In the passages considered here, *quasi* is given more or less force, according to the translation. Certain scholars argue that *quasi* always means 'as' or 'on the basis that', rather than 'as if' – explanation, rather than analogical extension.[24] In at least some of these instances, other scholars understand *quasi* in the 'as if' sense outlined above – an interpretative tool for bringing into the scope of the *lex* a situation that would, strictly speaking, fall outside it.[25] This chapter argues for the latter view in all four instances, afforced by the observation of an antiphonal structure to Ulpian's argument.

of the statutory action, even where the (now dead) slave 'cannot be brought into court to have his/her wound inspected and evaluated': W Ernst, Justinian's Digest 9.2.51 in the Western Legal Canon: Roman Legal Thought and Modern Causality Concepts (Cambridge, Intersentia, 2019), 117.

[22] eg, DJ Ibbetson, 'Buckland on the *Lex Aquilia* (Appendix to Chapter 2)' in PJ du Plessis (ed), *Wrongful Damage to Property in Roman Law: British Perspectives* (Edinburgh, Edinburgh University Press, 2018) 64, 76, 83–84; Musumeci, '«*Quasi ruperit*», «*quasi rupto*»' (n 8).

[23] On *quasi* in Pomponius's argument in D. 45.1.25, see R Quadrato, *Sulle tracce dell'annullabità: Quasi nullus nella giurisprudenza romana* (Naples, Jovene, 1983), 23–30.

[24] CA Cannata, 'Sul testo della *lex Aquilia* e la sua portata originaria' in L Vacca (ed), *La responsabilità civile da atto illecito nella prospettiva storico-comparatistica* (Turin, Giappichelli, 1995) 25, 48 n 65; Musumeci, '«*Quasi ruperit*», «*quasi rupto*»' (n 8); MV Sanna, '*Rumpere* e *quasi rumpere* tra *lex* e *interpretatio*' (2017) 111 *BIDR* 347, 366.

[25] Musumeci, '«*Quasi ruperit*», «*quasi rupto*»' (n 8), 350 (footnote omitted); F Musumeci, '*Molesta separatio, difficilis separatio* ed esperibilità dell'*actio legis aquiliae*' in *Studi in onore di Remo Martini*, vol II (Milan, Giuffrè, 2009) 821, 833–34. Lawson tentatively suggests that *quasi* might denote a decretal, rather than the edictal action: Lawson (n 6), 107 fn s 20. However, this is unsupported by the texts and inconsistent with *quasi*'s function, articulated above, of assimilating a new situation to an existing one, in order to treat them equally. See also A Corbino, *Il danno qualificato e la Lex Aquilia: Corso di diritto romano*, 2nd edn (Padua, CEDAM, 2008), 62; Musumeci, '«*Quasi ruperit*», «*quasi rupto*»' (n 8), 350 fn 6.

III. D. 9.2.27.13

Ulpian opens his commentary on *ruperit* by reporting, at 13:

> The lex says *ruperit*. Almost all the *veteres* understood the word *rupisse* as *corruperit*.[26]

This preface flags to the reader that Ulpian's subsequent exposition encompasses two legal concepts: the *ruptio* of the *lex* but also the *corruptio* of juristic interpretation; some of what follows is not commentary on *ruperit* at all.

Since he later mentions five jurists (Brutus, Sabinus, Vivianus, Octavenus and Celsus), 'almost all' is tantalising. Not least because we have no textual reference to *corruptio* before Celsus and Julian,[27] appreciating whom Ulpian regards as *veteres* might assist in understanding why he cites their views – for example, as affirming the elision between *rumpere* and *corrumpere*, or as historical hold-outs.[28] *Veteres* is, of course, a relative label – for Justinian, classical jurists, including Ulpian,[29] are *veteres*;[30] for the classical jurists, *veteres* normally means their late Republican predecessors.[31] Ulpian probably numbers Brutus, writing in the second half of the second century BCE, among the *veteres*, since he cites the younger Rutilius on a matter argued *apud veteres*.[32] Ulpian sometimes groups Sabinus, active under Tiberius,[33] with the *veteres*,[34] and sometimes not.[35] In no surviving text does Ulpian use *veteres* in conjunction with the first-century[36] jurists Vivianus and Octavenus. By quoting Celsus's approval of 'the *veteres*' opinion',[37] Ulpian perhaps distinguishes him from that class – but the inference is uncertain. By comparison, three texts more plainly suggest that Ulpian does not include Pomponius, writing in the mid-second century CE, not very long after Celsus, as one of the *veteres*.[38] While Ulpian's own use of the – non-technical – label *veteres* reveals little, it would be consistent with general usage for him to have included Brutus but not Sabinus, Vivianus, Octavenus or Celsus; for these later, Imperial, jurists, it would, then, be settled that *ruptio* includes *corruptio*.[39]

[26] D. 9.2.27.13 (Ulp. 18 *ad Ed.*): *Inquit lex 'ruperit'. Rupisse verbum fere omnes veteres sic intellexerunt 'corruperit'.*

[27] GD MacCormack, 'Aquilian Studies' (1971) 41 *SDHI* 1, 4.

[28] Lawson, eg, suggests that Brutus may have been in the minority and have preferred a statutory action for *quasi rumpere*, where the *res* itself was not changed: Lawson (n 6), 23. MacCormack suggests that Ulpian termed *corrumpere* what some earlier jurists termed *quasi rumpere*: MacCormack, 'Aquilian Studies' (n 27), 4–5. See also Von Lübtow (n 8), 115.

[29] C. 6.49.7.1b (Justinian to Johannes PP, 23 October 530).

[30] eg, C. 1.17.2.11, C 1.17.2.13 and C 1.17.2.20 (Justinian to the Senate and all the people, 16 December 533).

[31] AD Manfredini, *Contributi allo studio dell'«iniuria» in età repubblicana* (Milan, Giuffrè, 1977), 56.

[32] D. 7.8.10.3 (Ulp. 17 *ad Sab.*).

[33] D. 1.2.2.48 and D. 1.2.2.50 (Pomp. *l.s. Enchirid.*).

[34] eg, D. 17.2.52.18 (31 *ad Ed.*).

[35] eg, D. 12.5.6 (18 *ad Sab.*).

[36] C Russo Ruggeri, *Viviano giurista minore?* (Milano, Giuffrè, 1997), 13–25.

[37] eg, D. 7.8.10.3 (17 *ad Sab.*), D. 12.5.6 (18 *ad Sab.*).

[38] D. 2.4.4.2 (5 *ad Ed.*); D. 21.1.23.2 (1 *ad Ed. Aedil. Curul.*); D. 47.10.13.7 (57 *ad Ed.*).

[39] See, however, nn 113 and 122.

IV. D. 9.2.27.14

It is clear from 14 that Celsus understands *ruptio* as *corruptio*:

> And therefore [*ideo*] Celsus asks, if you sow tares or wild oats in another's field of standing corn [*seges*], by which you contaminate it, the *dominus* (or, if there is *locatio conductio* of the land, the *colonus*) may sue not only *quod vi aut clam* but may also sue *in factum*; and, if the *colonus* brings the action, he must undertake that there will be no further suit, that is, that the owner will not trouble the defendant further – since it is one [*nam alia*] sort of loss to spoil [*corrumpere*] and change [*mutare*] the thing itself, where the *lex Aquilia* has a place, and another to attach [*applicare*] something, without any change to the thing itself [*nulla ipsius mutatione*], separation of which is troublesome [*molesta separatio*].[40]

To illustrate that part of the point of 13 was to explain Celsus's discussion in 14 – discussion of a question that, on its face, has nothing to do with *ruperit* but instead with *corruperit* – we may look to *ideo* – 'therefore' or 'on that account'. This adverb is often referenced by a conjunction introducing a causal clause; in 14, we see this in *nam* – 'since'. Inverting the order of the Latin to bring out the effect in English, the structure of 14 is, 'Since [*nam*] it is one sort of loss to spoil and change the thing itself … on that account [*ideo*], Celsus asks …'. This reading is proposed with hesitation, given the noted linguistic defects of 14, attributed to serious compression by the compilers.[41] However, this reading explains why the *nam alia* clause is not in indirect speech: it is not a reason given by Celsus for his answer to the question posed; it is the reason given by Ulpian for Celsus's having posed the question in the first place.[42]

Having opened by telling us that almost all the *veteres* interpreted *ruperit* as *corruperit*, Ulpian reports Celsus's principle that, to qualify under the *lex*, there must be *corruptio* and *mutatio*: adverse change to the *res*.[43] If the proposed reading of the *nam alia* clause is sound, Ulpian himself is associated – albeit not unequivocally – with this *corrumpere et mutare* principle. In the example, Celsus says the owner or *colonus* of the cornfield contaminated by weeds should bring a decretal action *in factum* rather than the action under the *lex*; to the field of standing corn itself, there was *nulla mutatio* – 'no change'. As MacCormack contends, the cornfield – in law, a single *res*, the land – is not adversely changed, even though *damnum* – loss – may exist, in the form of a future harvest that may be diminished or will be

[40] D. 9.2.27.14 (Ulp. 18 *ad Ed.*): *Et ideo Celsus quaerit, si lolium aut avenam in segetem alienam inieceris, quo eam tu inquinares, non solum quod vi aut clam dominum posse agere vel, si locatus fundus sit, colonum, sed et in factum agendum, et si colonus eam exercuit, cavere eum debere amplius non agi, scilicet ne dominus amplius inquietet: nam alia quaedam species damni est ipsum quid corrumpere et mutare, ut lex Aquilia locum habeat, alia nulla ipsius mutatione applicare aliud, cuius molesta separatio sit.*

[41] *Index Interpolationum*, vol I, col 115. See also GD MacCormack, '*Celsus quaerit:* D.9.2.27.14' (1973) 20 *RIDA* 341, 341–42; eg, *posse agere* and *agendum*, no object for *eam exercuit*.

[42] Ulpian may nonetheless be explaining Celsus's view: Musumeci, '*Molesta separatio, difficilis separatio*' (n 25), 825.

[43] MacCormack, 'Aquilian Studies' (n 27), 6.

troublesome to separate.[44] The object in issue is the field, not the harvest: what is troublesome is separating the planted tares or oats from the land.[45] The reference to the interdict *quod vi aut clam* confirms this, since it concerns land and not fruits.[46] Like Servius's *raucis aut herbis segetes corruptae*,[47] which must refer to *corruptio* of cornfields – rather than harvests[48] – by worms or weeds, Celsus contemplates the field of standing corn, a field not itself damaged by the sowing of weeds.[49] A further feature, explored below,[50] is that the conduct is attachment – accession to the land by planting. While, in property law, the discrete identity of the accessory is lost in the merger, that of the principal remains unchanged – *nulla ipsius mutatio.*

V. D. 9.2.27.15

At 15, Ulpian further unpacks Celsus on *corruptio*:

> Celsus says there can plainly be an action under the Aquilian against one who pollutes [*spurcavit*] or pours out [*effudit*] wine, or makes it vinegar [*acetum fecit*], or in another way ruins it [*alio modo vitiavit*], because pouring out and making into vinegar are encompassed in the word *corruptum*.[51]

Whereas 14 was a negative case – no *corruptio*, absent change to the *res* – we now see four examples, in relation to wine, that do count: *spurcare* – 'pollute'; *effundere* – 'pour out'; *acetum facere* – 'turn into vinegar'; and *alio modo vitiare* – 'ruin in some other way'. Although much depends on how we translate *spurcare* and *vitiare*, the sense of these verbs is dilution, adulteration and perhaps total functional destruction. Albanese suspects compression or alteration of Celsus's discussion of *spurcare* and *effundere*, since he does not conceive of these as involving change to the thing; however, MacCormack and Musumeci are surely right that change occurs when wine is poured over or mixed with some other substance.[52]

[44] MacCormack, '*Celsus quaerit:* D.9.2.27.14' (n 41), 344.

[45] Buckland considers the (as yet inextant) crop the object: Ibbetson, 'Buckland on the *Lex Aquilia*' (n 22), 76. While admitting the alternative of damage to the land, Di Porto argues that the weeds are mixed with – and fall to be separated from – the harvested grain: A Di Porto, 'La Tutela della "salubritas" fra editto e giurisprudenza: il ruolo di Labeone' (1988) 91 *BIDR* 459, 495–96 fn 117. This view is rightly rejected: L Capogrossi Colognesi, 'L'interdetto «quod vi aut clam» e il suo àmbito di applicazione' (1993) 21 *Index* 278, 278.

[46] See D. 43.24.7.5 (Ulp. 71 *ad Ed.*); Celsus and Ulpian may differ on the scope of the interdict.

[47] D. 19.2.15.2 (Ulp. 32 *ad Ed.*).

[48] Compare, eg, D. 18.1.78.3 (Lab. 4 *Post. a Iav. Epit.*) (snow ruining the future harvest – *frumenta*, not *seges*).

[49] See also OE Tellegen-Couperus, 'The Tenant, the Borrower and the *lex Aquilia*' (1995) 42 *RIDA* 415, 425–26; Von Lübtow (n 8), 166.

[50] Below, section IX.

[51] D. 9.2.27.15 (Ulp. 18 *ad Ed.*): *Cum eo plane, qui vinum spurcavit vel effudit vel acetum fecit vel alio modo vitiavit, agi posse Aquilia Celsus ait, quia etiam effusum et acetum factum corrupti appellatione continentur.*

[52] MacCormack, 'Aquilian Studies' (n 27), 6; Musumeci, '*Molesta separatio, difficilis separatio*' (n 25), 834 fn 35. Albanese notes that, in D. 9.2.27.35, Ulpian reports Labeo as requiring an *actio in factum* for wine spilled out: B Albanese, 'Studi sulla legge Aquilia' (1950) 21 *AUPA* 1, 67. MacCormack suggests that the difference is the target of the conduct: the wine itself is poured out in D. 9.2.27.15 and recovery may be by

MacCormack observes that the statutory verbs *urere*, *rumpere* and *frangere* could hardly apply to liquids, and wonders whether Celsus might have borrowed a concept of *corrumpere* from another context, or developed the notion specifically for liquids.[53] The former is an intriguing suggestion: *corruptio* of the praetor's *album*,[54] coinage,[55] public measures[56] and wills,[57] or of the character of judges and witnesses,[58] slaves[59] and women,[60] or even of the enjoyment of incorporeal legal rights[61] all involve dilution or adulteration, in some sense. More fundamentally, the original meaning of *corrumpere* entails total destruction – the prefix *con-* denoting completeness – and there are many examples where what is described as *corruptio* can only amount to total destruction.[62]

VI. D. 9.2.27.16

After these more or less abstract statements of principle about *corruptio*, Ulpian returns to the *lex* at 16:

> Moreover, he [Celsus] does not deny that *fractum* and *ustum* are encompassed in the word *corruptum*; but he says that there is nothing new in a *lex* enumerating certain things specifically and then using a general word that comprises the specific ones; and this opinion is true.[63]

Discussion of conflicting views – over which Ulpian prefers Celsus's opinion that *rumpere* is to be understood as *corrumpere* – has been omitted.[64] Picking up the

actio directa; in D. 9.2.27.35, the punctured cask was the direct target of the conduct and the wine a consequential loss that may be recovered only by *actio in factum*: MacCormack, 'Aquilian Studies' (n 27), 19–20.

[53] MacCormack, 'Aquilian Studies' (n 27), 6.

[54] eg, D. 2.1.9.pr (Paul. 3 *ad Ed.*); D. 2.1.7.pr (Ulp 3 *ad Ed.*); Inst. 4.6.12.

[55] eg, PS 5.25.1.

[56] eg, D. 48.10.32.1 (Mod. 1 *de Poen.*).

[57] eg, D. 9.2.42 (Iul. 28 *Dig.*); D. 10.2.16.5 (Ulp. 19 *ad Ed.*).

[58] Among more than 40 relevant texts: D. 42.1.33 (Call. 5 *Cogn.*) (witnesses); D. 48.10.1.2 (Marcian. 14 *Inst.*) (judges and witnesses); D. 4.8.3.1 (Ulp. 13 *ad Ed.*) (arbitrators); D. 49.14.29.pr (Ulp. 8 *Disp.*) (*delatores*).

[59] See D. 11.3.

[60] eg, D. 24.3.47 (Scaev. 19 *Quaest.*); D. 48.19.38.3 (Paul. 5 *Sent.*).

[61] Among Gaius's frequent uses of *corruptio* in relation to rights: D. 4.5.8 (4 *ad Ed. Provinc.*) (*iura naturalia*); D. 39.2.19.pr (*ad Ed. Pu. de Damno Inf.*); G. 1.163 (*ius adgnationis*); G. 4.38 (contractual rights). See also D. 45.1.72.pr (Ulp 20 *ad Ed.*) (*stipulatio*); D. 39.3.11.pr (Paul. 49 *ad Ed.*) (water rights); D. 43.19.3.12 (Ulp. 70 *ad Ed.*) (right of way).

[62] eg, in addition to the legal rights cases (above, n 61): D. 19.2.62 (Lab. 1 *Pith.*) (subsidence destroys a channel); D. 19.2.35.1 (Afr. 8 *Quaest.*) (next year's crops); D. 19.5.14.3 (Ulp. 41 *ad Sab.*) (acorns); D. 10.2.4.1 (Ulp. 19 *ad Ed.*) (poisons and illicit objects). For a survey of things that may be the object of *corruptio*, see O Gradenwitz and others, *Vocabularium Iurisprudentiae Romanae*, vol I (A–C) (Berlin, G Reimeri, 1903), cols 1041–42.

[63] D. 9.2.27.16 (Ulp. 18 *ad Ed.*): *Et non negat fractum et ustum contineri corrupti appellatione, sed non esse novum, ut lex specialiter quibusdam enumeratis generale subiciat verbum, quo specialia complectatur: quae sententia vera est.*

[64] MacCormack, 'Aquilian Studies' (n 27), 6–7.

prefatory explanation of the link between *ruptio* and *corruptio*, this is a bridge passage, taking Ulpian back from *corruptio* to the text of the *lex* and to articulation of the other legal concept in his commentary: *ruptio*. The bridge is structurally significant because, from 17 to 24, Ulpian does not – as the opening in 13 might otherwise suggest – focus on *corruptio*. Rather – and as we might expect in lemmatic commentary – Ulpian explores *ruptio*, with only occasional asides about *corruptio*, on the authority of the *veteres*' assimilation of the concepts.

VII. D. 9.2.27.17

Fragment 17 is not about *corruptio*; it is about *ruptio*:[65]

> We will certainly accept as having *rupisse* the person who has wounded [*vulneravit*], or struck with rods or whips or fists, or with a weapon, or with something else, in such a way that he cuts [*scinderet*] open someone's body, or bruises it [*tumorem fecerit*], but only if loss is caused *iniuria*. It is otherwise if he does not cheapen the slave or make it less valuable, for then the Aquilian does not lie and he will only be able to bring the *actio iniuriarum*; for the Aquilian only addresses those *ruptiones* that cause loss [*quae damna dant*]. Therefore, if a slave has not been made less valuable, but expenses have been incurred towards his health and healing, loss seems to me to have been caused in these respects; and hence I can sue on the *lex Aquilia*.[66]

As introduced here, *ruptio* has three components: first, conduct of a *vulnerare* kind – wounding, characteristically by rods, whips, fists, weapons or the like;[67] second, a physical consequence, in the characteristic forms *scindere* – 'cutting open' – or *tumorem facere* – 'bruising', 'making a swelling'; and, third, an economic consequence, in the form of *damnum* – 'loss'.

Rodger contends that the third component derives not from Ulpian's interpretation of *ruperit* but from the 'overarching precondition for liability, *si quis alteri damnum faxit*'[68] – 'if someone should cause *damnum* to another'. However, given that Ulpian here sets out characteristic, and relatively narrow, conduct and physical consequence elements – perhaps taking over traditional conceptions

[65] Hausmaninger, 'Zur Gesetzesinterpretation des Celsus' (n 21), 266–67.

[66] D. 9.2.27.17 (Ulp. 18 *ad Ed.*): *Rupisse eum utique accipiemus, qui vulneraverit, vel virgis vel loris vel pugnis cecidit, vel telo vel quo alio, ut scinderet alicui corpus, vel tumorem fecerit, sed ita demum, si damnum iniuria datum est: ceterum si nullo servum pretio viliorem deterioremve fecerit, Aquilia cessat iniuriarumque erit agendum dumtaxat: Aquilia enim eas ruptiones, quae damna dant, persequitur. Ergo etsi pretio quidem non sit deterior servus factus, verum sumptus in salutem eius et sanitatem facti sunt, in haec mihi videri damnum datum: atque ideoque lege Aquilia agi posse.*

[67] Note the similarity to Ulpian's definition of *occidere* in D. 9.2.7.1: P Ziliotto, *L'imputazione del danno aquiliano: tra iniuria e damnum corpore datum* (Padua, CEDAM, 2000), 185.

[68] Rodger, 'The Palingenesia of the Commentaries Relating to the Lex Aquilia' (n 5), 176. Birks also resists the idea – albeit in relation to *corruptio* rather than *ruptio* – that interpretation could narrow the scope of the verb to conduct that occasioned economic loss, excluding burning, rupturing or fracturing that did not cause loss: Birks (n 3), 145–46.

derived from the XII Tables[69] – it is not obvious that he could not intend to convey that *ruptio* entailed a characteristic and narrow economic consequence. In saying, 'We will certainly accept as having *rupisse* … but only if loss is caused *iniuria*', Ulpian is ambiguous: he could be explaining a limit internal to *ruperit* as properly interpreted, or he could be pointing to the supervening requirement of *damnum* from the statutory phrase *si … damnum faxit*. The former is emphasised by 'those *ruptiones* that cause loss' – a clause omitted in the Collatio, where Ulpian's opinion about the medical expenses in the final sentence is also reversed. Some interpolation is likely.[70] Regardless of interpolation, however, the notion that *ruptio* is limited by *damnum* – whether inherent in the interpretation of *ruperit* or of *damnum faxit* – is present as a third component in Ulpian's exposition.

In light of the connection between the characteristically violent[71] *rumpere* and *vulnerare*, the expansion of *rumpere* to *corrumpere* has been cited to support the view that chapter III originally applied to wounding slaves and *quadrupedes pecudes* and was only later extended – *corruptio* being result-focused – to destroying inanimate objects.[72] On the other hand, those who consider that chapter III originally applied only to destroying inanimate objects read Ulpian's exposition of *ruperit* as substantively an explanation of *corruptio*, a wider notion that could include bruises, which plainly fall short of destruction.[73] Ulpian's specific vocabulary of *rumpere* and *vulnerare* arguably weighs against the latter view – again, perhaps given traditional conceptions derived from the XII Tables – but the original scope of chapter III is notoriously intractable.

Fragment 17 concludes the set-up of Ulpian's argument: he has flagged the two key concepts, *ruptio* and *corruptio* at 13; outlined *corruptio* at 14–15; explained the connection between *corruptio* and *ruptio* at (13 and) 16; and outlined *ruptio* at 17. The remaining texts in the passage refer back to one of these two concepts; it is argued here that, from 17 onwards, Ulpian pairs a text affirming a principle about *ruptio* or *corruptio* with an answering text illustrating pragmatic attenuation of that principle, signalled by *quasi*.

[69] JM Kelly, 'The Meaning of the Lex Aquilia' (1964) 80 *LQR* 73, 82–83; NH Andrews, '"*Occidere*" and the Lex Aquilia' (1987) 46 *CLJ* 315, 324, 328.

[70] Daube prefers the Digest: D Daube, 'On the Use of the Term *Damnum*' in V Arangio-Ruiz (ed), *Studi in Onore di Siro Solazzi nel Cinquantesimo Anniversario del Suo Insegnamento Universitario, 1899-1948* (Naples, Jovene, 1948) 93, 134–35 fn 201. Lawson considers that the Collatio more accurately states Ulpian's view: Lawson (n 6), 106–07 fn s 17. Both the Digest and the Collatio texts have probably been revised and shortened: A Samir, 'D.9.2.27.17 versus CO.2.4: Који текст је интерполисан?' (2012) 46 *Zbornik radova Pravnog fakulteta, Novi Sad* 375; FR Pringsheim, 'Die Verletzung Freier und die "lex Aquilia"' (1962) 28 *SDHI* 1, 7; M Kaser, *Zur Methodologie der römischen Rechtsquellenforschung* (Wien, Böhlau, 1972), 31–32.

[71] H Hausmaninger, *Das Schadenersatzrecht der lex Aquilia* (Vienna, Manz, 1976), 16; U Wesel, *Rhetorische Statuslehre und Gesetzesauslegung der römischen Juristen* (Cologne, Carl Heymann, 1967), 46.

[72] eg, Andrews (n 69), 325–26.

[73] eg, Musumeci, '«*Quasi ruperit*», «*quasi rupto*»' (n 8), 356 ff, commenting on the future *accipiemus* at 360.

VIII. D. 9.2.27.18

The first *quasi* appears in 18:

> If someone cuts [*sciderit*] or stains [*inquinaverit*] clothes, he is liable on the Aquilian as if [*quasi*] he *ruperit*.[74]

The text 'answers' two principles. It answers, first, the clear case of *ruptio* by wounding a slave in 17 – *scinderet alicui corpus* – with the example of cutting clothes – *vestimenta sciderit*. In contrast to the 'we will certainly accept' of 17, to cut clothes is only *quasi rumpere*. If Ulpian's focus is *ruptio*, as the repetition of *scindere* suggests, it is easy to see why cutting clothes is analogous to – but not the same as – cutting open a slave. Cutting with a knife or scissors is a little like wounding with a weapon; a rent or tear is a physical consequence equivalent to a bruise; and the economic consequence is diminished value. However, it is still not exactly wounding; it would be a misuse of language – legal language harking back to the XII Tables – to say that clothing, an inanimate thing, has been *rupta* in the core sense of wounding. There has been 'some physical damage but not enough to constitute to "breaking" or "smashing" [*rumpere*]'.[75] The defendant is liable to the statutory action but Ulpian's *quasi* in 18 signals a juristic fudge – a pragmatic, rather than a strictly principled, extension.[76]

Second, 18 answers the clear case of *corruptio* by polluting wine in 15 – *vinum spurcavit* – with the example of staining clothes – *vestimenta … inquinaverit*. The connection is less distinct, both because 18 has *quasi ruperit* and 15 is about *corruptio* and because, while 17 and 18 are paired by *scindere*, between 15 and 18 there is only the less precise – but conceptually identical – echo of *spurcare* in *inquinare*. Ulpian's focus is *ruptio*; it is clear that staining can only be *quasi rumpere*: in staining, there is no physical conduct analogous to wounding; and the physical consequence is nothing like cutting, bursting open, or even swelling.[77] Nor – comparing 18 to 15 – is staining clothes like *corruptio* of wine. Adulterated wine is changed and effectively destroyed – the resultant mixture, inseparable in law, is no longer drinkable as wine. Stained clothes are still clothes; the stain might be permanent (in which case the substance accedes to the clothes) or it might be removable.[78] The comparison to *corruptio* is, however, weak; 18 is focally about *ruptio*. The inclusion of *inquinare* as well as *scindere* in fact serves as a bridge

[74] D. 9.2.27.18 (Ulp. 18 *ad Ed.*): *Si quis vestimenta sciderit vel inquinaverit, Aquilia quasi ruperit tenetur.*

[75] MacCormack, 'Aquilian Studies' (n 27), 9.

[76] Arguing that *quasi* here signifies only the explanatory 'as', Musumeci is forced to say that *ruperit* actually has the sense of *corruperit*, there being no *ruptio* in the original: Musumeci, '«*Quasi ruperit*», «*quasi rupto*»' (n 8), 362. It is submitted that Ulpian's use of each verb in 13–28 is careful and calibrated to context; *ruperit* here means *ruperit* and *quasi* means 'as if'.

[77] Albanese suggests interpolation and that, in classical law, *spurcare* and *inquinare* necessitated an *actio in factum*, absent *mutatio rei*: Albanese (n 52), 66–67, 202.

[78] Musumeci, '«*Quasi ruperit*», «*quasi rupto*»' (n 8), 361.

to 19–20, which are expressly about *corruptio*. What 18 shows is that there are some matters – like cutting and staining clothes – that can be waved through under the statutory language as *quasi ruptio*; 19 and 20, however, are nothing like the ancient concept of *ruptio*, and have to be considered, instead, in terms of the juristic *corruptio*.

IX. D. 9.2.27.19–20

The facts of 19 and 20 are straightforward:

> 19. Next, if someone pours [*effuderit*] my millet or harvested grain [*frumentum*] into a river, the Aquilian action will lie.[79]
>
> 20. Also, if someone mixes [*immiscuit*] sand or something else with harvested grain [*frumento*], so that it is difficult to separate [*difficilis separatio*] them, he can be sued as if [*quasi*] it were *corruptum*.[80]

The verb *effuderit* expressly references a form of *corruptio* articulated in 15. Pouring grain into the river is like pouring wine out over the ground; while the positions of liquid and solid are reversed, each merger is inseparable and each accessory *res* destroyed. The *corrumpere et mutare* principle is clear, since 'the substance of the corn itself is affected by the water'.[81] Observing that the grain is swollen – as in *tumorem facere* – we might consider there to be *ruptio*; however, since *effundere* in 19 is linked to *corruptio* in 15, and 20, which is expressly about *corruptio*, is introduced by *item* – 'also', Ulpian's focus in 19 is likely *corruptio*, not *ruptio*.

In 20, Ulpian holds that action is possible only *quasi de corrupto* – 'as if it were *corruptum*'. In terms of conduct, while *immiscere* is not one of the *corruptio* verbs in 15, the idea is present in *spurcare* and *alio modo vitiare*; the conduct component thus suffices for *corruptio*. The economic loss component is also present: the owner incurs additional costs in sieving to separate the grain,[82] or else sells coarser, grittier meal, at a lower price.[83] However, the physical consequence component is absent: unlike 19, the mixture in 20 is separable, and the grain is not destroyed – or even altered. *Quasi* thus signals a conscious pragmatic attenuation of the *corrumpere et mutare* principle of 14 – affirmed by the swollen grain in 19 – to permit the statutory action in 20, even though there is no inseparable merger and

[79] D. 9.2.27.19 (Ulp. 18 *ad Ed.*): *Sed et si quis milium vel frumentum meum effuderit in flumen, sufficit Aquiliae actio.*

[80] D. 9.2.27.20 (Ulp. 18 *ad Ed.*): *Item si quis frumento harenam vel aliud quid immiscuit, ut difficilis separatio sit, quasi de corrupto agi poterit.*

[81] BE Grueber, *The Roman Law of Damage to Property: A Commentary on the Title of the Digest Ad Legem Aquiliam (IX.2)* (Oxford, Clarendon Press, 1886), 98. See also Albanese (n 52), 202.

[82] On Roman flour-sieves, see LA Moritz, *Grain-mills and Flour in Classical Antiquity* (Oxford, Oxford University Press, 1958), ch IV.

[83] On grades of flour for Roman bread, see ibid, chs V–VI; KD White, 'Food Requirements and Food Supplies in Classical Times in Relation to the Diet of the Various Classes' (1976) 2 *Progress in Food & Nutrition Science* 143, 160–62.

no adverse physical change. The conclusion that separation is not practically and economically worthwhile likely motivates this attenuation, as Musumeci observes, noting that Ulpian and Paul both treat the *difficilis* as if it were impossible in other contexts.[84]

Does this pragmatic attenuation *quasi corruptum* effectively destroy the *corrumpere et mutare* principle – can the limit case in 20 be reconciled with the original principle in 14? The *difficilis separatio* of grain and sand in 20 strongly echoes the *molesta separatio* of weeds and land in 14, yet in 14 an *actio in factum* is required and in 20 a statutory action *quasi de corrupto* is allowed. Albanese and others explain the apparent inconsistency by positing compilatorial distortion of 20.[85] Buckland contends of 14 that 'such dealings are *quasi corruptio*'.[86] Ziliotto holds that Celsus's view in 14 was outdated by Ulpian's time.[87] Valditara distinguishes *molesta separatio* – troublesome but still possible – and *difficilis separatio* – so practically impossible as to be considered an alteration, though he further suggests that the grain is physically altered by contact with the sand.[88] Musumeci afforces Valditara's *molesta–difficilis* distinction with the counterfactual signalled by *quasi*.[89]

These attempted reconciliations are unconvincing. Solutions amending the text should be a last resort. Differences between Celsus and Ulpian are entirely possible but, as suggested above, there are linguistic grounds for attributing the *corrumpere et mutare* view to Ulpian as much as to Celsus.[90] The adjectives *molesta* and *difficilis* differ but they are non-technical, and their meanings overlap too much to sustain different results in 14 and 20. If the grain were physically altered by contact with sand, 14 would be the same as 19 – and thus redundant. *Quasi* is certainly relevant but its presence in 20 simply begs the question why the same solution is not available in 14.

It may yet be possible to reconcile 14 and 20 by recognising in the facts and in the structure of Ulpian's analysis greater nuance in the notion of *corrumpere et mutare*. As foreshadowed above, the exposition of *corruptio* in 14 and 15 reveals principles connected with accession of movables to immovables, and with the distinctive treatment of 'damage' to liquids. In the *corruptio* fact-patterns (14–15 and 19–20), Ulpian investigates *mutatio* in three dimensions, according to whether the facts involve: merger (accession) or mixture; movables or immovables; and solids or liquids. Fragment 20, the limit case, is the final permutation in a sequence of object-combinations reflecting these three dimensions.

[84] Musumeci, '*Molesta separatio, difficilis separatio*' (n 25), 834–35.

[85] Albanese (n 52), 203–04; G Rotondi, 'Teorie postclassiche sull'*actio legis Aquiliae*' in G Rotondi, *Scritti giuridici*, vol II (E Albertario ed, Pavia, Tipografia e legatoria cooperativa, 1922) 411, 457 fn 3; Wesel (n 71), 47 n 13.

[86] Ibbetson, 'Buckland on the *Lex Aquilia*' (n 22), 76.

[87] Ziliotto (n 67), 183 n 4.

[88] G Valditara, *Sulle origini del concetto di damnum* (Turin, Giappichelli, 1998), 12 fn 57.

[89] Musumeci, '*Molesta separatio, difficilis separatio*' (n 25), 834, 836.

[90] Above, section IV.

The first two dimensions may be considered together. As argued above, the object in 14 is a cornfield, and the conduct effects accession – sowing (planting) movables in an immovable. In 20, the object is harvested grain, and the conduct produces not accession but mixture. It may be that, from the perspective of the principal thing, accession of movables to immovables is simply not contemplated – as to conduct or result – by the statutory verbs: *(cor)ruptio* of land may be conceptually subtractive only. When wine is poured out in 15, there is *corruptio* of the wine but no indication of *corruptio* of the land to which it presumably accedes. In D. 9.2.50, a wrongdoer demolishes another's house and constructs baths in its place; Ulpian allows an action for *damnum*, separately noting – *praeter ius* – that the baths accede to the land.[91] What constitutes the *damnum* is unexpressed but likely consists of the value of the house demolished (subtracted), since baths generate an income and enhance the value of the land. The construction of baths – even without the owner's consent – is addressed by the accession rule, not the Aquilian action. Similarly, actions for *damnum iniuria* are not mentioned – nor, admittedly, expressly denied – when a statue[92] or road[93] is repaired,[94] or when a pipe is laid through a house.[95] If accessions to land are conceptually outside *(cor)ruptio*, this would explain why 14 requires a decretal action – akin to when valuables are cast into water,[96] or another's wine or grain is consumed.[97] In contrast, no accession rule operates in 20 to preclude *(cor)ruptio*: sand and grain exemplify mixture, not accession.

The third dimension of Ulpian's investigation of *mutatio* – focusing on whether the facts involve solids or liquids – amplifies this possible explanation why 20 amounts only to *quasi corruptio*. Discounting impossible permutations,[98] Ulpian's three dimensions give rise to nine possible object-combinations. Of these, Ulpian does not consider three that involve accession of (movable or immovable) solids to solids, or (movable) liquids to liquids. True accession – not *specificatio* – in these cases consists only in augmenting quantity; consistently with the suggestion just advanced, it may be that, conceptually, statutory *(cor)ruptio* is only ever subtractive. The remaining cases are: accession of a solid movable to a solid immovable (sowing weeds in 14); accession of a liquid movable to a solid immovable (pouring out wine in 15); accession of a liquid movable to a solid movable (grain absorbing water in 19); mixture of a solid movable with a liquid movable (polluting wine in 15); mixture of two liquid movables (wine otherwise ruined in 15[99]);

[91] D. 9.2.50 (Ulp. 6 *Opin.*).
[92] D. 48.4.5.pr (Marcian. 5 *Reg.*).
[93] D. 43.19.3.12 (Ulp. 70 *ad Ed.*).
[94] Ulpian defines 'repair' as restoring something *corruptum* to its pristine state: D. 43.21.1.6 (70 *ad Ed.*).
[95] D. 9.2.29.1 (Ulp. 18 *ad Ed.*) – though accession operates differently in relation to building materials: D. 6.1.59 (Iul. 6 *ex Minic.*).
[96] D. 9.2.27.21 (Ulp. 18 *ad Ed.*); D. 19.5.23 (Alf. 3 *Dig. a Paulo Epit.*); D. 19.5.14.2 (Ulp. 41 *ad Sab.*).
[97] D. 9.2.30.2 (Paul. 22 *ad Ed.*).
[98] Accession of immovables to movables, accession of solids to liquids (dissolving salts in water is surely *specificatio*) and mixtures involving immovables.
[99] Making vinegar would be *specificatio*, not *confusio*.

and, finally, mixture of two solid movables (grain and sand in 20). As noted above, owing to their nature, a distinctive principle – dilution or adulteration – must apply for 'damage' to liquids; moreover, liquid mixtures are normally inseparable. The grain-and-sand mixture in 20 is a mixture of solids; it does not exactly involve dilution or adulteration but illustrates the closest equivalent for solids; and it is separable – in practice (by sieving), as well as in principle. Whereas 15 is straightforwardly *corruptio*, 20 is, on account of these differences – and the absence of physical alteration to the grain – only *quasi corruptio*.

Accordingly, having regard to this more nuanced investigation of *mutatio* attributed to Ulpian, it may be argued that 20 can be reconciled with 14, because it concerns mixture, not accession, and because it involves two movables, not a movable and an immovable. It may be argued, further, that 20 can be distinguished from 15, because it involves two solids, not one or more liquids.

X. D. 9.2.27.21–22

Though not often discussed together, 21 and 22 are linked by a shared verb-stem – the 'striking' in *excusserit* and *percussa*:

> 21. If someone knocks [*excusserit*] coins from my hand, Sabinus believes there is an action for *damnum iniuria*, provided they are lost and do not come to another person, as where they fall into a river, or the sea, or a drain. For if they come to another person, there will be an action for *furtum ope consilio*; the ancient jurists also accepted this. He [Sabinus] says that an *actio in factum* can also be given.[100]
>
> 22. If a woman or mare who has been hit [*percussa*] by you has a miscarriage, Brutus says that you are liable to the Aquilian as if [*quasi*] for *ruptum*.[101]

What action Sabinus allowed in 21 – statutory or decretal; Sabinus surely did not contemplate both[102] – is controversial. The linguistic precision of the last sentence is compelling, especially given the cases of the ring in the Tiber and the silver cup in the sea,[103] both actions *in factum*, and is arguably more likely to convey Sabinus's view.[104] Understood in this way, 21 is – analogously to 14 – a negative

[100] D. 9.2.27.21 (Ulp. 18 *ad Ed.*): *Si quis de manu mihi nummos excusserit, Sabinus existimat damni iniuriae esse actionem, si ita perierint, ne ad aliquem pervenirent, puta si in flumen vel in mare vel in cloacam ceciderunt: quod si ad aliquem pervenerunt, ope consilio furtum factum agendum, quod et antiquis placuit. idem etiam in factum dari posse actionem ait.*

[101] D. 9.2.27.22 (Ulp. 18 *ad Ed.*): *Si mulier pugno vel equa ictu a te percussa eiecerit, Brutus ait Aquilia teneri quasi rupto.*

[102] Albanese (n 52), 51; Lawson (n 6), 108 fn s 21. MacCormack suggests Sabinus may have intended both: MacCormack, 'Aquilian Studies' (n 27), 31. Barton suggests Sabinus may have taken different views in different works: JL Barton, 'The *Lex Aquilia* and Decretal Actions' in WAJ Watson (ed), *Daube Noster: Essays in Legal History for David Daube* (Edinburgh, Scottish Academic Press, 1974) 15, 19.

[103] D. 19.5.23 (Alf. 3 *Dig. a Paulo Epit.*) and D. 19.5.14.2 (Ulp. 41 *ad Sab.*); see also G. 3.202, as Albanese points out, noting consistency with Ulpian's opinions in D. 47.2.50.4: Albanese (n 52), 51–52.

[104] ibid, 59–62.

text, affirming a principle about *ruptio* by offering an example beyond its limit. The statutory action fails because, although striking is conduct of the appropriate kind, and although there is loss, the requisite physical consequence is absent: the coins suffers no wound or bruise (neither, for that matter, does their holder).[105]

The relevant object in 22 is disputed: Bignardi argues that it is the foetus that is *quasi ruptum* – *quasi* because it was not yet a distinct *res* at the time – though she admits this shifts the focus of *ruptio* from conduct to result.[106] However, the dominant view[107] holds that Brutus is, like Quintus Mucius in a comparable text from Pomponius,[108] concerned with *ruptio* of the mother, of which the foetus is, at the relevant time, part.[109] The latter view is more readily accepted: the mother is the only possible legal object of the *ruptio*; and valuation of the foetus, even considered as a future thing for chapter III, would be highly problematic.

Reading 21 and 22 together reveals Ulpian's point. Both are cases where something is expelled when the bearer is struck. In 21, there is a decretal action only, because there is no physical consequence: this is the principle of *ruptio* affirmed by the negative. In 22, the miscarriage is a physical consequence for the pregnant mother but, again, it would strain the ancient statutory concept of *ruptio* too far to say that there was literally *ruptio* of her,[110] both because she herself remained whole,[111] and perhaps also because the physical effect was, in some sense, only temporary.[112] While miscarriage is not a wound of the kind envisaged by *ruptio*, it is nonetheless sufficiently analogous that – combined with conduct of the right kind, striking, and with *damnum* – the jurists permit the fudge signalled by *quasi*, and allow the statutory action.[113]

[105] ibid, 51. MacCormack argues that Sabinus allowed the direct action, on the basis that irretrievable loss is equivalent to destruction of indestructible coins: MacCormack, 'Aquilian Studies' (n 27), 31.

[106] A Bignardi, 'Frangere e Rumpere nel Lessico Normativo e nella Interpretatio Prudentium' in S Romano (ed), *Nozione, Formazione e Interpretazione del Diritto: dall'Età Romana alle Esperienze Moderne: Ricerche Dedicate al Professor Filippo Gallo*, vol 1 (Naples, Jovene, 1997) 11, 40–48, with reference to scholia translating quasi as ὡσανεί.

[107] D Nörr, 'Zur Interdependenz von Prozeßrecht und materiellem Recht am Beispiel der lex Aquilia' (1987) 6 *Rechtshistorisches Journal* 99, 106–07; Cannata (n 24), 47; Corbino, *Il danno qualificato e la Lex Aquilia* (n 25), 101; A Corbino, '*Lex Aquilia* e procurato aborto' in E Chevreau, D Kremer and A Laquerrière-Lacroix (eds), *Carmina Iuris: Mélanges en l'honneur de Michel Humbert* (Paris, De Boccard, 2012) 159; Musumeci, '*«Quasi ruperit», «quasi rupto»*' (n 8), 372; G Valditara, 'In tema di stima del danno aquiliano' (2016) 44 *Index* 197, 200–01.

[108] D. 9.2.39.pr (Pomp. 17 *ad Q.Muc.*): *quia equam in iciendo ruperat.*

[109] D. 25.4.1.1 (Ulp. 24 *ad Ed.*): *partus enim antequam edatur, mulieris portio est vel viscerum.*

[110] Grueber (n 81), 100; Hausmaninger, *Das Schadenersatzrecht der lex Aquilia* (n 71), 16; O Behrends, 'Methodik der Fallbearbeitung' (1985) 11 *Juristische Schulung* 878, 881–82. Nörr considers that there was straightforwardly *ruptio* of the mother: Nörr, *Causa mortis* (n 8), 130–31.

[111] MacCormack, 'Aquilian Studies' (n 27), 3–4.

[112] Corbino, '*Lex Aquilia* e procurato aborto' (n 107), 164–65; Valditara, 'In tema di stima del danno aquiliano' (n 107), 205. The significance of the temporary character of the injury is disputed: Sanna (n 24), 367.

[113] Musumeci argues that: for Brutus, *rumpere* did not include *corrumpere*, and by *quasi* Brutus meant 'as if'; but, for Ulpian, *rumpere* actually meant *corrumpere*, and by *quasi* Ulpian meant simply 'as': Musumeci, '*«Quasi ruperit», «quasi rupto»*' (n 8), 358, 368, 375–83. It is submitted that Ulpian used *quasi* in the same sense attributed to Brutus. For Ulpian to use *rumpere* and *corrumpere* interchangeably

Considering the facts in a different light, 21 and 22 can be understood as cases where part of a thing is damaged. On this basis, 21 is *in factum* because coins are not really part of the person holding them. However, 22 is closer – close enough to be *quasi ruptio* – because, although the foetus is a separate thing when born, it is physically and legally part of the mother when she is struck. Whether the physical consequence or the object be taken as the focus of these texts, Ulpian offers a carefully structured discussion, in which a text affirming principle is answered by a pragmatic extension marked by *quasi*.

XI. D. 9.2.27.23–24

The connection between the next two texts is less immediately obvious:

> 23. And he [Brutus] says that, if someone had loaded [*oneraverit*] a mule more than is right and broke [*ruperit*] one of its limbs, there will be place for the Aquilian.[114]
>
> 24. If someone pierces [*perforasset*] a ship (full) of merchandise, Vivianus writes that there will be an Aquilian action as if [*quasi*] he *ruperit*.[115]

In 23, the mule – a *quadrupes pecus* – is burdened with cargo; the verb *onerare* could also characteristically be used for loading the ship full of wares in 24. The mule is, in fact, overburdened and there is *ruptio*[116] of a limb – entailing *os fractum*.[117] The ship is punctured – *perforasset*, the same verb used of the pearls in D. 9.2.27.30, which is part of a short lemmatic commentary on *frangere*.[118] Accordingly, the texts again form a pair: modes of transport loaded with goods, each of which suffers a *fractio*. In addressing *fractiones* considered as *ruptiones*, the pair indirectly references 16 – indirectly because 16 concerns *corruptio*, not *ruptio*.

The facts of 24 are incompletely stated;[119] it is unclear whether the relevant *res* is the cargo[120] or the ship.[121] The ship is arguably more likely: the conduct described

as exact synonyms would be incompatible with his separate explanations of *ruptio* in 17 and *corruptio* in 14–15, his express articulation of the relationship between the concepts in 13 and 16, and his careful choice of fact-patterns referencing each explanation.

[114] D. 9.2.27.23 (Ulp. 18 *ad Ed.*): *Et si mulum plus iusto oneraverit et aliquid membri ruperit, Aquiliae locum fore.*

[115] D. 9.2.27.24 (Ulp. 18 *ad Ed.*): *Si navem venaliciarum mercium perforasset, Aquiliae actionem esse, quasi ruperit, Vivianus scribit.*

[116] Musumeci's arguably unwarranted suggestion that Brutus meant *quasi ruperit* – not *ruperit* – is grounded in the contested supposition that, for Brutus, ch III applied only to total destruction of inanimate things: Musumeci, '«*Quasi ruperit*», «*quasi rupto*»' (n 8), 384.

[117] A Lorusso, 'Reflections on the Quantification of *Damnum*' in PJ du Plessis (ed), *Wrongful Damage to Property in Roman Law: British Perspectives* (Edinburgh, Edinburgh University Press, 2018) 183, 190.

[118] D. 9.2.27.30 (Ulp. 18 *ad Ed.*); see Rodger, 'The Palingenesia of the Commentaries Relating to the Lex Aquilia' (n 5), 196.

[119] Albanese (n 52), 69 fn 1; Musumeci, '«*Quasi ruperit*», «*quasi rupto*»' (n 8), 387.

[120] eg, Albanese (n 52), 69 fn 1, 201, suggesting the classical law action was *in factum*. See also Valditara, *Sulle origini del concetto di damnum* (n 88), 12; Sanna (n 24), 365–66.

[121] MacCormack, 'Aquilian Studies' (n 27), 5.

is directed at the ship; the paired text in 23 involves *ruptio* of the mule, not the goods; and focusing on the ship enables Ulpian to make novel points involving *fractio* as *ruptio* and causation, whereas he has already addressed goods damaged by water in 19 and (undamaged) goods lost in water in 21.

Fragment 23 illustrates the principle that there is *ruptio* where a limb is broken (*fractum*), even by non-violent *onerare*. Why is 24 only *quasi ruperit*?[122] Since *damnum* plainly results, one or both of the conduct and physical consequence components of *ruptio* must be lacking.[123] Description of the ship as loaded with merchandise – an otherwise otiose detail – may be significant to the conduct enquiry. Loaded cargo links 23 and 24 but the difference in the defendants' conduct affords that loading different consequences. The cargo's mass matters in both cases: if the mule were less loaded, there would have been no injury; if the ship were less loaded, it might not have sunk when pierced.[124] In 23, the defendant piles cargo on the mule and *aliquid membri ruperit*; he does not target the mule's limb but supplying the mass suffices for *ruptio* (*os fractum*). In 24, the defendant punctures (*frangere*) the cargo-laden ship and only *quasi ruperit*. Piercing is not very different from cutting, which qualifies as *ruptio* in 17–18; it may be *quasi ruptio* here because piercing does not suffice to sink the ship – the mass of the cargo is also required. If striking in 21–22 is the core case, loading without directed violence in 23 is at one remove but still causally sufficient. The conduct in 24 is not; it represents a pragmatic causal attenuation of the principle in 23: in modern terms, piercing is not a sufficient cause but a necessary element of a causally sufficient set. Accordingly, the conduct is only *quasi ruptio*.

In terms of physical consequence, 23 illustrates a characteristic *tumorem facere*, a wound from which bones or fluids burst outwards. Piercing – whether or not it sinks the ship[125] – may entail a clear *fractio* of the hull but there is less obviously *ruptio*: water rushing into the ship is 'bursting' in reverse. Merchandise does burst outwards; however, cargo – like the coins in 21 but unlike the foetus in 22 – is not regarded in law or fact as part of the ship. Accordingly, 24 may not strictly entail a *ruptio* but the physical consequence is sufficiently analogous in practice to count as *quasi ruptio*.

If the *res* in 24 is the ship, Ulpian in 23–24 considers overlap between *frangere* and *rumpere*; and, whether understood in terms of conduct or (the closely related) physical consequence, 24 entails pragmatic attenuation of the principle expounded in 23. Alternatively, if the *res* is the cargo, it is still possible to discern attenuation – but

[122] As for Brutus (see n 102), Musumeci argues that, for Vivianus, *rumpere* did not include *corrumpere*, and that, whereas by *quasi* Vivianus meant 'as if', Ulpian meant 'as'; in view of the period between Brutus and Vivianus, he argues in the alternative that, if Vivianus did understand *rumpere* as *corrumpere*, Vivianus, like Ulpian, meant by *quasi* only 'as': Musumeci, '*«Quasi ruperit», «quasi rupto»*' (n 8), 390–91. Both views are rejected here.

[123] Unlike 23, the object in 24 is not a *quadrupes pecus*; however, this is not a component of *ruptio* elaborated in 17 and it is unlikely that, for Vivianus, in the first century CE, ch III was confined to slaves and quadrupeds (if it ever was).

[124] Jettisoning cargo to save the ship is a stock example: Inst. 2.1.48; D. 41.1.9.8 (Gai. 2 *Rer. Cott.*).

[125] Compare: Russo Ruggeri, *Viviano giurista minore?* (n 36), 113; Musumeci, '*«Quasi ruperit», «quasi rupto»*' (n 8), 389.

only in terms of conduct. Scholars argue that the conduct is deficient, because there is no direct contact – wounding – of the merchandise by the defendant.[126] This is plausible, assuming the merchandise suffers some physical change.[127] In contrast, as noted above, water damage to the cargo would be *corruptio* according to 19, and the associated swelling might even be *ruptio* in the *tumorem facere* sense.

XII. *Damnum* in D. 9.2.27.25–28

Lenel, albeit hesitantly, treats D. 9.2.27.25 as the start of Ulpian's commentary on *si damnum faxit iniuria*.[128] Birks argues that Ulpian's lemma was *iniuria* – wrongfulness – but that the compilers distorted the original to focus on *damnum* – loss.[129] Rodger suggests that Lenel and Birks proceeded on the incorrect basis that *iniuria* signals wrongfulness, and argues instead that, in *nulla enim iniuria est* in 25, *iniuria* means 'unlawful injury or loss'.[130] Rodger's view is preferable: recognising 'that Ulpian is using *iniuria* as a virtual synonym for *damnum*'[131] renders unnecessary the reframing of the *damnum*-based explanation of expenses saved that Von Lübtow and Birks propose;[132] and recognising that 25–28 relate to the lemma *ruperit* coheres better with the commentary on *fregerit* that follows in 29–33.[133] Further, on the wider analysis of 13–28 proposed here, according to which Ulpian's examples pick up elements of the 'definitions' of *corruptio* in 14–15 and *ruptio* in 17, 25–28 are readily understood as unpacking 'but only if loss is caused *iniuria*' in 17, whether or not the phrase *eas ruptiones, quae damna dant* is original. The echo is clear not only in *nulla enim iniuria* in 25 but in the focus on loss in the examples 25–28.[134] Economic loss was the third component of *ruptio* described in 17; the only component not addressed in 18–24, it is addressed in 25–28, before Ulpian considers *fregerit*.[135]

[126] eg, Sanna (n 24), 366; Lorusso (n 117), 208.

[127] Absent both direct contact and physical change, 21 – like D. 19.5.23 (Alf. 3 *Dig. a Paulo Epit.*) – requires an *actio in factum*, not an action for *quasi ruptio*.

[128] Lenel (n 1), col 530 §625 fn 1.

[129] Birks (n 3), 153–63, 174–79.

[130] AF Rodger, 'What did *Damnum Iniuria* Actually Mean?' in AS Burrows and AF Rodger (eds), *Mapping the Law: Essays in Memory of Peter Birks* (Oxford, Oxford University Press, 2006) 421, 428–33.

[131] ibid, 432.

[132] Von Lübtow (n 8), 132; Birks (n 3), 158.

[133] Rodger, 'The Palingenesia of the Commentaries Relating to the Lex Aquilia' (n 5), 176–83.

[134] Albanese (n 52), 206; S Schipani, *Responsabilità «ex lege Aquilia»: Criteri di imputazione e problema della «culpa»* (Turin, Giappichelli, 1969), 340; Hausmaninger, *Das Schadenersatzrecht der lex Aquilia* (n 71), 31; Capogrossi Colognesi (n 45), 276–77; Russo Ruggeri, *Viviano giurista minore?* (n 36), 114–17; Corbino, *Il danno qualificato e la Lex Aquilia* (n 25), 106–07 – though Russo Ruggeri and Corbino also consider that proper use is not *corruptio*; see also Hausmaninger, *Das Schadenersatzrecht der lex Aquilia* (n 71), 17.

[135] Rodger, 'What did *Damnum Iniuria* Actually Mean?' (n 130), 429; Rodger, 'The Palingenesia of the Commentaries Relating to the Lex Aquilia' (n 5), 176; DF Pugsley, 'The Lex Aquilia' (1972) 89 *South African Law Journal* 489, 490.

Although not marked by *quasi* in alternate texts, 25–26 and 27–28 can be understood as pairs; each pair implicates one of the two species of *damnum* expressed by Ulpian's contemporary Paul: 'what we have had to expend' or 'what we could have gained'.[136]

XIII. D. 9.2.27.25–26

Agricultural examples characterise 25–26:

> 25. If someone picks unripe olives or harvests an unripe cornfield or an immature vineyard, he will be liable to the Aquilian. However, if they are already ripe, the Aquilian will not lie; for there is no *iniuria*, since he has in effect gifted you the expenses incurred in the collection of fruits of this sort. However, if he takes them away after they have been collected, he is liable for theft. Octavenus adds a proviso in relation to grapes: unless, he says, he threw them on the ground, such that they were squandered.[137]
>
> 26. He [Octavenus][138] writes the same about coppice woodland: if it is unripe, he is liable to the Aquilian; and, if he crops a mature wood, he is liable for theft and for cutting trees by stealth.[139]

Addressing the *damnum* component of *ruptio*, 25 articulates the principle that the statutory action lies for picking fruits only at a time when their immaturity occasions loss: there is no relevant *ruptio* of the land – the object being the olive grove, cornfield or vineyard – when the fruits are ripe. One species of *damnum* is 'what we have had to expend'; *saving* of necessary expense is the opposite of *damnum*; accordingly, picking ripe fruit – saving the owner the harvesting expenses – lacks the necessary *ruptio* occasioning *damnum*.

In earlier pairs, the second text indicates a pragmatic attenuation – signalled by *quasi* – of the principle of the first text. While there is no *quasi* in 26, imagining how *quasi* might have fit reveals the significance of its absence. Whereas the olives, corn and grapes in 25 are harvested annually and would separate from their parent plants naturally in time, the coppicing in 26 recurs only after a period of years – three to four years for birch but perhaps 50 years for oak – and there is no necessary, natural separation of branches. 'Ripeness' of coppice wood is less predictable than of olives; the necessity of harvesting expenses is less certain. Moreover, the 'fruit' is less obvious. The saving of expense is, accordingly, less clear – the putative gain by

[136] D. 9.2.33.pr (Paul. 2 *ad Plaut.*): … *In lege enim Aquilia damnum consequimur: et amisisse dicemur, quod aut consequi potuimus aut erogare cogimur.*

[137] D. 9.2.27.25 (Ulp. 18 *ad Ed.*): *Si olivam immaturam decerpserit vel segetem desecuerit inmaturam vel vineas crudas, Aquilia tenebitur: quod si iam maturas, cessat Aquilia: nulla enim iniuria est, cum tibi etiam impensas donaverit, quae in collectionem huiusmodi fructuum impenduntur: sed si collecta haec interceperit, furti tenetur. Octavenus in uvis adicit, nisi, inquit, in terram uvas proiecit, ut effunderentur.*

[138] Perhaps Vivianus: Russo Ruggeri, *Viviano giurista minore?* (n 36), 19, 113.

[139] D. 9.2.27.26 (Ulp. 18 *ad Ed.*): *Idem et in silva caedua scribit, ut, si immatura, Aquilia teneatur, quod si matura interceperit, furti teneri eum et arborum furtim caesarum.*

'saving' an expense that might not be incurred for several years, to harvest 'fruit' that need not have been harvested at all, might be considered too uncertain or too remote for the statutory action.

Pragmatic attenuation of the principle of 25 in the circumstances of 26 could be intelligible in both directions. Coppicing ripe wood might be treated as nonetheless occasioning *damnum*, because no necessary expense is saved and because it is not a naturally separating annual fruit. Alternatively, notwithstanding that it does not involve harvesting annual fruiting crops, coppicing ripe wood might be treated just like 25, 'as if' expense is saved – which would preclude *damnum*. The actual reported result reveals a principle of *damnum* so strict that there is no space for a pragmatic *quasi* in the first alternative and no need for it in the second: gain by a contingent saving of future expense of a valuable product (even if not fruit) does preclude *ruptio*, for want of *damnum*.

By omitting *quasi* from the 25–26 pair, Ulpian underscores the absolute character of *damnum*: there is no attenuation of principle when it comes to *damnum*. This absoluteness is discernible even in the decretal actions: recovery is occasionally possible for loss without damage but never for damage without loss.

XIV. D. 9.2.27.27–28

The final two texts do not appear to have much in common:

> 27. If you plunder a mature pollard willow-grove without harming the trunks [*stirpes*], the Aquilian will not lie [he says].[140]
>
> 28. And if someone castrates a slave boy and makes him more valuable, Vivianus writes that the Aquilian will not lie but an *actio iniuriarum* will have to be brought, or an action on the edict of the aediles or for fourfold.[141]

While 27 and 28 appear disparate, 27 appears similar to 26, with pollarding substituted for coppicing; however, it is what 27 adds to 26 that reveals the link to 28. The focus of 27 is the proviso 'without harming the trunks'. Whereas 25–26 consider necessary expense as *damnum* (and saving of necessary expense as gain precluding *damnum*), 27–28 concern present loss sustained in curtailment of future profitability – the 'what we could have gained' species of *damnum*. Pollarding mature willow saves present expense in harvesting but harming the trunks means there will be no future growth, forestalling future gains and depreciating the current value of the grove as a crop-producing asset.

Against this background (and linked by *stirpes* – 'roots' or 'trunks' but also 'stock' in the progeny sense), 27–28 cohere better. In 28 as in 27, there is a cutting

[140] D. 9.2.27.27 (Ulp. 18 *ad Ed.*): *Si salictum maturum ita, ne stirpes laederes, tuleris, cessare Aquiliam.*
[141] D. 9.2.27.28 (Ulp. 18 *ad Ed.*): *Et si puerum quis castraverit et pretiosiorem fecerit, Vivianus scribit cessare Aquiliam, sed iniuriarum erit agendum aut ex edicto aedilium aut in quadruplum.*

that prevents the asset from generating fruit in the future; however, unlike 27, the cutting in 28 causes appreciation, not depreciation, in the present value of the asset: castration normally increases the value of a slave (depending on the use envisaged and the aftermath of the operation).[142] Again, putative pragmatic attenuation in 28 of the principle in 27 that losing the capacity to generate fruits in the future constitutes *damnum* is intelligible in both directions. Castration might be treated as if it entailed depreciation, because the possibility of progeny is precluded, notwithstanding the increased market value of the slave; alternatively, castration might be treated as if it entailed no loss, because of the increased value, notwithstanding the lost capacity to procreate. As with 26, however, the principle of *damnum* actually applied is strict; it precludes a pragmatic *quasi* in the first alternative and obviates the need for it in the second: the immediate gain in market value precludes any *damnum* in the form of the lost opportunity for progeny (and, presumably, medical costs arising in connection with castration).

Again, the omission of *quasi* reveals a hard edge to the *damnum* component of *ruptio*: there is no loss where there is a gain, however debatable (25–26), or where there is a net[143] increase in market value, even if there are losses incurred along the way (27–28). Loss is an absolute requirement for *ruptio*, and no attenuation is entertained.

XV. Principle and Pragmatism in Ulpian's Argument

This chapter argues that Ulpian uses *quasi* in 18, 20, 22 and 24 to mean 'as if' – signalling an interpretation extending the *lex Aquilia* to situations that, strictly, fall outside its scope. It argues that each *quasi* text embodies the pragmatic extension of a principle affirmed in the immediately preceding text, such that Ulpian's analysis in 17–24 has an antiphonal structure of paired texts. It suggests that 25–28 also consists of paired texts, where the absence of *quasi* in the answering text of the pair in fact stresses Ulpian's point. It may even be possible to discern in 13–28 four blocks of four texts: a first, 'definitional' block (13–16); two blocks considering whether the conduct or the result was of the right kind for *ruptio* or *corruptio* (17–20 perhaps emphasising conduct and 21–24 perhaps emphasising result); and a final block examining the *damnum* requirement (25–28). This last suggestion is only tentative, because different themes may be discerned in 17–24, and because conduct and result are somewhat indiscriminately bound together in the

[142] eg, D. 39.4.16.7 (Marcian. *l.s. de Delator.*); C. 6.43.3.1 (Justinian to Johannes PP, 1 September 531). See D Dalla, *L'incapacità sessuale in diritto romano*, vol 1978 (Milan, Giuffrè, 1978), 74–75, 143. Where undisclosed, castration is nonetheless a flaw in sale: eg, D. 21.1.7 (Paul. 11 *ad Sab.*); D. 21.1.38.7 (Ulp. 2 *ad Ed. Aedil. Curul.*). See ibid, 144–48, explaining D. 21.1.6.2; C Russo Ruggeri, 'Brevi note critiche su D. 9.2.27.28' (1992) 43 *IVRA* 111, 112.

[143] That the castrated slave is worth more than the value of progeny forgone and medical costs incurred in connection with the procedure can reasonably be presumed; no issue would otherwise arise.

interpretation of the statutory verb. Whether this suggestion be accepted or not, understanding 13–28 as reconstructed in this chapter permits three more general observations about Ulpian's argument.

First, the proposed reconstruction of 13–28 demonstrates how carefully Ulpian delineates distinct concepts of *ruptio* (17) and *corruptio* (14–15), articulates the relationship between them (13 and 16), and selects fact-patterns that reference components of those concepts more or less expressly – by, for example, repeating key words. This careful delineation makes it unlikely that Ulpian uses the language of *quasi ruperit* and *quasi corruperit* idly, or that his concern throughout the passage is with an all-subsuming *corruptio*.[144] In fact, true to its lemmatic form, Ulpian's exegesis largely concerns *ruptio*, with a small handful of texts showing how *corruptio* fits into *ruptio*.

Second, the structure of 13–28 – relying on *quasi* and antiphonal pairs of principled and pragmatic texts – suggests that Ulpian's purpose is exposition of a layered legal position, probing 'the limits of a principle',[145] rather than critical appraisal or rebuttal of earlier jurists' views. The strongest potential indication of rebuttal lies in the apparent inconsistency of 14 and 20. While a possible reconciliation is sketched above, it may be that Ulpian does ultimately disagree with Celsus's view in 14, and answers Celsus in 14 and 15 with the similar case in 20 precisely to reveal the inconsistency in his predecessor's conclusion that *corruptio* requires *mutatio*. Nonetheless, a refutational purpose is not necessarily obvious: the focus of the intervening texts 17–19 is *ruptio*, not *corruptio*; Ulpian nowhere expressly disagrees with Celsus; and 20 includes nothing comparable to the closing remark *et ait Sabinus* that Ibbetson argues demonstrates Ulpian's sarcastic disagreement with Sabinus on *contrectatio*.[146] More generally than the problem of reconciling 14 and 20, it is, of course, plainly possible to read Ulpian's antiphonal pairs as systematically undermining each statement of principle with a pragmatic attenuation, in order to rebut the principles advanced. However, while principle and pragmatic attenuation are repeatedly juxtaposed in 17–24, the textual pairs do not jar in a way that unequivocally indicates rebuttal; each text in the pair is compatible with the other. This is the function of *quasi*: it signals a strained interpretation but one that is nonetheless permissible. Moreover, Ulpian does not, in terms or by example, advance any principle to replace *ruptio* and *corruptio* as unpacked in 17 and 14–15. Given Ulpian's didactic purpose – for the benefit of practitioners[147] but doubtless also scholars[148] – a purely destructive argument, rather than a reasoned preference for one stated view over another, is less likely than an essentially

[144] Compare Cannata (n 24), 48 n 65; Musumeci, '«*Quasi ruperit*», «*quasi rupto*»' (n 8), 358, 368, 375–83, 390–91.

[145] AM Honoré, *Ulpian: Pioneer of Human Rights*, 2nd edn (Oxford, Oxford University Press, 2002), 103.

[146] DJ Ibbetson, 'The danger of definition: *contrectatio* and appropriation' in ADE Lewis and DJ Ibbetson (eds), *The Roman Law Tradition* (Cambridge, Cambridge University Press, 1994) 54, 68.

[147] F Schulz, *History of Roman Legal Science* (Oxford, Oxford University Press, 1946), 198.

[148] Honoré (n 145), 127.

expository treatment, revealing historical layers of juristic interpretation of *ruptio*, *quasi ruptio*, *corruptio* and *quasi corruptio* as Ulpian endeavours to come to grips with each notion.[149]

Finally, from a method perspective, the reconstruction proposed affirms that Ulpian offers no mere congeries of examples, arranged according to similar πράγματα – circumstances – but, rather, a carefully constructed sequence of illustrations referring back to (components of) core concepts earlier explicated – an exploration of principles, organised on a principled basis. Pollarding a willow-grove in 27 and castrating a slave in 28 are linked not merely by a pun on *stirps* but by a controversy about present gain and future loss; the prospect of gain is part of the exploration of *damnum*; economic loss is identified as a component of *ruptio*. An initial sense of principle and pragmatism is revealed in the antiphonal pairing of affirmative and *quasi* texts; recognising these pairs – and perhaps larger blocks consisting of pairs of pairs – exposes this second, structural sense of principle, in what might otherwise be no more than fact-patterns, each linked pragmatically to the next by factual association.

In the work of a jurist who sought 'to cover the whole field of law',[150] it is no surprise to discern elements of both principle and pragmatism. What this chapter's exploration of an antiphonal structure of paired texts in this passage has sought to reveal is the distinctive intertwining of principle and pragmatism in both the substance and the method of Ulpian's commentary on *ruptio* and *corruptio*. Arguably, this is a remarkable feature, even for the jurist whose subtlety of thought and clarity of expression so commended his works to Justinian's compilers that they account for some third of the texts in the Digest.[151]

[149] For the view that Ulpian may have no settled interpretation of Aquilian *ruptio*, see: Hausmaninger, 'Zur Gesetzesinterpretation des Celsus' (n 21), 269.

[150] HF Jolowicz and JKBM Nicholas, *An Historical Introduction to the Study of Roman Law*, 3rd edn (Cambridge, Cambridge University Press, 1972), 393.

[151] ibid, 394.

BIBLIOGRAPHY

Aarnio, A and MacCormick, DN, 'Introduction' in A Aarnio and DN MacCormick (eds), *Legal Reasoning*, vol II (Aldershot, Dartmouth, 1992) xi.

Abbott, FF and Johnson, AC, *Municipal Administration in the Roman Empire* (New York, Russell & Russell, 1968).

Adams, C, 'Transport' in W Scheidel (ed), *The Cambridge Companion to the Roman Economy* (Cambridge, Cambridge University Press, 2012) 218.

Albanese, B, 'Studi sulla legge Aquilia' (1950) 21 *AUPA* 1.

Andreau, J, 'Concepts économiques dans les œuvres des juristes romains' in E Lo Cascio and D Mantovani (eds), *Diritto Romano e economia. Due modi di pensare e organizzare il mondo (nei primi tre secoli dell'Impero)* (Pavia, Pavia University Press, 2018) 223.

Andrés Santos, FJ, 'Brevissima storia della critica interpolazionistica nelle fonti giuridiche romane' (2011) 33 *Revista de estudios histórico-jurídicos* 65.

Andrews, NH, '"*Occidere*" and the Lex Aquilia' (1987) 46 *CLJ* 315.

Ankum, JA, '*Utilitatis causa receptum*, On the Pragmatical Methods of the Roman Lawyers' in JA Ankum, R Feenstra and WF Leemans (eds), *Symbolae iuridicae et historicae Martino David dedicatae* (Leiden, Brill, 1968) 1.

—— 'The Functions of Expressions with *Utilitatis Causa* in the Works of the Classical Roman Lawyers' (2010) 16 *Fundamina* 5.

Ankum, JA and Pool, E, '*Rem in bonis meis esse* and *rem in bonis meam esse*: Traces of the Development of Roman Double Ownership' in PBH Birks (ed), *New Perspectives in the Roman Law of Property* (Oxford, Oxford University Press, 1989) 5.

Ankum, JA, van Gessel-de Roo, M and Pool, E, 'Die verschiedenen Bedeutungen des Ausdrucks in bonis alicuius esse/in bonis habere im klassischen römischen Recht' (1981) 104 *ZRG RA* 238.

—— 'Die verschiedenen Bedeutungen des Ausdrucks in bonis alicuius esse/in bonis habere im klassischen römischen Recht: Teil 2' (1988) 188 *ZRG RA* 334.

—— 'Die verschiedenen Bedeutungen des Ausdrucks in bonis alicuius esse/in bonis habere im klassischen römischen Recht: Teil 3' (1990) 105 *ZRG RA* 155.

Apathy, P, *Die publizianische Klage: das relative dingliche Recht des rechtmässigen Besitzers* (Vienna, Österreichische Staatsdruckerei, 1981).

Appleton, CL, *Histoire de la propriété prétorienne et de l'action publicienne*, vol I (Paris, Ernest Thorin, 1889).

Arangio-Ruiz, V, 'L'application du droit romain en Égypte après la constitution antoninienne' (1948) 29 *Bulletin de l'Institut d'Égypte* 83.

Atiyah, PS, 'From Principles to Pragmatism: Changes in the Function of the Judicial Process and the Law' (1980) 65 *Iowa Law Review* 1249.

—— *Pragmatism and Theory in English Law* (London, Stevens & Sons, 1987).

Atiyah, PS and Summers, RS, *Form and Substance in Anglo-American Law: A Comparative Study in Legal Reasoning, Legal Theory, and Legal Institutions* (Oxford, Oxford University Press, 1987).

Aubert, J-J, *Business Managers in Ancient Rome: A Social and Economic Study of Institores, 200 B.C.-A.D. 250* (Leiden, Brill, 1994).

—— 'Les *institores* et le commerce maritime dans l'Empire romain' (1999) 9 *Topoi* 145.

Austin, J, *Lectures on Jurisprudence*, vol II, 5th edn (R Campbell ed, London, Murray, 1885)

Austin, JL, 'Performative Utterances' in JO Urmson and GJ Warnock (eds), JL Austin, *Philosophical Papers* (Oxford, Oxford University Press, 1979) 233.

Avenarius, M, *Der pseudo-ulpianische liber singularis regularum: Entstehung, Eigenart und Überlieferung einer hochklassischen Juristenschrift* (Gottingen, Wallstein, 2005).
Avenarius, M and others (eds), *Gradenwitz, Riccobono und die Entwicklung der Interpolationenkritik: Methodentransfer unter europäischen Juristen im späten 19. Jahrhundert = Gradenwitz, Riccobono e gli sviluppi della critica interpolazionistica: Circolazione di modelli e metodi fra giuristi europei nel tardo Ottocento* (Tübingen, Mohr Siebeck, 2018).
Babusiaux, U, '*Quod Graeci … vocant* – Emblematischer Codewechsel in den Juristenschriften' in J Hallebeek and others (eds), *Inter cives necnon peregrinos: Essays in honour of Boudewijn Sirks* (Göttingen Vandenhoeck & Ruprecht, 2014) 35.
Baldus, C and others (eds), *Dogmengeschichte und historische Individualität der römischen Juristen = Storia dei dogmi e individualità storica dei giuristi romani: atti del seminario internazionale (Montepluciano 14–17 giugno 2011)* (Trento, Università degli Studi di Trento, 2012).
Balsdon, JPVD, *Romans and Aliens* (Chapel Hill, University of North Carolina Press, 1979).
Banaji, J, *Agrarian Change in Late Antiquity: Gold, Labour, and Aristocratic Dominance* (Oxford, Oxford University Press, 2001).
Bannon, CJ, *The Brothers of Romulus: Fraternal Pietas in Roman Law, Literature, and Society* (Princeton, Princeton University Press, 1997).
Barton, JL, 'The *Lex Aquilia* and Decretal Actions' in WAJ Watson (ed), *Daube Noster: Essays in Legal History for David Daube* (Edinburgh, Scottish Academic Press, 1974) 15.
Beatson, J and Zimmermann, R (eds), *Jurists Uprooted: German-Speaking Emigré Lawyers in Twentieth Century Britain* (Oxford, Oxford University Press, 2004).
Becker, A, *Platons Politeia: Ein systematischer Kommentar* (Ditzingen, Reclam, 2017).
Behrends, O, 'Methodik der Fallbearbeitung' (1985) 11 *Juristische Schulung* 878.
Behrends, O and others (eds), *Corpus Iuris Civilis. Text und Übersetzung*, vol 2 (Heidelberg, CF Müller, 1995).
Beiser, FC, *The German Historicist Tradition* (Oxford, Oxford University Press, 2011).
Berger, A, *Encyclopedic Dictionary of Roman Law* (Philadelphia, The American Philosophical Society, 1953).
Beseler, G, *Beiträge zur Kritik der römischen Rechtsquellen*, vol 2 (Tübingen, Mohr, 1911).
Besta, MC, 'Pesca e pescatori nell'Egitto greco-romano' (1921) 2 *Aegyptus* 67.
Bignardi, A, '*Frangere* e *Rumpere* nel Lessico Normativo e nella *Interpretatio Prudentium*' in S Romano (ed), *Nozione, Formazione e Interpretazione del Diritto: dall'Età Romana alle Esperienze Moderne: Ricerche Dedicate al Professor Filippo Gallo*, vol 1 (Naples, Jovene, 1997) 11.
Birks, P, 'Fictions Ancient and Modern' in DN MacCormick and PBH Birks (eds), *The Legal Mind: Essays for Tony Honoré* (Oxford, Clarendon Press, 1986) 83.
Birks, PBH, 'Other Men's Meat: Aquilian Liability for Proper Use' (1981) 16 *Irish Jurist* 141.
—— *The Roman Law of Obligations* (E Descheemaeker ed, Oxford, Oxford University Press, 2014).
Bobzien, S, 'Stoic Logic' in B Inwood (ed), *The Cambridge Companion to the Stoics* (Cambridge, Cambridge University Press, 2003) 85.
Boethius, *Boethius's In Ciceronis Topica* (E Stump trans, Ithaca, Cornell University Press, 1988).
Bohlen, D, *Die Bedeutung der Fischerei für die antike Wirtschaft* (Hamburg, Diss U Hamburg, 1937).
Bonini, R, *I libri de cognitionibus di Callistrato: Ricerche sull'elaborazione giurisprudenziale della cognitio extra ordinem*, vol 1 (Milan, Giuffrè, 1964).
Bortolucci, G, 'Index verborum Graecorum quae in Institutionibus et Digestis occurrunt' (1906) 76 *Archivio giuridico Filippo Serafini* 353.
Boyancé, P, 'La main de Fides' (1964) 70 *Collection Latomus* 101.
Bradley, KR, *Slaves and Masters in the Roman Empire: A Study in Social Control* (Oxford, Oxford University Press, 1987).
Brennan, TC, *The Praetorship in the Roman Republic*, vol II (Oxford, Oxford University Press, 2000).
Broekaert, W, *Navicularii et Negotiantes: A prosopographical study of Roman merchants and shippers* (Rahden, Marie Leidorf, 2013).
—— 'Freedmen and Agency in Roman Business' in AI Wilson and M Flohr (eds), *Urban Craftsmen and Traders in the Roman World* (Oxford, Oxford University Press, 2016) 222.

Brown, WC, 'The *gesta municipalia* and the public validation of documents in Frankish Europe' in WC Brown and others (eds), *Documentary Culture and the Laity in the Early Middle Ages* (Cambridge, Cambridge University Press, 2013) 95.
Bryce, J, 'Inaugural Lecture: The Academical Study of the Civil Law' in *Studies in History and Jurisprudence*, vol II (Oxford, Clarendon Press, 1901) 475.
Bryen, AZ, 'Law in Many Pieces' (2014) 109 *Classical Philology* 346.
Buckland, WW, *The Roman Law of Slavery: The Condition of the Slave in Private Law from Augustus to Justinian* (Cambridge, Cambridge University Press, 1908).
—— *A Manual of Roman Private Law*, 2nd edn (Cambridge, Cambridge University Press, 1953).
—— *A Text-Book of Roman Law from Augustus to Justinian*, 3rd edn (PG Stein ed, Cambridge, Cambridge University Press, 1963).
Buckland, WW and McNair, AD, *Roman Law and Common Law*, 2nd edn (FH Lawson ed, Cambridge, Cambridge University Press, 1952).
Bund, E, *Untersuchungen zur Methode Julians* (Cologne, Böhlau, 1965).
Burrows, AA (ed), *English Private Law*, 2nd edn (Oxford, Oxford University Press, 2007).
Burton, GP, 'Tributum' in S Hornblower and A Spawforth (eds), *The Oxford Companion to Classical Civilization*, 2nd edn (Oxford, Oxford University Press, 2014) 814.
Cairns, JW and du Plessis, PJ (eds), *Beyond Dogmatics: Law and Society in the Roman World* (Edinburgh, Edinburgh University Press, 2007).
Camodeca, G (ed), *Tabulae Pompeianae Sulpiciorum*, vol I (Rome, Qasar, 1999).
Candy, P, 'Parallel Developments in Roman Law and Maritime Trade during the Late Republic and Early Principate' (2020) 33 *Journal of Roman Archaeology* (forthcoming).
Cannata, CA, 'Sul testo della *lex Aquilia* e la sua portata originaria' in L Vacca (ed), *La responsabilità civile da atto illecito nella prospettiva storico-comparatistica* (Turin, Giappichelli, 1995) 25.
Capogrossi Colognesi, L, 'L'interdetto «quod vi aut clam» e il suo àmbito di applicazione' (1993) 21 *Index* 278.
Carcaterra, A, *Il possesso dei diritti nel diritto romano* (Milan, Giuffrè, 1942).
Cerami, P, '"*Mutua pecunia a magistro 'navis reficiendae causa' sumpta*" e "*praepositio exercitoris*": Profilo storico-comparatistici' (2000) 46 *AUPA* 131.
Cerami, P and Petrucci, A, *Diritto commerciale romano: Profilo storico*, 3rd edn (Turin, Giappichelli, 2010).
Clinton, K, 'The Eleusinian Mysteries: Roman Initiates and Benefactors, Second Century B.C. to A.D. 267' in W Haase (ed), *Aufstieg und Niedergang der Römischen Welt*, vol II.18.2 (Berlin, De Gruyter, 1989) 1499.
Coch Roura, N, *La forma estipulatoria: Una aproximación al estudio del lenguaje directo en el Digesto* (Madrid, Dykinson, 2017).
Collinet, P, 'The General Problems Raised by the Codification of Justinian' (1923) 4 *Leg Hist Rev* 1.
Comune di Roma, *Ara Pacis*, new edn (S Fox trans, Milan, Electa, 2009).
Corbino, A, *Il danno qualificato e la Lex Aquilia: Corso di diritto romano*, 2nd edn (Padua, CEDAM, 2008).
—— '*Lex Aquilia* e procurato aborto' in E Chevreau, D Kremer and A Laquerrière-Lacroix (eds), *Carmina Iuris: Mélanges en l'honneur de Michel Humbert* (Paris, De Boccard, 2012) 159.
Corcoran, S, 'Collatio legum Mosaicarum et Romanarum' in RS Bagnall and others (eds), *The Encyclopedia of Ancient History* (Blackwell, 2012) DOI:10.1002/9781444338386.wbeah13050.
Cortés Copete, JM, 'Adriano y la regulación de los mercados cívicos: una nueva lectura de IG II2 1103' (2015) 46 *Habis* 239.
—— 'Koinoi Nomoi: Hadrian and the Harmonization of Local Laws' in O Hekster and K Verboven (eds), *The Impact of Justice on the Roman Empire: Proceedings of the Thirteenth Workshop of the International Network Impact of Empire (Gent, June 21–24, 2017)* (Leiden, Brill, 2019) 105.
Costa, E, *Il Diritto Privato Roman nelle Comedie di Plauto* (Turin, Bocca, 1890).
Cowell, J, *Institutiones Iuris Anglicani* (Cambridge, Legat, 1605).
Crawford, MH (ed), *Roman Statutes*, vol 1 (London, Institute of Classical Studies, 1996).
—— *Roman Statutes*, vol 2 (London, Institute of Classical Studies, 1996).

Curtius, C, 'Mittheilungen aus Athen und dem Piraeus' (1870) 29 *Philologus* 691.
D'Amelio, G, 'Il *Dictionarium Iuris* di Jacques de Revigny' (1972) 40 *Leg Hist Rev* 43.
D'Arms, JH, *Commerce and Social Standing in Ancient Rome* (Cambridge, Harvard University Press, 1981).
Daalder, ES, *De rechtspraakverzamelingen van Julius Paulus: Recht en rechtvaardigheid in de rechterlijke uitspraken van keizer Septimius Severus* (The Hague, Boom Juridisch, 2018).
Dalla, D, *L'incapacità sessuale in diritto romano*, vol 1978 (Milan, Giuffrè, 1978).
Daube, D, 'On the Use of the Term *Damnum*' in V Arangio-Ruiz (ed), *Studi in Onore di Siro Solazzi nel Cinquantesimo Anniversario del Suo Insegnamento Universitario, 1899-1948* (Naples, Jovene, 1948) 93.
Day, J, *An Economic History of Athens under Roman Domination* (New York, Columbia University Press, 1942).
de Ligt, L, *Fairs and Markets in the Roman Empire. Economic and Social Aspects of Periodic Trade in a Pre-Industrial Society* (Amsterdam, Gieben, 1993).
—— 'The Nundinae of L. Bellicius Sollers' in H Sancisi-Weerdenburg (ed), *De agricultura: in memoriam Pieter Willem de Neeve (1945–1990)* (Amsterdam, Gieben, 1993) 238.
—— 'Roman Law, Markets and Market Prices' in PJ du Plessis, C Ando and K Tuori (eds), *The Oxford Handbook of Roman Law and Society* (Oxford, Oxford University Press, 2016) 660.
De Martino, F, 'Studii sull'actio exercitoria' (1941) 7 *Rivista del Diritto della Navigazione* 7.
—— 'Ancora sull'«actio exercitoria»' (1958) 4 *Labeo* 274.
Di Porto, A, 'La Tutela della "salubritas" fra editto e giurisprudenza: il ruolo di Labeone' (1988) 91 *BIDR* 459.
Diósdi, G, *Ownership in Ancient and Preclassical Roman Law* (Budapest, Akadémiai Kiadó, 1970).
Dixon, S, *The Roman Family* (Baltimore, Johns Hopkins University Press, 1992).
Dondorp, H, '*Partes secanto*: Aulus Gellius and the Glossators' (2010) 57 *RIDA* 131.
Dovere, E, 'Le discours juridique et moral d'*utilitas* à Rome' (1999) 65 *SDHI* 239.
du Plessis, PJ, *Letting and Hiring in Roman Legal Thought: 27 BCE–284 CE* (Leiden, Brill, 2012).
—— *New Frontiers: Law and Society in the Roman World* (Edinburgh, Edinburgh University Press, 2013).
—— 'Notes on a fire' in F Sturm and others (eds), *Liber Amicorum Guido Tsuno* (Frankfurt, Vico, 2013) 309.
—— *Borkowski's Textbook on Roman Law*, 5th edn (Oxford, Oxford University Press, 2015).
—— (ed), *Cicero's Law: Rethinking Roman Law of the Late Republic* (Edinburgh, Edinburgh University Press, 2016).
—— 'Urban Landlords and Tenants' in PJ du Plessis, C Ando and K Tuori (eds), *The Oxford Handbook of Roman Law and Society* (Oxford, Oxford University Press, 2016) 635.
du Plessis, PJ, Ando, C and Tuori, K, *The Oxford Handbook of Roman Law and Society* (Oxford, Oxford University Press, 2016).
Dworkin, RM, *Taking Rights Seriously* (London, Duckworth, 1977).
—— *Law's Empire* (London, Fontana, 1986).
Eisele, F, 'Beiträge zur Erkenntniss der Digesteninterpolationen' (1897) 18 *ZRG RA* 1.
Ernst, W, Justinian's Digest 9.2.51 in the Western Legal Canon: Roman Legal Thought and Modern Causality Concepts (Cambridge, Intersentia, 2019).
Evans-Jones, R and MacCormack, GD, '*Iusta causa traditionis*' in PBH Birks (ed), *New Perspectives in the Roman Law of Property* (Oxford, Oxford University Press, 1989) 99.
Everett, N, 'Lay documents and archives in early medieval Spain and Italy, c. 400–700' in WC Brown and others (eds), *Documentary Culture and the Laity in the Early Middle Ages* (Cambridge, Cambridge University Press, 2013) 63.
Farrell, J and Putnam, MCJ (eds), *A Companion to Vergil's Aeneid and its Tradition* (Chichester, Wiley-Blackwell, 2010).
Feenstra, R, 'L'"Epistula" comme preuve d'une stipulation' in *Studi in onore di Emilio Betti*, vol 2 (Milan, Giuffrè, 1962) 405.
Felius, I (ed), *Corpus Iuris Civilis Iustinianei*, vol 3 (Lyons, 1627).

Fleming, R, *Kings and Lords in Conquest England* (Cambridge, Cambridge University Press, 1991).
Földi, A, 'Remarks on the legal structure of enterprises in Roman law' (1996) 43 *RIDA* 179.
Föllinger, S, 'Anthropologie und Ökonomie bei Platon' in W Enkelmann and B Priddat (eds), *Was ist? Wirtschaftsphilosophische Erkundungen: Definitonen, Ansätze, Methoden, Erkenntnisse, Wirkungen* (Marburg, Metropolis, 2015) 413.
—— *Ökonomie bei Platon* (Berlin, De Gruyter, 2016).
Föllinger, S and Korn, E, 'Glück und Ökonomie – ein interdisziplinäres Projekt zur Bedeutung von Institutionen bei Platon' in V Mammitzsch and others (eds), *Die Marburger Gelehrten-Gesellschaft: Universitas litterarum nach 1968* (Berlin, De Gruyter, 2016) 337.
Forschner, B, 'Law's Nature: Philosophy as a Legal Argument in Cicero's Writings' in PJ du Plessis (ed), *Cicero's Law: Rethinking Roman Law of the Late Republic* (Edinburgh, Edinburgh University Press, 2016) 50.
Frakes, RM, *Compiling the Collatio Legum Mosaicarum et Romanarum in Late Antiquity* (Oxford, Oxford University Press, 2011).
Frier, BW, *The Rise of the Roman Jurists: Studies in Cicero's pro Caecina* (Princeton, Princeton University Press, 1985).
—— *A Casebook on the Roman Law of Delict* (Atlanta, Scholars Press, 1989).
Gardner, JF, *Family and Familia in Roman Law and Life* (Oxford, Oxford University Press, 1998).
Gargola, DJ, *Lands, Laws, & Gods: Magistrates and Ceremony in the Regulation of Public Lands in Republican Rome* (Chapel Hill, University of North Carolina Press, 1995).
Garnett, G, *Conquered England: Kingship, Succession and Tenure, 1066–1166* (Oxford, Oxford University Press, 2007).
Gemoll, W and Vretska, K, 'ἄστυ' in *Griechisch-deutsches Schul- und Handwörterbuch*, 10th edn (Munich, Oldenbourg, 2012) 140.
George, H, *Progress and Poverty* (London, Reeves, 1884).
Georges, KE, *Ausführliches lateinisch-deutsches Handwörterbuch*, vol 2, 11th edn (H Georges ed, Hannover, Hahn, 1962).
Giaro, T, 'L'Art de comparer les cas' (1994) 60 *SDHI* 522.
—— 'Legal Tradition of Eastern Europe. Its Rise and Demise' (2011) 2 *Comparative Law Review* 1.
Gibbon, E, *The History of the Decline and Fall of the Roman Empire*, vol 4 (London, Strahan and Cadell, 1788).
Gilmore, MP, *Argument from Roman Law in Political Thought, 1200-1600* (Cambridge, Harvard University Press, 1941).
Giltaij, J, 'Greek Philosophy and Classical Roman Law: A Brief Overview' in PJ du Plessis, C Ando and K Tuori (eds), *The Oxford Handbook of Roman Law and Society* (Oxford, Oxford University Press, 2016) 188.
Girard, PF and Senn, F, *Textes de droit romain*, vol I, 7th edn (Paris, Dalloz, 1967).
Glare, PGW (ed), *Oxford Latin Dictionary*, vol I (A–L), 2nd edn (Oxford, Oxford University Press, 2012).
Goff, RLA, 'The Search for Principle' (1983) 69 *Proceedings of the British Academy* 169.
Goodhart, AL, *English Contributions to the Philosophy of Law* (New York, Oxford University Press, 1949).
Gordley, J, *The Jurists: A Critical History* (Oxford, Oxford University Press, 2013).
Gordon, WM, *Studies in the Transfer of Property by Traditio* (Aberdeen, University of Aberdeen Press, 1970).
—— 'Legal Tradition, with particular reference to Roman Law' in DN MacCormick and PBH Birks (eds), *The Legal Mind: Essays for Tony Honoré* (Oxford, Clarendon Press, 1986) 279.
—— 'The Importance of the *iusta causa* of *traditio*' in PBH Birks (ed), *New Perspectives in the Roman Law of Property* (Oxford, Oxford University Press, 1989) 123.
Gradenwitz, O and others, *Vocabularium Iurisprudentiae Romanae*, vol I (A–C) (Berlin, G Reimeri, 1903).
Graindor, P, *Athènes sous Hadrien* (Cairo, Imprimerie Nationale, 1934).
Graßl, H, 'Marktorganisation und Preisbildung in der römischen Kaiserzeit' in R Rollinger and C Ulf (eds), *Commerce and Monetary Systems in the Ancient World: Means of Transmission and Cultural Interaction* (Stuttgart, Steiner, 2004) 352.

Greengus, S, 'Old Babylonian Marriage Ceremonies and Rites' (1966) 20 *Journal of Cuneiform Studies* 55.
Gretton, GL, 'Ownership and its Objects' (2007) 71 *Rabels Zeitschrift für ausländisches und internationales Privatrecht* 802.
Grey, TC, 'Holmes and Legal Pragmatism' (1989) 41 *Stanford Law Review* 787.
—— 'Freestanding Legal Pragmatism' (1996) 18 *Cardozo Law Review* 21.
Grueber, BE, *The Roman Law of Damage to Property: A Commentary on the Title of the Digest Ad Legem Aquiliam (IX.2)* (Oxford, Clarendon Press, 1886).
Günther, S, *Vectigalia nervos esse rei publicae: Die indirekten Steuern in der Römischen Kaiserzeit von Augustus bis Diokletian* (Wiesbaden, Harrassowitz, 2008).
—— '(K)einer neuen Theorie wert? Neues zur Antiken Wirtschaftsgeschichte anhand Dig. 50,11,2 (Callist. 3 cognit.)' (2017) 124 *Gymnasium: Zeitschrift für Kultur der Antike und Humanistische Bildung* 131.
Guzmán Brito, A, 'El significado de "quasi" en el vocabulario de los juristas romanos' (2016) 38 *Revista de estudios histórico-jurídicos* 79.
Haack, S, 'On Legal Pragmatism: Where Does "the Path of the Law" Lead Us?' (2005) 50 *American Journal of Jurisprudence* 71.
Hackl, K, 'Sulla finzione nel diritto privato' in F Pastori (ed), *Studi in onore di Arnaldo Biscardi*, vol I (Milan, Cisalpino–La Goliardica, 1982) 245.
—— 'Vom „quasi" in römischen zum „als ob" im modernen Recht' in R Zimmermann, R Knütel and JP Meincke (eds), *Rechtsgeschichte und Privatrechtsdogmatik* (Heidelberg, CF Müller, 1999) 117.
Haferkamp, H-P and Repgen, T (eds), *Wie pandektistisch war die Pandektistik?* (Tübingen, Mohr Siebeck, 2017).
Hale, BM, 'Principle and Pragmatism in Developing Private Law' (Cambridge Freshfields Lecture 2019), available at: www.supremecourt.uk/docs/speech-190307.pdf.
Hammond, NGL and Scullard, HH (eds), *The Oxford Classical Dictionary*, 2nd edn (Oxford, Oxford University Press, 1970).
Hanbury, HG, 'The Place of Roman Law in the Teaching of Law To-day' [1931] *Journal of the Society of Public Teachers of Law* 14.
Harke, JD, *Si error aliquis intervenit - Irrtum im klassischen römischen Vertragsrecht* (Berlin, Duncker & Humblot, 2005).
Hart, HLA, 'American Jurisprudence through English Eyes: The Nightmare and the Noble Dream' (1970) in *Essays in Jurisprudence and Philosophy* (Oxford, Clarendon Press, 1983) 123.
—— 'Diamonds and String: Holmes on the Common Law' (1963) in *Essays in Jurisprudence and Philosophy* (Oxford, Clarendon Press, 1983) 178.
—— 'Jhering's Heaven of Concepts and Modern Analytical Jurisprudence' (1970) in *Essays in Jurisprudence and Philosophy* (Oxford, Clarendon Press, 1983) 265.
Harter-Uibopuu, K, 'Hadrian and the Athenian Oil Law' in R Alston and O van Nief (eds), *Feeding the Ancient Greek City* (Louvain, Peeters, 2008) 127.
Hausmaninger, H, 'Zur Gesetzesinterpretation des Celsus' in *Studi in onore di Giuseppe Grosso*, vol V (Turin, Giappichelli, 1972) 243.
—— *Das Schadenersatzrecht der lex Aquilia* (Vienna, Manz, 1976).
Heineccius, JG, *Elementa Juris Civilis secundum ordinem Pandectarum*, vol I (Amsterdam, Jansson-Waesberge, 1740).
Heumann, HG and Seckel, E, '*iubere*' in *Handlexikon zu den Quellen des römischen Rechts*, 10th edn (A Thon ed, Graz, Akademische Druck- und Verlagsanstalt, 1958) 290.
—— '*utensilia*' in *Handlexikon zu den Quellen des römischen Rechts*, 10th edn (A Thon ed, Graz, Akademische Druck- und Verlagsanstalt, 1958) 607.
Highwood, J, *The Influence of the Christian Religion on Roman and English Law* (Durham, Thomas Caldcleugh, 1903).
Hilder, J, 'Jurors, Jurists and Advocates: Law in the *Rhetorica ad Herennium* and *De Inventione*' in PJ du Plessis (ed), *Cicero's Law: Rethinking Roman Law of the Late Republic* (Edinburgh, Edinburgh University Press, 2016) 166.

Höbenreich, E, *Annona: juristische Aspekte der stadtrömischen Lebensmittelversorgung im Prinzipat* (Graz, Leykam, 1997).
Holmes, OW, *The Common Law* (London, Macmillan, 1882).
—— 'Law in Science and Science in Law' (1889) in *Collected Legal Papers* (New York, Harcourt, Brace and Co, 1920) 210.
—— 'Learning and Science' (1895) in *Collected Legal Papers* (New York, Harcourt, Brace and Co, 1920) 138.
—— 'The Path of the Law' (1897) in *Collected Legal Papers* (New York, Harcourt, Brace and Co, 1920) 167.
Honoré, AM, 'Ownership' in AG Guest (ed), *Oxford Essays in Jurisprudence* (Oxford, Oxford University Press, 1961) 107.
—— 'Legal Reasoning in Rome and Today' (1973) 4 *Cambrian Law Review* 58.
—— 'Conveyances of Land and Professional Standards in the Later Empire' in PBH Birks (ed), *New Perspectives in the Roman Law of Property* (Oxford, Oxford University Press, 1989) 137.
—— *Ulpian: Pioneer of Human Rights*, 2nd edn (Oxford, Oxford University Press, 2002).
—— 'Ulpian, Natural Law and Stoic Influence' (2010) 78 *Leg Hist Rev* 199.
Horak, F, *Rationes decidendi: Entscheidungsbegründungen bei den älteren römischen Juristen bis Labeo* (Aalen, Scientia, 1969).
Hornblower, S, Spawforth, A and Eidinow, E (eds), *Oxford Classical Dictionary* (Oxford, Oxford University Press, 2012).
Howarth, D, *Law as Engineering: Thinking About What Lawyers Do* (Cheltenham, Edward Elgar, 2013).
Humfress, C, 'Telling Stories About (Roman) Law' in P Dresch and J Scheele (eds), *Legalism: Rules and Categories* (Oxford, Oxford University Press, 2015) 79.
Huschke, PE, *Iurisprudentiae Anteiustinianae quae svpersvnt* (Leipzig, Teubner, 1861).
Huvelin, P, *Études d'histoire du droit commercial romain (histoire externe - droit maritime)* (H Lévy-Bruhl ed, Paris, Sirey, 1929).
Hyamson, M (ed), *Mosaicarum et Romanarum Legum Collatio* (London, Oxford University Press, 1913).
Ibbetson, DJ, 'The danger of definition: *contrectatio* and appropriation' in ADE Lewis and DJ Ibbetson (eds), *The Roman Law Tradition* (Cambridge, Cambridge University Press, 1994) 54.
—— '*Obligatio* in Roman Law and Society' in PJ du Plessis, C Ando and K Tuori (eds), *The Oxford Handbook of Roman Law and Society* (Oxford, Oxford University Press, 2016) 569.
—— 'Buckland on the *Lex Aquilia* (Appendix to Chapter 2)' in PJ du Plessis (ed), *Wrongful Damage to Property in Roman Law: British Perspectives* (Edinburgh, Edinburgh University Press, 2018) 64.
—— 'Natural Law in Early Modern Legal Thought' in H Pihlajamäki, MD Dubber and M Godfrey (eds), *The Oxford Handbook of European Legal History* (Oxford, Oxford University Press, 2018) 566.
Ibbetson, DJ and Lewis, ADE, 'The Roman law tradition' in ADE Lewis and DJ Ibbetson (eds), *The Roman Law Tradition* (Cambridge, Cambridge University Press, 1994) 1.
Jahr, G, 'Zur iusta causa tradtitionis' (1963) 80 *ZRG RA* 141.
James, W, *Pragmatism: A New Name for Some Old Ways of Thinking* (London, Longmans, 1907).
Jenkins, D (ed), *The Law of Hywel Dda: Law Texts from Medieval Wales* (Llandysul, Gomer, 1986).
Jhering, CRR, *Geist des römischen Rechts auf den verschiedenen Stufen seiner Entwicklung*, vol 4 (Leipzig, Breitkopf und Härtel, 1867).
—— *L'Esprit du droit romain dans les diverses phases de son développement*, vol 4, 3rd edn (O de Meulenaere trans, Paris, Marescq, 1886).
—— 'In the Heaven for Legal Concepts: A Fantasy' (1985) 58 *Temple Law Quarterly* 799.
—— *Ist die Jurisprudenz eine Wissenschaft?: Jherings Wiener Antrittsvorlesung vom 16. Oktober 1868*, 2nd rev edn (O Behrends ed, Göttingen, Wallstein, 2009).
Johnston, DEL, *The Roman Law of Trusts* (Oxford, Oxford University Press, 1988).
—— 'Limiting Liability: Roman Law and the Civil Law Tradition' (1995) 70 *Chicago-Kent Law Review* 1515.
—— 'Suing the *Paterfamilias*: Theory and Practice' in JW Cairns and PJ du Plessis (eds), *Beyond Dogmatics: Law and Society in the Roman World* (Edinburgh, Edinburgh University Press, 2007) 173.

Jolowicz, HF, 'Academic Elements in Roman Law' (1932) 48 *LQR* 171.
—— 'Utility and Elegance in Civil Law Studies' (1949) 65 *LQR* 322.
Jolowicz, HF and Nicholas, JKBM, *An Historical Introduction to the Study of Roman Law*, 3rd edn (Cambridge, Cambridge University Press, 1972).
Jones, AHM, 'In eo solo dominivm Populi Romani est vel Caesaris' (1941) 31 *Journal of Roman Studies* 26.
Kacprzak, A, 'Rhetoric and Roman Law' in PJ du Plessis, C Ando and K Tuori (eds), *The Oxford Handbook of Roman Law and Society* (Oxford, Oxford University Press, 2016) 200.
Kantor, G, 'Property in Land in Roman Provinces' in G Kantor, T Lambert and H Skoda (eds), *Legalism: Property and Ownership* (Oxford, Oxford University Press, 2017) 55.
Karlović, T, 'Propter celeritatem dirimendarum litium – Presumptions and Stipulatio in Roman Law' in CH van Rhee and A Uzelac (eds), *Truth and Efficiency in Civil Litigation: Fundamental Aspects of Fact-finding and Evidence-taking in a Comparative Context* (Cambridge, Intersentia, 2012) 375.
Kaser, M, 'Zur „iusta causa traditionis"' (1961) 34 *BIDR* 61.
—— 'Sur la Méthode des Jurisconsultes Romains' (1962) 5 *Romanitas* 107.
—— *Das römische Privatrecht*, 2nd rev edn (Munich, Beck, 1971).
—— *Zur Methodologie der römischen Rechtsquellenforschung* (Wien, Böhlau, 1972).
—— 'Nochmals zu *in bonis habere*' (1984) in M Kaser, *Römische Rechtsquellen und angewandte Juristenmethode* (Vienna, Böhlau, 1986) 346.
—— *Römische Rechtsquellen und angewandte Juristenmethode* (Vienna, Böhlau, 1986).
Kehoe, DP, *Investment, Profit, and Tenancy: The Jurists and the Roman Agrarian Economy* (Ann Arbor, University of Michigan Press, 1997).
—— 'Contracts, Agency, and Transaction Costs in the Roman Economy' in DP Kehoe, DM Ratzan and U Yiftach (eds), *Law and Transaction Costs in the Ancient Economy* (Ann Arbor, University of Michigan Press, 2015) 231.
Keller, FL, *Ueber Litis Contestation und Urtheil nach classischem Römischem Recht* (Zurich, Gessner, 1827).
Kelly, JM, 'The Meaning of the Lex Aquilia' (1964) 80 *LQR* 73.
—— *Roman Litigation* (Oxford, Oxford University Press, 1966).
—— *Studies in the Civil Judicature of the Roman Republic* (Oxford, Oxford University Press, 1976).
Kern, O, 'Eleusis 1' in A Pauly and others (eds), *Paulys Realencyclopädie der classischen Altertumswissenschaft*, vol V.2 (Stuttgart, JB Metzler, 1905) col 2336.
—— 'Mysterien (eleusinische Weihen)' in A Paulyand others (eds), *Paulys Realencyclopädie der classischen Altertumswissenschaft*, vol XVI.2 (Stuttgart, Alfred Druckenmüller, 1935) col 1211.
Kim, K, *Aliens in Medieval Law: The Origins of Modern Citizenship* (Cambridge, Cambridge University Press, 2000).
Kirschenbaum, A, *Sons, Slaves and Freedmen in Roman Commerce* (Jerusalem, Magnes, 1987).
Kramer, MH, 'The Philosopher-Judge: Some Friendly Criticisms of Richard Posner's Jurisprudence' (1996) 59 *MLR* 465.
Krampe, C, 'Julian im Dialog über *Mutuum*, *Traditio* und *Causa*' (2014) 20 *Fundamina* 489.
Kroger, JR, 'The Philosophical Foundations of Roman Law: Aristotle, the Stoics, and Roman Theories of Natural Law' [2004] *Wisconsin Law Review* 905.
Krueger, P and others (eds), *Corpus Iuris Civilis* (Berlin, Weidmann, 1872–95).
Lactantius, *Lactantius: Divine Institutes* (A Bowen and P Garnsey trans, Liverpool, Liverpool University Press, 2003).
Lawson, FH, *Negligence in the Civil Law* (Oxford, Oxford University Press, 1950).
Lazo, P, 'La interpretación de la cláusula *eius rei nomine* de los edictos *de exercitoria* y *de institoria actione*' (2016) 43 *Revista Chileana de Derecho* 1081.
Le Conte, A (ed), *Corpus juris civilis glossatum ex recens. Dionys. Gothofredi*, vol IV (Lyon, 1604).
Leadbetter, B, *Galerius and the Will of Diocletian* (London, Routledge, 2009).
Leese, M, 'Greek Influences on Roman Dowry Law' (2019) 40 *Journal of Legal History* 130.
Leesen, TG, *Gaius meets Cicero: Law and Rhetoric in the School Controversies* (Leiden, Brill, 2010).
Lenel, O, *Palingenesia Iuris Civilis*, vol 1 (Leipzig, Tauchnitz, 1889).
—— *Palingenesia Iuris Civilis*, vol 2 (Leipzig, Tauchnitz, 1889).
—— *Das Edictum Perpetuum*, 3rd rev edn (Leipzig, Tauchnitz, 1927).

Leptien, U, '"Utilitatis causa": Zweckmässigkeitsentscheidungen im römischen Recht' (1969) 35 *SDHI* 51.
Letwin, SR, *On the History of the Idea of Law* (Cambridge, Cambridge University Press, 2005).
Levy, E, Rabel, E and Mitteis, L, *Index interpolationum quae in Justiniani Digestis inesse dicuntur* (Weimar, Böhlau, 1929).
Liebs, D, 'Compte rendu: Roberto Bonini, I libri de cognitionibus di Callistrato, Ricerche sull'elaborazione giurisprudenziale della cognitio extra ordinem, vol 1, Giuffrè, Milano, 1964' (1966) 34 *Leg Hist Rev* 254.
—— 'Römische Provinzialjurisprudenz' in H Temporini (ed), *Aufstieg und Niedergang der römischen Welt*, vol II.15 (Berlin, De Gruyter, 1976) 288.
—— 'Wenn Fachliteratur Gesetz wird: Inwieweit wurden römische Juristenschriften im Lauf der Jahrhunderte überarbeitet' (2018) 135 *ZRG RA* 395.
Locke, J, *Two Treatises of Government* (first published 1689, P Laslett ed, Cambridge, Cambridge University Press, 1988).
Lokin, JHA, 'The End of an Epoch: Epilegomena to a Century of Interpolation Criticism' in R Feenstra and others (eds), *Collatio Iuris Romani*, vol I (Amsterdam, Gieben, 1995) 261.
Lokin, JHA, Meijering, R and Stolte, BH (eds), *Theophili Antecessoris Paraphrasis institutionum* (AF Murison trans, Groningen, Chimaira, 2010).
Longo, G, 'Actio exercitoria – Actio institoria – Actio quasi institoria' in G Grosso (ed), *Studi in onore di Gaetano Scherillo*, vol II (Milan, Cisalpino-La Goliardica, 1972) 581.
Lorusso, A, 'Reflections on the Quantification of *Damnum*' in PJ du Plessis (ed), *Wrongful Damage to Property in Roman Law: British Perspectives* (Edinburgh, Edinburgh University Press, 2018) 183.
Lovato, A, *Studi sulle Disputationes di Ulpiano* (Bari, Cacucci, 2003).
Luban, DJ, 'What's Pragmatic about Legal Pragmatism?' (1996) 18 *Cardozo Law Review* 43.
Lucrezi, F, *Il procurato incendio in diritto ebraico e romano* (Turin, Giappichelli, 2012).
—— 'Ancora sulla data della "Collatio"' in F Sturm and others (eds), *Liber Amicorum Guido Tsuno* (Frankfurt, Vico, 2013) 193.
Lytle, E, 'Fishless mysteries or high prices at Athens? Re-examining IG II 1103' (2007) 64 *Museum Helveticum* 100.
MacCormack, GD, '*Partes secanto*' (1968) 36 *Leg Hist Rev* 509.
—— 'Formalism, Symbolism and Magic in Early Roman Law' (1969) 37 *Leg Hist Rev* 439.
—— '*Celsus quaerit:* D.9.2.27.14' (1973) 20 *RIDA* 341.
—— 'Aquilian Studies' (1971) 41 *SDHI* 1.
—— 'The Oral and Written Stipulations in the Institutes' in PG Stein and ADE Lewis (eds), *Studies in Justinian's Institutes in memory of J. A. C. Thomas* (London, Sweet & Maxwell, 1983) 96.
MacCormick, DN, *Legal Reasoning and Legal Theory* (Oxford, Oxford University Press, 1978).
Maine, HJS, *Lectures on the Early History of Institutions* (London, Murray, 1875).
—— *Early Law and Custom*, new edn (London, Murray, 1890).
—— *Ancient Law*, repr edn (first published 1861, London, Oxford University Press, 1954).
Maitland, FW, *Township and Borough* (Cambridge, Cambridge University Press, 1898).
Manfredini, AD, *Contributi allo studio dell'«iniuria» in età repubblicana* (Milan, Giuffrè, 1977).
Manthe, U, 'Collatio 6,7 pr. isdem abstipulantibus' in M Avenarius, R Meyer-Pritzl and C Möller (eds), *Ars Iuris: Festschrift für Okko Behrends zum 70. Geburtstag* (Göttingen, Wallstein, 2009) 351.
—— 'Dubletten im Text der Collatio als Spuren der Redaktionstätigkeit' in K Muscheler (ed), *Römische Jurisprudenz – Dogmatik, Überlieferung, Rezeption: Festschrift für Detlef Liebs zum 75. Geburtstag* (Berlin, Duncker & Humblot, 2011) 395.
—— 'Die Collatio: Inhalt, Textkritik und Verfasserfrage' in U Manthe, S Nishimura and M Igimi (eds), *Aus der Werkstatt römischer Juristen: Vorträge der Europäisch-Ostasiatischen Tagung 2013 in Fukuoka* (Berlin, Duncker & Humblot, 2016) 197.
Marotta, V, 'I giuristi romani come "intellettuali": la cultura di Callistrato' (1992) 1 *Ostraka* 287.
Mayer-Maly, T, *Das Putativtitelproblem bei der usucapio* (Graz, Böhlau, 1962).
Mazhuga, VI, 'Сцены стипуляции в комедиях Плавта' (1997) 3 *Hyperboreus* 10.
Meyer, EA, *Legitimacy and Law in the Roman World: Tabulae in Roman Belief and Practice* (Cambridge, Cambridge University Press, 2004).

Miceli, M, *Sulla struttura formulare delle 'actiones adiecticiae qualitatis'* (Turin, Giappichelli, 2001).
—— *Studi sulla «rappresentanza» nel diritto romano* (Milan, Giuffrè, 2008).
Migne, J-P (ed), *Patrologiae cursus completus*, vol 54, Series Latina (Paris, Migne, 1860).
Minieri, L, *Exurere, adurere, incendere: Studi sul procurato incendio in diritto romano* (Naples, Satura, 2012).
—— 'Sul *quasi incendarius*' in F Sturm and others (eds), *Liber Amicorum Guido Tsuno* (Frankfurt, Vico, 2013) 251.
Mitteis, L, 'Storia del diritto antico e studio del diritto romano' (1929) 12 *AUPA* 477.
Mommsen, T, *Römisches Strafrecht* (Leipzig, Duncker & Humblot, 1899).
Montemayor Aceves, ME, *Comparación de leyes mosaicas y romanas*, 2nd edn (Mexico City, Universidad Nacional Autónoma de México, 2006).
Moritz, LA, *Grain-mills and Flour in Classical Antiquity* (Oxford, Oxford University Press, 1958).
Mouritsen, H, *The Freedman in the Roman World* (Cambridge, Cambridge University Press, 2011).
Mussawir, E, 'To isolate the law: the activity of the jurist in Digest 9.2.27.12 and Digest 45.3.18.2' (2019) 10 *Jurisprudence* 54.
Musumeci, F, '*Molesta separatio, difficilis separatio* ed esperibilità dell'*actio legis aquiliae*' in *Studi in onore di Remo Martini*, vol II (Milan, Giuffrè, 2009) 821.
—— '*«Quasi ruperit», «quasi rupto»*. In tema di applicazione concreta del terzo capitolo della *lex Aquilia*' in C Russo Ruggeri (ed), *Studi in onore di Antonino Metro*, vol IV (Milan, Giuffrè, 2010) 347.
Navarra, M, *Ricerche sulla utilitas nel pensiero dei giuristi romani* (Torino, Giappichelli, 2002).
Nicholas, JKBM, 'The Form of the Stipulation in Roman Law II' (1953) 69 *LQR* 233.
—— *An Introduction to Roman Law* (Oxford, Oxford University Press, 1962).
Nichols, R, *Settling the Frontier: Land, Law and Society in the Peshawar Valley, 1500–1900* (Oxford, Oxford University Press, 2001).
Nörr, D, 'Book Review: Wolfram Kerber, Die Quasi-Institute als Methode der römischen Rechtsfindung' (1973) 90 *ZRG RA* 421.
—— *Causa mortis: auf den Spuren einer Redewendung* (Munich, Beck, 1986).
—— 'Zur Interdependenz von Prozeßrecht und materiellem Recht am Beispiel der lex Aquilia' (1987) 6 *Rechtshistorisches Journal* 99.
Northwood, S, 'Census and Tributum' in L de Ligt and S Northwood (eds), *People, Land, and Politics: Demographic Developments and the Transformation of Roman Italy 300 BC-AD 14* (Leiden, Brill, 2008) 257.
Nowak, M, 'Manicipatio and its life in Late-Roman law' (2011) 41 *The Journal of Juristic Papyrology* 103.
Nozick, R, *Anarchy, State and Utopia* (Oxford, Blackwell, 1974).
Obituaries, 'Toni Morrison' *The Times* (7 August 2019) 47.
Oliver, JH, *Greek Constitutions of Early Roman Emperors from Inscriptions and Papyri* (Philadelphia, American Philosophical Society, 1989).
Osler, DJ, 'The Myth of European Legal History' (1997) 16 *Rechtshistorisches Journal* 393.
Otto, CE, Schilling, B and Sintenis, CFF (eds), *Das Corpus Juris Civilis in's Deutsche übersetzt*, vol 4 (Leipzig, Carl Focke, 1832).
Palmer, RC, 'The Economic and Cultural Impact of the Origins of Property: 1180-1220' (1985) 3 *Law and History Review* 375.
Pellecchi, L, 'L'Azione in ripetizione e le qualificazioni del *dare* in Paul. 17 *ad Plaut.* D. 12.6.65: Contributo allo studio della *condictio*' (1998) 64 *SDHI* 69.
Petrucci, A, 'Ulteriori osservazioni sulla protezione dei contraenti con gli *institores* ed i *magistri navis* nel diritto romano dell'età commerciale' (2002) 53 *IVRA* 17.
Piccinelli, F, *Studi e ricerche intorno alla definizione «Dominium est ius utendi et abutendi re sua quatenus iuris rati patitur»*, repr edn (Naples, Joneve, 1980).
Pilipow, R, 'The Jeweled Jurist: Late Roman Legal Aesthetics' (2020) 4 *Studies in Late Antiquity* 185.
Plisecka, A, 'The Use of Greek by Roman Jurists' in L Beck Varela, P Gutiérrez Vega and A Spinosa (eds), *Crossing Legal Cultures* (Frankfurt am Main, Peter Lang, 2009) 59.
Pollock, F and Wright, RS, *An Essay on Possession in the Common Law* (Oxford, Oxford University Press, 1888).
Pölönen, J, 'Framing "Law and Society" in the Roman World' in PJ du Plessis, C Ando and K Tuori (eds), *The Oxford Handbook of Roman Law and Society* (Oxford, Oxford University Press, 2016) 8.

Posner, RA, *Overcoming Law* (London, Harvard University Press, 1995).
—— 'Pragmatic Adjudication' (1996) 18 *Cardozo Law Review* 1.
—— *The Problematics of Moral and Legal Theory* (London, Belknap Press, 1999).
Pothier, RJ, *Traité du droit du domaine, de propriété*, vol 1 (Paris, Debure, 1772).
Pound, NR, 'Mechanical Jurisprudence' (1908) 8 *Columbia Law Review* 605.
Powell, L, *Marcus Agrippa: Right-Hand Man of Caesar Augustus* (Barnsley, Pen & Sword, 2015).
Prichard, AM, *Leage's Roman Private Law*, 3rd edn (London, Macmillan, 1961).
Pringsheim, FR, *Gesammelte Abhandlungen*, vol 1 (Heidelberg, Carl Winter, 1961).
—— 'Die Verletzung Freier und die "lex Aquilia"' (1962) 28 *SDHI* 1.
Proudhon, P-J, *What is Property?* (DR Kelley and BG Smith eds, Cambridge, Cambridge University Press, 1994).
Pufendorf, S, *Of the Law of Nature and Nations: Eight books*, 4th edn (B Kennett trans, London, J. Walthoe and others, 1729).
—— *De Jure Naturae et Gentium Libri Octo*, repr edn (Oxford, Oxford University Press, 1934).
Pugliese, G, 'In tema di «actio exercitoria»' (1957) 3 *Labeo* 308.
Pugsley, DF, 'The Lex Aquilia' (1972) 89 *South African Law Journal* 489.
—— 'Was *justa causa* necessary for *traditio* in Roman law?' in DF Pugsley, *Americans Are Aliens: and other essays on Roman Law* (Exeter, University of Exeter, 1989) 27.
Puliatti, S, *Il de iure fisci di Callistrato e il processo fiscale in età severiana* (Milan, Giuffrè, 1992).
Quadrato, R, *Sulle tracce dell'annullabità: Quasi nullus nella giurisprudenza romana* (Naples, Jovene, 1983).
Rabello, AM, 'Collatio Legum Mosaicarum et Romanarum' in F Skolnik and M Berenbaum (eds), *Encyclopaedia Judaica*, vol 5, 2nd edn (Farmington Hills, Macmillan, 2007) 57.
Rainer, JM, 'Zur *insula* im Römischen Recht' in MJ Schermaier, JM Rainer and LC Winkel (eds), *Iurisprudentia universalis: Festschrift für Theo Mayer-Maly zum 70. Geburtstag* (Cologne, Böhlau, 2002) 609.
Raz, J, 'Legal Principles and the Limits of Law' (1972) 81 *Yale Law Journal* 823.
Riccobono, S, 'Studi critici sulle fonte del diritto romano' (1895) 8 *BIDR* 169.
—— 'Analisi delle decisioni di Paolo in confronto alle riforme giustinianee: Appendice III: Analogia, assimilazione, approssimazione nell'opera dei giuristi romani ed in particolare dell'uso dell'avverbio "quasi"' (1917) 3–4 *AUPA* 697.
—— 'Outlines of the Evolution of Roman Law' (1925) 74 *University of Pennsylvania Law Review* 1.
—— 'La Giurisprudenza classica come fattore di evoluzione nel diritto romano' in GG Archi (ed), *Scritti di diritto romano in onore di Contardo Ferrini* (Milan, Hoepli, 1946) 18.
—— *Stipulation and the Theory of Contract* (B Beinart and J Kerr-Wylie trans, Amsterdam, Balkema, 1957).
Ritter, J and Gründer, K (eds), *Historisches Wörterbuch der Philosophie*, vol 7: P–Q (Darmstadt, Wissenschaftliche Buchhandlung, 1971).
Robinson, OF, *The Criminal Law of Ancient Rome* (London, Duckworth, 1995).
Roddaz, J-M, *Marcus Agrippa* (Rome, École française de Rome, 1984).
Rodger, AF, 'What did *Damnum Iniuria* Actually Mean?' in AS Burrows and AF Rodger (eds), *Mapping the Law: Essays in Memory of Peter Birks* (Oxford, Oxford University Press, 2006) 421.
—— 'The Palingenesia of the Commentaries Relating to the Lex Aquilia' (2007) 124 *ZRG RA* 145.
Rodríguez, C and Azaustre Fernández, MJ, 'Algunas consideraciones sobre las ferias y los mercados en Derecho Romano y su recepción en Derecho Español' (2016) 17 *Revista Internacional de Derecho Romano* 145.
Rosenfeld, M, 'Pragmatism, Pluralism, and Legal Interpretation: Posner's and Rorty's Justice without Metaphysics Meets Hate Speech' (1996) 18 *Cardozo Law Review* 97.
Rostovtzeff, M, *The Social and Economic History of the Roman Empire*, vol 2, 2nd edn (Oxford, Oxford University Press, 1957).
Roth, A, *Who Gets What – and Why: The New Economics of Matchmaking and Market Design* (Boston, Houghton Mifflin Harcourt, 2015).
Rotondi, G, 'Teorie postclassiche sull'*actio legis Aquiliae*' in G Rotondi, *Scritti giuridici*, vol II (E Albertaria ed, Pavia, Tipografia e legatoria cooperativa, 1922) 411.

Ruffing, K, 'Auctions and Markets in the Roman Empire' in M Frass (ed), *Kauf, Konsum und Märkte. Wirtschaftswelten im Fokus – Von der römischen Antike bis zur Gegenwart* (Wiesbaden, Harrassowitz, 2013) 213.

Rüfner, T, 'Imperial *Cognitio* Process' in PJ du Plessis, C Ando and K Tuori (eds), *The Oxford Handbook of Roman Law and Society* (Oxford, Oxford University Press, 2016) 257.

Russo Ruggeri, C, 'Brevi note critiche su D. 9.2.27.28' (1992) 43 *IVRA* 111.

—— *Viviano giurista minore?* (Milano, Giuffrè, 1997).

Saccoccio, A, *Si certum petetur: Dalla condictio dei veteres alle condictiones giustinianee* (Milan, Giuffrè, 2002).

Saller, RP, *Personal Patronage under the Early Empire* (Cambridge, Cambridge University Press, 1982).

Sambrian, T, 'La *mancipatio* nei trittici della Transilvania' (2005) *Diritto@Storia: Rivista Internazionale di Scienza Giuridiche e Tradizione Romana*, available at: www.dirittoestoria.it/4/Tradizione-Romana/Sambrian-Mancipatio-trittici-Transilvania.htm.

Samir, A, 'D.9.2.27.17 versus CO.2.4: Који текст je интерполисан?' (2012) 46 *Zbornik radova Pravnog fakulteta, Novi Sad* 375.

Sampson, JW, '*lex Aquilia* on wrongful damage to property' in *Oxford Classical Dictionary* (Oxford, Oxford University Press, 2018) DOI:10.1093/acrefore/9780199381135.013.8261.

Sanna, MV, '*Rumpere* e *quasi rumpere* tra *lex* e *interpretatio*' (2017) 111 *BIDR* 347.

Scarano Ussani, V, *L'Utilità e la certezza* (Milan, Giuffrè, 1987).

Schanbacher, D, 'Zur Bedeutung der Leistungszweckbestimmung bei der Übereignung durch *Traditio* und beim Leistungsversprechen durch *Stipulatio*' (1992) 60 *Leg Hist Rev* 1.

Schiavone, A, *Nascita della giurisprudenza: Cultura aristocratica e pensiero giuridico nella Roma tardo repubblicana* (Roma, Laterza, 1976).

—— 'Forme normative e generi letterari. La cristallizzazione del ius civile e dell'editto fra tarda repubblica e primo principato' in E Dovere (ed), *La codificazione del diritto dall'antico al moderno* (Naples, Editoriale Scientifica, 1998) 51.

Schiller, AA, 'Sources and Influences of the Roman Law, III-VI Centuries A. D.' (1933) 21 *Georgetown Law Journal* 147.

—— *Roman Law: Mechanisms of Development* (The Hague, Mouton, 1978).

Schipani, S, *Responsabilità «ex lege Aquilia»: Criteri di imputazione e problema della 'culpa'* (Turin, Giappichelli, 1969).

Schofield, M, 'Plato on the economy' in M Hansen (ed), *The Ancient Greek City-state: Symposium on the Occasion of the 250th Anniversary of the Royal Danish Academy of Sciences and Letters, July, 1-4, 1992* (Copenhagen, Det Kongelige Danske Videnskabernes Selskab, 1993).

Schulz, F, *Principles of Roman Law* (M Wolff trans, Oxford, Oxford University Press, 1936).

—— *History of Roman Legal Science* (Oxford, Oxford University Press, 1946).

—— *Classical Roman Law* (Oxford, Oxford University Press, 1951).

Seckel, E, 'Ceterus' in *Heumanns Handlexikon zu den Quellen des römischen Rechts*, 9th edn (Jena, Fischer, 1926) 67.

Sedley, S, 'Declining the brief' in S Sedley, *Ashes and Sparks: Essays On Law and Justice* (Cambridge, Cambridge University Press, 2011) 153.

Silver, M, 'In Dubious Battle: An Economic Analysis of Emperor Hadrian's Fish and Olive Oil Laws' (2011) 7 *Roman Legal Tradition* 1.

Sirks, AJB, *The Theodosian Code: A Study* (Friedrichsdorf, Tortuga, 2007).

—— 'The slave who was slain twice: causality and the *lex Aquilia* (Iulian. 86 *dig*. D. 9,2,51)' (2011) 79 *Leg Hist Rev* 313.

—— 'What did *in bonis* in the *actio Serviana* include?' in H Dondorp, MJ Schermaier and AJB Sirks (eds), *De rebus divinis et humanis: Essays in honour of Jan Hallebeek* (Göttingen, Vandenhoeck & Ruprecht, 2019) 323.

—— 'The causa Rutiliana' (forthcoming).

Sohm, R, *The Institutes of Roman Law*, 4th edn (JC Ledlie trans, Oxford, Oxford University Press, 1892).

Stanojević, O, 'Gaius and Pomponius: Notes on David Pugsley' (1997) 44 *RIDA* 333.

Steel, CEW, *Roman Oratory* (Cambridge, Cambridge University Press, 2006).

Stein, PG, *Regulae Iuris: From Juristic Rules to Legal Maxims* (Edinburgh, Edinburgh University Press, 1966).
—— 'Franz Horak – *Rationes decidendi* [review]' (1970) 36 *SDHI* 460.
—— 'Logic and Experience in Roman and Common Law' in *The Character and Influence of the Roman Civil Law: Historical Essays* (London, Hambledon, 1988) 37.
—— 'Roman Law, Common Law, and Civil Law' (1992) 66 *Tulane Law Review* 1591.
—— 'Interpretation and Legal Reasoning in Roman Law' (1995) 70 *Chicago-Kent Law Review* 1539.
—— *Roman Law in European History* (Cambridge, Cambridge University Press, 1999).
—— 'The Roman Jurists' Conception of Law' in A Padovani and PG Stein (eds), *A Treatise of Legal Philosophy and General Jurisprudence*, vol 7: The Jurists' Philosophy of Law from Rome to the Seventeenth Century (Dordrecht, Springer, 2007) 1.
Stephen, JF, *A History of the Criminal Law of England*, vol I (London, Macmillan, 1883).
Strabo, *Geography*, vol III: Books 6–7 (HL Jones trans, Cambridge, Harvard University Press, 1924).
Sutherland, DW, *The Assize of Novel Disseisin* (Oxford, Oxford University Press, 1973).
Szanto, E, 'Δεῖγμα' in A Pauly and others (eds), *Paulys Realencyclopädie der classischen Altertumswissenschaft*, vol IV.2 (Stuttgart, JB Metzler, 1901) col 2383.
Tchernia, A, *The Romans and Trade* (J Grieve and E Minchin trans, Oxford, Oxford University Press, 2016).
Tellegen-Couperus, OE, 'The Tenant, the Borrower and the *lex Aquilia*' (1995) 42 *RIDA* 415.
—— *Quintilian and the Law: The Art of Persuasion in Law and Politics* (Leuven, Leuven University Press, 2003).
Tellegen-Couperus, OE and Tellegen, JW, 'Reading a Dead Man's Mind: Hellenistic Philosophy, Rhetoric and Roman Law' in PJ du Plessis (ed), *Cicero's Law: Rethinking Roman Law of the Late Republic* (Edinburgh, Edinburgh University Press, 2016) 26.
Thomas, JAC, 'Form and Substance in Roman Law' (1966) 19 *Current Legal Problems* 145.
—— *Textbook of Roman Law* (Amsterdam, North-Holland, 1976).
Troje, H, *Graeca leguntur* (Cologne, Böhlau, 1971).
Tuori, K, *Ancient Roman Lawyers and Modern Legal Ideals: Studies on the Impact of Contemporary Concerns in the Interpretation of Ancient Roman Legal History*, 2nd corrected edn (Frankfurt am Main, Vittorio Klostermann, 2007).
Vacca, L, '«Iusta causa» e «bona fides» nell'«usucapio» romana: A proposito del titolo «pro suo»' in V Giuffrè (ed), *Sodalitas: Scritti in Onore de Antonio Guarino*, vol 4 (Naples, Jovene, 1984) 1955.
Valditara, G, *Sulle origini del concetto di damnum* (Turin, Giappichelli, 1998).
—— 'In tema di stima del danno aquiliano' (2016) 44 *Index* 197.
Valiño, E, 'Las relaciones básicas de las acciones adyecticias' (1968) 38 *Anuario de Historia del Derecho Español* 377.
van Oven, JC, 'La Stipulation a-t-elle dégénéré' (1958) 26 *Leg Hist Rev* 409.
Vatin, C, 'Le tarif des poissons d'Akraiphia' in F Salviat and C Vatin (eds), *Inscriptions de Grèce centrale* (Paris, De Boccard, 1971) 95.
Viehweg, T, *Topik und Jurisprudenz* (Munich, Beck, 1953).
Vivenza, G, 'Roman Economic Thought' in W Scheidel (ed), *The Cambridge Companion to the Roman Economy* (Cambridge, Cambridge University Press, 2012) 25.
Von Lübtow, U, *Untersuchungen zur lex Aquilia de damno iniuria dato* (Berlin, Duncker & Humblot, 1971).
Voss, WE, *Recht und Rhetorik in den Kaisergesetzen der Spätantike: eine Untersuchung zum nachklassischen Kauf- und Übereignungsrecht* (Frankfurt, Löwenklau, 1982).
Wachsmuth, C, *Die Stadt Athen im Alterthum*, vol 2.1 (Leipzig, Teubner, 1890).
Wagenvoort, H, *Pietas: Selected Studies in Roman Religion* (Leiden, Brill, 1980).
Wallace-Hadrill, A, *Herculaneum: Past and Future* (London, Frances Lincoln, 2011).
Watkins, TH, '*Coloniae* and *Ius Italicum* in the Early Empire' (1983) 78 *Classical Journal* 319.
Watson, WAJ, *The Law of Obligations in the Later Roman Republic* (Oxford, Oxford University Press, 1965).
—— *The Law of Persons in the Later Roman Republic* (Oxford, Oxford University Press, 1967).
—— *The Law of Property in the Later Roman Republic* (Oxford, Oxford University Press, 1968).

—— *Limits of Juristic Decision in the Later Roman Republic*, Inaugural Lecture No 36 (Edinburgh, University of Edinburgh, 1969).
—— 'Narrow, Rigid and Literal Interpretation in the Later Roman Republic' (1969) 37 *Leg Hist Rev* 351.
—— *The Law of Succession in the Later Roman Republic* (Oxford, Oxford University Press, 1971).
—— *Roman Private Law around 200 BC* (Edinburgh, Edinburgh University Press, 1971).
—— 'Illogicality and Roman Law' (1972) 7 *Israel Law Review* 14.
—— *Roman Slave Law* (Baltimore, Johns Hopkins University Press, 1987).
—— 'Two Studies in Textual History' in WAJ Watson, *Studies in Roman Private Law* (London, Hambledon Press, 1991) 345.
Watson, WAJ (ed), *The Digest of Justinian*, rev edn (Philadelphia, University of Pennsylvania Press, 1998).
Watson, WAJ and El Fadl, KA, 'Fox Hunting, Pheasant Shooting, and Comparative Law' (2000) 48 *American Journal of Comparative Law* 1.
Weinfeld, M, 'תיִרְּב *b^erith*' in GJ Botterweck and H Ringgren (eds), *Theological Dictionary of the Old Testament*, vol II, rev edn (JT Willis trans, Grand Rapids, William B Eerdmans, 1975) 253.
Weinrib, EJ, 'Legal Formalism' in D Patterson (ed), *A Companion to Philosophy of Law and Legal Theory* (Chichester, Blackwell, 2010) 327.
Wesel, U, *Rhetorische Statuslehre und Gesetzesauslegung der römischen Juristen* (Cologne, Carl Heymann, 1967).
Wesener, G, 'Zur Denkform des "quasi" in der römischen Jurisprudenz' in Università di Parma Facoltà di giurisprudenza (ed), *Studi in memoria di Guido Donatuti*, vol 3 (Milan, Cisalpino-La goliardica, 1973) 1387.
White, KD, 'Food Requirements and Food Supplies in Classical Times in Relation to the Diet of the Various Classes' (1976) 2 *Progress in Food & Nutrition Science* 143.
Whitman, JQ, *The Legacy of Roman Law in the German Romantic Era* (Princeton, Princeton University Press, 1990).
Wibier, M, 'Cicero's Reception in the Juristic Tradition of the Early Empire' in PJ du Plessis (ed), *Cicero's Law: Rethinking Roman Law of the Late Republic* (Edinburgh, Edinburgh University Press, 2016) 100.
Wieacker, F, *Textstufen klassischer Juristen* (Göttingen, Vandenhoeck & Ruprecht, 1960).
—— *A History of Private Law in Europe* (AD Weir trans, Oxford, Oxford University Press, 1995).
Wilhelm, A, 'Inschriften aus Erythrai und Chios' (1909) 12 *Jahreshefte des österreichischen archäologischen Instituts in Wien* 126.
Willems, C, '„Urbanes" Mietrecht? Der römische Wohnungsmarkt zwischen Preismechanismus und Intervention' (2019) 136 *ZRG RA* 233.
—— 'Kognitionsprozess' in U Babusiaux and others (eds), *Handbuch des Römischen Privatrechts* (Tübingen, Mohr Siebeck, 2020) § 15 (forthcoming).
—— 'Markt und Recht in der Spätantike' in K Droß-Krüpe and K Ruffing (eds), *Market(s) – Market Buildings – Market Squares* (Wiesbaden, Harrassowitz, 2020) (forthcoming).
Wilson, AI, 'Developments in Mediterranean shipping and maritime trade from the Hellenistic period to AD 1000' in D Robinson and AI Wilson (eds), *Maritime Archaeology and Ancient Trade in the Mediterranean* (Oxford, Oxford Centre for Maritime Archaeology, 2011) 33.
—— 'Roman Economic Thought' in W Scheidel (ed), The Cambridge Companion to the *Roman Economy* (Cambridge, Cambridge University Press, 2012) 287.
Winkel, LC, '*Usucapio pro suo* and the Classification of the *causae usucapionis* by the Roman Jurists' in PBH Birks (ed), *New Perspectives in the Roman Law of Property: Essays for Barry Nicholas* (Oxford, Oxford University Press, 1989) 215.
—— 'L'histore du droit, exemple d'une science interdisciplinaire' (1996) 9 *Sartoniana* 125.
—— 'The Role of General Principles in Roman Law' (1996) 2 *Fundamina* 103.
—— 'Le droit romain et la philosophie grecque, quelques problèmes de méthode' (1997) 65 *Leg Hist Rev* 373.
Wolff, HJ, 'Ulpian XVIII ad edictum in collatio and digest and the problem of postclassical editions of classical works' in Università cattolica del Sacro Cuore (ed), *Scritti in onore di Contardo Ferrini: pubblicati in occasione della sua beatificazione*, vol 4 (Milan, Vita e pensiero, 1949) 64.

Wonnacott, M, *Possession of Land* (Cambridge, Cambridge University Press, 2006).

Wood, I, 'Disputes in late fifth- and sixth-century Gaul: some problems' in W Davies and P Fouracre (eds), *The Settlement of Disputes in Early Medieval Europe* (Cambridge, Cambridge University Press, 1986) 7.

Wubbe, FBJ, 'Quelques remarques sur la fonction et l'origine de l'action Publicienne' (1961) 8 *RIDA* 417.

Ziliotto, P, *L'imputazione del danno aquiliano: tra iniuria e damnum corpore datum* (Padua, CEDAM, 2000).

Zimmermann, R, *The Law of Obligations: Roman Foundations of the Civilian Tradition* (Oxford, Oxford University Press, 1996).

—— *Roman Law, Contemporary Law, European Law: The Civilian Tradition Today* (Oxford, Oxford University Press, 2001).

—— 'Roman Law in the Modern World' in DEL Johnston (ed), *The Cambridge Companion to Roman Law* (New York, Cambridge University Press, 2015) 452.

Zweigert, K and Kötz, H, *An Introduction to Comparative Law*, 3rd edn (AD Weir trans, Oxford, Oxford University Press, 1998).

INDEX OF PRIMARY SOURCES

Introductory Note

This Index encompasses references to the surviving primary sources, legal and literary. References to named sources that have not survived directly – for example, the *lex Atinia* or the XII Tables – are included in the General Index.

Modern Sources

GENERAL INDEX

Introductory Note

References such as '178–79' indicate (not necessarily continuous) discussion of a topic across a range of pages. In the case of topics frequently traversed, references have been divided into sub-topics, where possible; otherwise, only the most significant references are listed. Since they are the concern of the volume as a whole, references to 'principle' and 'pragmatism', and to certain other terms used frequently throughout the book, have been minimised; information will be found under the more specific relevant topics.

www.ingramcontent.com/pod-product-compliance
Ingram Content Group UK Ltd.
Pitfield, Milton Keynes, MK11 3LW, UK
UKHW020810290926
15470UKWH00003B/1061

9 781509 938957